To
Angela & Don –
Kindred Spirits
(and all the little spirits♡ **W9-ASM-700**
Love –
Floyd

Being
and Becoming

Recent Titles in
Contributions in Philosophy

Coercion and Autonomy: Philosophical Foundations, Issues, and Practices
Alan S. Rosenbaum

Einstein and the Humanities
Dennis P. Ryan, editor

From Science to Subjectivity: An Interpretation of Descartes' *Meditations*
Walter Soffer

José Ortega y Gasset: Proceedings of the *Espectador universal* International
Interdisciplinary Conference
Nora de Marval-McNair, editor

The Dynamics of Knowledge: A Contemporary View
David Z. Rich

Dilthey Today: A Critical Appraisal of the Contemporary Relevance of His Work
H. P. Rickman

The Structure and Confirmation of Evolutionary Theory
Elisabeth A. Lloyd

Make Room for Dreams: Spiritual Challenges to Zionism
Haim Gordon

Beyond the Secular Mind: A Judaic Response to the Problems of Modern
Civilization
Paul Eidelberg

Question-Reply Argumentation
Douglas N. Walton

The Last Choice: Preemptive Suicide in Advanced Age
C. G. Prado

Victims and Values: A History and a Theory of Suffering
Joseph A. Amato

The Life and Death Debate: Moral Issues of Our Time
J. P. Moreland and Norman L. Geisler

BEING ─────────

and BECOMING

A Critique of Post-Modernism

F. F. CENTORE

Contributions in Philosophy, Number 44

Greenwood Press

New York • Westport, Connecticut • London

Library of Congress Cataloging-in-Publication Data

Centore, F. F.
    Being and becoming : a critique of post-modernism / F. F. Centore.
        p.   cm. — (Contributions in philosophy, ISSN 0084-926X ; no.
    44)
    Includes bibliographical references and index.
    ISBN 0-313-27616-1
    1. Postmodernism. 2. Thomists. I. Title. II. Series.
    B831.2.C38 1991
    190–dc20   90-45070

British Library Cataloguing in Publication Data is available.

Copyright © 1991 by F. F. Centore

All rights reserved. No portion of this book may be
reproduced, by any process or technique, without the
express written consent of the publisher.

Library of Congress Catalog Card Number: 90-45070
ISBN: 0-313-27616-1
ISSN: 0084-926X

First published in 1991

Greenwood Press, 88 Post Road West, Westport, CT 06881
An imprint of Greenwood Publishing Group, Inc.

Printed in the United States of America

The paper used in this book complies with the
Permanent Paper Standard issued by the National
Information Standards Organization (Z39.48–1984).

10 9 8 7 6 5 4 3 2 1

To
Professor Larry Azar

teacher and friend
friend and teacher

Realism always was and still remains the source of our personal liberty. Let us add that, for the same reason, it remains the only guarantee of our social liberty.

Etienne Gilson
"Medieval Universalism,"
Harvard Tercentenary Celebration (1936)

Only now can the great dialectical puzzle of the one and the many, . . . be given its true and fundamental ground. . . . All human speaking is finite in such a way that there is laid up within it an infinity of meaning to be explicated and laid out. That is why the hermeneutical phenomenon also can be illuminated only in light of the fundamental finitude of being, which is wholly verbal in character.

H.-G. Gadamer
Truth and Method (1989): pp. 457–58

CONTENTS

Preface   xi

Prologue: On Post-Modernism as the Current Orthodoxy   1

1   Nietzsche and Friends: The Attack on Being,
    Knowledge, and Morals   21

2   Descartes, Kant, and James: As If Theism,
    Proto-Deconstructionism   71

3   Hegel and Kueng: Pantheism, the Polite
    Form of Atheism   105

4   Heidegger and Sartre: Essence-Phobia,
    with a Vengeance   135

5   Thomas Aquinas: Super-Modernity Superseded,
    "Being" Remembered   173

Epilogue: On the Ethical Importance of "And"   207

Appendix: A Summary of Hume's Deduction
Leading to Skepticism   229

Notes   237

Bibliography   255

Index   277

PREFACE

Everyone by nature loves trying to solve a mystery. Philosophy marks the height of this general rule of human nature. The most interesting problems and puzzles in philosophy are those concerned with reconciling apparently irreconcilable opposites, such as stability/flux, reality/appearance, sameness/difference, eternity/time, universal/particular, absolute/relative, substance/accident, subject/object, determinism/freedom, discipline/creativity, hierarchy/democracy, individual/group, security/adventure, intimacy/substantiality, faith/reason, mysticism/ordinary life, and the like.

Over the centuries these problems have evoked a second order of dichotomies and conflicts, this time between and among competing theories which are designed to resolve the first order puzzles. Some of these competing theories are realism/idealism, essentialism/existentialism, theism/atheism, theocentrism/anthropocentrism, absolutism/libertarianism, capitalism/communism, and so forth. Even today there seems to be no end to these philosophical debates. There is, nonetheless, progress in philosophy, which can be measured by the degree to which contemporary thinkers have at their disposal, thanks to the work of their predecessors, a more comprehensive view of the various possible alternatives for resolving the first order problems, as well as a history of what has actually happened when certain views are put into practice.

The purpose of this study is to look into this nest of problems more deeply, and ultimately to resolve, in principle at least, all of the paradoxes and puzzles on the basis of an old insight into the nature of reality. It is not a defense of classical philosophy in general, after the fashion of Leo Strauss. Neither is it an attempt to go back and live in the past. Such a thing is not even possible. It is possible, though, to apply to the present certain principles which, because they are so fundamental to the human condition, possess a timeless element about them.

We live in a constantly changing world, and we cannot be sure that life will be better in the future than it is now. At the present time we have lived long enough to witness with our own eyes the demise of the Left. This complements the death of the Right in 1945. But what will replace the Left among the intelligentsia? Unfortunately, post-modernism is superficially attractive enough to capture the East just as it has already overpowered the West, where the extreme position of hyper-modernism now dominates. This is even now leading to social disintegration, just as the extreme of collectivism has led to civil war in the East.

Today, while philosophers fiddle, our intellectual and moral social structure is burning to the ground. Strife and conflict are rampant. But must we be continuously in a state of war, and more and more often in a state of civil war — the cold war, the war on AIDS, the war on poverty, the war on drugs, the war on crime, the war on racism, the war on child abuse, the war on wife abuse, the war on pornography, the war on terrorism, the war on pollution, not to mention the war on the deficit, and so forth? The answer is in the negative, but the foundation for the "no" answer is something positive, rational, and in keeping with religious faith. This combination, though, is something which the contemporary world has been trained *not* to understand.

It may be that the world of human experience does provide a solid foundation for a series of well-balanced doctrines on the great speculative and practical issues of human existence and life. It may also be the case that a certain amount of dogmatism is *necessary* to the preservation of the good life in the good society. It would certainly seem to be necessary for social stability. G. K. Chesterton once observed that those caught up in a state of moral confusion will never change the world for the better because they are too busy always changing their minds. Even Freud was not opposed to dogmatism in principle. What he opposed was the combination of being dogmatic and being wrong simultaneously. Toleration, justice, privacy, and so forth, are undoubtedly good things, but how can we act on them rationally if we do not know precisely what they mean?

On the basis of a totally amorphous reality, deprived of any intrinsic natures or essences which might found natural physical and moral laws, the post-modern fallibilistic approach to the world wants to emphasize toleration, justice, privacy, and so on, to the point of a totally amorphous morality, at least in principle. Not surprisingly we are beset with conflicting signals from every side. According to the super-popular TV show M.A.S.H., war is fun. Others tell us war is hell. Is revenge good or a great evil? Is unfaithfulness in marriage good or a great evil? Is there any problem which can't be solved by getting a gun and killing? Are the Cosbys the ideal family? Is there any such thing as an ideal family? How long can a house so divided continue to stand? Are we going to end up, because of our extremisms, imitating Colombia or Lebanon?

To glance at only two examples out of the many which could be mentioned, consider the current heated debates over the moral and legal aspects of abortion and homosexuality. How often have we heard news reports about the "pro-choice" side of the abortion issue accusing the "pro-life" side of being fascist in character because it wants to curtail a woman's freedom? Those who see homosexuality as a rightful, and even beautiful, option often do the same with respect to those who are opposed to it in principle. The prevailing orthodoxy in both cases is that anyone is free to do whatever he or she wishes, and no one else (including the government) has the right to interfere and impose his or her will upon the genuine, authentic, and free decisions of the autonomous individual. This is the consensus of society and *therefore* must be honored.

Obviously, where there is a spectrum with two extremes, any move away from one extreme must be a move toward the other extreme. *If* it is a choice between abortion on demand and no freedom of choice at all, or between homophilia and homophobia, then it follows that when one option is eliminated the other must be advocated. Unless one can avoid acting at all, this is reasonable.

But why assume in advance that that's the way things are? Or why assume that a move away from one extreme must be a move all the way to the other extreme? Without passing moral judgment on the issues, it is still possible to raise a more primitive question concerning why the issues of abortion and homosexuality should be treated, especially in the popular media, as two-part disjunctions in the first place. Is it that the masters of the modern media cannot imagine anything more complex? Or is it that the audiences, to which they must cater, cannot do so? Even though one or both of these may be the case, I think that there's more to it than this. The purpose of this work is to investigate what the more fundamental situation might be.

There are many to whom I owe thanks for helping me complete this work. These would include all of my colleagues, friends, and acquaintances, both known and unknown to me, who have bestowed upon me, and on this work in particular, their intellectual help, stimulation, and constructive criticisms over the years. That I owe a special debt to the historical-analytical methodology and Christian philosophy content of thinkers such as Etienne Gilson, Joseph Owens, and Larry Azar will be recognized by anyone familiar with the "Toronto School" of Thomistic philosophy. As Jacques Maritain once pointed out, many contemporary thinkers believe themselves to be under the influence of some powerful compulsion forcing them to pour corrosive acid over the very things ordinary people (including themselves) most need in order to live normal lives. I regard myself as being extraordinarily fortunate in having acquired a very effective means for neutralizing such acid. The debt one owes to one's teachers is beyond measure; I can do no more than say "thank you."

Others to be thanked include Professor John Whiton, Department of Germanic and Slavic Languages and Literatures, University of Waterloo, and Professor John Finn, C.R. (retired), Department of French, St. Jerome's College, University of Waterloo, for their help with some of the translations; my many students, especially Douglas McManaman, for their challenging questioning; the members of the Board of Governors of my College for their generous financial support during my sabbatical leave; the several typists, particularly Susan Bell, whose skill with word processors have greatly lightened my task; and also Cathy Fitzgerald for her help with the arduous task of proofreading.

*Being
and Becoming*

PROLOGUE: ON POST-MODERNISM AS THE CURRENT ORTHODOXY

> Unde, si nullus intellectus esset aeternus, nulla veritas esset aeterna. (Thus if there were no eternal intellect, then there would be no eternal truth.)
>
> St. Thomas Aquinas
> *Summa Theologiae* I: 16, 7

> Since there is no infinite and perfect consciousness to think it, there can no longer be any *a priori* good.
>
> J.-P. Sartre
> *Existentialism and Humanism* (1982): p. 33

Must "reality" always be written enclosed within quotation marks? Should a thing-word be used (mentioned) only for the purpose of showing that it should not be taken literally? Is it really possible to create and destroy things by our personal use and disuse of words? Gain a word, gain a thing; lose a word, lose a thing? Is the house of being-something constructed of my words? Or can it only be done by means of a widespread community effort; a social consensus? Nietzsche asserted in his *The Gay Science* (II: 58) that it is enough to create new names in order to create new essences, that is, new "things." Heidegger agreed. In his *Being and Time* (Intro.: 6; I: 10), we are told that we should not even talk about the I, ego, spirit, soul, reason, mind, psyche, person, conscious subject, and the like, because just talking about such a thing immediately prejudices the thinker in favor of the real existence of such a "thing." In post-modernism essences are *willed* into existence. Is this the last word on the subject?

But then one must ponder, Is there really any world of definite types of things out there at all? Or is it only a case of the local locus of activity which we call human being-there (*Dasein*) imposing upon an amorphous I-Know-Not-What the various definitions of worldly things, as a cookie-cutter cuts out definite shapes from a nondescript layer of dough? Are all things, including human beings, really only "things?"

The post-modern world-view says yes. In its effort to overcome the old dichotomies found within the traditional doctrines of science, philosophy, and theology, the hyper-modern school has reacted by rolling everything together into one Great Unknown and then calling upon the creative powers of human nature in order to provide people and societies with the *appearance* of definite types and sorts of things which *appear* to possess independent acts of existence relative to each other. But is the knower really there at all as an independent subject and substance? Apparently he or she really is, and isn't, and at the same time.

In the process of trying to maintain this strange situation, all of our most basic common-sense knowledge of reality is taken apart, reinterpreted, deconstructed, and restructured, not once but, potentially at least, over and over again forever into the future. Not only that, the theory, since it purports to instruct us about the way the world and the human condition *really* is, demands that this has indeed *always* been the case throughout the whole history of human existence. Objectivity is what the spirit-of-the-world (people) *want* to be the case. Man-the-world-builder is radicalized. Not only is the historical process of scientific development relativized, but the very *truths* of science are also deconstructed.

Moreover, not only does this do great violence to our everyday world, it also negates most of the traditional theological notions of the Judaeo-Christian and Islamic religions. Personal immortality vanishes under the new radical hermeneutic of the One. The line between good and evil is blurred to the point where, like the Becoming which is Reality, the very idea of guilt and sin become unintelligible. The sacraments become merely superficial social signs of community involvement. Theology and philosophy are transmuted into anthropology, psychology, and sociology. God himself is melded and kneaded into the uncreated, never-ending universe.

In the case of extreme positions, however, as in the case of pendulums, the extreme view must soon enough move back toward center under its own weight. The force of reality is strong enough to overcome any power some given philosophical theory may possess to pull us off-center for a short time. And what our life-centered experience of reality demands is *both* essence *and* existence, fixed meanings *and* multiple variations, the traditional *and* the modern, and so forth. However *avant-garde* it may appear at the moment, any philosophy, interpretation, or hermeneutic which affirms one at the expense of the other is doomed to failure.

Explaining *how* we can have both aspects of reality simultaneously is within the province of the philosophy of being. *That* we do in fact have both is a fact of experience. Even the hyper-moderns themselves, for all their emphasis upon Becoming, must, in the very process of speaking about Process, constantly make reference to essence and the essential. Likewise in moral matters: There is no escaping the need for *per se* goods. This is no mere matter of grammar or linguistic convention, but something inherent in the very nature of reality itself and our knowledge of reality. There is nothing at all "unrealistic" about adjusting one's moral behavior, whether political, economic, sexual, and so on, to an objective set of rigorous standards.

We already know from the history of our own century that any philosophy of reality which fails to account for the objective universality and necessity of mathematics and science, and hence for the possibility of the predictability of natural events, is bound sooner or later to be publicly discredited. In the first half of our century the Logical Positivists built their whole reputation upon their ability to defend mathematics and science, while discarding "metaphysics" and religion as being composed of unverifiable, meaningless statements. All of reality was reduced to a material extension, perhaps atomistic in nature, but always unknown in itself. Determinism and laboratory work were accepted; freely chosen human values were rejected. Today, however, Logical Positivism has passed away, mainly because it threw out the baby with the bathwater: that is, because, in its effort to discredit "metaphysics" and religion, it also discredited that which it most desired to serve, namely, objective, deterministic science.

In the second half of our century the shoe is on the other foot. All forms of determinism are rejected while freedom is emphasized. Hard-nosed scientism is out of favor; variability and reinterpretation are at the center of everything. The hyper-moderns do not hesitate to declare themselves to be the prophets of a New Age, one which will have finally and forever passed over and beyond all previous patterns of philosophical and religious thought (subject and object, inside and outside, theory and data, and so on). In this New Era, man and nature, God and the world, the theoretical and the practical, and the like, become united in one ever-changing universe. Lacking any definite guide "out there," it is now up to human beings to remake the world after their own image. Anyone who defends "fixity" is considered a fool. The Dionysian, authentic, autonomous man of the Atheistic Existentialists is the hero of the day. Living according to eternal verities and unwavering principles is discarded as nonsense. In general, anthropocentrism holds the field while theocentrism is not even allowed into the game.

Nietzsche once complained (*Antichrist* I: 43) that the main reason for the historical success of Christianity was that people were flattered into thinking that everyone was of equal value before God and could live forever with God. It's selfishness raised to an infinite degree, he thought, and yet it was precisely this miserable flattery of personal vanity that brought all the little prigs, madmen, failures, and the whole scum and refuse of the world, into the Church. If nothing else, we at least cannot accuse Nietzsche of pulling his punches.

But is post-modernism any better? What does the secular humanist offer us if not the power to eat of the tree of the knowledge of good and evil and not die? After Deconstructionism has done its work, *we* end up being able to take great pride in our uniqueness and autonomy. We are the masters of our fate, the captains of our ship, the creators of the world. And let there be no doubt about it, it is *our* world and not the property of Anyone else.

Under the influence of Heideggerian hermeneutics, for instance, and in contrast to Logical Positivism, we are now allowed to talk endlessly about the divine, but only in a mythological way, for even the gods are only real as human creations. We are faced today with a strange mixture of a deep-seated despair concerning, not just the contents of knowledge, but the very nature of the rational process itself, combined with a self-generated exultation over our new-found autonomy. With respect to knowledge, even science has lost its objective status. Today the super-moderns will not allow anyone to be dogmatic about anything, regardless of his or her discipline. Instead, everyone is free to do his or her "own thing." One must then wonder, is there any longer any such thing as a discipline at all? How can anyone claim to have a definitive, expert knowledge of anything?

At one extreme there are those who promote deterministic science at the expense of everything else. At the other there are those who strenuously fight against this determinism. A thinker such as Sartre would be an outstanding example of this other extreme. He is so taken aback by the implications of modern science that he would turn against science in order to preserve freedom. He would even turn against nature in order to avoid being determined by his own nature. Furthermore, he would even turn against reason itself by declaring that our human nature is rooted in "nothingness," and that this "nothingness," in contrast to the something (i.e., "being," or the material world), is the source of our distinctively human trait of autonomy. It is our *non*-nature that allows us to be free amid the deterministic, scientific natural world of material things.

Today, especially in moral matters, the anti-scientific group is in the ascendancy. Undoubtedly, as a new group on the intellectual scene, even though individual members often sound very much like Hume or Hegel, the post-moderns are interesting to read, and their speculations are philosophically stimulating. Without a doubt, the emphasis on flux, even though much too one-sided to accurately reflect our actual being-in-the-world, is *an* important aspect of our experience.

Moreover, even though it is true that we do not begin by knowing ourself or our own soul first and foremost in our *Lebens-Welt,* as even St. Thomas Aquinas would maintain in agreement with Heidegger but contra Descartes and Locke, it isn't true that we must end in agnosticism and skepticism with respect to the existence and nature of the self. The hyper-moderns, however, true to their twentieth-century phenomenological roots, begin with ideas which are somehow suspended between an apparent "well-defined world" and an apparent "knowing self," and end by denying both "things." The only thing that really exists is *Dasein,* the reified Question Question-ing, which both is and is not there. How can such a situation be comprehended in a rational way? Neither can Aquinas, for example, allow the rational use of nothing to explain something, whereas some leading twentieth-century thinkers want to do just that.

In all, despite their efforts on behalf of phenomenological understanding, universal integration, and human unity, the post-moderns do in fact end up endorsing the most eccentric and downright abnormal views. Yet, as far as the popular media and popular education are concerned, it is all very normal; indeed, it is *the* standard to be taught and promulgated.

In a nutshell, the current situation in the West, and very likely more and more so in the East, is this. From the perspective most familiar to the ordinary citizen, it is widely thought and taught that, in order to exist, a liberal democracy depends upon toleration, which in turn depends upon a moral ambiguity and relativism (the liberal consensus). Exactly what the necessity for a moral relativism depends upon is not clear to the average person. When viewed philosophically, though, it is possible to penetrate to deeper levels of explanation. Philosophically speaking, the claim is that nihilism is necessary to support an anti-essentialism, which is necessary to support a moral ambiguity, which is necessary to support toleration, which is necessary to support a liberal democracy.

The ultimate foundation for post-modernism is located on the level of the philosophy of being. At this level it is generally assumed, without very much argumentation or consideration of alternatives, that Becoming-Temporality is the only reality. At this level, in order to maintain this view, as with Hegel, ordinary logic must be suspended and replaced with some new transcendental mode of thought. The result is the now-familiar nihilistic, God-Is-Dead doctrine.

This foundation produces some necessary design requirements in the superstructure. Ordinary logic is now restored so that these consequences can be drawn out. In terms of cognitive theory, there can be no essence to anything, nothing fixed and permanent, no eternal truths which temporal and finite minds must take into account. There are now only localized and particularized perspectives. The most one can hope for are temporary coherences between and among our temporary sets of sensations. Instead of the mind conforming to reality, reality must conform to the mind. *This is the very essence of anthropocentrism.*

The ethics based upon such an epistemology is an amoralism in which everyone must invent meaning for himself and herself, and will essences into existence. All decisions are now pragmatic and exploratory. The autonomous self reigns supreme, unless it voluntarily subjugates itself to some temporary leader within some wider social scheme. The autonomous self can justify doing anything just so long as it is pleasing to the self and one is honest and sincere about it. My own will is the only standard of anything good, and anything that goes against it, such as objective rules of behavior, accusations of individual and personal guilt, personal punishment, and so on, is not only evil but the greatest evil. So, for instance, for the independent woman abortion is good because she freely wills it, while rape is evil because she does not will it.

The natural deduction from this state of affairs in the political sphere is the liberal consensus which is supposed to be essential to a liberal democracy. This largely unconsciously held doctrine is "liberal" because it emphasizes the individual's right to make and remake the world after his or her own image, and it is a "consensus" because it is something with which everyone must go along (or so it is assumed) if one's personal freedom and privacy are to be maintained.

Precisely because there is no final and absolute Truth about anything, no one can claim any sort of final and absolute authority over anyone else. This is supposed to guarantee individual freedom in a liberal democracy. To the post-modern thinker the real danger to democratic life is not error but intolerance. Moral relativism is the order of the day. Claiming you're absolutely right in some objective way is the only real sin today. This attitude, in the terminology of Allan Bloom, is the essential part of the "democratic personality." Anyone who shares this attitude, according to the popular media and public education, is mainstream. Anyone else is at best only marginal, and at worst a Right-Wing, reactionary fanatic. The amazing thing, which shows the power of the present-day mind-set, is that this is so even in many schools still claiming some religious affiliation.

"Pro-choice" on abortion, for instance, is mainstream while "fundamentalist" Protestants and "papist" Catholics are fringe people, and thus not deserving of complete news coverage and classroom discussion. Pro-life people are merely narrow-minded anti-abortionists whereas those holding the opposing view are broad-minded pro-choice defenders of women's rights. There is no talk of a woman's obligations toward her family and society because it is presumed that her *only* obligation is toward herself. According to the prevailing orthodoxy this is the way things *should* be. But how can this be when Western values are supposed to support life and the right to life, liberty, and the pursuit of happiness? It is because liberty and happiness are more important than life (i.e., someone else's life).

Being fair to all sides on some basic moral and legal issue means being intolerant *only* of intolerance. As soon as someone is perceived as wanting to restrict someone else's right to do as he or she pleases, that someone, by a sort of inbred intuition endemic to society, is immediately at least psychologically rejected as being an enemy of the good life in the good society. Moral ambiguity must be preserved at all costs. The idea is to support *only* those who support a maximized amount of freedom of action for anyone with the needed mental and physical health, and the desire, to exercise his or her freedom. This is the message conveyed, whether directly or indirectly, by the popular media, as anyone can verify by watching any one of the national evening news broadcasts.

Likewise for an issue such as artificial contraception, which strikes at the very heart of natural law ethics. Of the four possible moral combinations concerning birth control and/or disease control via either some artificial method or abstention — namely, (1) the first wrong and the second right (the Roman Catholic view); (2) the first right and the second wrong (the hedonistic view); (3) both wrong (the Darwinian evolutionary view); (4) both equally right and proper — *only* (4) is regarded as currently acceptable, non-judgmental, and orthodox. This is the *only* view treated in a favorable light by the popular media and popular education. Even though such treatment is very propagandistic, because of the *Zeitgeist* it is hardly ever recognized for what it is, even by the most "liberal" of reporters.

Judging by what is taken for granted these days, even science is not strong enough to overcome the moral imperative of post-modernism. At first sight it might seem odd, considering the fact that we certainly live in a highly scientific and technological age, that the moral consequences of the Darwinian evolutionary world-view are not more widely promoted. No doubt this is due, in part at least, to the fact that we have learned a lesson from the Nazis, who used Darwin to help justify their policies. This, though, is not the most fundamental reason. The more pertinent reason today goes deeper than politics and confirms the prevalent role of post-modernism. The central notion today is that nothing is to stand in the way of the new "religion" of post-modernism, neither some other religious or political doctrine nor science. The authentic self, either alone or in groups, must decide.

At the end of his *Descent of Man,* chapter 21, "General Summary and Conclusion," Darwin makes a public statement concerning his views on birth control, sexual mores, and evolution via natural selection. He states that, despite the possibility of overpopulation and the ensuing hardships which are sure to follow, birth control should not be practiced by human beings. In the later 1870s he even refused to come to the aid of Charles Bradlaugh and Annie Besant, who were on trial in England for publishing a manual on birth control. He was, though, all in favor of "free love," *if* it helped advance the species. He taught that there should not be any restrictions on mating practices, such as those demanded by traditional religions. Instead, the best males should be allowed to mate (and reproduce) with the best females as often as they like. Also, if possible, inferior specimens should not be allowed to mate (and reproduce) at all.

Nevertheless, despite all the praise given to Darwin, and the constant lip service paid to his evolutionary views in the classroom and by the public media, his ethical views are usually ignored, and are even treated as an embarrassment when they are mentioned. Educators today want to forget that even the most benign and kindly form of passive differential reproduction still means the elimination of inferior specimens, and even whole races if they are maladjusted, by means of constant conflict and struggle.

I would suggest that, although ignoring nature is inconsistent from the perspective of the lip service we pay to the importance of modern science, it is consistent from the post-modern viewpoint. Even Nietzsche's notion of the completely "naturalized man" didn't mean following nature; it meant following one's own will (the Super-man). To understand Nietzsche and his many modern disciples we have to see them as attempting to undermine and contradict practically every tenet, on a line-by-line basis, of traditional religious doctrine. In effect, each individual now becomes his or her own little god. Instead of one Author of Nature we now have millions and millions of authors. "True science" is as much a matter of sociological consensus as is "true religion." The effect of this is not only to undermine religion but also to undermine nature and science.

To actually practice Darwinian evolutionary ethics would mean conforming the individual will to the facts of nature (assuming of course that Darwin was right). This would mean that someone was being controlled by something outside of one's own willfulness. This is not allowed. Regardless of whether the motive force is some Super-Subjectivity flowing through the subject or some autonomy coming from within the subject alone, the internal will power must never be frustrated. Such willfulness also possesses the added advantage of allowing the post-modern thinker to arbitrarily negate, for example, the Nazi-like attempts to help evolution along by deliberate social policies. Thus we (supposedly) avoid genocide, Spanish Inquisitions, witch hunts, and the like.

The same sort of thing is seen today in the abortion debate: Because it is supposed to be irrelevant, scientific evidence concerning the human status of the fetus is almost always ruled out of court. One's choices must not be controlled by anything external, whether God or objective scientific evidence. The *only* really relevant sort of information is what the individual, the judge, the jury, the social consensus, and so on, wants to be the case. Nature may have its ways and laws, but the thing that really counts is *my* way, and *our* way, of doing things. This means, for instance, that it's up to me to decide, or for my society to decide, what is or isn't a human being with human rights and privileges. Anti-racist policies, for example, then become as arbitrary as pro-racist policies. This is considered by post-modernism to be anthropocentric humanism, and produces what is called legal positivism, which also fits in well with the super-modern mind-set. Along the way, utilizing whatever technological means are available to help satisfy our wants is encouraged.

The same phenomenon appears in other areas of contemporary life as well. For example, it is widely held that to be a member of a certain religious denomination it is sufficient for someone to simply *claim* to be a member, thus making oneself an actual member of the group. Likewise, there is no need to worry about environmental pollution. For a long time now the popular attitude has been that as long as we think everything will work out in the end, then everything will work out in the end. Also, to make life worth living (following the advice of William James, given to the Harvard YMCA in 1895) all we need do is to believe that life is worth living and then it is worth living. In the absence of some fixed standard acting as a measure of the individual's (or group's) mind and will, everything becomes a self-fulfilling promise. The difference between the "is" and the "ought" is erased. Since there is no objective measure, there cannot be any need for anyone to conform to some objective measure. Going simply on the basis of what one wants, what should be the case and what is the case must be the same thing.

Generally speaking in moral matters, what one wants, and the "truth" of the matter, are the same thing. Practically everything that happens in our society today can be accounted for on the basis of the prevalent orthodoxy of post-modernism. In addition to the examples given above, one could also mention, among many others, the areas of contemporary comedy and money matters. With respect to modern entertainment, the point of contemporary comedy is to be pointless. We cannot expect the modern comedian to measure our current situation against an objective standard because there is no such rule of life. Neither can one expect the government to worry too much about national deficits. In post-modern economics, what we owe to ourselves can be wished away as easily as anything else. This is the great modern myth of capitalism, parallel to the great myth of socialism, which is that wealth will somehow create itself, and all the central planners need do is worry about how to distribute the wealth.

Since these last two points may not be immediately obvious to everyone, I will take a moment to expand upon them. It is an old saying that tragedy unites while comedy divides. What this means is that those elements of human life which are generally considered tragic, such as death, loss of opportunity, frustration, and so forth, are fairly universal; they can be recognized as tragic by the vast majority of people in the world regardless of their cultural or ethnic backgrounds. Comedy, on the other hand, is much more geared to particular cultures and societies, and even to different subgroups within a society. Making an "ethnic" joke may be great fun for one group within a society but poison for another. Some people might get a good laugh out of things such as:

"Did you hear about the Catholic priest who had to go *under cover* because of his liberal views on sex?"

"I say, with these new laws, we can make a *killing* in the abortion business."

"Do you think that 210 is a good I.Q.? — For *all* of Italy!"

Others will regard such lines as being in bad taste and maybe even worthy of censorship. As all politicians, teachers, and others in the public eye know very well, one must be very careful about the jokes one makes in public.

This being the case, it is really of great significance when, in the process of trying to figure out what is going on beneath the surface in society, one runs across a very basic agreement in the public sphere about what's funny. Now, as a matter of fact, we do find today that there is a great deal of basic agreement about what humor *should* be. From the Flintstones to the Cosbys to the Simpsons, the effort to merely maintain a middle class existence is the main source of humor. Life's highest aspiration is to be able to continue running in circles. *Under*achievement is the norm.

The core of contemporary comedy is this: You can say anything you want as long as it is ultimately pointless. The purpose of modern humor is to be purposeless. Good humor is amoral, anti-hero, aimless humor. Over and over again this point is brought home to us. The mere fact that people generally know and love their prime time TV comedy shows so well proves the point. The audience tells the producers what it wants. Working on the assumption that the popular media (otherwise they wouldn't be popular) give their audiences what they want, we have a very strong indication that post-modernism is the current orthodoxy.

In the past the typical form of humor was satire. The names of Aristophanes and Juvenal among the ancient writers, and Cervantes, Swift, and Voltaire among more recent authors, represent the typical humorists of the Western world until very recent times. Others, such as Shakespeare, Rabelais, and Hans Christian Andersen, could also be added to the list. When these writers told a story it had a point to it. They wrote with a purpose. Their aim was to reveal to the people of their own society certain facts about themselves. Standing back from the actual events depicted in their stories, the writers of satires attempt to break down the ethnocentric prejudices of their own societies so that the people can see themselves as they would appear to an objective and disinterested outside observer viewing them from a distance. There is such a thing as a privileged perspective on what is good and evil.

Sometimes, as in Cervantes's *Don Quixote,* it is the whole human race that is being shown to itself. At other times, as in Aristophanes's *The Birds,* the satirist's barbs are directed against the tender skins of those in his own limited society, rather than against the human race at large. In all cases, though, the "joke," once it hits home, bears an unmistakable message for the audience. Look at yourselves, Jonathan Swift says in his *Gulliver's Travels,* worrying about unimportant little things like at which end to open your eggs — and actually going to war over it! What small-minded fools you are! In true satire, underneath all the comedy, farce, jibs, and ego-busting jabs, there is a serious message to be digested by the audience.

Not so in current comedy. Take any of the recent and widely popular examples of amusement as seen on the most popular of the popular media, television. What is the one thing all these shows have in common? The answer: Their aimlessness. They are all devoted to diversion for the sake of diversion. Their message is that there is no message, or that we must be so "open-minded" about everything that no one moral perspective is any better than any other one.

In the case of a familiar children's cartoon program, for instance, we are repeatedly treated to the same format over and over again. First the coyote attempts to capture the roadrunner. Then the poor beast ignominiously fails, usually by himself falling into the trap which he had cleverly set for the bird. His injuries are always grotesquely grave and gruesome. Nevertheless, he always manages to pull himself (literally oftentimes) back together again. Instead of Nietzsche's self-legislative Superman we have the self-creating super-coyote, not subject to the laws of nature. The same sort of thing is then repeated over again. This has been going on now for many years, and the poor beast has yet to lay his paw upon the speedy little bird. After all, the roadrunner is entitled to get what he wants as well.

Other programs show the same aimlessness. They exhibit to the viewer, usually in very quick succession, animations in which funny little people are seen sliding down a leg into a belly button, or in which we follow an insane-looking bishop through the mechanical bowels of a washing machine. Then there are demonstrations of all sorts of funny ways to walk. Caricatures of well-known people are also commonplace. Also ever-popular are the unexpected reversals: Celebrities asking for a teenager's autograph, the crooks arresting the cops, the wild-eyed romantic old ladies chasing after the young men, and the store clerk who simply refuses to sell anything.

We can also count upon numerous "cameo" appearances by famous people from all walks of life, usually saying and doing all kinds of out-of-character things. Taking a cue from Harold Lloyd, Buster Keaton, and Charlie Chaplin, many programs delight us with slapstick amusements. There's always a great deal of action, but the ungainly super-heroes of comedy never seem to get hurt. As long as you are funny you can get away with anything — including getting hit on the head with a sixteen-ton weight and walking away with a smile. In this regard, every comedian is a Superman or Superwoman.

Next we have the outlandish puppets, the ridiculing of the place from which the show originates, the unending jokes about artists, politicians, actors and actresses, clerics of all denominations, the different races, and so on and so forth. Then there are the mild ethnic and religious (but never about post-modernism) jokes, the lampoons upon famous scientific studies, especially any concerned with sex, as well as upon novel and movie plots, all the major human social ceremonies, such as funerals, weddings, and elections, and, never to be left out these days, skits about mixed marriages and homosexual relationships.

Intertwined with all this are songs with outlandish lyrics, a deliberate lack of synchronization between words and mouth movements, and the frequent changing of bizarre and fantastic costumes. Finally, we are treated to the repetition of basically the same skit with a hundred and one ridiculous variations. In the modern comedy the important thing is a continuous stream of fast and unexpected developments — all leading nowhere.

As was already pointed out, in a satire the writer stands outside of the action the better to craftily lambast the shortcomings of his audience. But more often than not in contemporary comedy, as Ronald Knox discerningly observed in his early twentieth-century work *Essays in Satire,* many years before the advent of popular television, the comedian is now the butt of his or her own jokes. This is a sure sign that something radical has occurred in the contemporary approach to comedy. Instead of laughing at the foibles of humankind at large or at the follies of one's own society, modern amusement laughs at itself. The whole enterprise is like a snake attempting to swallow its own tail. The distance between the subject and the object is gone. The jokers delight is being the object of their own insults. When someone, or someone close to him or her such as his wife or her husband, goes down in a shower of ridicule, it is not the universal faults of the human species, or the foolish antics of one's own society, that are shown up for what they are, but the comics themselves that suffer the abuse.

Post-modernism teaches the compression together of the objective and the subjective. Everything comes around full circle sooner or later. To laugh at the world is to laugh at yourself. There is no external platform upon which you can stand and view the outlandish antics of the human race. No matter where you stand you are always looking at yourself in a mirror. Like the bent blade of a crazy sword or the twisted barrel of a weird rifle, the point of every joke is always twisted around so as to come back upon the comic. The joke is always on ourselves.

The great classical comic writers and the great classical philosophers have at least this much in common: They always plagiarized reality. The contemporary comic, however, reflects our newly nihilized world. There is no reality. Everything is mere verbiage. What the "Theatre of the Absurd" is to the intelligentsia, current popular comedy is to the less educated people in society. Hence the predominance of the one-liner, which reflects the disintegration of everything, rather than the well-developed and drawn out satire. Moreover, special effects replace plot; short shocking scenes substitute for story line; and the public keeps buying it.

How can anyone remain sane in such a world? This is also mirrored in popular comedy. The present-day comic is always walking on the edge; always, like John Cleese's comic characters, just on the verge of going over the edge, of going completely insane. The fact that he doesn't actually "go off the deep end," but instead continues to teeter on the brink, is precisely what makes his characters so believable and pertinent in post-modern times. We can empathize with such beleaguered characters, because that is the kind of world in which we ourselves live.

The influence of post-modernism also holds in financial matters. We don't literally worship money today, but it is revered as the *sign* of what is of greatest importance in an anthropocentric world-view. Social consensus decides what the culture holds up to itself as its highest value. And in our contemporary world, taken as a whole, the general consensus is that the business of the world is business. We have decided that business is best for us. This is now, throughout the world, the great new religious myth of our times. Descartes wanted to make the world safe for science. Today we are much more interested in perpetuating our comfortable life-style by making the world safe for business. *Because* this is what *we want,* it *must* be right.

Although this sort of thing was certainly not unknown in the past, it did not dominate human life. Aristotle, for instance, in the fourth century B.C., was certainly aware of the importance of money relative to other things which might be prized in life. He states in his *Rhetoric:*

> If you have money there are always plenty of people fawning after you. Hence the remark of Simonides, when asked by Hiero's wife whether it's better to be wise or rich, about the relative roles of the scholar and the rich man: "Rich of course, for I see the scholars spending all their time at the doors of the rich men." (II: 16)

Today, though, money does dominate. Why is it that when a man abandons his wife and children for a younger and better-looking woman he is not condemned but is instead often regarded with envy by other men in society? If the man is an older movie star or politician, such behavior is usually regarded as an indication, not of an evil character, but of his everlasting virility and youthful sexual powers.

But now let this same man rob a bank, run off with all the money in the office, embezzle millions from a client's trust fund, or fail to pay his "fair share" of taxes, and see what happens to him. The same judge who would remain calm when dealing with a case of fornication, adultery, or abortion now becomes quite angry and proceeds to "throw the book at him."

Let a manager of a large corporation "fool around" with the wife of a fellow manager of the same company and there is no way the boss can fire him according to the laws of the land. Legally one is not allowed to argue that, because of his actions, he is no longer fit to be a member of the company "team." However, let the same man take so much as a dollar from the company's bank account and he is on his way out the door before he can say "post-modernism."

The same sort of thing applies to the waitress down the street to whom you give your tip each day after lunch. Let her spend every night in someone else's bed and she is above reproach by all around her. No one can censure or reprimand her. Yet, let her fail to report her tips to the tax collector and see what ill fate befalls her. Will the judge have pity on her? Not in the least. She must pay the full amount plus interest and a fine in order to be set free. Why? Because of the "principle of the thing."

The same "principle" applies to the businessperson who fails to turn over the sales tax he or she has collected for the government. If the person owns a restaurant he or she can get away with all kinds of things, such as watering down the soup or overpowering your brain cells with monosodium glutamate, but not *that*. If the person runs a nightclub featuring the sexploitation of women, the law cannot lay a finger on him or her. But let that same person fail to fill out the proper small business forms, or neglect to send in the proper quarterly payment of taxes, and the government is down on the place in a minute, padlocking the doors and nailing shut the windows.

At first sight none of these events would seem to make any sense. Why should we distinguish among temptations? Offhand one would think that it is just as good (or bad) to covet your neighbor's winnings at the track or on the stock market as it is to covet his or her spouse. But that's not the case today. Why isn't lusting after a million dollars, even if it belongs to somebody else, and actually doing something about getting it into your own pocket, as much a matter of easy-going good humor in the *actual* operation of society as is lusting after somebody else's husband or wife, and doing something concrete about getting him or her into your own bed?

The answer to this question is that right and wrong are decided by social consensus, not by some divine standard or the like, and that the social consensus today is that giving in to the one type of temptation is fine while succumbing to the other kind is evil. What's right and wrong can be changed *at will*. Tomorrow things may be different, but the *justification* for the way things are will remain the same regardless of the particular content of the social mores. Now, granted that this is the case at the more fundamental philosophical level, that is to say, granted that post-modernism is the current orthodoxy, how do we go about enforcing the prevailing world-view?

The answer to this latter question is to look to the government for the appropriate laws. Once the government knows what is sacred and what is profane, it can establish the proper rules and regulations to enforce the will of the people. There's no such thing as the separation of religion and state. Religion and philosophical world-view are of primary importance in society. The only serious issue is *which* religion and *which* philosophy the state is to regard as the current orthodoxy. Today money has become the sign and symbol of what is sacred. Money does not have any intrinsic value in itself. It rather plays the role of a medium between the government and the social consensus. It's comparable to the role of prayer (the medium between human beings and God) in the Supernatural Theism religions of Judaeism, Christianity, and Islam, for instance.

Few people these days fully realize what has been happening to the relationship between human beings in society and the government's role as the keeper of the sacred prayers. Money is everything to the government. First, they actually make it. Then they have absolute control over all the institutions which distribute it. They command interest rates, the "flow" of money, and the investment of it. Governments also superintend the collection of money from businesses and individuals. It is the opinion of most governments that they can tax anything, at any time, to any extent.

In addition, the government possesses extraordinary power to intervene in each and every one of your financial affairs. Your bank accounts can be confiscated, the contents of your safe appropriated, and your very wages seized — and all legally. There is not a penny in your pocket that cannot be shaken out. Not only that, the ordinary citizen can be thrown into jail for being "uncooperative," or for failing to "confess" his or her money to the all-powerful tax collector. In post-modern society confession is good for your state.

At one time in the past (1895), for example, before the roots of the present-day liberal consensus became firmly fixed, the United States Supreme Court declared the newly introduced personal income tax to be unconstitutional. Today, of course, even without a constitutional amendment allowing it, such a move would be utterly unthinkable. This is so not merely because of the enormous amounts of money required by the government to give people what they want, but for a much more profound reason.

The more hidden reason for the present-day situation is that the government has the *right* to control what is sacred and to oversee the means necessary to salvation. As the socially appointed mediators between the new divine "reality" and human beings, all prayers must go through the government agents. The relationship between the government's interest in money and the decisions of the courts is no accident. Once one admits that money is the sign of the sacred, the means whereby we are incorporated into the state religion, the new myth of salvation via semi-socialized business, everything that follows fits neatly into place.

Within the new state religion actions such as homosexuality or adultery must hold a rather superficial place. On the other hand, however, doing something to disrupt the prayers of society must be considered as a deplorable crime. The state can tolerate almost anything other than a dispoiling of its body and blood, that is, of its money, which is a sign of the sacred. The only really grievous or mortal sins are monetary sins. Such sins offend against the very nature of the state, as justified by post-modernism, and cry to "God" for vengeance.

For those who violate the monetary code, who plunder the straight and narrow path to salvation, who rape the department of internal revenue, retribution is swift and sure. Like an Original Sin affecting our relationship to the divine, we are all, in the eyes of the mediators between The Holy and humans, guilty until proven innocent when it comes to money matters. And being "uncooperative," such as demanding something on the basis of another religion, can only make matters worse. Abandon your family and nothing will happen to you; murder your spouse and you can get away with ten to twenty; but offend the contemporary caretakers of the common consensus and you are condemned to hell (on earth) for as long as you live.

This is all perfectly justified, according to the post-modern mind-set. Although the state's attitude toward monetary matters may appear inconsistent with respect to matters of personal privacy and freedom, it does make sense within the anthropocentric world-view of thinkers such as Heidegger and Gadamer. Whereas the extreme libertarian branch of post-modernism is constantly missing the forest because of all the individual trees, the more typical post-modernism is supplied with an anti-chaos safety valve in the form of a social consensus which binds together the otherwise disintegrated members of the species. This allows certain legal rules and regulations to be regarded as if they were objectively true and certain, even though in fact they are not. Thus, according to this interpretation of reality, oppressive government policies with respect to financial matters are not really oppressive, but only another vindication of our right to rule ourselves.

To summarize, post-modernism has become in effect the unofficial new state religion, the new salvation myth, with universal validity, to which every good citizen must adhere. In effect, someone who fails to follow the liberal consensus is guilty of treason. The common standard of good behavior is no longer some inspired scripture, such as the Bible, but the pragmatic rules and regulations required for carrying on profit-making businesses (including many colleges, athletic teams, and so on). The government's business is to keep businesses going and profits flowing. To this extent, and only to this extent, it must be concerned about social welfare and stability. This takes money, the new *means* of salvation. Hence the *central* importance of the tax collector. In more ancient times heretics were burned at the stake; today the uncooperative dissident is grilled by inquisitors from the IRS, the new Holy Office.

Going under such names as Radical Hermeneutics, Deconstructionism, Neo-pragmatism, or Post-modernism, the current orthodoxy teaches that the modern world (1600–1945), with its separately existing God and objective science, has passed away forever, replaced by a much more fluid and amorphous world of process, thus calling for a much more radical mode of interpretation (hermeneutics). It holds that everything is only a metaphor and a symbol for a reality which really is not there. Everything is a function of history; all cultures and religions are only temporal, temporary, and mythological. In the beginning was not the Word of God but hermeneutics — and also in the middle and at the end.

Philosophically its roots lie in the rejection of Greek Being, that is, in the rejection of anything which is self-identical, immutable, unchanging, and absolute. The foundation for this attitude was laid down by the Epistemological Idealism of Descartes and Kant, and has reached its culmination in the twentieth-century Phenomenologists such as Martin Heidegger, Jean-Paul Sartre, and their many followers, including many nominally traditionally religious thinkers. They see being and becoming, essence and existence, tradition and novelty, object and subject, science and history, and so on, as absolutely irreconcilable. Truth to them means mainly internal coherence. There is no Truth, only local "truths." There can be no correspondence to reality because there is no reality. The most we can ever expect to "find" or "discover" is "reality." Everything is human-generated, anthropomorphized, and historicized.

Moreover, there is a moral dimension to the scene. The post-modern is good; the opposition is bad. Whereas post-moderns are *avant-garde,* liberal, and progressive, the uninitiated are fundamentalists, reactionary, and static. While the traditionalist is a medieval witch-hunter, the trans-modern is open-minded and tolerant. Where the backward ones are institutional, hierarchical, rigid, object-based, conservative, and unidirectional, the intellectually and morally superior ones are egalitarian, freedom-loving, process-based, subject-oriented, contextual, symbiotic, and self-transcending. Certainly the dogmatic ones cannot experience pathos, sympathy, and open-mindedness to the same high degree as the super-moderns.

Even though it is the orthodox view these days, nothing could be falser when applied to the basic principles of a thinker such as Thomas Aquinas, for instance. What *is* certain, however, is that post-modernism itself is not above criticism. The post-modern professionals completely overlook the fact that Deconstructionism is itself a dogmatic position. Even though it is the heritage of our age, as a doctrine its foundation is totally unnecessary and unsound, its assumptions are gratuitous, and its neutrality and open-mindedness are purely mythological. Practically speaking, as Plato saw a long time ago with respect to the Sophists, the doctrine of neo-modernity is completely unworkable, even in ordinary day-to-day affairs, and must sooner or later (if its full practical consequences were ever to be actually put into practice) lead to utter chaos and destruction.

One must wonder, "Can't we find a better alternative?" Backing up a few steps, we would also want to know: What more precisely does the doctrine attempt to teach us? What are its origins? And, given the great importance and need for interpretation (good hermeneutics) in all aspects of our understanding of both the past and the present, what can be salvaged from the extreme and exaggerated form of the hermeneutical doctrine which would still be true and useful to us today?

The purpose of this work is to review what the Deconstructionists have to say, to account in historical terms for why they feel it is necessary to say it, and to explain why it is in fact not at all necessary to make such claims. This can only be done in the philosophy of being, that science of the ordinary which deals with the meaning of "to be," essence and existence, the meaning of "reality," science and religion, and the ultimate source of all human life and understanding, whether God or the Primaeval Sea Soup. However, I do not expect my efforts to be received with open arms by everyone.

Back in the 1940s, based upon the unhappy experience of trying to get *Animal Farm* published, George Orwell pointed out that at any given time in history there is an "orthodox" world-view which all "right-thinking" people accept without question. Any challenger *deserves* to be silenced, and usually is. A genuinely unfashionable opinion is almost never given a fair hearing, either in the popular press or in professional books and journals. This is especially true when the movers and shakers of society are not even aware themselves of exactly what it is they hold and why they hold it. In Orwell's time and place, the Western intelligentsia was leaning heavily toward the Left. In 1946 even Harry S Truman was afraid of offending Stalin.

In the later 1980s Allan Bloom had to face a similar situation following the publication of his *The Closing of the American Mind: How Higher Education Has Failed Democracy and Impoverished the Souls of Today's Students*. In this work he argues that we must be very dogmatic about what is needed for a liberal democracy and its preservation. The *last* thing in the world we need is an infinite toleration and indifference in morals and politics. Calm, cool reason should rule, not popular special interests, especially in those institutions, such as the universities, where a criticism of the current assumptions of society is supposed to take place. The *last* thing in the world a university should be is merely a reflection of popular culture. What could be more level-headed and well-balanced?

Astonishingly, though, Bloom was vehemently attacked for even suggesting such a thing. Perhaps not so astonishingly, however, once we understand post-modernism, and how it has captured the mind of our contemporary world. To the typical secular post-modern the notions that authority and freedom, or dogma and toleration, are *not* incompatible is sheer heresy. Reviewers attacked him from every side. How could any really modern, up-to-date person possibly criticize the open-mindedness of Heidegger, or possibly object to the schools being taken over by Social Reformers, Feminists, Gays, Animal Rightists — or even Post-Modernists for that matter — and the like? He was rejected out-of-hand as being reactionary, and was widely diagnosed as suffering from the dread disease AIDS — Absolutist Illiberal Dogmatic Syndrome.

The same attitude can even be found today among various religious thinkers. Among some Roman Catholics, for instance, the very idea of a Universal Catechism dictated by Rome is regarded with deep repugnance. This is not because of some particular doctrine or other, such as whether or not Adam and Eve really existed, but because of the very idea of an objective measure whereby the authentic Catholic teacher can be distinguished from the pseudo-Catholic teacher. It is the very notion of a stable and enduring, eternal and non-historical, Truth that's repugnant. It's not so much a dispute between one doctrine and its contrary as it is a dispute between authority and freedom, which are assumed to be incompatible. The dissidents are especially troubled by this incompatibility in the area of "academic freedom" within Church-supported schools.

Even the Bible is not immune from the post-modern "paradigm shift." Some dissidents, following the lead of Nietzsche and others who cast aside scholarship and who regard Scripture as just another totally human production, think nothing of rewriting Holy Writ to suit themselves. Since the ultimate power of creation and destruction rests with human beings, they believe that they have every right to do so. *They* represent the vanguard, the will of "the people," the wave of the future. They can do no wrong; the rear guard can do no right. From the Judaeo-Christian viewpoint, the "new morality," which wants to supplant the "old" religion and alter Scripture to suit itself, is mainly the old paganism. Yet today many Church leaders (perhaps out of ignorance), instead of doing everything they can within the bounds of love and reason to curtail such activity, are actually encouraging it. Truly post-modernism is a universal phenomenon today.

If this is true, then post-modernism cannot be overthrown by some particularized counterattack. It must instead be attacked at its very *root*. This, I think, is the most effective way to proceed. Whereas thinkers such as Allan Bloom concentrate more on the political philosophy level, my intention is to address the issue on the more fundamental philosophy-of-being level. This is the foundational analysis approach. An historical-analytical approach will reveal the weakness at the foundation of post-modernism. An historical analysis of the road up to our later twentieth-century state of affairs, in other words, this work as a whole, *is itself* the major argument against the post-modern position. Once we clearly see what it takes for granted, and how in fact there exists a more commonsensical, well-balanced, logical, scientific, and true-to-life alternative, the back of super-modernism, theoretically at least, will have been broken. Thus, will Deconstructionism be deconstructed — undone by its own inattention to its own most basic assumptions?

NIETZSCHE AND FRIENDS:
THE ATTACK ON BEING,
KNOWLEDGE, AND MORALS

> ...bis der Text unter der Interpretation verschwand (... till the
> text vanished under the interpretation).
>
> F. W. Nietzsche
> *Beyond Good and Evil:* 38

> What if Nietzsche himself meant to say nothing, or at least not
> much of anything, or anything whatever? Then again, what if
> Nietzsche was only pretending to say something?
>
> J. Derrida
> *Spurs* (1979): 125, 127

Modernity has several meanings. As it is currently understood in
contemporary philosophy it means modern philosophy, or those
traits and characteristics that were stamped upon modern thought
by the seventeenth-century philosophers and scientists, most notably
Descartes and Newton. These traits and characteristics are
primarily the various forms of dualism that were initiated in the
seventeenth century and continued into our own century. These
would include the split between subject and object, private and public,
body and mind, matter and mind, matter and energy, space and
time, hard data or facts and theory or explanatory systems, the world
and experience, concrete and abstract, empiricism and rationalism,
senses and consciousness, the universe and God, and other forms of
bifurcation.

The most fundamental split of all, though, and the one that post-
moderns use to summarize all the others, is the one between Being
and Becoming, that is, between that which is eternally fixed,
immutable, permanent, unchanging, non-historical, and isolated
within itself, and that which is forever in flux, changing, temporal,
developing, growing, evolving, dynamic, and implicated in
everything, everywhere.

If this be modernity, then post-modernity must be that which moves beyond all such divisions in order to establish (or reestablish) a unity and integration among all of the many and various separations that have so dominated the world of the recent past. In this regard new developments in science, such as Einstein's relativity theory, Niels Bohr's interpretation of physical properties, quantum mechanics, high energy physics, and unified field theory, have helped the cause of integration a great deal.

But why should the philosopher always lag behind? Instead of being a follower the philosopher should lead the way in the process of breaking down the old rigid structures and erecting in their place a new palace of knowledge better suited to our present times. This is the task of the hyper-modern thinker, and if he or she has erred by replacing one extreme view with another extreme view, it can at least be understood and sympathized with even if such extremism is not accepted as being truly the last word on the subject. After all, the deep-seated desire for integration is as basic to the human mind as the need for all human beings to know the source and origin of their existence, and so should be treated with great respect. Indeed, it may well be that finding the answer to the first problem would also prove to be a great help in finding the answer to the second problem.

The general direction taken by post-modern thinkers is toward the submerging of everything in one general all-consuming flux in which everything is dissolved together in one world of Becoming. *Everything* must be relativized, even science, and even God if indeed there is such a being. They propose to radicalize the ancient need for interpreting the spoken and written word to such an extent that little if anything is left of the original work of art, philosophical, scientific, or theological text, and so on. This is because there is no Self. To discover an author's meaning, in the old-fashioned, outmoded way of looking at hermeneutics, requires that you have an author. But to have an author means having a person, which means having an enduring and unified Self. Deconstruct the Self and the whole series collapses, resulting in nothing but a naked text to be looked at anew each time by various interpreters.[1]

The post-moderns take their lead largely from the Phenomenologists and Atheistic Existentialists of the twentieth century, especially Martin Heidegger. At all times, though, they retain the right to reject whatever they consider to be too traditional in such philosophies. In their own view of themselves, they have transcended all of the old, classical categories of all past philosophy, science, and theology. All the traditional distinctions, such as those between absolutism and relativism, Idealism and Realism, objectivism and subjectivism, and so on, are rejected as inherently incoherent. Such divisions have never really existed; they have only recently been invented by various Western philosophers. We *now* see how all such dichotomies coalesce into unity.

The modernity school affirms that all such categories are now outmoded and that we have now entered into a new era of Radical Hermeneutics and Deconstructionism. In this New Age everything is so historically conditioned and sociologically relativized that nothing remains of past rational thought. All is new and different. Even rationality itself must be reinterpreted. The old emphasis on logical thought, of building up a case based upon true and certain premises, of working with fixed definitions, of getting the facts right, and so forth, has now all gone by the board; it is now all ancient water under the philosophical bridge of time, ever flowing in the river in which we can never step twice — or even once. Serious study is still allowed, but only in a humanized, anthropocentric form. In the beginning was *hermēneutikos*; and now also in the end.

This also explains why no one in the modernity school can allow science to be taken seriously as true and certain, necessary and universal, knowledge. The natural world must be as open to many and various interpretations as any other aspect of the human world, whether literature, morals, or anything else. Once you admit that there is objective knowledge not subject to social consensus and historical conditioning, you would have *ipso facto* destroyed the universal nature of Deconstructionism. Science, as a human endeavor, cannot be allowed to transcend particular times and places any more than anything else. Hence, the theory cannot allow for one person to be right (e.g., a Copernicus or a Galileo) while everyone else in the society is wrong. This would be the hole in the dyke which would allow all the old dichotomies to flood back in again.

Certainly the world must be allowed to be what it is. But *what* is it? Certainly we can presume that as long as there has been language there has been the need for hermeneutics, that is, for interpretation, for letting the true meaning of the words show itself. But what if there is no true meaning? What if there is no text at all? What if all we have is the human subject, forever locked within himself or herself, unable to speak the truth about God or anything else, including the Self? Is the ultimate meaning of reality that it has no meaning, and — as with some of the ancient Sophists such as Gorgias — isn't even there?[2]

Although the need for hermeneutics has always been recognized and accepted by reasonable people, Deconstructionism is a horse of a different color. Deconstructionism is an extreme and radical form of hermeneutics. Saying that we must be circumspect and cautious in our attempts to understand something, that we must be aware of the difficulties inherent in any attempt to comprehend the meaning of some text from the past, and even of the present, is one thing. But to claim that it is impossible in principle to ever understand the true meaning of the original text, or that in fact there is no true meaning at all, is quite another sort of thing.

In literary circles Deconstructionism means that the critic is more important than the text; that the interpreter is superior to the original artist when it comes to understanding the work. In effect it implies that there is nothing really objective about the piece to be analyzed; there is only a more or less circumspect collection of different perspectives and critical viewpoints. It can also mean that the only real meaning in the work under review is what the reviewer puts into it. Interpretation becomes a sort of game, a never-ending "playing around." Being creative is reduced to being relatively different.

Generally speaking, it means that the methodology, principles, and process of interpretation and explanation are *everything* of importance in our anthropocentric understanding of the world. Although this process might be temporarily suspended or held in abeyance, usually by arbitrary human convention, especially for the sake of social and political stability, it can never be replaced with anything final and definitive. The center of reality, where we might expect to find The Truth, is in fact empty. The best we can do is to circle the hollow hub forever, providing our own projections and holographs as we go through life.

But does such a view really make any sense? Even while admitting the literary abilities of writers such as Roland Barthes, Jacques Derrida, Michel Foucault, Hans-Georg Gadamer, and Richard Rorty, someone still has the right to ask: Is the thought of thinkers such as Heidegger and his many disciples really something different *in kind* from everything that has gone before? Or is it only some old drink in a new bottle, some old clay in a new shape, some ancient philosophy dressed in lederhosen rather than togas? Is the contemporary way really "post-" or only very much "pre-" modern? Have we "advanced" to the point of being positively prehistoric? Is it the way of the future for evermore, or is it simply ancient sophism in disguise?

This modern form of agnosticism and skepticism extends not only to the results of reasoning but to the reasoning power itself. The world is divided and subdivided into innumerable parts and aspects, none of which is actually coherent with any other part, even though we might "see" some degree of coherence by arbitrarily projecting such into the world. The self, the ordinary world, and scientific laws, in any objective sense, all disappear in a cloud of unknowing. In parallel fashion, the verbal expression of this non-knowledge is also broken up and scattered, *never* to be reunited in some intelligible way.

However, when one looks into the background and foundation for this current fashion in human thought, one finds that it is precariously perched upon a false assumption. The stage has been set for this modern mind-set by a series of recent thinkers going back several centuries. In the more recent past the key figure is Martin Heidegger, who took his inspiration from Hegel and Nietzsche. Descartes, Kant, William James, and Jean-Paul Sartre have also been key players in our time.

If we dilate a moment on Nietzsche, we find that many of the familiar terms of twentieth-century philosophy, such as "absurd" and "nausea," were already present in his works and were used in basically the same way as they are used today. The total desubstantialization of everything is also found in his works. In addition, Nietzsche's phobia for divine, personal authority-figures — as if being true to yourself, or to the forces of nature which are (supposedly) surging through you, stood in contradictory opposition to being true to God or to God's earthly vicars — is still a common theme in many modern circles (even religious ones!). His lamentations over the decline of European culture, with the emphasis on German culture, might also be mentioned as something very pertinent to the twentieth century, especially as seen in Martin Heidegger.

Neither did Nietzsche hesitate to reinterpret the Judaeo-Christian Scriptures, usually in some very strange ways, when it suited his purposes to do so. In our own time, thinkers such as Hans Kueng and the late J. L. Mackie can be found doing the same sort of thing. For example, what can a secularist do with all the talk in the Bible and Church tradition about love, "love thy neighbor," "God is Love," and so on? The answer given in the *Antichrist* I: 23 (Kaufmann ed.) is that, since love is blind, since love is the state in which we see things the least clearly and distinctly, it is the state in which we are most susceptible to being deceived and lied to. The emphasis upon love was therefore only a clever and shrewd invention on the part of the early Christian leaders, deliberately designed to make Christianity's early devotees more willing to sacrifice themselves for the sake of God and Church.

As far as Jesus Christ himself is concerned, he was not such a bad person after all. He was in fact very much like Nietzsche himself. As we learn in sections 33–36 of the *Antichrist,* the *true* meaning of the Gospels and Christianity, something which was lost from the day of the Cross to this, is the unity of God and man. Sounding very much like Hegel who came before him and Kueng who comes after him, for Nietzsche the purely human, naturalized Christ figure is simply a window on Reality; a symbolist who showed us how to live in a completely guiltless way in a completely naturalized world.

There is nothing divine about Redemption. The *true* historical Christ did nothing more (nor less — because it is of great importance) than show us how to save ourselves; to pull ourselves up by our own bootstraps. According to this nihilized version of Christ only inner realities are really real. Everything else of a natural, temporal, spatial, and historical nature is only a sign and an occasion for stories. Everything is symbolic, a sign of the truth about the human condition, which is for each of us to be an individualized, finite, mortal, suffering nothing (as in Buddhism), struggling to get by amid the Great Unknown.

The vast majority of us are weak — all too weak — and end up being members of the security- and comfort-seeking herd. A few especially bold and enlightened ones (that is, those who agree with Nietzsche and have the Will to act) might become Supermen. It is the role of the Superman (there is no Superwoman for Nietzsche) to remake the world according to his own image, even if it means great self-discipline and suffering on his part. In general, the world *is* a projection of human desires anyway. It is not only that the past is an interpretation imposed upon it by a future generation; it is that the *present* is an invention, an ever-ongoing interpretation, here and now. In this regard, all of society is parallel to the individual insofar as it invents its own stories, myths, narratives, "histories," and the like, about itself as it goes along. And society, in order to keep going and to be progressive, requires strong leaders.

More often than not these attitudes are simply taken for granted, not only among the common folk to whom they have seeped down from the philosophers and the masters of the modern media, but also among the academics and intellectuals. They go completely unchallenged; they pass for the obvious and the "reasonable"; there is little, if any, questioning of one's presuppositions. And, as Allan Bloom points out at the beginning of his *The Closing of the American Mind,* if and when they are questioned there is disbelief and consternation, and sometimes obviously overt hostility, toward the challenger. How can such a one be so backward, regressive, and just plain "out of it"? As Bloom anticipated, it is for this reason that his work caused such an uproar among the conservative academic defenders of the *status quo.*

This rejection, of course, is precisely what I reject. In its place I would suggest that the whole modern, *avant-garde* mind-set is founded upon a radically false, or at least unnecessary, initial starting point. Once this first false step is exposed to the sunlight, certain consequences are sure to follow in the thinking of any truly open-minded person, the main one being a serious reconsideration of the whole Deconstructionism doctrine.

The major basic false assumption upon which rests the whole case for the post-modern mind-set, and which uses hermeneutics in such a way so as to destroy in advance any possibility for true and certain knowledge in science, philosophy, and theology, is that Being and Becoming cannot be reconciled, and thus the modern thinker is forced to choose one and reject the other. The thinking today, ironically enough often appealing to supposedly uncertain science for support, is that the up-to-date, modern, *avant-garde* thinker must choose Becoming and jettison Being.

Nietzsche is very far from being the first to face this issue. However, he did it in such an impudent and stark style that he has now come to epitomize the issue in the modern milieu. Although he never really challenged his own first principles, the whole situation is sharply spelled out for us in his works. For instance, in his *Twilight of the Idols* he asserts:

> Whatever has being does not become; whatever becomes does not have being. Now they [all the classical philosophers] all believe, desperately even, in what has being. . . . But Heraclitus will remain eternally right with his assertion that being is an empty fiction. The "apparent" world is the only one: the "true" world is merely added by a lie. (Kaufmann ed. IV: 1–2)

We are also taught by Nietzsche that there are no things, no substances, that there is nothing permanent, and that there is no unity to anything (if there were things). Ironically for a defender of bold, free actions, he also insists that there is no free will in human beings (if there were human beings and human nature).

In his *Antichrist* I: 15, 25, we are told about the basic opposition between Being and Becoming in the form of the opposition between God and Nature. This, proclaims Nietzsche, explains *everything* with respect to the modern world and the continued existence of traditional religion, especially Judaeo-Christianity. It is only the empty, hot-air belief in Being which keeps religion afloat. But Being, God, the permanent, the unchanging, the absolute, and so forth, are pure fictions and lies. Nature, though, is good and real. As a first approximation we can say that the mere outward *appearance* of things *is* the really real. However, when we come to fully understand what this means for us in practical terms, we will soon realize that neither the essence nor the appearance, the apparently stable nor the changeable, the conceptual nor the sensible, are really real. If there are no things, there cannot be any appearances of things. *Everything* is disorganized, disunited, deconstructed (*Twilight* V: 6).

Generally speaking, though, the changeable, the historical, the superficial must be accepted; the divine, the immutable, the morally fixed and absolute must be rejected. Since we cannot have both at the same time, and since we must go with what our immediate experiences tell us, we have no choice but to jettison the old-fashioned, outmoded notion of God as Being and accept with open arms and great joy the fact that we are alone in an absurd world. We are forever on the brink, always about to fall over, forever rocking back and forth and being tossed about on a meaningless sea; it is no wonder that we feel nauseated in such a world.

But what is the alternative? Within the very limited confines of Nietzsche's absolute dichotomy it can only be a return to the unnatural, that is, to Being. We would then be back inside the straitjacket of some divine moral world-order, whether of a Platonic, Judaeo-Christian, Kantian, or whatever kind. Once grant "Being" and everything bad in human life is sure to follow. He tells us in his *Antichrist* "When, through [divine, fear-of-God] reward and punishment, one has done away with natural causality, an *anti-natural* causality is required: now everything that is unnatural follows" (I: 25).

Supernatural causality or natural causality represents an absolute dichotomy for Nietzsche. Once you accept the former, *everything* bad follows. This terrible denaturing of everything that is humanistic and ennobling is the legacy of the Jews and of their religious offspring, the first Christians after Jesus Christ himself. Instead of living a healthy, happy life, without feelings of guilt and remorse over our actions (some of which must naturally be dark and terrible), traditional religion has besmirched us with the lie of sinfulness. Because of religion we regard the exercise of our natural functions as dangerous temptations; we are poisoned by the worm of conscience, and in general, we lose the innocence of change. We lose the sense and the joy of the momentary and of the purely sensual; of the new (relatively speaking at least) because it is the new, and only because it is the new; of the wonderfully gratuitous, accidental, airy, and even of the trivial, fickle, and flighty Superficial.

This must necessarily be the case because the human race has stubbornly clung to the outmoded, old-fashioned, and so on, idea of Being. When will we ever wake up to the fact that The Fixed (essences, substances, meanings) is incompatible with The Changeable and that we must adhere to the latter in order to really and truly be ourselves? All the while, of course, we must realize that there is no self; we are as much a part of the "apparent" natural world as anything else (keeping in mind that there are no things — not even mind-things).

Although he is interesting as a literary figure, no intelligent person can take Nietzsche seriously. The very best one can do is to only *appear* to do so. It is no exaggeration to say that *if* we take Nietzsche seriously (which no one can really do), literally everything is gone, including Nietzsche and everything he ever wrote and said. The end result is utter confusion and universal unintelligibility. There would be absolutely nothing left for anyone to be tolerant of or relative to.

Moreover, it is, strictly speaking, impossible to say what *is not* real, true, and good without knowing, at least in one's own mind and to one's own satisfaction, what *is* real, true, and good. For Nietzsche to imply that everything is unreal, both essence and existence, permanence and change, fixed meaning and word, also implies that he knows what is real. One cannot compare something to something else without a conscious knowledge of both things. To know, to speak in such a way as to imply knowledge (rather than simply uttering gibberish), to say that one thing does not correspond in some way or other to another thing, demands that we know, or at least seriously think we know, the pertinent information about both the one and the other thing. Despite what he may want, or have the ability to superficially say in words, Nietzsche cannot both eat his cake and have it too. Without something to become there cannot be any becoming. We might conceive of being without becoming, but not vice versa. In parallel fashion, even to think of non-being (nothingness) demands thinking of being (somethingness).

Since there is no reality for Nietzsche, he must forever abandon any hope of finding reality. To hope at all in the sense of hoping for the "beyond," for heaven, for Being, is a great evil for Nietzsche. He praises the Greek mythologists for leaving hope behind in Pandora's Box of evils (*Antichrist* I: 23). This is just before asserting that the Virgin Mary was invented by the early Church in order to stimulate lust and thereby help attract pagan males to Christianity, which occurs just before asserting his interpretation of love mentioned above.

This absolute knowledge of non-knowledge on Nietzsche's part is an amazingly bold assertion, but one which is impossible to maintain. His permanent knowledge of non-permanence destroys non-permanence. Nietzsche is constantly *relating* to us *why* he declares himself on this or that subject, the *reasons* for his hard-and-fast conclusions, the evidence that *proves* he is right beyond any shadow of a doubt. How can this be unless he really knows something? What are we to make of the great faith he has in his own intellect to understand evidence, reasons, proofs, conclusions, and so on? Did he start out with hope and end with certitude? Is his position now true and fixed forever? Has he given us The Truth about Reality?

Even Kant, for all his hard work devoted to institutionalizing Descartes, knew this. Reality in itself is unknown, he claimed, but science is possible because *all* human beings have born within themselves the *same* set of interpretive categories, to be applied in basically the *same* way. His Duty and Categorical Moral Imperative served the same purpose in ethics. This is Kant's version of scientific objectivity. In fact, it is not a real scientific objectivity, as we know today after the breakdown of Newtonian physics, the discovery of non-Euclidean geometries, and so on. Nevertheless, he at least recognized the need for some sort of universal and constant standards whereby human knowledge and morals can be judged; which may help explain why thinkers such as Nietzsche, James, Heidegger,

Gadamer, Rorty, and others, despite Kant's subjectivism, want little to do with him.

It is not clear what constitutes the overwhelmingly convincing modern situation of which Nietzsche speaks. Is it based primarily upon the results of modern science, or does it derive from Hegel? On the one hand Nietzsche keeps insisting upon the unity of God and man, and upon the profound self-overcoming of the spirit. On the other hand he attacks speculative knowledge as certainly not the basis for action, and even impossible in principle. Speculative knowledge depends upon having things with essences, things which can be known in themselves. But if there are no such things, we are left with *only* instinct, intuition, drives, and practice. In other words, we are left with only practical knowledge and *pragmatism*. He thinks it is a gross indecency on the part of modern man not to recognize this and henceforth act accordingly. In this light he attacks Hegel's Pure Spirit as pure stupidity and the Absolute as pure nonsense.

Science, though, he thinks, seems to fit in well with an emphasis upon sensations, and it is this sensate becoming which has pushed God out of the world (*Twilight* IV: 3; cf. *Antichrist* I: 48). If indeed science (meaning primarily the biological and physical sciences) is basically the work of the senses, somehow carefully organized and interrelated, a view which he may have gotten from Hume and Comte, then we would again be back in the world of the Atomistic Pre-Socratic philosophers who could not rise above the level of their senses to contemplate that which is spiritually permanent, unchanging, and essentially fixed. Once again it is Being against Becoming, with the ever-shifting sands of the senses providing no basis for stability and permanence in the world as we know (sense) it.

Some later thinkers, such as Rorty, when faced with the traditional problems of philosophy, would just as soon change the subject. What the subject is changed to, though, in no way solves the problems. Neither does it cause them to simply go away. The issues are so basic to human thought that there is in fact nowhere to which the post-modern thinker can transcend. This urge to escape, to transcend, is totally in vain, a mere matter of wishful thinking.

A foundational analysis may in fact reveal that science, poetry, novels, depth psychology, anthropology, mysticism, and so on, are *not* all on a par insofar as their speculative value is concerned. One might find that there is no reason why we cannot have, at the same time, both the truth about extramental things and intramental coherence, a conformity and correspondence (but not in the form of representations and pictures) of the mind to reality and the internal accommodation of one proposition to another, of public and private knowledge, and so forth. Why must we assume, at the outset and at any time, that it is a case of *either* essences (Plato, correspondence,

God, religion) *or* existence (science, coherence, positivism, agnosticism, skepticism, consensus) with no possibility for a reconciliation or for a unifying middle position?

Nietzsche suffers nausea when he sees the way his contemporary human beings, especially the more learned ones and the social and political leaders, keep calling themselves Christians when in fact they all know in their own minds and consciences that modern science has destroyed anything like the Beyond, the Last Judgment, the immortality of the soul, the existence of God, sin, redemption, and even free will in humans (*Antichrist* I: 38). Yet he himself continually keeps exhorting his readers to rise up, throw off the chains forged about their bodies by priests and atavistic theologians, and become examples of his new, naturalized man. Once again he wants to eat his cake and have it too. According to his own theory there is no possible basis for any sort of free action, either on his part or on the part of his readers. Are we to assume then that his thinking and writing are the work of an automaton? Is it a case of one tape recorder "talking" to other tape recorders?

In any event, it is the real world which must act as the guide and measure of the mind's judgments, not vice versa. Abandon reality as the criterion of what is true and all other forms of mental activity become meaningless, if not outrightly impossible. No one given theory, however elegant and internally coherent within itself, would be any more worthy of being accepted by honest, intelligent people than any other one. The theory must adjust to the facts, to the real world, not vice versa.

Even the very best fiction writers cannot exceed the limits of their own experiences of the real world. This is why the truth is in fact always stranger than fiction and always must be so. One's imagination is always dependent upon one's real-life experiences. A budding fiction writer is always advised to write of what he or she knows best. We can only speak of what we know, even if we are just speaking fables. But Nietzsche would have us believe that he does not really know anything; yet, he keeps on talking.

Anyone who tries to take Nietzsche seriously would be back in the world of the ancient Sophists, verbally claiming that all points of view are equally true and valid, and finally reduced to silence and the mere wiggling of fingers, while all the time actually acting and living on the basis of their knowledge of unified, substantial entities with fixed natures pursuing fixed goals, including the self. Is a radical hypocrisy the final product of a radical, hyper-modern "authenticity"? Why not? If you are going to sin or to make a fool of yourself you should, according to Nietzsche, at least do so boldly and even egregiously. Yet, given its radical impracticality, one wonders, could it be that Nietzsche's whole output is one long deliberate joke foisted upon gullible followers? Could it be the perverse palming off of a playful lunacy by a master prankster? As Derrida asks, is Nietzsche really saying anything at all?

However we look at it, though, in modern as well as in ancient times, whether in Europe or in any other part of the world, the whole deduction is asserted on the basis of a supposedly irreconcilable war between Being and Becoming. This is the great false premise of the Deconstructionist outlook and is, therefore, the main issue to be discussed in this book.

Anyone who, like Nietzsche, attacks Being must pay a heavy penalty for doing so. All intelligibility depends upon having something to know. Nothing accounts for nothing. Neither can a pure Becoming be comprehended. Whether in science, philosophy, or theology, there must be something fixed, or "tethered" as Plato would say.[3] Any knowledge worthy of the name must give an account or explanation of why things, including the things of the senses, are the way they are. This means finding the unifying concept, idea, formula, definition, and so on, which gives the investigator the pattern for interpreting the world of experience as it *really* is. Denying the existence of natures or essences is tantamount to denying the possibility of any kind of mathematics and science. The alternative to a nature composed of substantial centers of action (natures) capable of being known, at least indirectly via a process which investigates the activities performed by the substantial entities so that we come to know things as they really are, is an amorphous world in which everything melts into everything else. Such a world, were it to really exist that way, would be utterly unintelligible to us.

Yet, this is the sort of world the post-moderns would have us believe in. Some post-moderns adopt as their model the reductionistic physicalist metaphysics of David Hume in their efforts to bring a kind of uniformity and homogeneity to things. Others adopt the pantheism of the Stoics or of a Georg Hegel in order to achieve the same all-comprehensive view of *one* world without fundamental dichotomies, especially the existence of God as a separately existing Supreme Being. All post-moderns, despite their various differences, begin with Nietzsche's God-is-dead nihilism. Some, generally the Humeans, refuse to discuss God at all in any serious way. Others, generally the Hegelians, are willing to retain some notion of God, but only in what they consider to be the updated, modified version of some form of process philosophy and theology. In either case, relativism reigns supreme.

There is also general agreement on the need for an anthropocentric rather than a theocentric approach to human life. The motto "Man is the measure" of the ancient Sophist Protagoras of Abdera is emphasized.[4] Exactly *how* man is the measure, though, is open to various interpretations. Some adopt the highly subjective view which Hume derived from Descartes (see Appendix), while others take the more roundabout approach of Hegel. With respect to this latter way, John Macquarrie, for instance, in his *In Search of Deity* (1985) follows very closely in the footsteps of Hegel in this regard. Hegel claimed that he was not a pantheist because Spinoza was a pantheist and he (Hegel) was not like Spinoza. Spinoza's one substance was static and acosmic while Hegel's God was dynamic. Hegel also claimed that his doctrine was compatible with Christianity, and was indeed the highest and best form of Christianity.

Macquarrie makes similar claims. His dialectical theism is not a pantheism, he claims, because it is like Hegel's doctrine, which was not a pantheism. He defines pantheism as a doctrine which asserts the homogeneous presence of God throughout nature; indeed, God is Nature; the world is God. Macquarrie, however, denies that this is the way the world really is. He may not know why there is evil in the world but he does know that God, although *in* the world and *continuous with* the world, is not equally immanent everywhere and equally expressed in everything.[5]

Following Hegel, Macquarrie regards the human species as the greatest manifestation of God. Man is the Absolute coming to know Itself. Changing Christian doctrine to accommodate his dialectical theism, he claims that the *whole* human race is the "incarnation" of God. Jesus Christ, although certainly an exalted figure in religious history, cannot claim any really special status in this regard. It is only through man that we know God, not vice versa. It is human nature rather than divine nature (because all men are divine to a high degree) which is at the center of his natural theology. Thus is an apparent theocentrism transmuted into an anthropocentrism.

In addition, few post-moderns are willing to accept the completely amoral personal, social, and political consequences of Nietzsche's God-is-dead dictum. As unsatisfactory as their attempts may be, over and over again they attempt to circumvent the necessarily amoral consequences of both the reductionistic materialistic and the amorphous pantheistic positions. Neither approach provides any basis for an objective and binding moral code for human behavior. Both are completely relativistic, which is to say, both leave us completely at sea as far as any secure shoreline or steady horizon for ethical behavior is concerned. The "moral holiday" denied by William James is in fact guaranteed by post-modernism, and it is not a very pleasant cruise.

For example, taking his lead from Heidegger, Gadamer proposes a doctrine of a thoroughgoing historical-cultural relativism, of a complete becoming/duration/temporality conditioning. According to Gadamer, in his *Truth and Method* (1989), there is no method that can give us the truth. He insists that the human condition is never freed of its historical context. Even in those periods of world history in which there is an emphasis upon the absolute, absolutism is not really the case. Even non-historical culture is itself the result of historical conditioning. There is no escaping the web of time. Everything is caught up in the net of temporality. This is as true of philosophy itself as it is of anything else, even of those philosophies of the Absolute. Those who would escape the trap of temporality and historically conditioned truth and being are attempting to do the impossible. Even the best philosophical broom cannot sweep out the ocean of time. Only a god could have such an atemporal, ahistorical knowledge, and man is not a god, but only a man.

This attitude also has its implications for social and political philosophy. Given a situation in which we are free to discuss God and the gods as much as we wish, can anyone ever expect to come up with any sort of definitive resolution of the God Question based upon philosophical reasoning? And if we cannot, on what basis are we to establish our rules and laws for the regulation of our interpersonal social and political lives? Remembering that even the physical and social sciences are as much relativized as anything else, and so cannot be called upon to rescue us, can we have any hope that such truths can ever come out of philosophical reasoning concerning the ultimate questions of human life? Granted that science cannot solve for us any of our ethical and moral problems, can we ever hope to find the answers in some philosophical *method*?

According to at least one contemporary thinker, the answer is no. After Descartes's attempt to overcome skepticism and the failure of this attempt as shown in Hume; after Kant's attempt to overcome Hume's skepticism and the failure of Kant's attempt as seen in Comte and J. S. Mill; and after the attempts of thinkers such as Karl Marx, Edmund Husserl, Bertrand Russell, and A. J. Ayer to overcome the skepticisms previous to themselves, we are once again in the depths of dark depression as far as rational thought is concerned. This, at least, seems to be the view of Richard Rorty in his work *Philosophy and the Mirror of Nature* (1979). Rorty's point is that philosophy cannot be the mirror of nature. No philosophical system can be objectively true. The aim of philosophy is not truth but criticism. Its role is not to systematize truth but to edify in the sense of constantly analyzing and questioning.

But does this mean then that we can live on bread alone? Is it then no longer true that a nation without vision perishes? Not exactly. Human beings and human societies still require values by which to live. Saying that these values cannot be supplied by philosophy, science, or theology does not mean that we can therefore forget about them or do away with them. But how then do we get and keep them? Rorty's answer is that we *must* get and keep them through social convention. Philosophical systems, which are really attempted justifications for the historically conditioned behavior of people and societies, are arrived at by subtle social inculcation and cultural decisions. Values are not derived from nature, but are projections into nature of what a society wants. Civic virtue is the only virtue.

In philosophy, claims Rorty, there can be no "privileged representations." Taking his cue from Wilfrid Sellars and W.V.O. Quine, two followers of Russell, but who are "heretical" because of their skepticism relative to Russell's dogmatism, Rorty claims that the *appearance* of the objective truth of philosophical (justificational) systems is *really* due to a process of social dialectic, social "conversation," and social practice. "The crucial premise of this argument is that we understand knowledge when we understand the social justification of belief, and thus have no need to view it as accuracy of representation."[6]

Philosophy, therefore, can never be true and certain knowledge. And any theory which claims it has *the* method for discovering the truth in philosophy is sure to be overturned sooner or later. For a long time this emphasis upon the study of knowledge (epistemology) first, and the philosophy of nature, or being, or ethics, and so on, later, has led us astray. Now we know that no theory of knowledge can claim a privileged relationship to reality. In the end, it seems, even philosophy is deconstructed.

This theme is continued in Rorty's *Consequences of Pragmatism* (1982). Pragmatism is characterized by Rorty as being a form of anti-essentialism applied to epistemological issues and moral philosophy. It also declares that there is no basic epistemological difference between the "is" and the "ought" of ordinary language, the "facts" and "values" of metaphysical language, and "morality" and "science" in methodological discourse. In addition, pragmatism means "there are no constraints on inquiry save conversational ones — no wholesale constraints derived from the nature of the objects, or of the mind, or of language, but only those retail constraints provided by the remarks of our fellow-inquirers."[7] What Rorty wants is a Pure Dialectic sort of situation. With shades of James's terminology, the wholesale market in truth is shut down. The only thing that counts is whether something works, and this is decided solely by the way in which it is accepted or rejected by the ever-ongoing process of societal discussion. Sooner or later there will be a consensus, even if only for a short time. That this does happen in society is a matter of fact.

Conversation is *a good in itself, its own end,* and *its own justification*; its success is measured by the mere fact that it continues. Rorty thinks that this goes a long way in reducing the charges of moral relativism and irrationalism that are often leveled against pragmatism. Rather than condemning pragmatism as an invitation to moral holidays, we should be proud of the fact that William James and John Dewey could provide us with no guarantees about the actual success and future outcome of our efforts. With respect to results, in true pragmatic fashion, Rorty says wait and see. In effect, we are invited to play a game of Russian roulette with individual lives and the life of society.

Yet, this is the best he can do. Today, thinks Rorty, those who continue to talk about Being and essences are merely comic figures who give philosophy a bad name. Anyone who takes Being seriously is an outdated old fogy. What Rorty wants is a greater sense of human community, and the way to get it is to see ourselves as thrown together in a great rudderless, motorless, sailless ship at sea, going nowhere in particular, following a non-course unchartered by any Divine Will or Mind, and facing unknown dangers over every new wave we encounter. But, all is not hopeless; we can and must go on, deciding amongst ourselves, through the means of open and free discussion, *which is a good in itself,* how fast, how far, and in what direction we will paddle our own canoe, using our own power, might, and will. Heidegger said we must face death bravely on our own; Rorty says we must bravely face the future, and maybe death also, on our own.

Rorty begins by adopting Nietzsche's nihilism, that is, by agreeing that all the religious, traditional theological thought patterns, and traditional philosophical justifications for human moral behavior based upon objective standards are now dead and gone *forever.* This situation is epitomized in the death-of-God slogan. However, the state of emptiness and nothingness which follows upon nihilism is not meant to be a final state of despair but the opening up to something better in the future. For Nietzsche it freed the Superman to pursue his own goals without any feelings of guilt. For Rorty it means that we are now on our own as a community. The Herd Mentality, which Nietzsche so despised, is elevated by Rorty into a place of honor. The Collective Superman replaces the Individual Superman. And all because we must continue to live in society without Being. I think Rorty is speaking in his own name when he says, "Being is what Nietzsche, as spokesman for the concluding moment of the dialectic of the last two thousand years, said it was: a 'vapor and a fallacy.'"[8]

When we put this together with Rorty's belief that the fact of social discourse, and its continuity forever, is a *per se* good, we can reach the conclusion that all of mankind has an obligation not to destroy or outlaw various subdivisions of the one human race for any reason whatsoever. Even though unjustified and ungrounded, toleration is the last word on the subject. Even though unsupported by any external aids, such as God, Science, Knowledge, Rationality, or Truth, we *must* nevertheless continue to forge ahead and make the best of it. The basic moral dictum is be tolerant.[9]

Running counter to the old adage that "When philosophers disagree blood is shed," Rorty insists that we had best learn a real respect for each other, regardless of how outlandish our views may appear to each other. With respect to academics, it means that no one should call a colleague a bad name, and the last thing we should see are fistfights breaking out in the Common Room. Taking philosophy seriously is one thing, but actually acting it out socially and politically is quite another. Simply, don't do it.[10]

Rorty is not a religious thinker in any easily recognizable sense. This does not mean, though, that openly religious thinkers have not also been deeply influenced by the super-modernity school. In the recent past we have the examples of Paul Tillich, Hans Kueng, and John Macquarrie to show us the great influence of Hegel on traditional monotheistic religious thought. More recently, Mark C. Taylor in the Protestant tradition and John D. Caputo in the Roman Catholic tradition can serve as examples of the influence of Radical Hermeneutics and Deconstructionism on religious thought.

Taylor, for instance, in his *Deconstructing Theology* (1982), quotes with approval Gadamer's observation that, in the last analysis, Goethe's statement that everything is a symbol is the most comprehensive formulation of the hermeneutical idea, meaning that everything points to something else.[11] To Taylor, everything must be contextualized and re-historicized. Nothing can exist apart from everything else. Everything is implicated in everything else. In order to understand something, even God, you must also understand its opposite. Thus the absolute and the relative are necessarily fused into one. Absoluteness is the structure of relationships, while the relative is the content of that structure. "In a more theological idiom, God and world cannot exist apart from one another."[12]

Deconstruction, he states, is best understood as post-modernism "raised to method." From a religious perspective, however, he does not think we must accept the notion of absence as somehow absolute. Taylor observes that "One can agree with Derrida's criticism of a metaphysics which venerates atemporal being or presence at the expense of temporal becoming without accepting his virtual absolutizing of absence."[13]

Taylor wants both absence and presence, but more in the fashion of Hegel than of the more extreme deconstructionists who would dissolve everything into a virtual nothingness. In line with Hegel and Kueng, Taylor concludes that "The death of the transcendent Father need not be the complete disappearance of God, but can be seen as the birth of the divine, which now is grasped as an immanent and eternal process of dialectical development."[14] Likewise for the human self. This Hegelian pantheism is taken by Taylor to be the *only* way to go in our present age. It is the only way to fill the empty mirror of reality.

Thus, the "metaphysics of presence" is to be taken at least somewhat seriously. These days, however, under the influence of the Phenomenologists and Atheistic Existentialists, it is almost *de rigueur* to deride the traditional Judaeo-Christian emphasis upon the personal presence of God as an existentially separate personal being. For instance, in the case of John D. Caputo, who considers himself to be very *avant-garde* with respect to modern philosophy, the notion of *Deus absconditus* is carried to an extreme and elevated into a mystical doctrine for all future religions, especially the Judaeo-Christian religion. God's essence is not to be, but to be absent. Everything coming before Heidegger is merely *avant-propos* with respect to the modern age. Any attempt to maintain the more or less outdated and reactionary notions of a traditional philosophy is greeted with a *Deus avertat!*

True religion, Caputo claims, is both protestant and catholic. The "religious attitude arises precisely as a *protest* against suffering."[15] It is catholic because suffering, and the protest against suffering, is universal. Nevertheless, this protest against the degradation and violation of our lives should not attempt to do away with the primacy of flux. Religion does not begin from above with God, but from below with suffering, with people grappling with the flux. A healthy and robust religion does not accept suffering as "God's will or as a punishment for sin or as a means of sanctification."[16] Apparently, in harmony with the anti-religious philosophy of someone such as Nietzsche, the authentic, genuine, and honest religious person must reject the doctrine of Original Sin. Consequently, one may ask, what need is there for divine grace, or even the religious doctrine of the Incarnation?

Philosophically speaking, Caputo has ruled out the very possibility of ever getting a fix on the flux. Being and Becoming are forever irreconcilable. The Aristotelian aim of calming the Heraclitean waters must be rejected as impossible in principle. The repetitious rapids of flowing flux must go on forever. Any appeal to divine grace to help us out is a cop-out. Any religious appeal to Jesus Christ to help tell us who God is, and who we are, is philosophically negated in advance. As with his hero Heidegger, as well as with shades of Hegel and Hans Kueng, it would seem that for Caputo revelation and theology are controlled by philosophy. True religion must own up to the contingency of its symbols. It is genuine only insofar as it owns up to the fact that we are all situated in an abyss. Undecidability and ambiguity engulf everything and everybody. "We do not know who we are, not if we are honest, or whether or not we believe in God: that is the point of departure for any genuine faith."[17]

For Caputo's "radical hermeneutics," it also turns out to be the end of the process. Whether following the tragic, atheistic train of thought or the religious approach to suffering, we must always come to the same basic philosophical conclusion; namely, that learned unknowing is the final answer. Any attempt to resolve the issue of *being* in one way or another once and for all is simply to engage in the anti-Heideggerian metaphysics of presence and identity. Caputo, apparently identifying "being" with Greek Being, will not have any of it. If we face the cold truth, *the* truth, we do not know whether or not we believe in God. Instead we must be prepared to be constantly moving back and forth between the biblical Abraham, someone (imaginary?) who did really believe, and Nietzsche's Zarathustra, someone (definitely imaginary) who did not believe.[18]

The best we can hope for in the New Age of the future is to keep the flux flowing, to keep the play in play, to honor non-identity, difference, and the Heraclitean tides of time. And this indeed is where we find ourselves even today, after having been enlightened by Heidegger. We humans are a community of unknowers who can never rise above the temporal tide in order to explain its motions. It is the *lack* of something which makes us all the same. We must be prepared to let loose the flux even in our own souls. The person (Heidegger's *Dasein*) is the opening through which becoming resonates.

Distance apart is what keeps us together. Our non-being is what makes us be. Like Sartre's donut, it is the center that is not there that keeps us together. As with Camus's absurd man, the tension of the awareness of nothingness must not be relaxed. We must forever be disarming the pretensions of presence, Caputo asserts. And if we should ask *what* it is that is speaking through the *per-sona,* we cannot expect any answer. Is it some sort of World-Soul after the fashion of William James? Is it the natural world? Is it God? Or, I might ask, is the world God?[19]

Ethically speaking we are required to engage in a universal letting-be, a generalized *Ge-lassen-heit.* Whatever was previously subordinated, hierarchized, and marginalized must now be put on a par. Gods and men, earth and sky, male and female, Greek and Jew, East and West, weak and strong, healthy and sick, animal and human, and so forth, are to be allowed to be what and how they are. This universal hands-off policy is supposed to produce, Caputo claims, an ethics of liberation, toleration, and solidarity.

In this regard, says Caputo, a *radical* hermeneutics must save Nietzsche from himself. The ethics of Phenomenological-Atheistic Existentialism must be turned to the service of universal emancipation. A tremendous task considering the fact that Nietzsche himself would have wanted nothing to do with it. Nevertheless, Nietzsche (like Kierkegaard and Heidegger too) is a subversive political figure. To the extent that God is defined *in practice* for the theist as he who stands with those who suffer, such thinkers may even be regarded as godly people. Nietzsche and Heidegger become Leftists; they are the friends of the economically and culturally oppressed, thinks Caputo, and therefore friends of goodness and light, regardless of what they may have looked like in the past.[20]

Apparently, the *lethe* (forgetfulness) of being, and even of God, does not rule out the whole series of Judaeo-Christian virtues. One must wonder, though, whether or not the forgetfulness of being and God is compensated for by the remembrance of things past, of what is right derived from other sources, perhaps going back to one's childhood, such as Church teachings coming through the Scriptures, Councils, and saint-scholars.[21]

The same sort of thing is found if we look into the work of the late John Leslie Mackie, a modern-day defender of Hume. Following in the footsteps of Mill, Darwin, and Ayer, he wishes to preserve the morality of mankind while eliminating the need for any sort of objective standard. In his extended commentary on Hume's *Dialogues Concerning Natural Religion,* entitled *The Miracle of Theism* (1982), Mackie puts his faith in the natural human instinct for survival. He comes to the conclusion that the existence of the Judaeo-Christian God, defined (following Richard Swinburne) as a spiritual person, omnipresent, creator and sustainer of the universe, a free agent, omnipotent, all-knowing, all-good, immutable, eternal, a necessary being, all-holy, worthy of worship, and the source of moral obligation, is highly improbable. Nevertheless, true to Hume's own position, whether such a God exists or not makes no difference to human moral behavior. As long as you *act* as if you want to live in society, it makes little difference whether you call yourself, or even think yourself, religious.[22]

However, my contention is that the deconstructionist-pragmatic approach to morality is in fact very impractical. The absence or presence of God *does* make a difference to one's moral behavior if one is a rational person. It is especially important that you be created by God as a free person. This is because ethics presupposes the existence of free choice in the individual human agent. But there is no room for free choice in Hume's atomistic, physicalist philosophy of being, as there is none for those who are consistent in following out his doctrine, such as Ayer. To the extent Mackie agrees with this he cannot talk about ethics *at all.*

Also, Mackie, in attempting to apply the Humean-Darwinian doctrine in our contemporary age, runs into all the same problems as Rorty, and without any better means for resolving them. For Mackie, nothing is certain, nothing is above criticism, nothing is to be *a priori,* nothing is to be taken for granted, everything is to be built up out of little bits of sense perception, and so forth. Nothing is to be regarded as good *in se, per se,* and *secundum se.* There is no need to explain the world, nature, human instincts, human intentionality, and purposefulness. The brute fact of human life and society is to be regarded as reasonable in itself. Likewise, the existence of the *need* for human morality is reasonable in its own right and requires no further explanation or support. It is just there and we *must* accept it.

Hence, as Epicurus and Hume had said before him, there is no need to fear chaos and destruction because God is not present.

Mackie, however, like Rorty, involves himself in a string of contradictions. Simultaneously we both are and are not committed to *per se* goods. He states that we *must* be confident that we can find principles of cooperation in the midst of competitiveness, that we *must* be able to live together without destroying each other, that we *must* achieve harmony, and that we *must* stress intellectual honesty, tolerance, free inquiry, and individual rights. Before he finishes his "Conclusions and Implications" he has gone through, either directly or indirectly, practically the whole litany of human rights derived from the world's Judaeo-Christian heritage. Strangely, he says that there is such a thing as the truth and that we *must* go after it. This is what makes "empiricists" like James (and himself) optimistic and willing to take risks. "As James says, a risk which gives us our only chance of discovering the truth, or even approaching it, is indeed a reasonable risk."[23]

What Mackie completely overlooks, however, is that someone such as Nietzsche, beginning with the same view of evolutionary reality as Darwin and James, came to decidedly anti-democratic conclusions. Mackie hardly mentions Nietzsche, but then, to Mackie's credit, neither does he attempt to retread him as a Leftist. He does mention with approval the fact that Hans Kueng recognizes the possibility of a Nietzsche-type naturalistic genealogy of morals based upon a socio-historical process in which human beings work out for themselves on earth various solutions to their pressing problems. What is overlooked, though, is that in order to do so in a binding way we must be guided by objective standards of a *per se* kind.[24]

For his part, Nietzsche must be given credit for understanding certain aspects of traditional religion very well. Nietzsche, of course, like all modern thinkers on the subject of God, has been greatly influenced by Judaeo-Christian theology. In the Bible, and in the philosophies concerned with it, when taken at their best, existentialism reigns supreme. God is the totally *free* creator; "*He Who Is*" is he who bestows existence in a completely free, novel, and unpredictable way. Now, *if* man is to replace God, then, according to Nietzsche, *man* must be the one to possess such power.[25]

How then can anyone talk about the necessity of a democratic society, tolerant behavior, loving relationships, and communal solidarity, as if we somehow know where we are going before we get there? In Nietzsche's world, to the extent one's consciousness is raised to the full awareness of what being a god means, one is a Superman. To the extent one is not aware, one participates in the slave mentality, the morality of the herd. In the herd, huddled together to protect itself against the pressures of existing in a careless world, pity, mutual help and cooperation, warm-heartedness, patience, industriousness, humility, and friendliness are fostered. How spiritless and small-minded, thinks Nietzsche. Traditional morality is simply the herd instinct showing up in the individual.

And what is Mackie's answer to this situation? He simply asserts that Kueng's emphasis upon taking care of ourselves, of being responsible for our own morality, is "strikingly similar" to his own solution to the problem of potential chaos; "it is in itself an adequate *reply* to nihilism about value."[26]

It is, however, totally inadequate from the viewpoint of human peace and harmony. When Nietzsche took over Darwin's evolutionary struggle for survival, which would continue to produce new and better species, and applied it (theoretically) to social and political affairs, he knew full well that it meant anything but peace and harmony. It did *not* mean never using other humans to further your own ends; it did *not* mean never using others as means rather than regarding them as ends in themselves. If Mackie is really basing his optimism and hope solely upon the self-legislative personality, but without the added feature of objective measures, he is indeed engaging in a very deadly form of wishful thinking.

The same can be said about those who operate within an explicitly religious context. Caputo, for instance, states:

> Far from being able to see God everywhere, the believer has perhaps the sharpest sense of all of the withdrawal of God, His absence from the world. His faith consists precisely in bending in the direction of the God who withdraws. . . . I mean that, for a radical hermeneutic, God is always and everywhere, in all the epochs, essentially withdrawn from the world, even as faith says He is omnipresent. His very self-giving is self-withdrawing, a-lethic.[27]

Or is it that the "lethe" is only a form of lethargy, languor, and lassitude? One would hope that, as far as social and political philosophy is concerned, it does not end up being lethal. For example, this sort of mysterious approach can very easily shade off into various forms of neo-pagan mystery cults, which may or may not be benign. If we survey what has gone on under the auspices of such cults in the past, we certainly cannot be assured of peace and tranquility. The same is true of those which exist today. I am speaking here about the doctrine which is taught by the cults, not about the actual practice of the members, which may or may not conform to the doctrine. We are all aware of Christians who do not practice what they preach. This, however, is no argument against the value of the doctrine, anymore than the value of a medicine can be judged by those who *do not* take it. In the case of the cults, though, the doctrine, when practiced, is often deliberately meant to be destructive.[28]

In any event, the movement toward mystery cults is certainly a far cry from orthodox monotheism. For instance, in regard to any cult which tends to identify God with nature, or with some aspect of nature, the practical tendency has to be toward a nature worship. In such a situation Jesus Christ loses his historical status, becoming instead merely an archetypal figure representing the constant cycles of birth, death, and rebirth going on in the body of Mother Nature. The divine is everywhere and in everything. A pantheistic cosmology replaces the living God of the Bible. Rites of Spring replace the mass. Ecological emblems, such as garlands of ivy, replace traditional religious symbols such as the crucifix.

In such a system all of human life becomes a playground for the spirits of the woods, waters, and mountains. Sub-human, sub-rational nature is exalted. In nature everything is natural, including all varieties of sex-organ usage. If the doctrine of Original Sin and if being "up tight" about sex is going to hamper our "natural" activities, then so much the worse for the Bible and the Church. Indeed, it might even be declared, as is done by Matthew Fox, for instance, that if the New Age Mysticism is not immediately adopted by the present religious leaders, the Church, and maybe the whole world, is doomed.

It could even be asserted that our salvation depends upon going *back* to the pre-Christian wellsprings of earthly life. In the ancient Dionysian Mystery Cults, for instance, it was said that those who honored Nature and her gods prospered, while those who did not went insane. Because of the maternal aspects of Nature (the one God, the one Reality), some of the Dionysian ceremonies were restricted to females, while women often acted as priests in others. Some of the ceremonies even included the use of human sacrifices and canni-balism. In addition, playfulness and playacting were emphasized throughout, and the upswelling of youth. In their later Roman versions, these Dionysian rituals, although tamer in their sensual excesses, were called the *Ludi Liberales,* a free playing around. Is this the last word of Radical Hermeneutics?

I note that both Caputo's *Radical Hermeneutics* and Bloom's *The Closing of the American Mind* were published about the same time (1987), but without any cross-pollination between them. Caputo has a definite leaning toward Left-Wing causes, such as Liberation Theology in Latin America and Radical Feminism everywhere, even in the Church. The original Nietzsche, however, was certainly no friend of women's rights and of the classless society, while the original Heidegger looked to the German youth, and their apotheosized leader (Hitler), for salvation. Yet Caputo's position would certainly not surprise Bloom.

Which is more important to the preservation of a self-creative, inner-directed, caring personality: peace, democracy, prosperity,

harmony, rationality, orderliness, stability, justice, truth, and *being*
— or perpetual tension, ambiguous flux, fractured identities,
disruption, and even chaos? For the super-modern it must be the
latter. The poor who are always with you (Matthew 26:11) has taken
on a new meaning. In Bloom's analysis, to the post-modern the poor
represent an opportunity to show commitment, not to the elimination
of poverty and injustice, but simply to *commitment.* Self-assertion
and will become ends in themselves. Bloom states: "Thus
determination, will, commitment, caring (here is where this now
silly expression got its force, concern, or what have you, become the
new virtues."[29]

For Bloom, Caputo could well be another example of a well-
meaning modern thinker trying to turn Nazis into Marxists; and
also trying to reinterpret Marx so as to allow for the permanent
revolution entailed by the newly discovered ambiguity, meaninglessness, and mysteriousness of Being. *Die Bewegnung* (the
Movement) becomes the goal. Movement itself, in the sense of just
going, becomes the new ideal. It is change for the sake of change;
modernity for the sake of modernity. Progress, in the sense of aim-
ing for a fixed, objective standard, is out. The gratuitous act is in.
Bloom states that "today virtually every Nietzschean, as well as
Heideggerian, is a leftist."[30]

But they are not just old-fashioned Leftists. They are the new
mutant breed of Leftists who have deconstructed the doctrinaire
teleological aspects of Marx in favor of a more flexible non-aim suitable to the flowing flux. This indeterminate, fence-sitting, un-know-
ing, non-being sort of agnostic, skeptical New Man is the new hybrid
species of the super-modern era. And none too soon either, considering the fact that after 1989–1990 the old-fashioned Left is dead.

According to Bloom's analysis, this new breed is achieved by
doing some fancy footwork around the old notions of the proletariat,
the bourgeoisie, and the Superman. The old notion of progress
implied a fixed ideal to be achieved in a finite time. In Nietzsche's
scheme neither women nor the slavish "herd" were shown any
respect. In Marx's scientific dialectic the workers would overpower
the capitalists and bring justice into the world. In the new scenario
the Superman becomes the whole proletarian class counteracting the
dull, mundane, comfort-seeking, spiritless, complacent, enemy-of-
the-creative-artist bourgeoisie mentality. The philistine shopkeepers
are seen as opposed to the youthful upwelling of creative energy
which requires nothing more than the deconstruction of the old
industrial-military-governmental-religious-educational complex in
order to reach full bloom. The resurgence of culture is the main
thing, not a chicken in every pot.

Thus, Nietzsche and Heidegger, the enemies of democracy, are
transmuted into friends of egalitarianism by virtue of the fact that

they possessed a true consciousness of the power of the dispossessed (the geniuses, the artists, the inner-directed, the spirited) to lead a grass-roots revolution which would sooner or later make society a better place for *everyone*. In this way elitism and egalitarianism are combined, using as a justification that what the *avant-garde* is doing today everyone will be doing tomorrow. With respect to the free, gratuitous act: Today the few; tomorrow the many. The liberated, charismatic, self-legislative person, whether in civil society, educational institutions, or the Church, becomes the new prophet leading the people into a brave new world of socialistic egalitarianism.[31] Anyone who disagrees with this world-vision of how Future Man is going to supplant the old, last man of the present era is regarded as being behind the times, reactionary, regressive, and so on.

However, let us be a bit more careful about just who is or is not outmoded. Bloom insists that Heidegger, for instance, like Marx, was certainly no friend of democracy and toleration. Bloom recognizes the fact that much of modern thought is enthralled by Deconstruction-ism, so much so that it despairs of ever achieving the truth by rational means. Both Rorty and Bloom value free and open discus-sion, but they support their view on entirely different grounds. Rorty thinks pragmatism is sufficient; Bloom knows it is not.

Bloom's work is one long lament on the politicization of many major universities over the past three decades. He attributes this sad state of affairs primarily to the breakdown of an emphasis upon classical learning and the study of the Great Books (Ideas) of the Western World in the undergraduate Arts faculty classroom. Into their place have gone all sorts of "contemporary" and "relevant" things, but nothing of really lasting value. In fact, he claims, the classical thinkers, such as Plato, Aristotle, Aquinas, Locke, and Rousseau, *are* the really relevant thinkers of *our* time. Both from the individual and the social viewpoints, they form the solid foundation we need to understand and preserve a relatively free, democratic way of life; and their main home should be the universities.

In Bloom's view, a university should be largely free of any sort of political pressure, whether from the Left or Right. All too often, though, since the 1930s in Europe and the 1960s in America, professors have substituted what was currently fashionable and supposedly relevant for what was of lasting value, thus breaking a tradition with the past, and depriving their students of a firm foundation for understanding their world, whether past or present. Once the great university tradition of continuity with the great minds of the past is lost, it is very difficult to restore, especially in the short run. This tradition has been broken, thinks Bloom, and now accounts in large part for the lack of respect many people have for the liberal arts and the humanities, as well as for the feeling of inferiority many

Arts professors have for themselves, especially relative to those in science, engineering, and mathematics.

The university should be a place of reflective scholarship, not a hotbed of Left-Wing, Right-Wing, Feminist, Black, Church Dissident, Animal Rights, Gay Rights, or whatever, activism. It should be a place where rational dialogue and calm thinking is more respected than being a popular personality or being up to date simply for the sake of modernity. Content is more important than style. Being a good teacher and being a popular teacher may, of course, coincide, but they should not be assumed to be equivalent in all cases. The important thing for Bloom is that professors actually profess something significant, that they demand some hard thinking on the part of their students, and that they do more than preach agnosticism, skepticism, unteaching, moral relativism, mythology, and "do your own thing," all with the aid of a constant stream of movies and tapes.

Bloom takes Socrates and Plato as prime examples of what intellectuals should be doing; Nietzsche and Heidegger as prime examples of the enemies of toleration. Calm, reflective thought cannot be a handmaiden to any Movement, however popular and culturally relevant it may seem to be at the moment. Bloom dilates on Heidegger by noting that Heidegger's mysterious Being is so morally amorphous that it can accommodate almost any political system, even Nazism. Heidegger, even though "the most interesting thinker of our century," was no match for the *Anschluss* of blood and steel.[32] Having emptied his own thinking of anything that could withstand the powerful anti-democratic forces of his own day, he surrendered to the *Volk* his duty to defend responsible freedom of thought.

Up until the twentieth century, professors had defended Socrates and Plato against the masses. But now, with Heidegger, the teacher follows the populace, even when it is in one of its more irrational moods. Bloom thinks that this sort of obsequiousness is a tragedy.

> Thus it was no accident that Heidegger came forward just after Hitler's accession to power to address the university community in Freiburg as the new rector, and urged commitment to National Socialism. His argument was not without subtlety and its own special kind of irony, but in sum the *decision* to devote wholeheartedly the life of the mind to an emerging revelation of being, incarnated in a mass movement, was what Heidegger encouraged. That he did so was not a result of his political innocence but a corollary of his critique of rationalism. . . . The university may have come near to its death when Heidegger joined the German people — especially the youngest part of that people, which he said had already

made an irreversible commitment to the future — and put philosophy at the service of German culture.[33]

This was no aberration on Heidegger's part, but a necessary result of his studied rationalized irrationalism, his anti-philosophical philosophy, his deconstruction of the stable safeguards protecting the West from decline and barbarism. For Bloom, Deconstruction is simply destruction with an added syllable. Praising Deconstructionism is like praising the organic body which is so open to its environment that it allows in just anything at all, including deadly infections.

Regardless of what one thinks about Bloom's critique of the contemporary university, at the very least he has challenged us to imagine some viable alternatives to civil law as the highest source of morality. Is there some definitive doctrine that can act as a secure bulwark against the twin evils of Fascism and Communism, under whatever form they may appear, for ages to come? Traditional monotheistic religion, for instance, would seem to be at least one possible candidate. The existence of a personal God, present to his creatures, with a right to command, and in fact commanding them to love one another, to care for widows and orphans, to refrain from convenience killing, not to abuse the weak, not to engage in acts of vengeance, and so on, would seem to fill the bill.

This, of course, is rejected by thinkers such as Rorty, as well as other post-moderns. Remember, following Nietzsche, God is dead and gone *forever*. Nevertheless, how then can anyone any longer speak of something as "evil" or "bad"? Are we really content simply begging the question concerning the existence of *per se* goods? Rorty has no real defense and justification for pragmatism as an answer to nihilism. All he can do is draw a moral from the history of human thought, the lesson of which, he claims, is that all methodologies and dogmas of the past have failed to provide us with a universally accepted and eternal truth.[34]

Regardless of whether this is truly the case (I do not think it is), I still want to know *today* what I should accept as good and reject as evil. Rorty is still left with the key question, What does "evil" mean? Is a lump of lead in the earth something evil? Should galena (lead ore) be condemned as bad? Can we say that any particular thing or group of things is evil? This does not seem to be the case when things are taken simply by themselves.

However, if a mugger puts a piece of lead into your head I think we would all agree that such a "thing" is evil. Even here, though, we must ask, For whom or what is it evil? It is evil for the victim, but perhaps not so for the criminal; after all, he got the money, which is good for him. Such examples and questions can be multiplied over and over again. The end result, though, will be, I think, that *things* are not evil, but that the way things are arranged relative to each other may be evil. A piece of lead in the earth is not evil, but in your head it is. Lead is not *supposed* to be in your head in that way.

Any talk about good and evil necessarily involves talk about the way things are *supposed* to be, either by themselves or in relation to other things. To say that something is evil means, most fundamentally and basically, that it does against the way something is *supposed* to be. There is a violation of a standard, a rule, a law, a criterion of what is right and proper.

It is natural at this juncture to inquire about the origin of such standards. Are they self-generated, the result of social dialogue, the result of whim or fancy, given from above, and so on? The most obvious case of laws and lawmaking is within the civil context. The government makes laws about which side of the road to drive on, where and when to pay taxes, how much, and so forth.

Normally, though, we do not think of someone as evil for getting a parking ticket; unlucky maybe, but not evil. To be evil there must be something more profound involved. Perhaps a traitor, someone who goes against the whole nation and the common good in some very basic way, is evil. More likely, however, the term is reserved for a religious context. To be evil means to go against God's law. There is a moral dimension assumed, one which is more radical than any civil law. Hitler was evil, even though most of the horrible things he did were perfectly legal according to the formalities of civil government. Apartheid in South Africa can be called evil, even though quite legal. The crushing of the student-worker pro-democracy movement in China in June of 1989 was evil and yet completely lawful, and so on.

In this sense there is always some law above the civil law which determines whether or not the civil law is just. As a consequence, no civil law can dictate morality precisely because it is morality which must dictate to the civil law. This, of course, assumes that there is a "higher" law. If there is no such law, then one of the lower levels must take on the ultimate lawmaking role. The most likely candidate for this function would be the civil law at the national level.

I submit, however, that this is not acceptable to the vast majority of human beings in the world. We are in fact always passing judgment on the civil laws, praising them as good or condemning them as bad. This would not be rationally possible if there were not some outside measure whereby the law was evaluated, either something peculiar to ourselves, such as our basic, positive human nature, or something which transcends ourselves and all individual human beings, such as the dictates of a divine being, or both.

In a situation where each individual were a law unto himself or herself, sheer chaos would reign. There would be no safety, peace, or prosperity for anyone. Every act of "stealing," "revenge," "rape," "murder," and so forth, would be allowed and *justified* when judged against the standard of the freedom of choice to do what *I* deemed best *for me,* whether now or in the long run.

Even if someone decided not to steal and rape, out of fear of punishment or enlightened self-interest, or through some mutual agreement, the theoretical possibility to *justly* do so would always remain. He or she could always decide at one time or another (say, when she thought she could really get away with it) to change her mind and claim her primordial right to being the final arbiter of what is really and ultimately good and evil, even with respect to any "deal" she might have previously made with other consenting adults.

Therefore there must be some standard of rightness which is not based solely on one's will. There must be some transcendental criterion of justice, some objective measure of good and evil, which is binding on all humans alike, as well as on the governments they form and the nations they create. We can call this objective measure the divine law, or the voice of heaven speaking in the world, or the dictate of reasonable human nature when acting in the way it was designed to act (the natural moral law), and so on. We can look for it in Plato's World of Ideas, in Scripture, in our own essential nature, or in some direct personal communication with God. In any event, it has to be there *if* we are going to make sense of any discussion of fair-unfair, just-unjust, good-evil, and the like. This is good to know because it helps us solve the problem of evil, but it also creates a problem for us when we must specify more exactly what this standard is, and how we are to relate to it.

Nevertheless, the *fact* of evil (for instance, floods, disease, birth defects, murders, rapes, racism, and so on, that is, both natural and man-made evils) presupposes that evil is something real in the sense of being the violation of an actually existing transcendent law or arrangement of things. But this could not be the case if there were nothing really transcendent. Hence the fact and reality of evil necessarily leads us to see that there is a factual and really existing transcendental standard of morality to which I must adhere, using my free will and good judgment to do so. Without some such standard evil would be gone, even though personal pain and suffering remained.

Consequently, a cool, rational mind must conclude that the existence and reality of evil is not an argument against some transcendental reality; it is rather an irrefutable argument *for* the existence of such a thing. It is not a matter of probability, however high. Regardless of how we ultimately reconcile the nature of the transcendental with the reality of evil, the point is that there would be nothing to be reconciled in the first place if there were no such standard acting as an objective measure of good and evil. Denying transcendental reality is a non-solution to the problem of evil taken seriously.

As we know from human experience, human action always requires a goal to be achieved, something to aim at. In the moral sphere this means having *per se* goods to act as guides whereby our advance toward or retreat from where we should be can be measured. It is the serious, adult version of the childhood game of "hot and cold." Now, both Rorty and Mackie admit the existence of *per se* goods. Yet it is a fact that we cannot make something intrinsically relative into something absolute. We can pretend to do so, but we cannot really do so. Neither will merely postulating a goal, in some arbitrary manner, whether individually or socially, be sufficient to guide our behavior. Even pretending to be a theist because, for instance, that is the social consensus in Rome and we must always do what the Romans do when in Rome, will not work.

A postulate is of its very nature something unnecessary. *If* I go to the store, *then* I will buy a newspaper. The statement of this compound proposition in no way obliges me to actually go to the store. I can postulate my going to the store. I can imagine myself going to the store. But at no time need I actually ever go to the store.

Moreover, even the postulation is not necessary. Backing up one step further, I am in no way obliged to state such a hypothetical case in the first place. I may or may not wish to set up a relationship in which buying a newspaper depends upon my going to the store. I may, in fact, have no desire whatsoever for a newspaper. I may, in fact, care absolutely nothing for newspapers under any circumstances. The same sort of thing can be said of the pragmatic-deconstructionist approach to morality.

It works on the assumption that society is good and should be preserved. It assumes that there is such a thing as the good life in the good society. It is deeply interested in world peace, equal rights for women, human rights in general, human harmony, and the like. It thinks that the way to get these results is to respect one another and practice widespread toleration. It could very well be true that in order to achieve universal harmony and peace it is necessary to follow such a program, but that is not the point here.

The real question is, Why must we desire such a situation in the first place? At first sight Rorty's approach might appear very practical, useful, utilitarian, and the height of enlightened self-interest. But what can we say about those cases in which someone refuses to make the initial commitment?

Also, even assuming that we should be nice to other people, not because it is good in itself, but because we ourselves, in one way or another, benefit from such behavior, and because society as a whole will ultimately benefit from such conduct, how are we to handle exceptional cases? Say, for example, that someone has great political power and/or great wealth, great enough to insulate himself or herself completely and successfully from any personal repercussions that may result from his or her actions. Why then should such a person behave ethically? What need is there for such a one to worry about other people or the society at large, as long as he or she could get away with it during his or her own lifetime?

Or assume that someone, either alone or in conjunction with some "radical" group, cares little for human beings as individuals. The "Cause" is everything! After carefully and rationally considering all the circumstances of his or her life and times, such a person might decide that the consequences of harm or even death to himself or herself, or to others in society, is well worth it. What can the "Let us be pragmatic about this" view do in such a case? Really nothing. After all, it is the very self-interest and utilitarian interests of such people, as decided by themselves, which provide the motivation for their actions in the first place. Regardless of the social conversation, the whole process easily backfires when we run into people who either need not or *will* not worry about such things.

Is there any way to circumvent this sort of problem, perhaps by using literature and the public media to graphically show everyone exactly what harm and destruction is caused by the IRA, the Central American "death squads," the Near East radical groups, and so forth? Would actual pictures and detailed descriptions of murdered victims and destroyed property turn the tide of public opinion against such actions, and do it to the point of actually convincing young people, regardless of the "rightness" of their Cause, not to engage in such actions as a means to their ends? In a way this approach would be parallel to showing the world the tortured and mutilated victims of Nazi oppression, or showing people pictures of dismembered fetuses, as a means for combatting anti-Semitism and abortion. Recently Rorty has suggested just such an approach in his *Contingency, Irony, and Solidarity* (1989).

Near the beginning of chapter 9, the last chapter in his *Contingency, Irony, and Solidarity,* Rorty states:

> I have been urging in this book that we try *not* to want something which stands beyond history and institutions. The fundamental premise of the book is that a belief can still regulate action, can still be thought worth dying for, among people who are quite aware that this belief is caused by nothing deeper than contingent historical circumstance.

Rorty then goes on to insist that a "sense" of human solidarity can continue to exist even though its religious and semi-religious foundations have been removed. He even maintains that there will very likely be moral progress in the world, and that this progress consists in our gradually abandoning the tribal attitude in favor of a greatly expanded liberal "we" or "us" which will come to include the whole human race. This *universalized* ethnocentrism is the heart of the "liberal" view of life and the foundation for the democratic political program, even though there is no non-circular way to rationally defend it. Logically, we are always bound to beg the question. Rorty is *absolutely* certain that *all* "metaphysical" systems are equally indefensible.

It has only been by chance and our good fortune that we have managed to live through the horrors of twentieth-century pain, humiliation, and cruelty so that we can now see that peace and human solidarity are preferable to the death camps. Democracies can now afford to throw away the religious and quasi-religious ladders which have been used in their own construction. We now have a new capital upon which to draw interest. Compared with its alternatives, it is now obvious that the liberal democracy approach of J. S. Mill is good while the systems of Hitler, Stalin, and Mao Tse-tung are evil. We have now reached the point where our very *vocabulary,* which inculcates democratic values into our lives, is itself a sufficient and final justification for voting liberal. Through language we impose our values upon the world, not vice versa.

It is hard to imagine a greater naïveté than that of post-modernism. A belief, *known* to be without any objective foundation, *known* to be merely the result of an accidental set of historico-sociological conditions, *known* to be the outcome of nothing more than a tribal propinquity and sentimentality, *known* to be a mere nominalistic projection, is sure to have precisely the opposite effect of that desired by Rorty. No rational human being (if there were such a thing as human nature, which Rorty asserts there is not) could possibly go along with such a situation. In Rorty's proposed cure, honesty spoils the therapy.

This may help explain why he tends to play down the role of speculative reason in human life. As with Derrida, he realizes that too much rationality and reasoning is no good for his proposed program. It is much better to be satisfied, or at least claim to be satisfied, with a playful deconstruction and breaking down of all past thinkers (or at least all those who thought too much) so that the present-day post-modern thinker cannot be accused of merely doing the same sort of thing they were doing but with a somewhat changed content. The price one pays for this forced and fantastic novelty is, I submit, utter unintelligibility. Rorty, because he knows in advance the conclusions he wants to reach, is at least partially blind to this fact. Being cruel he claims is a *per se* evil; it is the worst thing we can do. This is the conclusion we *must* reach regardless of the intelligibility or non-intelligibility, or even the non-existence, of the premises.

No doubt, in general, on average, over the long haul, people are inclined to sympathize with other people who are in the same real-life situations as they are. Someone with children to care for, for instance, but who is not being persecuted, will suffer with someone she knows who has children to care for and who is being persecuted, and the like. No doubt, in general, on average, in the long run, people prefer peace and harmony to bloodshed, strife, pain, humiliation, and cruelty. These are facts of life and human experience which could just as well be explained, and perhaps explained better, by someone rejected by Rorty, such as Aquinas following the natural moral law.

But what about the exceptional cases? What about the short run? What about individuals or societies deciding that, for their immediate purposes, for the time being, under these given circumstances, and so on, pain and cruelty are fine and good things? Is a pro-abortionist anti-baby or just pro-women? Was Hitler anti-Jewish or just pro-German? Should the "hippie" who is being beaten by a bully cop, and the bully cop who is beating him, feel a strange sort of sympathy for each other because they are both misfits? And what about the self-legislative autonomous individual who freely, with complete self-awareness, arbitrarily decides that eliminating one's enemies with an axe, or "liberating" money from a bank at gunpoint, and so forth, *is* the right and honorable thing to do?

Those who think like Rorty cannot answer these hard questions of real life. When faced with a real, breathing terrorist the best Rorty's analysis of the ultimate metaphysical truth about reality can do is to *try* to get him to stop inflicting pain long enough so that the super-modern thinker can point out to him that, when given a chance to compare and choose among various ways of life, the chances are that the ordinary person will usually pick the non-terrorist approach. But can this really be seriously offered as an alternative to raising someone up from his or her earliest youth in the belief that there are objective standards of morality to which everyone is obliged to adhere; that evil and sin are objectively real, and that we must conform to reality rather than vice versa?

Despite the lip service he pays to nominalism, Rorty is pretty good at knowing for sure what is and is not, *in a moral sense,* humiliating and cruel. He apparently knows the difference between a non-cruel doctor or coach causing pain and a cruel terrorist causing pain. In addition, he seems to know a human being when he sees one. He is able to group, categorize, and classify with a high degree of accuracy. He has no doubts about the fact that there is *one* human species. To do this, though, requires that there be something objectively the same about all the individuals in the set, something which, according to his own asserted nominalism, is not and cannot be the case. So, which Rorty are we to believe? The theoretical (nominalistic) Rorty or the practical, real-life (non-nominalistic) Rorty?

He is also certain about his Humean materialistic view of the world and everything in it, including human beings. He is certain about the *lack* of a unified self and human nature, about the way the mind is reducible to the brain, about the little folds in the cortex producing thought, about the non-existence of anything spiritual, and so on. Rather than expanding the realm of the possible, he is constantly contracting it. Yet he regards his position as more advanced than anything that has gone before; as superior to any other one, as if it were really something unique and new. It is as if no one had ever heard of Hume or Darwin before.

Without retracting his skeptical super-modern position, Rorty must still struggle with the problem of morality in a nihilistic world. If there are no transcendent ideals to guide the actions of all people at all times, how can we ever hope to gain a consensus on what is mean and cruel and therefore to be rejected by both individuals and society? Rorty suggests that the "ideals" of a Liberal Democracy can still be fostered (even though there are no real ideals, objectively speaking) by an emphasis upon the power of the pen and pictures in literature and the popular media to demonstrate to people that certain social practices are mean and cruel and run counter to the objective of social solidarity. Writers such as George Orwell (Eric Blair, 1903–1950) have already done this for us with respect to Communist dictatorships; others, such as Vladimir Nabokov (1899–1977), have done similar things for us by showing us the dangers of inordinate and uncontrolled sexual involvements.

What Rorty says, I think, is true as far as it goes; we *are* moved by images to a large extent. What his view cannot account for is why certain images should be fostered and others not. Should images depicting the fact that "war is hell" have been used in the 1940s to form a popular consensus against continuing the war against Hitler? Being sensitive to suffering is certainly a fine thing, but what if the suffering is a necessary means to a good end? Literature as an expression of ideals is to be recommended, but which ideals should it express? Rorty should be praised for his efforts to reestablish some objective moral norms, but at the same time we should not forget that a similar approach has been tried before, by thinkers such as Hume and Darwin, and for the same basic reason; namely, they wanted *both* to keep faith with their strong *a priori* moral commitment to the basic Christian ideal of "love thy neighbor" *and* to keep faith with their intellectual rejection of God's existence and presence in any providential, immediate, meaningful sense. All such schizophrenic positions, however, are bound to fail because of their basic irrationalism.

According to Hume, for instance, the existence of a transcendental set of ideals or of a God who is constantly near us is completely unnecessary when it comes to having an orderly life in an orderly society. Take away traditional religion and no one would really miss it. Life, for example, under an Epicurean world-view, the one favored by Hume himself, could go on as usual. The real forces of law and order would still continue to operate. Consequently, Hume, according to his own evaluation of himself in his own time, cannot be looked upon as some sort of wild anarchist, fit for public punishment, because he favors the ancient doctrine of Epicureanism over that of the Church of England.

We should not suppose that this means for Hume a completely arbitrary way of decision-making. Hume and those who followed him in his approach, such as Mill and Darwin, still maintained a certain sort of objectivism in morals. One cannot make some set of moral principles work simply because one wishes them to work, or wants them to work, or passes some law saying that they must work. Regardless of what man does, in the end nature will out.

We can see this in Darwin, for example, who is known to have been much influenced by Hume. If we are to base our moral system on what is conducive to adaptation and survival here and now, for instance, it is obvious that nature, not man, must have the last word on the subject. In his *Descent of Man,* chapter 4, for example, Darwin states that conscience is the most important difference between humans and animals. Conscience is our ability to feel remorse, repentance, regret, and shame concerning our past deeds. Such a feeling is founded almost exclusively upon the judgments which are passed upon us by our closest circle of fellow human beings; in other words, social consensus and public opinion are paramount.

But, upon what bases are such judgments made? As it turns out, they are made in the long run upon considerations of social instinct, the common good, and those sentiments and sympathies we have developed over the course of our lives. In the long run, in order to survive, prosper, and conquer, certain virtues will come to dominate. Courage, temperance, chastity, universal respect for all humans and animals, and so on, as we see when we compare savage societies with civilized societies, must in the long run come to the fore, while our baser selfish instincts must recede. The evil that we see about us cannot be denied, but it is not due mainly to sin but only to the gap between the savage and the civilized traits to be found in individuals and in society at large.

Like Hume, Darwin distinguishes between the *standards* of morality and the *motives* for acting morally. The *standards* are those virtues which have been built up and transmitted over long periods of time from one generation to another, and which are primarily generally conducive to the overall welfare and good of society, and secondarily to the happiness of the great mass of humankind. This means for Darwin the rearing of the greatest number of individuals in the fullness of vigor and health, with all their faculties fully developed given the conditions of the world to which they must adapt.

The *motive* for proper behavior, on the other hand, is our sense of sympathy with others and, generally, the approbation and disapprobation we receive from others; in other words, social consensus and public opinion. Fortunately, we can count upon the fact that the fulfillment of our own desire for self-preservation and self-development, and the needs of society, usually coincide. As Ospovat has documented very well in his *The Development of Darwin's Theory* (1981), as Darwin got older his commitment to the necessary progress of nature and society, not with respect to the details but with respect to a long-run overall development, got stronger. Even without God's providence such progress will *necessarily* take place.

I think we can make some sense out of this approach, as did thinkers like Marx, given the reality of necessary progress in the world, and given the "love thy neighbor" Golden Rule as the final product of the process. But, today this notion is regarded, by Rorty at least, as being as dead as God. He even seems to realize that, after the Death of God, things may go on as usual for a while, but this would only be due to inertia, to a superstition carried over from traditional religion. The problem then becomes one of finding some substitute for God, generally acceptable to the population, once society at large takes in Nietzsche's nihilism. I submit that this cannot be done on the basis of drama, poetry, literature, and so on. What if slavery were to once again become socially acceptable, as today is the case with divorce and remarriage, abortion, and even drugs to a certain degree? Why can't such a custom be reinstated and once again become customary, to be reinforced by the society's writers and masters of the popular media?

Rorty's approach suffers from the same difficulty as Hume's and Darwin's; namely, we may know what is factually repulsive and disgusting, but we do not know thereby what is *really* good and evil. Through social conditioning, many things can come to be regarded as attractive or repulsive. Hume, for instance, seems to have forgotten that the law and order of the "civilized" Greeks of Epicurus's day was founded on legal arbitrariness, slavery, infanticide, prostitution, warfare, and a host of other practices Hume himself (I think) rejected. The more basic question is why slavery, for instance, is enforced by public opinion in one place but not in another? Could it be that one place has been Christianized and another not? If so, traditional religion *is* crucial.

In addition, it is even doubtful if moral sentiments as a motive for action could work outside the confines of a small tribal setting. On this point one might look into Hume's *Treatise,* Book III, Part II, wherein he explains the need, in large societies, to augment natural sentiments with elaborate legal devices in order to maintain law and order. The ideal is to have everyone embrace the civil conventions as if they were proximate and immediate natural virtues. But where this does not happen, the state must use its police power to enforce law and order. Although without reference to God, Hume still wants to maintain most of the basic Christian civil virtues. However, as he tells us in his *Principles of Morals,* Section IX, Part I, certain "'monkish virtues" (for instance, celibacy, fasting, penance, humility) should be eliminated. He continues to maintain, however, that modesty for women is a good thing.

But to talk like this is to miss the main point. In order to survive, a society needs common ideals, common truths, common standards. All the thinkers mentioned above would agree that any attempt to "do one's own thing" or to "march to the beat of a different drummer" in some fundamentally divergent way is completely out of the question. The usual rebuttal to this from the radical libertarians is to say that since my sense of justice, fairness, right and wrong, and so on, differs from yours, there can be no such common standards or truths in society. We must therefore allow for the possibility that chaos and destruction will prevail in society, and all in the name of freedom. The problem with this attitude, though, is that it in no way does away with the need for a common standard of justice for society. If anything it reaffirms such a need. The result of a lack of common standards is not an enduring nation basking in the benefits of freedom but the production of more than one nation.

Even if there is no immediate physical separation, there is at least a spiritual one. This has already been described in St. Augustine's *City of God,* wherein the Christians of his day found it necessary to withdraw from the pagan society of the time in order to live out their ideals. Even though living in the same area, Christians and pagans could not live in the same world. The mixture of the heavenly city and the earthly city was like oil and water, a superficial arrangement at best. In time, though, the contradiction had to be resolved in one way or another. As it turned out, classical paganism was destroyed and practices such as slavery outlawed.

This sort of thing is still happening today all over the world. We are beset today with all kinds of fundamental world-view disagreements. These intellectual divisions are sooner or later translated into moral divisions. We may be able to compromise on how far we want the window open in the office, but, given the fact of very basic moral differences, how do we compromise on the fundamental issues of life and death? Sooner or later we must stop talking and *act* one way or another. On certain very basic issues there is no way to compromise. But then what? The answer, I think, is that sooner or later, like it or not, some sort of segregation of the antagonistic parties must take place.

The segregation process, which seems to be the natural human solution to this sort of situation, can be either forced or voluntary, and always tends to go toward a physical separation. If the parties cannot live together, and if they nevertheless are to go on living, then they must somehow or other manage to live apart. Our present society contains many examples of both forced and voluntary types of segregation.

Smokers, for example, to take a relatively superficial case, are often forced by law to remain apart from non-smokers in various public places such as restaurants, while they are actually smoking. More serious and profound examples would be situations in which people are segregated on the basis of skin color or political party affiliation. But even these latter cases are superficial when compared to cases of segregation based upon one's basic world-view or religion. In this sort of case it is no longer possible to remain part of *one* nation. This situation is the type we find today in Cyprus, India, the Middle East, Sri Lanka, and so forth around the world, including the Soviet Union which, it turns out, is not so unified.

As long as compromise is possible, or as long as the different parties accept their lot in life as right and just (for example, as long as the lower caste in India thinks of itself as really lower, slaves really think they should be slaves, and so on) the society can go on. The question is, however, how far can we go before it becomes painfully obvious that union is no longer possible? How then can literature and the arts promote human solidarity when a clearly written statement of one's case would only serve to highlight the differences and divergences among the various factions? So what will this approach net Rorty? Ironically, just the reverse of what he wants.

And so, even though human history and past personal experiences may act as conservative forces (as James realized), the theoretical problem remains. In order to act, human beings must have goals. Individuals and societies must know where they are going *before* they go, at least tentatively. They might later discover that it was a mistake, but even to make *that* judgment requires some objective standard of what is really good for them.

Throughout their works modern atheists give the impression that certain things are in fact good *per se* and *in se,* things such as bodily health, the education of the mind, social harmony, and so on. Yet, if, according to pragmatism, you must always wait until you see the actual consequences of your acts, if such consequences are constantly being put off into the future, and if, in effect, the future never comes, how can anyone possibly make a judgment about what is good or useful? The future postponed is the future denied. Both to know what to aim at, and to know whether or not we have hit the target, requires a target. In the realm of human action this means that, *to be useful as a theory,* ethics must define the good in a *per se* way. Such goods demand a certain kind of God, and fixed natures, none of which the typical post-modern will allow us to have.

In this matter there is only one way to stand upright. The inner logic of the case will not allow any non-transcendental theory to survive, regardless of what variations may be attempted. For example, a fashionable form of enlightened self-interest today, going back to Hobbes, is contractarianism. But how could such a situation ever get started? Even if you could imagine yourself in a "state of nature" where it is all against all and each against each, and where you are about to make a deal with others in order to live a little better than the beasts, as some modern moralists like to imagine, what kind of bargain *should* you make? We were, of course, never in such a state; it is a pure myth. The existence of such a pre-social state is in fact a *deduction* from an atomistic, reductionistic view of the world and of human nature — human nature — something we are not even supposed to possess in any substantial, body and soul, sense.

Assume for the sake of argument that there is no one human nature shared by all human beings, and which in fact justifies placing us all together in the one species. Imagine instead that each individual is a unique specimen, yet possessing a will which goes out after things in the world. Among such creatures there would be no *natural* unity. The clashes which would occur among these atomistic entities, as each one tries to impose its will upon others, would soon make life mean, brutish, and short.

Suppose further that these pre-social beings should simultaneously decide in large numbers to give up their primordial state of natural warfare and enter into some form of cooperative relationship. Regardless of what form of society was set up by their mutual agreements, it would always have to be something unnatural to them. The strain of having to conform to laws which restrict their wills would always remain. Every cop would be their enemy. Is this state of affairs really *better* than another? Is having our will frustrated really better than taking a chance on exercising it to its fullest and perhaps dying in the process? Is there not instead some potency in human beings urging them to transcend the sense level so as to make them *want* to live better than the beasts?

The point is that even if a pre-social existence were the case, we still could not decide upon the best form of interpersonal relationships, upon the *ideal* society, with *ideals* of equality, freedom, and justice, without *ideals,* without some knowledge of what we were made for, what our aim *should* be. Without a transcendental definition of the good (for us), meaning something objectively fixed and which cannot be altered merely by our own will, we could not even begin to make up contracts, much less stick to them.

As Sartre emphasizes in his Paris lecture of 1945, *Existentialism is a Humanism,* you cannot do away with the principal sum and still expect to keep drawing interest on your money. Around 1880 in France there was a plan proposed by some Secular Humanists to do away with the God of the Bible but to keep all the same norms of honesty, progress, humanism, freedom, and justice. To do this, though, they had to postulate an *ideal* world, a Heaven of Ideas, which would serve as a standard of good for all human beings. Thus it would still be obligatory *a priori* to be honest (which would include keeping to your contracts), to have children, not to beat your wife, and so on.

Sartre rejects this as nugatory nostalgia. Without God there can be no Ideals or ideal situations of any kind. Nowhere is it Thought or Written that Good exists. This cannot be the case precisely because there is nothing higher than man in the whole universe, and all men are on a plane relative to each other (*"puisque précisément nous sommes sur un plan où il y a seulement des hommes"*). Thus, because making rational deals based upon enlightened self-interest requires ideals, transcendental standards, and some definite notion of what is absolutely good for human beings, contractarianism as a moral system is impossible in principle. We must instead, Sartre thinks, forever remain in a condition where each man is a solitary consciousness, where hell is other people, and in which the gratuitous, unjustifiable act reigns supreme.

To summarize then, some kind of really existing transcendental set of standards is required in order for us to speak meaningfully about evil. This is something recognized even among some of the God-is-dead philosophers. For instance, to quote from Nietzsche's *Beyond Good and Evil*:

> "Wie? Heisst das nicht, populaer geredet: Gott ist widerlegt, der Teufel aber nicht — ?" Im Gegentheil! Im Gegentheil, meine Freunde! ("What? Does not that mean in popular language: God has been disproved, but not the devil?" — On the contrary! On the contrary, my friends!) (37)

Sartre's play *Les Mouches* (*The Flies,* 1943) can also be seen this way: With the rejection of God goes the rejection of *ba'al zebub,* the Devil, the lord of the flies.

The notion that some sort of non-transcendent-based ethics might work at all is based upon the illusion that, although such an ethics has never worked in the past, it may work in the future. The logic of the position goes like this. It is a fact that society is surviving and that individuals in the society are more or less content with the way things are going along. It is also a fact that the present basis for the society is some sort of religious doctrine. Where this is (officially) not the case, such as in China, Russia, and Eastern Europe, the social system sooner or later (usually sooner — within a generation or two) collapses, and must be replaced by something more obviously theocentric. The result is that in the long run, and over the whole range of human history, stability and meaning in society is provided by some sort of theocentric doctrine. People are, either directly or indirectly, raised amid such a doctrine and, at least implicitly, accept it as objectively true and certain.

But now, the post-modern reasons, if we had something which was non-religious but nevertheless truly rational and motivating, we could gradually wean people away from their religious orientation, replacing it with some new attitude such as post-modern consensus, utilitarianism, contractarianism, neo-pragmatism, libertarianism, and the like. After all, since the theocentric position is known (by our cult at least) to be objectively wrong and even foolish, it could not have been the *real* foundation for society in the past any more than it is now. However, we accept the fact that the society is surviving, based upon the false foundation of some sort of supernatural theism. Whatever patterns of behavior that exist now are therefore fairly well ingrained and not likely to change in the near future. So, while people are adjusting to the new, *avant-garde* standard of morality, we can expect things to go on as usual. The principle of inertia applies to societies as well as to spaceships.

If and when some non-religious system is tried, as for instance the secular humanism of Marxism, or some modified socialistic system, as in Sweden, and the system results in the breakdown of society, we can, for a while at least, using Orwell's Reversal, claim that things are really not so bad after all, but in fact are better the new (broken-down) way than they were previously. As time goes on and things get worse (according to current predictions, for instance, because of birth control and abortion, by the middle of the twenty-first century there won't be any native Swedes left in Sweden) there is nothing to do but reverse directions, as in Russia and Eastern Europe, for example, and reestablish the "old" ways, which now become the new, up-to-date, *avant-garde* way to behave. As always in politics, today's liberals are tomorrow's conservatives.

As long as there is a settled background of stable social behavior, based upon some supernatural foundation, it is possible for the society to support a few people who claim that they can do just fine without God, or who claim that the whole society can get along just as well without its theocentric underpinning. However, once let such a view gain the upper hand, even for a short time, such as during the Russian Revolution, or even the Feminist or Sexual Revolution in some parts of the world, and we begin immediately to see the beginning of the end for that society. To save the society from complete breakdown there must be a reversal of the atheistic policy and a restoration of the theocentric underpinning. Once restored and resettled, there can then arise once again that small group within society preaching the "living on bread alone" message, and maybe expanding its influence so as to become the majority. And so the cycle goes on. But at what terrible cost in human lives and suffering during the periods of breakdown, atheistic domination, and restoration?

It is true, no doubt, that under some religious systems of government, such as during some periods in Europe under some of the bad popes, under some extremist Protestant leaders such as Queen Elizabeth I in England, under the fanatical Muslims in Iran or Iraq, or the like, there can also be tyranny and destruction, but this is due, not to religion *per se* but to its misuse and abuse, or perhaps to having the wrong religion to begin with. In any event, the same cannot be said for a secular system which, *by its very nature and definition,* does not allow for any truly objective (transcendent) standards of fair-unfair, right-wrong, good-evil, and so on. There is no way to bring such a system back to its true self or to its true essential nature, because the whole point of the doctrine is to insist that there is no true self or stable essence to be brought back to. The result can *only* be a downhill run into destruction.

The irony of the situation, from the post-modern perspective, is that, although a disciple of Yahweh, for instance, at least has the possibility of rightfully charging a post-modern with wrongdoing, a post-modern does not have even the possibility of doing so with respect to anyone at all. Where there is a supra-human standard, of justice for example, someone can be accused of acting unjustly. But where there is no objective measure, but instead only a social consensus or the like (in other words, where man is subject only to those laws which he gives to himself, either individually or in groups), the very possibility of a truly binding dictate is lacking. As a basis for ethical *theory,* therefore, post-modernism is quite useless.

The most that a post-modern can throw at someone who operates on a transcendent basis (which supposedly really is not there), is the charge that he or she is acting inconsistently, that is, that he or she is not practicing what he or she preaches. This charge, however, is of little rational significance. After all, the autonomous will is as absolutely free when it comes to acting inconsistently as it is with respect to anything else. This is the isolated, enclosed theoretical ballpark in which the post-moderns must play out their little game, regardless of how much they might wish it were otherwise.

By eliminating God, or at least the divine, which acts as an ultimate objective measure of what is just and unjust, fair and unfair, right and wrong, good, better, and best, and so on, we are left completely at sea insofar as our moral standards are concerned. We must then forge a new morality for ourselves, as Nietzsche, Sartre, and others realized. Certainly personal pain, suffering, anxiety, negative emotions, and so on, would still be part of our human experience, but we would no longer be able to say that such things are evil. The most we could claim is that *I* personally regard them as bad for me. This is hardly a suitable basis for righting the many injustices in the world.[35]

Finally, a word must be said about the reliability of science and the fact of physical necessity in nature. Hume denied the reality of necessary connections outside the mind based upon a deduction from the premises supplied to him by Descartes and others in the Cartesian family (see Appendix). Today the Deconstructionists also rebuff the scientist's claim to true and certain knowledge, also as the conclusion of a line of reasoning which takes for granted the desubstantialization of everything in the universe. In a world of pure becoming *everything* is dissolved in the vat of flux, essences are decomposed, and all fixed meanings disappear forever. But what if their philosophy of being is wrong? In this regard it is instructive to take a look at what happened to the Logical Positivists.

Today we have lived through the rise *and fall* of Logical Positivism. Thanks to the work of thinkers such as W. V. O. Quine, G. Bergmann, K. R. Popper, and the later Wittgenstein, the initial enthusiasm of the Vienna Circle, as developed by Rudolf Carnap and Ayer, has been greatly dampened and largely diverted into other streams of thought, such as James's pragmatism.

The attack of the Logical Positivists on traditional philosophy had already found its way through the minds of thinkers such as Hume and Auguste Comte, as well as the minds of a whole host of others who were developing a "physics" approach to mind and spirit, and who seriously thought that they could do away with all such things as mind, spirit, and God once and for all. The twentieth-century doctrine of the Logical Positivists brought this trend to a head by declaring that *only* certain sets of certain types of statements could be regarded as worthwhile and meaningful. *All* others must be rejected. This whole program was itself based upon a very narrow definition of science. Science became *a* method, and *the* method, the only way to achieve certitude.

More specifically speaking, the method of the Logical Positivistic program, as summarized in the verifiability principle, demanded that no statement be regarded as meaningful unless it could be tested for truth or falsity, at least in principle, by some combination of mathematics and particularized sense experiences. It soon became evident, however, as Kant had already realized relative to Hume, that any and all significant scientific statements could not be verified in such a manner. For instance, that *all* uninterferred-with bodies will travel in a straight line *forever,* or that *all* hydrogen (throughout the whole universe) burns, and so on, would become meaningless statements according to the verifiability principle. Scientific laws are *universal* and *necessary* within their given parameters and boundary conditions, and the Logical Positivistic program simply could not accommodate any sort of meaningful universality and necessity. It therefore had to be rejected by the very scientists it was supposed to be serving. As a result, today even Ayer himself no longer defends it.[36]

The fact is that much of modern science is certain and dependable knowledge. My statement is not based on some theory about the way things should be, or upon some outmoded and insular worldview, but upon the way science actually exists today. The well-established scientific laws of nature tell us what is really going on in nature, so much so that we can make accurate predictions about future events.

This does not mean that being able to make accurate predictions on the basis of a particular theory in and of itself proves that the particular theory is correct. To insist that it does would be to commit the logical fallacy of "affirming the consequent," which has the general form of "if p then q; q; therefore p." A particular example of this would be: "If the golf and country club deliberately discriminates against Catholics then it will have no Catholic members; it has no Catholic members (the consequent is affirmed); therefore it deliberately discriminates against Catholics." Although this sort of fallacy is quite common, it is not valid reasoning on the basis of the sufficient conditional compound proposition, the reason for this being that the same conclusion may be brought about by some other cause (for instance, if no Catholics have ever applied for membership then the club will have no Catholic members, and so on).

There must be universality and necessity, which is to say, there must be essences, *in nature* in order to have the *possibility* of accurate predictions. Usually, however, this does not necessarily mean that, in any given case, a particular theory is the only one which could have produced the given predictions. It is for this reason that we must still be careful today to talk about Darwin's special theory (natural selection) of the origin of organic species by a process of descent with modifications from a common ancestor, Einstein's theory of relativity, and the like.

Indeed, to talk about purpose and goal-seeking *in nature* is simply to give voice to the empirical fact that natural operations are generally predictable and regular (rule-like). This does not rule out accidents, unpredictability, and chance in nature. However, the more we engage in science the more we come to appreciate that, in order to apprehend whatever chaotic, non-linear elements there are in the world, the more we must see such events against a background of order and stability. There is no static noise without music. All snowflakes (the same) are different. God does not make wallpaper; God makes tapestries. In fine, there really are natural laws, which should not be confused with theories about nature.

Scientific laws are not merely arrangements of words within other sets of words (theories). Neither are they sociologically determined. Nor do they depend upon my knowing them for them to be true. When I hit a pothole with my car, the tire takes the blow and evenly distributes the pressure around the inside wall of the tire. The action is taking place *in the tire,* not in me, and not within the verbal framework of some internally coherent theory.

Within their boundary conditions, the well-established laws of nature are not just highly probable or temporarily correct; they are completely trustworthy and dependable within their specified parameters. Examples illustrating this point are too numerous to mention. They are as numerous as the textbooks in the biological, physical, and medical sciences. When, for instance, you drive a car, you are in fact betting your life on the fact that Pascal's Principle is true and certain. A pressure applied to an enclosed fluid is transmitted equally throughout that fluid, and thus your car stops when you apply the brakes. When you go into a room and turn on the lights, the lights must go on 100 percent of the time. If they should fail to go on, you do not say, "Well, it's only probable that they should work. After all, the laws of electrodynamics are only probable, and this time was the exception." No, what you do is change the lightbulb. If the lights fail to go on, you want to know why, because they should work *every* time.

When we think of all the well-established scientific laws (which should not be confused with their human applications via technology) which go into the design and function of so many different things which we so much take for granted these days, the truth, certainty, and dependability of science becomes more and more credible. The laws of electrodynamics, of aerodynamics (are you fearful of flying in an airplane?), fluid dynamics, heat transfer, and so forth, have allowed human beings to safely plunge to the depths of the sea and soar to the stars. When we add to this the accomplishments of those in medical science, in astronomy, and so on, the possibility of taking away the certitude which science so richly deserves shrinks to zero.

Yes, but is it not true that all these laws are based upon probability functions? Because we cannot get exact solutions to the activities of nature on the atomic and subatomic levels, we are forced, are we not, to rely upon gross averages in order to *represent* the actual activities of nature? Therefore, at its most fundamental level, nature is not really law-like, is it?

An interesting point, but beside the point. It is a fact of scientific experience that there are laws of nature on the level of ordinary human observation. These include the laws of probability. The laws of probability are not themselves probable, they are certain.

Also, the fact that we are presently uncertain concerning exact solutions to problems of matter in motion or energy and change on the microcosmic scale does not mean that there are no such solutions, but only that we are currently ignorant of what they are.

Furthermore, even assuming that we could *never* obtain such solutions, this state of affairs could still be regarded as a lack of power on our part rather than as a lack of lawfulness on the part of nature.

Of greatest significance, however, is that the issue of *how* the laws of nature are *explained* does not in the least do away with the fact that there are laws of nature. The well-established laws of nature are just that: well-established. Whether we account for them by the known or unknown movements of nature on the microcosmic level, or by the direct supervision of God, or both, or some other scheme of things, is beside the point. Questions concerning the origin of the laws, or of their maintenance, important though they may be, especially for the philosopher and theologian, do not in any way lead to a denial of the existence of such laws in the first place.

Those who would degrade science should also bear in mind that such an attitude will not make it easier to converse intelligently with scientists. The scientists themselves realize that regardless of how many times they may fail, they can never forfeit the goal of truth. Such a forfeiture, even though it may appear to be a sign of humility, and even great toleration, would in fact mean the destruction of their very rationality. To maintain, based upon the claim that the diversity of contradictory opinions is virtue itself, that the best ideal is to have no ideal at all, means the end of all human science, philosophy, and theology. Any intellectual progress at all requires the realization that we do not now know what we should know and that we are capable of achieving a more perfect knowledge.

We should observe that science itself wants nothing to do with such an agnostic attitude. Scientific caution should not be confused with professional agnosticism and skepticism. When a rocket is fired off into space, but instead falls in flames into the ocean, the scientists involved are deeply dismayed. They immediately set out to discover what went wrong. There is a right way to get a rocket into orbit, and if they know the truth about rocket engines, fuels, gravity, locking rings, weather conditions, and the like, the thing will work right. Truth, correctness, and rightness are what they struggle and strain to achieve, not error and falsehood. And when they get it right they are intellectually satisfied and emotionally happy.

Let us be clear about this: It is the actual possession of truth that is good and satisfying to the scientist, not merely the searching for truth. The only reason the process of truth-finding is at all satisfying is because of the prospect of actually achieving the goal of finding the truth, even if it is only a little bit of truth for the time being. Saying that the search for truth is preferable to the actual possession of truth is like saying that the search for a hamburger is preferable to having a real hamburger in your real stomach when you're dying for food. Scientific knowledge, as with meaning in life, cannot come merely from the search for truth, whether you search alone or with a group.

Thus philosophy, even in the area of the philosophy of being, is in no way opposed to scientific investigation. Where the scientist asks, "Why does the pancreas secrete insulin?" the philosopher asks, "What does it mean to be alive?" Where the scientist asks, "Why does iron rust?" the philosopher asks, "What is a substance?" or "What is change?" or "Why is there any world at all?" The main difference between the two areas is in the level of questioning, not in the rationality of their respective procedures.

By whatever means available, both the modern scientist and the traditional philosopher, having put aside the temporary detour of Logical Positivism, are searching for the truth about themselves and the world. There is no rational *a priori* reason for stopping this questioning process at some relatively proximate level of inquiry. Neither should we assume in advance that obtaining well-founded rational answers to the more ultimate questions is impossible in principle, as the post-moderns now claim.

Moreover, I do not see that there is any necessary opposition between the conclusions of philosophy and the results of theological speculation. Theology, *beginning* with an acceptance of Scripture (for instance, the Bible, the Koran) as true and certain, may or may not coincide with the results of philosophical speculation. But to claim *in advance* that they *must* contradict one another would be unwarranted. The *a priori* rejection of at least the possibility of a fruitful interrelationship between philosophy and theology must be rejected as being nothing more than a gratuitous assertion.

The sum total of all this is to say that recent reports about the death of traditional philosophy have been greatly exaggerated. But how did such reports get started in the first place? The next part of this book is devoted to answering that question. Within a historical-analytical context I will be making three main points.

1. The Being-Question is unavoidable to thinking human beings. As Kant recognized, what he called "metaphysics" was both unavoidable and necessarily vacuous because it was merely a play of ideas in the mind without any contact with the world of sense experience. Kant, however, confused metaphysics, which he thought must, by definition, deal only with concepts and abstractions within the mind, and the philosophy of being, which need not be restricted in such a manner.[37]

The key area of concern in the philosophy of being is the nature of being. What does it mean *to be*? Can being be defined? Is it a *what*? If not, how can it be understood at all? Are being and becoming, essence and existence, eternity and temporality, fixed meanings and multiple interpretations, and the like, compatible? This is the area of foundational analysis.

2. The failure to resolve the Being-Question in such a way so as to do justice to all aspects of human experience will inevitably lead to the most extreme positions imaginable. There is no change at all; or everything is only change with no real permanence in anything at all, which means that there are no substantial things at all. Then again, the result of such a failure may be a very confused and ultimately irrational attempt to blend everything together with everything else. We may end up with some sort of pantheistic doctrine which, in order to support itself rationally at some more superficial level, must deny the principle of non-contradiction on the most fundamental level of explanation. Or again, the result may be a totally disconnected Humean-type doctrine on the nature of the world.

3. This in turn produces the most profound amorphism in all areas of human intellectual and moral life. Such thinkers are thrown into a schizophrenic state of confusion, first running this way and then that, finally throwing in the towel completely and retiring to a mental residence of reticence and resignation to the futility of all "metaphysical" endeavors. This is the "sour grapes" syndrome in modern philosophy, the disparagement of something which has turned out to be, to some thinkers, unattainable.

What can be done then except to adopt an aimless pragmatism, hoping thereby to partially counteract the effects of one's unsuccessful philosophy of being. Rather than committing suicide, which was in fact retained as an option by Nietzsche for "when the time was right," we must continue to live a life of quiet desperation, inventing short-term goals, games, and diversions for ourselves, hoping thereby to muddle through life on a day-to-day basis. William James thought that we had to *feel* that life was serious, even if it were not; that it had some eternal and cosmic significance, even if it really did not.

But post-moderns no longer feel that way. If Plato were right we could really be justified in feeling that way. But he was definitely wrong, and James was definitely right. However, James was inconsistent; he did not push his own reasoning to its limit. If pragmatism is really taken seriously, then we can no longer really feel that way, says Rorty. If the vast majority of society ever catches up with the *avant-garde,* Rorty doesn't know what will happen.

We do not know how it *would* feel. We do not even know whether, given such a change in tone, the conversation of

Europe might not falter and die away. We just do not know. James and Dewey offered us no guarantees. They simply pointed to the situation we stand in, now that both the Age of Faith [religion] and the Enlightenment [science] seem beyond recovery.[38]

Rorty's whole tone and attitude is one of despair, compensated for by a forced optimism. His only *solatium* is the hope that things won't completely fall apart. For his part, M. C. Taylor quotes with approval the final thoughts of Wallace Stevens, namely, that there is no truth, only criticism, meta-criticism, and interpreting interpretation ad infinitum. There is nothing but fiction all around. The final belief is to believe in a myth known to be a myth. "The exquisite truth is to know that it is a fiction and that you believe it willingly."[39] Apparently there is at least *some* truth left in the world. The exquisite pain of a toothache is the last word in dental health; a deliberate self-deception is the epitome of human authenticity and honesty; we shout "eureka" upon discovering that we are ever more in error. Our capacity for merciful self-delusion is evolution's greatest gift to us. And it is all said with a straight face!

My primary interest here is not directly with thinkers such as Derrida, Foucault, Gadamer, Rorty, and others. It is rather with those who have provided the intellectual foundation for their current beliefs. To my mind, these are primarily Descartes, Kant, James, Hegel, Nietzsche, Heidegger, and Sartre. Nietzsche has already been discussed. Hans Kueng is also included as an example of a postmodern theological thinker greatly influenced by Hegel, and who in turn has greatly influenced many others today. But even here it is not my intention to work out a complete exposition of their philosophies. My only interest will be in those aspects of their thought that are specially salient and particularly pertinent to the main points about Being and Becoming I wish to make.

DESCARTES, KANT, AND JAMES: AS IF THEISM, PROTO-DECONSTRUCTIONISM

> I cannot forgive Descartes. In all his philosophy he would have been quite willing to dispense with God. But he had to make Him give a fillip to set the world in motion; beyond this, he has no further need of God.
>
> Blaise Pascal
> *Pensées* (Modern Library ed.) 77

> So, this is the religion we are to gain from the study of Nature; how miserable! The god we attain is our own mind; our veneration is even professedly the worship of self.... Well does Lord Brougham call it "the great architect of nature"; it is an instinct, or a soul of the world, or a vital power; it is not the Almighty God.
>
> John Henry Newman
> "Science and Religion"
> *Selections* (1895) 105

> My first characterization of pragmatism is that it is simply anti-essentialism applied to notions like "truth," "knowledge," "language," "morality," and similar objects of philosophical theorizing. Let me illustrate this by James's definition of "the true" as "what is good in the way of belief."
>
> Richard Rorty
> *Consequences of Pragmatism* (1982) 162

As we have seen, a *per se* good or evil is something which is good or evil in itself regardless of the motives or intentions of the human agent. For instance, if a hunter shoots to death another human being in the woods, the act of one human being killing another innocent human being is an evil act even though the hunter may be freed of guilt and punishment because of his ignorance, assuming that he had taken reasonable precautions, and so on. The existence of such *per se* good or evil actions depends upon the existence of some objective standard which provides us with fixed principles of behavior. Without God, Plato's Ideas, essential human nature, or the like, the very possibility of *per se* good and evil would disappear.[1]

This is the situation described by the post-modern thinkers. Theoretically speaking, they claim that all such standards have been washed away by the tides of modern science and hermeneutics. Practically speaking, however, this position cannot be maintained *if* we are to continue to have moral human activity and meaningful decision-making. In order to act in a rational way individuals and societies must have fixed goals and universal standards of goodness and justice to be achieved. Upon closer examination it turns out that the post-moderns, despite their protestations to the contrary, do in fact possess such goals and standards.

Why, though, would anyone feel obliged to fly in the face of the evidence and deny it? Judging by the history of ideas in the West, it is because, when the real extramental world is reduced to an amorphous mass, there is no other way to go than in the direction of claiming that all meaning in the world is a projection of the intramental world onto the extramental world of nature. The only reason there is something rather than nothing is because human beings create it. Even if we talk about Being speaking through human nature, the fact remains that without humanity there would be nothing to talk about. It is human nature that supplies the world with definite, separate, and determined *things*.

Long before Nietzsche, the foundation for the hyper-modern position was laid down by Descartes, whose intention was to do just the opposite. Employing the same easy essay *style* of Michel Montaigne, but hoping to overcome once and for all his skeptical *content,* Descartes set out to redesign the whole universe to suit his goal. In the process, though, God, as a separately existing Supreme Being, was destroyed, and Being was reduced to the humanistic and subjective. The extramental world became an amorphous extension or space to be worked on by the mind. Whether continuous or broken up into little pieces (atoms), there could only be one homogeneous substance "out there." The observed fact of nature as composed of individuated substances was deduced away. All of nature, the *whole* universe, was reduced to *one* essence. This is in sharp and contradictory contrast to the best of ancient and medieval philosophy and theology.[2]

The modern doctrine of Deconstructionism is largely a matter of desubstantialization. According to this anti-essentialism, Nature is not an orderly collection of natures, as it was for Aristotle and Aquinas, for instance. In this regard, the ancient Greek had to reject both Parmenides, who placed his faith entirely in reason, and the Atomists, who went entirely on the basis of sense knowledge when it came to discussing how human beings know things. The way of Pure Reason leads to the Immobile One Being. The way of the senses, which are forever diverse and variable, leads to the opposite extreme. Cratylus, for instance, the disciple of Heraclitus, went to the extreme of declaring that being was so changeable that it was impossible for anyone to say anything definite about anything. And so he just sat, moving his finger.[3]

As a rebuttal to this, Aristotle points to the *fact* of knowledge, just as Plato had done in his *Theaetetus.*[4] Knowledge is a *fact* of human experience. It means knowing *what* something is in a definite way. If Cratylus, and the Sophists in general, for all their "humanism," were right, there would be no possibility of knowing anything. There would be no essences; that is, there would be nothing to know. But everyone knows this is not the case.

Even ordinary people realize that there is a difference between a real physician, who really knows something, and a quack who does not. People might argue, because of different lighting, about the color of a wine bottle and, because of some variation in the condition of their health, about the sweetness of the wine, but the wine, the bottle, the table, the chairs, and so on, are there, and are known to be there.

Moreover, they can be defined and discussed in a public way. Communication and discussion is a *fact* of public life. The world is *not* an amorphous mass of non-things, in which everything ends up being everything else. If this is not true, there's no possibility for any sort of conversation, social or otherwise, in order to solve any problems, whether speculative or practical.

Where did this modern phobia for essences begin in modern times? What is the origin of the mind-set which now dominates so much of modern thought, and which we see in the anthropocentric secular humanism of Gadamer, the secular fideistic moralism of Rorty, and the strange, self-contradictory, convoluted word games of Derrida and others? Allow me to propose for further discussion the following sequence of events, beginning with Descartes's attempt to establish an unshakable and eternally secure foundation for science.

With good reason René Descartes is generally recognized as the father of modern philosophy. It was Descartes who inaugurated the habit in philosophical thinking of going from the mind to the world outside the mind in order to determine what the extramental world *really* is. This is the approach of Epistemological Idealism, the doctrine that consciousness determines reality rather than vice versa. As a way of figuring out things about the world it stands in contrast to the typical approach of ancient and medieval philosophy, which was an Epistemological Realism, that is, the view that our senses and mental faculties give us a very accurate account of what the world outside the mind is really like in itself. This is, in fact, the ordinary, common-sense approach of the average person. It is not, however, a "correspondence" or "picture" view of knowledge. It is also the approach which Hume called vulgar (commonplace) and Kant called naïve.[5]

However, regardless of what evaluation we make of Descartes, he remains the most important figure in the historical sequence of events. In effect he began a chain reaction which is still continuing today. Those who reacted against Descartes were themselves reacted against by others, and so on down the years until our present day. In this respect, Descartes holds a position in modern thought comparable to that held by Parmenides in ancient Greek thought. For good or ill, the challenge, stimulation, and ideas he threw out upon the intellectual scene could not be ignored or avoided. One way or another they cried out for a response. After Descartes, just as after Parmenides, many able minds rose up to meet the challenge, some of them, it turns out, perhaps even greater than that of the instigator himself.

Descartes's aim in life was to be both a good mathematical physicist and a faithful Christian in the Roman Catholic tradition. As far as he could see, the two went hand in hand. God is required in order that the world be an orderly cosmos in which neither matter nor motion can be either lost or gained in terms of their respective sum totals. Matter, which is the same as extension or space, can be subdivided to an unlimited extent, and its various subdivisions can be moved around relative to each, but no part can ever be completely lost, nor can any new parts ever come into existence. Likewise for motion. Whatever amount of motion is lost at one place is gained at another, and vice versa.

Because of this conservation of matter and motion (the basis for the principle of inertia) we can be sure of at least two things: (1) that nothing can ever move itself because of some internal principle of activity (i.e., all matter is inert); (2) that all formulas used to describe the changes in nature will ultimately balance. In this way the world would be made eternally and absolutely safe for science. Any other sort of universe, thought Descartes, would be unsuitable for a strictly scientific analysis of nature.

If we were to remove God and spiritual beings from such a world, we would be left with the familiar world of reductionistic materialism or physicalism. This, however, was what Descartes would not allow. He always insisted upon the absolute need for God, not only to act as the necessary guarantor of universal stability, but also because of our personal need for salvation. Human beings are not just matter in motion but spiritual souls as well. Although not a psychosomaticist, Descartes was a vitalist in the Platonic tradition who took the existence of the soul, as a separate spiritual substance whose essence is the act of thinking, quite seriously. He could not, however, like the pagan Platonic tradition, condemn the body as something either evil in itself or conducive to evil (the prison in which the psyche is chained up). Because of his religion, Descartes maintained the essential goodness of everything created by God, including the material world.[6]

Even though, after Descartes's day, because of his identification of soul with the activity of thinking, we are more likely to refer to our "mind" rather than our "soul" (the "mind-body problem" rather than the "soul-body problem," for example) when we speak of our spiritual nature, the importance of the absolute division between the soul and body (or consciousness and body) still remains for us today an important topic of discussion. If there is something very special about the soul, if it can have thoughts and ideas of things which cannot in any way come from the body, then we would be forced into the position of having to search outside of the physical world for the source of such thoughts and ideas.

Descartes is sure that such a situation actually exists with respect to the mind. First of all, and if for no other reason, the mind and the body must be absolutely separate in their very essences because one (the mind) is indivisible while the other (the body) is divisible to an unlimited extent. This is just another way of saying that mind is unextended while matter is extended. Thought has no dimensions at all. Matter is nothing but three dimensions.

This is, I think, the best interpretation for Descartes's famous *Cogito*. Descartes's "discovery" is not meant so much to say something about the existence of something as to say something about the nature of something. Even later, at the end of the *Meditations* (VI) for instance, when he sets out to prove the existence of the external material world, he is really not interested so much in its existence as he is in its nature. He is primarily concerned with *what* sort of thing it is rather than with whether or not it exists. Even though it is true that mathematicians usually regard anything unproven as uncertain, I do not think it applies in this case. All along, as a normal human being, Descartes *knew* that the existence of the extramental physical world is above suspicion.

Likewise for the mind. Obviously, something exists in some way or another, even if it is only as an illusion. The real problem is in figuring out exactly how such things should be *defined*. In the case of the soul it turns out that its proper definition must be a thinking thing. I think, therefore I am a thinking thing, at least insofar as my soul is concerned. This is the one solid certitude which can then act as a prototype for all other certitudes. Whenever we know for certain *what* something is (clarity), and thereby also know what something is not (distinctness, separateness), we will know with certitude that that is exactly how it exists in the world.

In the case of human nature, for example, we have an absolute division between human beings and all subhuman creatures. This shows up on the level of observation in the fact that human minds are capable of having concepts or ideas, whereas subhumans do not and cannot have such things. In a letter to Asa Gray (17 September 1861), Darwin states:

> Your question what would convince me of Design is a poser. If I saw an angel come down to teach us good, and if I was convinced from others seeing him that I was not mad, I should believe in design. If I could be convinced thoroughly that life and mind was in an unknown way a function of other imponderable force, I should be convinced. If man was made of brass or iron and in no way connected with any other organism which had ever lived, I should perhaps be convinced. But this is childish writing.

This illustrates very well the contrast between Descartes and the attitude of those later thinkers who wished to dispose of man's mind as a separate spiritual substance, and who attempted to account for mind in terms of refined sensations, the brain, and the like. For Descartes, human beings, insofar as our minds are concerned, are in fact in no way connected with any other sort of organism. And furthermore, we *have been* visited by angels when we consider the origin of certain of our ideas. In general terms, there is certainly no continuity between humans and subhuman organisms, and this becomes obvious, Descartes thinks, as soon as we consider scientific knowledge, which, because of his deconstruction of physical nature, is reduced to pure mathematics.

Realizing that there is an unbridgeable gap between the human mind and all subhuman creatures is extremely important to Descartes. Human beings can *think* about God; animals, plants, and minerals cannot. Moreover, we can think in terms of right and wrong, better and best, imperfect and perfect, truth and falsity, and so forth. We have ideas and concepts; things of a subhuman nature do not. Now, as a matter of common human experience, we are always making comparisons of one thing with another thing in terms of good, better, and best. In addition, it is obvious that whatever conclusions we might reach on the perfection of something or other, we could never do so without some underlying background idea of what it means to be perfect, regardless of the specific content of our judgment.

Descartes's approach, as expressed in chapter III of his *Meditations on First Philosophy,* entitled "Of God, That He Exists," should be compared to that of Saint Anselm when he speaks of the "ineffable." Even though we cannot speak of that to which the term refers in any particular case (otherwise that to which it refers would not be ineffable after all), we can still understand the meaning of "ineffable." Likewise with respect to the "perfect." We have some idea of what it means to be perfect, even though we are not able directly to sense or know of some particular perfect thing in a direct and immediate manner.

Moreover, we are all aware of the fact that whatever comes into existence must have a cause which accounts for its being here rather than its not being here. According to Descartes, it is just plain foolishness to say that something can come from nothing. The only thing that could come from nothing is more nothing. In other words, from nothing we get nothing. The only way to think of the production of anything, including our ideas, is in terms of something producing something else. The only serious question for Descartes in this context is the *source* of the thing produced. Does the thing I am experiencing come from something outside of my own mind, or does it come from within my own thinking?

It is obvious to Descartes that his ideas of things at least appear to come from different sources. Some of our ideas seem to come to us as strangers, unexpected and often unwanted. Others seem to be the result of our own fertile imaginations, composing and decomposing things based upon our previous experiences. If I should burn my hand, for instance, it would certainly appear to be the case that the burn is the result of some extramental cause rather than something which I impose upon myself. However, if I should invent a new species of animal, such as a flying horse, composed of various parts derived from my ideas of other animals, it is clear that what I am doing is the result of my own mind.

Now for the key question: What of my idea of God? Descartes tells us that "By the word God I mean an infinite, eternal, immutable, and independent substance, all-knowing and all-powerful, cause and creator of myself and of anything else whatsoever that may exist."[7] But where did such an idea come from? His whole idea of God can be summed up under the heading of a Perfect Being. The question for Descartes is how the notion of a Perfect Being could have come into the mind of an imperfect creature. Could he have put it together from previously known pieces of this or that from the world of finite human experience? Animals don't have such a notion. How could humans have come up with it?

In order to render Descartes's approach to God as clear as possible, at least in terms of the reasoning involved, I will express his reasoning in a series of traditionally formed syllogisms. Concisely arranged and rationally expressed, Descartes's reasoning in chapter III of his *Meditations* is as follows:

1. Everything has a cause.
   My idea of a perfect being is something.
   Hence, my idea of a perfect being has a cause.

2. The cause of anything is at least as real as the thing caused
   (the effect).
   The cause of my idea of a perfect being is the cause of
   something.
   Hence, the cause of my idea of a perfect being is at least as
   real as the thing caused (the effect — that is, my idea of
   a perfect being).
3. No imperfect thing can be the cause of my own idea of a
   perfect being.
   I am an imperfect thing.
   Hence, I cannot be the cause of my own idea of a perfect
   being.
4. The idea of a perfect being is either from outside or from
   inside of my own mind.
   It cannot come from inside of my own mind. (See #3 above.)
   Hence, it comes from outside of my own mind.
5. This extramental cause of my idea of a perfect being is
   either perfect *per se* or imperfect.
   It cannot be imperfect. (See #2 above.)
   Hence, it is perfect *per se*.

Descartes's arguments are quite cogent as far as the reasoning itself is concerned. He takes it as a fact of experience that we do in fact have an idea of an infinite, sovereignly perfect being. The only real question is, Where does it come from? Descartes tells us that such an idea is not merely the negation of the finite, or the composition of many finite things, or somehow derived from an imagined extension of my own inherent potencies for further development and knowledge, or anything else of the sort. My idea of a perfect being is a *positive* idea; the very idea of an actually *existing* being, of a *personal* nature, who is the *unity* of all perfections.

Descartes is not saying that he has a perfect idea of God. The very nature of the infinite is such that it must surpass the capacity of our finite mind. Descartes's main point is that we do in fact possess a positive idea of something infinitely perfect, even if it is only up to the limit of our capacity to do so. In fact, Descartes insists, the idea I have of God is "at once the truest, the clearest, and the most distinct of all the ideas I have in my mind."[8] In other words, after myself, I know God better than anything else, including the material world.

We should not suppose that there is some sort of symmetrical relationship between our comprehension of the infinite and the finite, the perfect and the imperfect. One is not the negation of the other, or vice versa. Is the glass half full or half empty? Is light the absence of darkness, or is darkness the absence of light? Is motion the absence of rest, or is rest the absence of motion? The infinite is not merely the negation of the finite, nor is the perfect the negation of the imperfect.

This approach will never resolve the issue. To Descartes's way of thinking, the only way to resolve the issue is to carefully examine our own consciousness in order to determine what ideas we have, and then to figure out where and when they could have come to us.

On the basis of this methodology, Descartes makes the assertion that *he* at least has an idea of infinite perfection, and that it could not have come from what appear to be external objects, nor from the fictions created by *his own* mind. This leaves only one other possibility, namely, the idea of God must be an *innate* idea. The idea of God is implanted in us at conception, and is anterior to our idea of the finite and the imperfect. Also, the idea of God is better known than the ideas we have of the nature and constitution of the extramental material world which is known through the senses. As an innate idea, the idea of God is forever fixed in us by God himself. It cannot be either diminished or augmented by us. We can thus add another segment to Descartes's reasoning:

6. The idea of an extramental perfect *per se* being is either derived from our accidental sense experiences or it is innate.

It cannot have come from our accidental sense experiences.

Hence, it is innate.

As Descartes summarizes his own reasoning for us:

The whole force of the argument I have used in proving the existence of God resides in this, that I understand that my nature could not be what it is, that I could not have in me, that is to say, the idea of God, if God did not truly exist, that same God whose idea inhabits me, who possesses all those perfections of which I have some idea without, indeed, being able to comprehend them altogether, and who is subject to no defects.[9]

Finding fault with Descartes has been a major preoccupation among scientists, philosophers, and theologians ever since Descartes's own day. One of the earliest thinkers to offer his criticisms was Thomas Hobbes, who was responsible for submitting the third set of objections to Descartes's *Meditations*. These objections, along with Descartes's replies, were published along with the *Meditations* in 1641.

One of the most obvious objections to Descartes's proof for the existence of God in a Supernatural Theistic sense is that we *do not* in fact have an idea of God as a perfect and infinite being. This must certainly be the case if by "idea" I mean a sort of picture or image of something. It would then be impossible to have an "idea" of anything immaterial, whether of souls, angels, or God.

Descartes's response is that he only used the term "idea" because it was in common usage in his day. What he means by it is not necessarily a material image, but whatever the mind is directly aware of. Thus, the awareness of wanting something, or the perception of the fact that I am fearful at a particular time and place, would count as ideas for the Frenchman. As far as the idea of God is concerned, then, says Descartes, "I think I did explain the idea of God well enough for those who want to attend to my meaning; I could never give an explanation that would satisfy people who choose to take my words otherwise than I intended."[10]

In reply to further objections along the same lines, Descartes takes the same attitude. Hobbes states that Descartes does not prove that there is an idea of God. The divine substance, if he indeed exists, must be inconceivable.

Descartes replies that it is clear that there is an idea of God present to the human mind. This is not something which needs to be proven; it must only be attended to. We must pay attention to it. It is not something which is necessarily always actively present to us. Once attended to, though, it is present and self-evident. As far as conceivability is concerned, it is clear that we cannot have divine knowledge of the divine nature. We can, though, by an extrapolation from the knowledge we do possess in a direct way, come to a clear and distinct appreciation of the divine nature. In summation Descartes concludes: "When God is called inconceivable this refers to a concept that should adequately comprehend him. In what way we have an idea of God, I have repeated *ad nauseam*; and there is nothing brought forward here to overthrow my demonstration."[11]

Assuming that we do in fact have an innate idea of God, that it is sufficiently clear and distinct for us to recognize it as such given our finite and imperfect being, and that it is the same for all human beings, the criticisms offered by Hobbes do not in fact carry much weight. But are these assumptions true, especially the primary one about the immediate presence of God in the first place? I don't think the primary one is true. Even those who, in good conscience, and with great attentiveness, do their best to concentrate on the *idea* of God find it very difficult, if not impossible, to arrive at one and the same idea of God recognized as being inherent in their thoughts from the very earliest moments of their existence.

After Descartes's death, the thinker most responsible for driving home this point is John Locke. The Protestant Locke, who set out to examine his own ideas in a new and honest fashion, and who at the end of the seventeenth century entered into a controversy with the Cartesians, especially Edward Stillingfleet (1635–1699) and John Norris (1657–1711), showed that there was no such innate idea of God. The point that Locke wanted to make is quite simple; namely, that if it were true that all human beings have an innate idea of God, then it would not be necessary to get into a *controversy* over the point. As Gilson has summarized the historical situation:

> Edward Stillingfleet, Bishop of Worcester, provides us with a vivid illustration of what was then a not uncommon state of mind. He had been persuaded by Descartes that innate ideas were the only means to prove the existence of God; Locke was now trying to prove that there are no such ideas; but then, asked Stillingfleet in his *Discourse in Vindication of the Doctrine of the Trinity* (1696), how are we to refute the atheists, if there is no innate idea of God? To which Locke replied, that if there really were in man an innate idea of God, there would be no atheists: "I would crave leave to ask your Lordship, were there ever in the world any atheists, or not?" That was enough to settle the whole question.12

In more modern times those who have attempted to unsettle the issue have not fared any better. We might even say that they are worse off than Stillingfleet. John Hick, for instance, in a recent attempt to claim that *all* religious traditions truly and objectively maintain the *same idea* of the divine, must so dilute and water down the notion of God that God becomes both personal and impersonal at the same time. According to Hick, there are only two basic religious concepts: "One is the concept of God, or of the Real experienced as personal, which presides over the theistic forms of religion. The other is the concept of the Absolute, or of the Real experienced as nonpersonal, which presides over the various nontheistic forms of religion."13
Underneath both, though, is the same reality. As an alternative to a complete and total skepticism with regard to the idea of God among human beings throughout the whole world, why not look for some common content which would show that all human beings, including the vast majority of those who would not be considered as believers in God from the viewpoint of Judaeo-Christianity, do in fact hold a common idea of God? Such an idea of God would be the idea of the "same limitless ultimate Reality" experienced in various ways. For Hick, "the great religious traditions of the world represent different human perceptions of and response to the same infinite divine Reality."14 I doubt if many traditional believers would be satisfied with such vagueness.
In addition, the definition of God given by Hick would certainly not gladden the hearts of Descartes and Stillingfleet. To be of any use to the Cartesians the idea of God had to be of a certain fixed nature, suitable to a world of scientific rigor and personal religion. To reduce God to a vague sort of undefined ultimate reality, which could just as well be identified with the whole physical world as not, was worse than useless for their purposes.

If for no other reason, it would not have allowed Descartes to go on, as he does at the end of his *Meditations,* to redefine nature solely in terms of matter in motion. A vague, amorphous divine natural world, complete with all of its shifting and mathematically unanalyzable qualities, a world more suitable to a Hegel, Nietzsche, or Heidegger, was exactly what Descartes did not want. If the natural world *is* God, then God could not be called upon deliberately to create a world consisting solely of certain primary qualities such as size, shape, and so on. What would then become of science? The answer is that we would have the science of the East, where such views did in fact predominate; which is to say, we would have no science worth speaking of at all.[15]

Also, it would not have served very well the personal religious purposes of the Cartesians. We must remember that Descartes was not a "liberal" mind in the manner of Hegel or Marx. He would not reject the principle of non-contradiction, that is, he would not turn irrational, at some very fundamental level of thinking, in order to account for something he wanted to explain on a more superficial level. There is no way God could be both Being and Non-Being or Personal and Impersonal, or any other such thing(s) both at the same time and in the same respect.

There is, however, another problem which Descartes had to face. Even assuming that he could overcome the problem of the innateness of the idea of God, how could he overcome the problem, so clearly to be seen in the outline of Descartes's argument as presented above, that whatever idea he had was exclusively his and only his idea? This is why, I think, he made a point of coming back to the proof for the existence of God in chapter V of the *Meditations,* "Of the Essence of Material Things, and, again, Of God, that He Exists."

What Descartes does, in effect, is pretty well to repeat Anselm's argument for the existence of God based upon the very definition of God as "that than which nothing greater can be conceived."[16] Descartes's problem is how he can overcome the nagging question about whether or not he can be sure that there is really something extramental corresponding to his intramental idea. Maybe the whole process is going on only inside his own mind. Is he committing the logical fallacy of begging the question, that is, assuming as true the very thing he is supposed to be proving to be true in an objective, extramental way?

This, I think, is precisely where the real problem with this approach to God arises. It looks like the definitional avenue to God's existence is a frame-up, a contrived set-up with a predetermined outcome. Defining something into existence is *too* easy. There is an important difference between an essentialistic judgment and an existentialistic judgment. Existential-type judgments are of a very special nature, such that it is not possible to have an idea or concept of existence. That is to say, the thought or idea of existence or of something existing is not the same as our immediate apprehension of real existence. Put otherwise, the *concept* of existence is as much within the realm of the abstract and essential as is the concept (the "what," the definition) of anything else. And this, in a nutshell, is the basic reason why the approach of Anselm and Descartes is always sure to fail.

In their efforts firmly to "construct" God, they did just the opposite. By reducing God to a concept in their sincere efforts to understand God, they in effect deconstructed God as a separately existing being with whom we can communicate and to whom we can become present. *If* our *understanding* of God is to be the basis for a personal relationship with God, then we have failed. God ends up being simply ourselves. All we have managed really to construct is a mirror, and as it was later explicitly recognized, an empty mirror.

Kant's way of putting this is to point out that "being" or "existence" cannot be a predicate. Saying that "God is omnipotent" is a proposition which can be understood and analyzed because the predicate "omnipotent" adds something to our understanding of the subject "God." It is a trait or characteristic which increases the definition or "what" of the subject term. However, saying "God is" or "God exists" does not add anything to what we already understand by the term "God." At most it is a way of emphasizing the subject, or perhaps a way of repeating the subject, such as saying "God is God." This, though, would be of very little help in a scientific context. After knowing that something is there, say, the planets and their motions, science wants to know more and more about *what* something is, not simply a repetition of the fact that something is there. Because, after all, what does existence mean if not simply to be there, to be found, to be instantiated?

In order to know that something is there it must be given in sense experience. It cannot be deduced or projected by the mind. The role of the mind is to organize existence, not provide it. Only sense experience can grant to the mind the raw data upon which the mind works its categories. How then can we ever find out about the existence of something by simply thinking about it? The simple answer is that we cannot. My idea of a hundred dollars remains the concept of one times a hundred dollars regardless of how long I think about it. The only way to make the money real is to have it given to me in one way or another. The same holds for God. Unless God is given to me in terms of sense data, there is no way I can reason my way to God's reality by any act of pure cognition alone.

In his *Critique of Pure Reason* (1781, 2nd ed. 1787), after discussing the above points, Kant states that there are three, and only three, ways to attempt proving the existence of God by reasoning. One way is the well-respected "physico-theological" approach of Aristotle,

Newton, and many others, which reasons from the given fact that things are in orderly and predictable motion in the world. These orderly changes and motions require causes. These causes, though, cannot go on to infinity. So ultimately there must be a first cause of motion.

The second way is the "cosmological" approach which begins with the fact that the world is a contingent place, meaning that the things in the world were not here yesterday, are here today, and will be gone tomorrow. But if everything were capable of not-being, nothing could have gotten started in the first place. Hence there must be a necessary being. A third way is the definitional or "ontological" approach.

If I am interpreting Kant correctly, despite whatever other difficulties there may be with the proofs, there is to Kant's way of thinking one central problem which can never be overcome regardless of how much we try modifying the various approaches. As he states in his *Critique of Pure Reason* II, chapter 3, sections 3–7, the first and second approaches reduce to the third. But the third must always fail, and therefore so must the first two. If my analysis of his reasoning is correct, he proceeds in the following way.

In order to understand the path to a God who transcends all present and future sense experience based upon the physico-theological proof, we must admit that everything which changes and moves, especially in an orderly and predictable fashion, requires a cause. This, though, presupposes that the things in question are not self-moved and self-sufficient. They are all dependent upon something else in order to show purpose, unity of organization, and so on. In other words, they are all contingent.

Yet this is exactly what the cosmological argument is based upon. We look around and find that for everything it is possible not-to-be-here. Everything within our experience comes and goes. Yet again, though, if we examine how it is that we can say that everything experienced is contingent in this sense, it turns out that we can only do so in contrast to the notion of necessary things. But where are these necessary things? That two and two make four is necessary. But this is only *within* the mind. And so it must also be for the idea of a transcendent supreme being existentially separate from his creation. We have a concept of God but no sense experience of God. It follows then that if we are to prove the existence of God, we must move from the intramental concept to the extramental reality, which is impossible. So it is that the argument from order rests upon the argument from contingency, which rests upon the ontological argument, which itself is without any rational foundation.

This means that we cannot, under any circumstances, reach the truth about the nature, providence, and personal presence of God by the use of our ordinary, scientific, experiential sort of reasoning.

Struggle as it might, the intellect is always sure to fail in this area. This is because the concept of God, as well as the concepts of his main attributes, are all purely transcendental ideas without worldly foundation. At the end of section 7 Kant states: "The attributes of necessity, infinitude, unity, existence apart from the world (and not as a world-soul), eternity — free from the conditions of time, omnipresence — free from the conditions of space, omnipotence and others, are pure transcendental predicates."[17]

What then, if anything, can we know about God? If God is an objectively real being, "out there" in the world of reality outside of our minds, how can we possibly find him? Unless God is an innate scientific category, such as cause and effect, which Kant is sure he is not, how can we ever prove the existence of God? Kant's answer to this problem, one generated within his own system designed to save science from skepticism, is to take a reasonable yet non-scientific approach to the existence of God. Although not the conclusion of a scientific reasoning process, God becomes a *postulate* of reason, needed in order to take care of certain moral needs equal in importance to the scientific needs of human nature.

Kant defines science in terms of universal and necessary knowledge, which means a heavy emphasis on mathematics. For Kant, there is as much science in the philosophy of nature as there is mathematics. However, unlike Bishop George Berkeley, Kant insists upon the existence of a material world outside the mind. The mathematical physicist (the ideal scientist) must have something out there to work on. Hence it is important to keep in contact with the sense world in order to have science. Science can only be science if, in addition to its mathematical formulation, it also has a data base in sense experience. For Kant, this is a matter of definition.

Consequently, science cannot be equated with what is reasonable. A religious belief in God may be reasonable, and reasoned to, even though it is not scientific according to his use of the term. Kant carries out this reasoning process in a straightforward deductive fashion in his *Critique of Practical Reason* (1788), a follow-up work to his *Critique of Pure Reason*. The topic is also discussed in his *Critique of Judgment* (1790), and in at least two other works on the metaphysical presuppositions needed to establish a solid moral life for human beings living in society. The result of Kant's "reasoned faith" has been called by Lewis White Beck "perhaps the most important and profound philosophy of morals produced in modern times."[18]

Kant, who was very pragmatic-minded in his own way, bases his view on the need for a rigid standard of behavior if we wish to preserve a civilized, decent human society. On the negative side, this means a need for self-control and restraint. On the positive side, it means a need for a caring, reliable, dutiful approach to our interpersonal relationships. Every right carries with it a corresponding obligation. Our primary obligation on the positive side is to exercise our will power in such a way as never to deliberately will to do something which could not be made into a standard mode of behavior for everyone else in the world. On the negative side, our duty is to never engage in special pleading for ourselves, that is, attempting to make an exception for ourselves relative to others. For example, stealing must be regarded as a violation of the moral law because, if universalized, it would result in the elimination of the very civilized society we want to preserve.

But what conditions are necessary in order for us to make sense out of human moral obligations? First of all we must have a truly free will with respect to our specifically human-type moral choices. A free will is required so that we might be justly blamed or praised for what we will or do not will, for what we do or do not do, based upon our own intentions. Since we cannot *know* the nature of something in itself, there can be no natural moral law for Kant. The will, therefore, must substitute for the intellect.

Second, we must possess at least an immortal soul so that our pure will to Duty might have an opportunity for reaching perfection. The highest and greatest good for each human being is the complete satisfaction of his or her self-consciousness. This can only come about via a combination of complete self-respect, which means the perfect practice of Duty, and a complete and perfect state of self-conscious happiness. In fact, neither of these can be achieved in our earthly life. Hence the need for our personal immortality in order that we might be able to complete the first part of the two requirements in our life after death.

In the same way, that is, in order to account for the very possibility of our highest good, God must exist. In this life there is no necessary proportion between our good moral behavior and our own happiness. The good often suffer while the evil prosper. As soon as we consider the situation, we discover just how limited we are in our power to bring about a coincidence of will and happiness. As a result, if we are to achieve happiness at all, it must be on a different plane of existence and in a different world of being. According to Kant, when speaking of an individual's will to duty, "Not being nature's cause, his will cannot by its own strength bring nature, as it touches on his happiness, into complete harmony with his practical principles."[19] Nevertheless, the need to combine Duty and Happiness remains. "Therefore also the existence is postulated of a cause of the whole of nature, itself distinct from nature, which contains the ground of the exact coincidence of happiness with morality."[20]

The exact coincidence is important. In order to have an exact coincidence, God must be personal, all-knowing, and all-powerful. The case of each individual is different from every other individual.

In order to provide for an exact coincidence God must personally know each case in its own personal individuality, and be in a position to hand out reward and punishment as each case deserves. What Kant is saying, in effect, is that without God there would be no exact justice. If God did not exist it would mean that if someone could get away with an evil act until he or she died, he or she would have gotten away with it *forever*.

In order to avoid this situation, which is so ruinous for both individuals and society, we must postulate a Supreme Being in the Supernatural Theism tradition. For Kant the proper name of God is the Supreme Moralist. In fact, from a religious perspective according to Kant, God means the moral (action) oriented traits of holy (law-maker, world-maker), ruler (executive power, morality-sustainer), and wise (rewarder and punisher, judge). Religion, the best of which is Christianity for Kant, is the recognition of the practical fact that all duties are divine commands welling up from within us, based upon our internal will to Duty, rather than some set of impersonal rules enforced from outside of us. It is by acting morally within this religious (Protestant non-denominational-Christian) context that we make ourselves worthy of eternal happiness. God did not create the world for our happiness within the world, but as a testing ground for our worthiness for happiness in the next world.[21]

To what extent, though, has Kant really improved upon Descartes and Anselm with respect to the presence of God? Hans Vaihinger rightly calls Kant's proof for the existence of God an "as if" approach. According to Vaihinger, looking upon God as the supreme ruler of a moral kingdom is *not* to be taken literally. Even though Kant substituted his own *ratio fecit Deum* (reason creates God) for the more ancient *timor fecit deos* (fear creates the gods), he nevertheless was a continuator of the hypothetical or "as if" mode of argumentation. The concepts of freedom, God, and immortality are simply the projections of the supersensuous within us, above us, and after us, respectively. In terms of any literal meaning which these concepts might have, they can refer only to those things with which we are in immediate contact, namely, ourselves and our environment.

Nevertheless, it is possible to say sincerely "I believe in God" in the Kantian philosophy of morality. Since the whole point of Kant's approach is to elicit action, that is, to bring about practical results on a day-to-day basis, saying "I believe in God" and saying "I act as if God really existed" amounts to saying the same thing. Those who go about crying "Lord, Lord" are not those who get into the kingdom of heaven, but only those who actually follow God's commands. Regardless of how much someone may talk about God, in the end there is still a great deal of truth in the old motto that actions speak louder than words. God is really present *only* to those who *act* in a godly way.

"But," asks Vaihinger, "is it not, from an ethical standpoint, a reprehensible lie to speak in this manner of a 'belief in a future world-judge' whose reality we do not assume?"[22] Referring back to Kant himself, Vaihinger claims that this is not the case. Once the existence of God is taken to heart, once God is internalized, and once we actually act and behave on the assumption of God's presence, then God does in fact exist within us.

A hypocrite, on the other hand, may say that he is acting in such and such a way because of his belief in God, while in fact the real motive for action is only the fear of punishment or some other worldly aspiration, such as fame, money, pleasure, and so on. To be "real" the belief must be sincere, "For the truly ethical man really finds this belief in himself, in the sense that it is efficacious within him to such a degree that the moral law is as sacred to him as if there really were a divine law-giver; and, in this sense, he sincerely believes in God."[23]

As far as Vaihinger can see, the meaning of Kant's approach to God is equal to the kind of action that results from the belief in God. Regardless of what you may call yourself, it is by your works that you shall be named. It's the practical belief in God that counts, not the theoretical belief. In this sense all ethically moral conduct presupposes the presence of God and the immortality of the human soul. Your actions are good and *therefore* you believe. "This Kantian *recte agis, ergo credis* is the basic axiom of practical philosophy and, as such, the counterpart to the basic axiom of Descartes's theoretical philosophy as rightly understood: *cogito, ergo sum.*"[24] Just as Descartes established the basic principle of knowing the truth in the speculative order, so Kant provided the basic principle of morality in the practical order.

Nevertheless, however true this may be psychologically speaking, how can I have a relationship with someone who is not there? Vaihinger, himself a neo-Kantian in his own philosophical outlook, has a thorough knowledge of all of Kant's writings, including the more obscure ones, such as *Kants Opus Posthumum*. In this collection of late Kantian works, written in the later 1790s but not published until 1881–1884, Vaihinger finds the final confirmation of Kant's "as if" approach to everything outside the thinker's own mind, including the *Ding an sich* (the thing in itself), for example, that tree as it exists independently of the knower. The same is certainly true of God as well.

Kant states that it makes no practical difference whether we place the source of the divine commandments in ourselves or in an objectively and independently existing Supreme Being. As Kant himself says, "God is not a being outside me, but only a thought in me. God is the morally practical self-legislative reason" (*Kants Opus Posthumum,* sec. 341, p. 819). In fact God does not exist outside me, but is only a moral relationship within me. In short, one part of my reason commands while another aspect of my reason moves me to action. In a word, to be religious in a Supernatural Theistic sense simply means being true to yourself. We are once again, as with Anselm and Descartes, only looking into an empty mirror.[25]

Is the situation with respect to the systematic deconstruction of God in William James's pragmatism any different? Going back to the seventeenth and eighteenth centuries for a moment, we might note in passing that Voltaire had criticized Pascal for claiming that sincerely believing something to be so somehow makes it actually be so. Being convinced you are the ruler of the world may get you into an insane asylum but it won't get you into the halls of world power, Voltaire pointed out.[26] According to James, however, this is really not completely true. There is a way of *becoming* the ruler of the world even if you are not really such a potentate to begin with, and that is to get the vast majority of the other people in the world to go along with your subjective belief. It is possible for something to become true via some forward-looking projective process which turns out to be useful and expedient at a certain time under certain circumstances. This is the insight James had early in his philosophical career, and which he later developed in his doctrine of pragmatism.

This doctrine calls for a redefinition of "true" and "truth." In ordinary usage in the English language, "true" means that there is a match-up or correspondence between something and something else. "This is a true diamond" ordinarily means that this particular piece of mineral corresponds to the specific chemical composition and crystalline structure of what scientists define as diamondness. A "true friend" is someone who corresponds to the definition of a friend, usually as defined by the person making the statement, but without ruling out the possibility that there may be a universal definition of friendship for the whole human race. Also, to say that you are "telling the truth" normally means that there is a correspondence between what you are saying and what you are thinking at the time.

By the same token, a "true statement" means that there is a correspondence between the mental, written, or spoken statement and the situation referred to by the statement. "You are now holding a book in your hands" is true if in fact, objectively speaking, you are holding a book in your hands here and now. Generally speaking, saying, "It is a fact that you are holding a book in your hands" and saying, "It is true that you are holding a book in your hands" are equivalent expressions. A fact is a truth; a truth is a fact. When dealing with extramental things and situations, it is normal and usual to regard the external world of nature as a given. It is reality that determines consciousness, not vice versa. The knower does not invent or create reality. He or she rather discovers it.

From James's perspective, the trouble with this approach to truth, commonsensical as it may be, is that it tends to pull us into the rationalist or intellectualist frame of mind. According to this mental "temperament," we should look down upon ordinary day-to-day experience as something inferior to pure thought. Knowledge gained through the senses is, if not totally worthless, at least misleading. In the fashion of Plato and Hegel, we are led away from the facts of experience to a realm of ideas in which the real-life events of our actual day-to-day existence are degraded to the point of being regarded as contradictory to the Truth. The Absolute wars with the concrete and the relative.

To use James's own language, the world of ideas becomes a closed system, finally fixed forever, non-utilitarian, haughty, remote, removed from the senses, pale, spectral, empty, pallid, abstract, sterile, simple, inert, static, stagnant, complete, an end in itself, preestablished, *a priori,* timeless, immutable, ready-made, unconditioned, transcendental, and generally so vague as to have no consequences for personal behavior. It doesn't really *exist* at all; it only *holds* or *obtains.* It lives, if it can be said to live at all, only in the world of logic. And if it has any friends it can only be in the world of mathematics.

In sharp contrast to this James pits the doctrine of pragmatism. How can the dead Absolute, which swallows up into itself all contradictions, as Kierkegaard had already noted, have anything to do with the "lived world" of becoming, change, and development? James, like John Dewey, sees a deep division between *being* and *becoming.* Being is defined as it was for the Greeks, that is, as the self-identical, as that which is absolutely opposed to alteration, change, and development. But the world of experience is not like that at all. What to do? If the world of essence, of the universal and the necessary, of Plato's Ideas and Hegel's Absolute, cannot be reconciled with the world of shifting sense experience, then so much the worse for Plato and Hegel.

James struggles with a love-hate relationship with Greek Being. It seems to work in areas such as logic and mathematics, but it in no way satisfies his obvious and overpowering experience of change. Part of his solution to his problem is to modify science so as to get it away from the fixity of essences and deterministic, eternally true, laws. Science itself is to be interpreted pragmatically. Science is not a reflection of reality out there in the extramental world. Its laws are only an expression of a scientist's point of view. Of what use are scientific laws supposedly telling us what the world is really like? "Their great use is to summarize old facts and to lead to new ones. They are only a man-made language, a conceptual shorthand, as some one calls them, in which we write our reports of nature; and languages, as is well known, tolerate much choice of expression and many dialects."27

Laws are expressed in language. And, since language is arbitrary, the scientific laws must be arbitrary also. Regardless of what we might think of James's reasoning, we can at least sympathize with his problem. But this does not really get to the root of his problem. Human arbitrariness may or may not have driven divine necessity from science, but even if it has, science is only one form of truth. What about truth in general?

He must somehow redefine it. He is not out to destroy it, or do away with most of it; only to redefine it. To accuse pragmatism of throwing out truth is an abominable misunderstanding and an impudent slander, James insists. In contrast to the medieval scholastics, who took an objectivist view of truth, James wants an instrumentalist or consequentialist view of truth.

> But please observe, now, that when as empiricists we give up the doctrine of objective certitude, we do not thereby give up the quest or hope of truth itself. We still pin our faith on its existence, and still believe that we gain an ever better position towards it by systematically continuing to roll up experiences and think. Our great difference from the scholastic lies in the way we face. The strength of his system lies in the principles, the origin, the *terminus a quo* of his thought; for us the strength is in the outcome, the upshot, the *terminus ad quem*. Not where it comes from but what it leads to is to decide. It matters not to an empiricist from what quarter an hypothesis may come to him: he may have acquired it by fair means or by foul; passion may have whispered or accident suggested it; but if the total drift of thinking continues to confirm it, that is what he means by its being true.28

But true to what? James's problem is compounded by the fact that he must do some strange things with the King's English. The ordinary view of "true" as used in English means a *conformity*. The picture of the clock is a true picture because it matches up with the real clock. "Two plus two is four" is a true statement because it matches up with the way these concepts must be related to each other. James is willing to admit universality and necessity in mathematics because mathematics is a strictly intramental phenomenon. But the outside world is not that way. There is no *being* out there in the real world of sense experience. If truth seems to presuppose fixity and abstractness, then something must be done with either truth or the real world. James decides to do something with both.

James says that "Names are arbitrary, but once understood they must be kept to."[29] If you want to communicate you cannot disrupt common usage. James, however, does not follow his own advice. If truth means a conformity, but if outside the mind there is no *being* to conform to, then it would seem that we should drop the term "truth" when dealing with extramental things and events. For instance, he might have decided to talk about "meaningfulness" and "meaninglessness" rather than "true" and "false," as was done later by the Logical Positivists.

Instead, however, he decided to try redefining truth in terms of an experiential process whereby we come to the realization that some idea or proposition about the extramental world is good and useful to us in our actual day-to-day real-life existence. Thereby pragmatism becomes a theory about theories rather than a theory about truth. What used to be called truth is now called the factual. Truths (theories) are founded in facts, and constantly move back and forth between and among facts, but they are not, strictly speaking, facts. "The 'facts' themselves meanwhile are not *true*. They simply *are*. Truth is the function of the beliefs that start and terminate among them."[30]

How does this affect our knowledge of God? We obviously cannot put God into a test tube. How then do we experience God so that we can make a true (good, useful) statement about him? We cannot. However, we may be able to justify a belief in God because such a belief is good and useful to us. It might be a fact that the *presence* of God is a true-good-useful belief, even though the *existence* of God is not a fact. As with Kant, what the intellect cannot do on the basis of straightforward sense experience, the will must handle in some other way. On the three assumptions that certain things, such as life, health, peace, progress, and so on, are of primitive importance, that these cannot be maintained without some sort of trans-human sanction, and that the intellect is not capable of establishing such a sanction, we have no alternative but to appeal to the will.

James takes up this issue in his essay *The Will to Believe* (1896). The question he raises is whether it is reasonable to hold religious views of the Supernatural Theistic type in the absence of a strictly logical and scientific proof founded upon sense experiences. James thinks it is, and proceeds to tell his Yale and Brown student audience why they, who are still religious, in contrast to his own Harvard students, have the better side of the issue.

First, he must dismiss Pascal's approach. Pascal was a well-meaning mathematician, but he had no deep appreciation of the inner workings of the mind. His Wager Argument thus ended up being a rather cold and calculating piece of mathematical probability. James, on the other hand, being a psychologist, wants to talk in terms of something much more congenial to the average human being. He says of Pascal's approach:

> You probably feel that when religious faith expresses itself thus, in the language of the gaming-table, it is put to its last trumps. Surely Pascal's own personal belief in masses and holy water had far other springs; and this celebrated page of his is but an argument for others, a last desperate snatch at a weapon against the hardness of the unbelieving heart. We feel that a faith in masses and holy water adopted willfully after such a mechanical calculation would lack the inner soul of faith's reality; and if we were ourselves in the place of the Deity, we should probably take particular pleasure in cutting off believers of this pattern from their infinite reward. It is evident that unless there be some pre-existing tendency to believe in masses and holy water, the option offered to the will by Pascal is not a living option. Certainly no Turk ever took to masses and holy water on its account; and even to us Protestants these means of salvation seem such foregone impossibilities that Pascal's logic, invoked for them specifically, leaves us unmoved.[31]

In fairness to Pascal it should be mentioned that James has not really done as much damage to Pascal as he thinks. Pascal had already answered, in part at least, James's contention about the lack of holiness and reverence of the Wager Argument. Pascal was not out to prove the existence of God at all; only the naïveté of the atheist. In addition, however, James misses two other points. One is that Pascal would not have tried his argument on Muslims and Protestants because, presumably, they *already* believe in God and thus have no need for the argument in the first place. In the second place, James underestimates the flexibility of the human psyche and its ability to adjust when it is convinced that it must do so. Masses and holy water are in fact live options, as shown by the fact that conversions have in fact taken place and are therefore at least possible.[32]

According to James's technical distinctions, an *hypothesis* is a candidate for belief; it is *alive* if you might actually act on it; a live *option* is a choice between live hypotheses. An option is *forced* if it is unavoidable, that is, if you must choose one hypothesis or the other whether you want to or not; it is *momentous* if you must choose now rather than later, if there is a great deal at stake, and if the decision is irreversible. A *genuine* option possesses all three traits of being alive, forced, and momentous.

Is there anything irrational about acting upon a genuine option in the absence of scientific proof? James thinks not. In fact, many intelligent people believe in such things as atoms, molecules, progressive evolution, democracy, and even in the possibility of attaining truth, without a complete justification by scientific evidence. This is because the real springs of human action lie much deeper than the level of reasoning. Our emotional natures must act, whereas our intellects might ponder things forever without acting. Even to try leaving the question open for some emotional reason is itself a non-rational decision, and is in as much danger of losing the truth as would be an outright decision against the issue in question.

This is especially true in moral matters. Waiting for *all* the evidence to come in before acting means, in effect, not to act at all. But life cannot go on this way. We must act on a minute-to-minute basis if we are to go on living in any kind of society. Even if we choose not to act, that is itself a choice for which we are responsible. All ordinary human life is dominated by the need to work with other people in society. To ask for absolute certitude in such situations before acting would put a quick end to all social relationships.

What James is talking about can be summarized under the heading of faith. For James, faith is another name for a working hypothesis. We must have such hypotheses in order to advance in our research. In human affairs, faith is even more important. It becomes part of the data which goes into the final solution. For example, if someone wants someone else to like him, how he acts toward the other person will have a great deal to do with the outcome. By starting with the faith that the other person *already* likes him, he can possibly change the situation in his favor. He cannot wait until all the evidence is in before he acts, because his actions are part of the evidence. Faith is as much a secular phenomenon as it is a religious one. All of secular society depends upon it. We must anticipate cooperation, or not act at all. In such cases it is perfectly rational to have faith run ahead of scientific evidence. We thereby set up a positive cycle. Indeed, if it were not for faith there would be no society, and consequently no possibility for the development of science at all.

Equally important, though, is the possibility for a negative cycle, caused by the anticipation of what might *not* happen. James used the then timely all-American example of robbers attacking a train to illustrate this point. How is it that a few people — robbers, terrorists, and so on — can control the behavior of large groups of other people? It is because they can count upon each other; they stick together. They know in advance what they can expect from each other.

In contrast, the many people being robbed or held hostage cannot count upon each other. Each one says to himself or herself: "If I act to stop this attack, what can I expect the others to do, and how effectively will they move to support me?" More often than not the answer that comes back is: "I really can't expect anything of the others." As James pointed out, if the attackers expected a unified front in opposition to the attack, say from a well trained army unit with high morale, they would never attack in the first place.

Under such circumstances, those who preach skepticism to us are really the irrational ones. First of all, as with all other human beings, their passions, their reasons of the heart which the head knows not of, to quote Pascal, must dominate anyway. Secular faith, at least, is inevitable.

Second, they are being silly when they tell us that we are better off risking the loss of truth than we would be if we took a chance and found out we were wrong. How can anyone live an exciting life without taking chances somehow or other sooner or later? How could any progress be made anywhere, even in science? James cannot imagine anything more impossible and duller than the position of the philosophical skeptics.

In the third place, even choosing not to act is itself an action. It means actively discouraging us from acting in a religious way. The skeptic dupes himself or herself if he or she thinks that he or she can really be neutral in the religious question. Either there is some ideal perfection to be gained by action, and it is better to believe such a thing than not to believe it, or there is no ideal perfection and to believe there is would be a great immorality. But to vote against the rationality of the will to believe would mean to choose the latter. In that event we could rightfully be expected to act differently than we would act if we had chosen the former. So, he or she who is not with me on this, thinks James, is definitely against me.

In all, therefore, there is no good reason for rejecting out of hand the rationality of the *will* to believe. James himself thinks that it is better to be a believer than a non-believer. For James, to be really open-minded and liberal means not ruling out in advance the truth that God exists, or that there is some far-off divine perfection toward which the whole creation is moving, or some other sort of trans-experiential possibility. Put this together with the pressing sociological, psychological, and pragmatic needs of people in everyday life, and James has no qualms whatsoever about taking a *risk* on faith, and behaving like a good Christian gentleman as a result.

Can we get James to be a little more specific about the meaning of faith and the presence of the trans-experiential reality, be it God or whatever? Concerning the definition of faith, which he also calls trust, James says the following in an 1880 address to the Harvard Philosophical Club:

> Now, there is one element of our active nature which the Christian religion has emphatically recognized, but which philosophers as a rule have with great insincerity tried to huddle out of sight in their pretension to found systems of

absolute certainty. I mean the element of faith. Faith means belief in something concerning which doubt is still theoretically possible; and as the test of belief is willingness to act, one may say that faith is the readiness to act in a cause the prosperous issue of which is not certified to us in advance. It is in fact the same moral quality which we call courage in practical affairs; and there will be a very widespread tendency in men of vigorous nature to enjoy a certain amount of uncertainty in their philosophic creed, just as risk lends a zest to worldly activity.[33]

Faith can also be called a "working hypothesis."[34] James does this in order to show that faith and science are far from incompatible, provided that faith is defined in the way that he wants it defined.

It seems clear from James's definition of faith that early on in his career he sees it as a pure act of the will, completely divorced from the intellect. Not surprisingly, other thinkers, such as Bertrand Russell, could feel very comfortable with James's approach and proceed to define faith as believing on the basis of no evidence whatsoever. As a pure act of the will, faith is totally gratuitous. If any evidence were available, doubt would be greatly reduced. But as it is, since it is possible at least to imagine the truth of the opposite of the proposition under consideration, it cannot be held as a truth in the ordinary usage of the term truth. At best it can be held as an opinion; and all opinions are open to revision upon the arrival of new evidence pro or con.

Believing on the basis of no evidence means no evidence external to the knowing subject. It does not rule out the subject himself, of course. The entire motive for willing on the part of the willing subject is in the will. In this sense faith is a leap, a way of bridging over a gap left in the structure of the world by the weakness of the intellect. Like Pascal and Kant, James sees the need to use the will to make up for the deficiencies of the intellect in religious matters. The healthy person sticks to sense knowledge, but not to the point of being a fanatic about it.

I think the real reason James does not care much for Pascal is not because the Frenchman talks about stakes and games and so on (James talks this way himself), but because Pascal insists that in order to be rational you *must* choose God. To James this is as fanatical as the scientist who insists that we must choose against God. As a teacher, James was noted for always saying in class, "*If* there is a God. . . ." The decision someone makes must always remain a purely gratuitous act of the will.

Nevertheless, as a social animal James thinks it best to believe that the belief in God is better than the disbelief in God. If this sounds rather removed from the fact of God's reality it is because it is.

Religion is basically a social phenomenon, but it must be acted upon privately. As normal people in the world we must act. "The whole defence of religious faith hinges upon action," states James.[35] If religion did not make any difference in the way we act, thinks James, he wouldn't bother with it at all. However, as it is, given our present state of evolution, if we want a decent civilization we need the right to believe in God.

But who or what is God? James answers this question for us at the end of his *Varieties of Religious Experience* (1902). The purpose of James's study is to determine what is common among all the religious traditions of humankind over a long period of time. At the end of the work he asks two questions. One is concerned with the "common nucleus" which underlies all the creeds despite their many discrepancies. The other is whether or not the unanimous testimony of the creeds is true (true here, I think, in the normal sense of the term).

In answer to the first question, James concludes that all religions involve some doctrine of salvation, which presupposes that there is some need for salvation. This need is based upon the fact that there is an uneasiness and discontentment which we find within ourselves. Then there is a proposed solution to the problem which always involves making some connection with some "higher power." This connection is always there, at least in potency, even though it may never be developed. If and when it is developed, however, the religious person becomes conscious of a *more,* which is a continuous extension of himself, which is operative in the world outside of himself, which can be contacted, and which will preserve the believer when everything around him has gone to wreck and ruin.[36]

Taking advantage of the newly developing science of the unconscious mind, James takes it as a fact (not a theory) that "The *subconscious self* is nowadays a well-accredited psychological entity; and I believe that in it we have exactly the mediating term required."[37] It is the unconscious or subconscious self which mediates between the conscious believer and the *more.* In his desire to be a good scientific psychologist, James feels secure in appealing to this budding science as a way of making a novel contribution to the philosophy of religion. Something must mediate between the "here" and the "beyond." Why cannot that something be our own unconscious minds, that hidden part of us which usually remains unexplored and unmanifested?

Many insights of genius might come from this area and *appear* as revelations. Invasions from this area seem to have a great deal to do with religious conversions, mystical experiences, and the communicational aspects of prayer. In all it seems like a good candidate to explain the rest of religion as well. And this is just what James proceeds to do with respect to "God."

Let me then propose, as an hypothesis, that whatever it may be on its *farther* side, the "more" with which in religious experience we feel ourselves connected is on its *hither* side the subconscious continuation of our conscious life. Starting thus with a recognized psychological fact as our basis, we seem to preserve a contact with "science" which the ordinary theologian lacks. At the same time the theologian's contention that the religious man is moved by an external power is vindicated, for it is one of the peculiarities of invasions from the subconscious region to take on objective appearances, and to suggest to the Subject an external control. In the religious life the control is felt as "higher"; but since in our hypothesis it is primarily the higher faculties of our own hidden mind which are controlling, the sense of union with the power beyond us is a sense of something, not merely apparently, but literally true.[38]

Although presented as an hypothesis, James seems to be much more sure of himself than that. In any event, the "hypothesis" that God might be a real, objectively existing transcendent Supreme Being is not even mentioned here.

What James is saying is unambiguous enough. The existence of a transcendent Supreme Being is only an appearance. What is literally true in the ordinary usage of the word true is that we exist, that we think, and that we have certain unconscious aspects to our thinking which can be used to account for our religious experiences. It is a fact that I think; it is a theory that God exists, but, because it is a good, useful theory, we can say it is true that God exists.

In reality what is God? God is really the Higher Self which occasionally breaks out of the confines of the unconscious mind and into our conscious mind. In other words, as with Kant, God is an *idea in me*. As a psychologist James is willing to accept the presence of God in a Supernatural Theistic sense as a fiction so long as it is a psychological fiction. God is the Wider Self. The positive content of the idea of God for religion is objectively and literally true as far as it goes, but it goes no further than the inside of one's mind (which is itself a function of the human organism).

Yet James insists that God is real. He can do this because he has already changed the meaning of "true" or "real" in a pragmatic, utilitarian, consequentialist direction. Believing in God, that is, in this Higher Self which we do not immediately recognize as being part of ourself, produces actual changes in our behavior. This changed behavior, if applied correctly in a social context, makes life better for everyone, and indeed makes possible the very existence of society. "But that which produces effects within another reality must be termed a reality itself, so I feel as if we had no philosophic excuse for calling the unseen or mystical world unreal."[39]

He also has no qualms about calling the Higher Self God. "God is the natural appelation, for us Christians at least, for the supreme reality, so I will call this higher part of the universe by the name of God."[40] James, in conformity with the usual belief of Christians, wants to emphasize the presence of God, rather than God as simply the "world-soul" or "logos" or overriding animating principle of the world. God is a personal cause; we have business with God; we make covenants with God which lead to a better society. The total expression of human personality and society is altered by our belief in God. Therefore "God is real since he produces real effects."[41]

If James is willing to make any concessions at all to the objective existence of a Supernatural Divine Being it can only be of a "piecemeal" sort. In the Postscript to his *Varieties of Religious Experience* he states that anything more than the experience of something *more* than ourself, which grants us greater peace of soul when we are in communion with it, would be superfluous in religious matters. All we require is a larger power, not a unique infinite power, to make us feel and act better. The concern over the immortality of the personal soul, for instance, is regarded by James as such a superfluous doctrine.

Likewise for monotheism. "Upholders of the monistic view will say to such a polytheism (which, by the way, has always been the real religion of common people, and is so still today) that unless there is one all-inclusive God, our guarantee of security is left imperfect."[42] This is because, under the rule of diverse gods, there might be parts of the universe left without divine providence; aspects of the world, including perhaps even some human beings, which are not ultimately "saved" or otherwise accounted for. The world would then become a place of fighting factions, depending upon which god rules where.

James can see nothing basically wrong with this scheme of things. In fact, it pretty well represents what the world is really like. It does seem that disorders in nature, and evils among humankind, do abound in the world. Parts of the world *are* lost, or at least it seems so. In any event, he says he is only toying with these notions and will not commit himself further.

James, however, is a little less noncommittal about the World-Soul. James, both in his 1890 two-volume work *The Principles of Psychology,* and in his *Psychology: The Briefer Course* (1892), chapter 3 (Gordon Allport edition), tentatively maintains the existence of the World-Soul. It might even be that what we call our own personal soul is really only a part of the World-Soul.

What is the self? asks James. He decides that whatever it may be, it must be something unified. When we talk about ourselves, thinks James, what we are really talking about is our own self-consciousness. James, who was never overly impressed with the so-called scientific finality of anything in psychology, thinks that the best the psychologist can do with self-consciousness is to take it as he finds it, and not attempt to get too "metaphysical" about it. By this he means that we should not attempt to explain all appearances in terms of some more fundamental mental being, such as an individual soul.

Observationally, self-consciousness is a "stream of thought." At any given moment there is a single thought summing up in itself all previous thoughts. The thought "appropriates" to itself all previous thoughts. The self, however, is not a mere aggregate of thoughts as Hume taught, but neither must we assume a single individual substance or soul underlying the thoughts. All we really know directly and immediately is the present thought; the thought *is* the knower; the act of knowing is identified with the power or potency to know. This failure on James's part to note the real distinction between potency and act is not uncommon.

Our problem, though, is not yet solved. Under such circumstances, how can there be any unity and stability in the thinker? James sees two possible solutions. One is an individual soul in each thinker. The other is a World-Soul, or Spirit of the World. It is as if the whole universe were one great living thing with its own soul. As far as James is concerned, the notion of a World-Soul, in which all individual persons somehow participate, would do the job of accounting for mental unity as well as the idea of individual personal souls.

The context for pragmatism is evolutionary theory. In order to have survived in its long upward struggle the human brain must have consistently served a useful function in the differential reproduction of semihuman and human-type creatures. And what other function could it have served than one which allowed the semihuman and human animals the opportunity to advance themselves relative to other creatures in the world? All the ideas we have in our mind, therefore, could not have come about unrelated to our changing environment. In order to have survived, our minds and our ideas must have served a *useful* function over and over again in the life history of the developing human species. Ideas are instruments or tools in our biological development.

As a result, the modern scientific thinker cannot be interested in simple "truth," as if truth somehow existed in a separate world, a world fit only for passive contemplation rather than biological action. Because of the surging, ever-changing character of nature, the truth can never be anything more than a label temporarily attached to some of our ideas which seem to have worked out well in practice. *Everything,* in the end, is only experimental. No statement about the world outside our own minds can be regarded as being above revision. Everything is in *process* and *becoming,* including the very laws of nature themselves.

Therefore, when James worries about the way truth changes, about the way no statement made about the extramental world of sense experience is ever final, what he is really worried about is the nature of God. If what we call "God" is just an *idea in me,* just an aspect of myself, and if the real "God" is only an aspect of the natural world, we really have no foundation for any long-lasting stability in the universe. Even the universality and necessity of scientific laws are called into question. It may take millions of years, but it would still be true to say "here today, gone tomorrow."

There is no doubt that James was an Epistemological Idealist. He tells us so himself. The only abiding absolute truth (in the common English sense) is his own self-consciousness. This, combined with evolutionary theory, is the heart of his world-view. He tells us in his *Will to Believe* VI:

> Objective evidence and certitude are doubtless very fine ideals to play with, but where on this moonlit and dream-visited planet are they found? I am, therefore, myself a complete empiricist so far as my theory of human knowledge goes. I live, to be sure, by the practical faith that we must go on experiencing and thinking over our experience, for only thus can our opinions grow more true; but to hold any one of them — I absolutely do not care which — as if it never could be reinterpretable or corrigible, I believe to be a tremendously mistaken attitude, and I think that the whole history of philosophy will bear me out. There is but one indefectibly certain truth, and that is the truth that pyrrhonistic scepticism itself leaves standing, — the truth that the present phenomenon of consciousness exists.

Does James mean major revisions or superficial revisions? Is he going from "The earth is spherical" to "The earth is flat like a dish" or to "The earth is spherical with such-and-such exact dimensions"? If the former, he is certainly wrong and outmoded; if the latter, he is not any different from the medieval scholastics he claims to reject.

In any event, he is certainly a Cartesian Idealist in epistemology. In Descartes's case, at the end of his methodical doubt, the only certitude left to him was his own existence as a thinking substance. This then gave him the *method* for establishing other certitudes; namely, whatever is as clear and distinct as his own idea of himself must also be accepted as equally true and certain knowledge. The clear and distinct *idea* of something *is* that something just as it really exists extramentally. In James's case, modern science, in the form of evolutionary doctrine, teaches him that everything is in constant alteration, ending up I-know-not-where. Paradoxically, his certitude about a universal evolutionism leads him to deny all other certitudes except the one about his own existence.

But there is more to it than that. Descartes at least held out the possibility of establishing other certitudes, while Kant at least continued to maintain the trustworthiness of science. James, though, is led into the position of denying the very possibility of any further certitudes in principle. If everything is in constant flux, always developing, but never arriving anywhere definite in some fixed and final, definable, *per se* way, then there simply is no Being. There is only becoming, and even the self, which I cannot possibly deny really exists, must somehow also exist in some stage of flowing flux, as a "stream" which begins and ends I-know-not-where. Everything must be held on faith, but a faith restricted to the secular and this-worldly stream of events.

In the case of someone such as Thomas Henry Huxley, the father of "Agnosticism," there is at least the hope that rational procedures, meaning the methodologies of the various biological and physical sciences, will surely produce in time true and certain, universal and necessary, dependable and trustworthy knowledge of the material universe. The only faith he would allow was that in the scientific method. With James, though, agnosticism is institutionalized as skepticism. James must thus greatly broaden the realm of faith *if* human life is to go on more or less as before.

So once again God is deconstructed. The only absolute is James's own thinking process. And it is only in the unity of his present state of mind that we find the *more*. God is himself, or some aspect of the world, which may or may not be there. To someone interested in the presence of God as a personal, separately existing being in direct contact with himself or herself this is not especially reassuring. According to Etienne Gilson:

> It is psychologically interesting to know that it does one good to *believe* there is a God; but that is not at all what the believer believes; what he actually believes is, that there *is* a God. . . . After reading W. James, I still want to know if my religious experience is an experience of God, or an experience of myself. For in both cases there can be a psychological religious experience, but in the first case only can there be a religion.[43]

Gilson cannot see how there can be a religion without the objective existence of a Being to whom we are bound, or how there can be a Judaeo-Christian religion without an authentic revelation to which we must bow.

A. J. Ayer, also, certainly no friend of Supernatural Theism and revealed religion, has something similar to say on the subject:

This is in line with the view of some contemporary theists that the doctrine associated with the religious practices in which they engage is acceptable as a useful myth. This view is so modest that it is hard to take issue with it, unless one wants to argue that the myth is harmful, but it does appear open to the practical objection that the satisfaction which most believers derive from their acceptance of religious doctrine depends upon their not judging it as mythical. A myth which is generally seen to be a myth must be in some danger of losing its utility.[44]

One could not ask for a better example of British understatement. Ayer, an erstwhile Logical Positivist who at one time would not allow any rational person to talk about God at all, seems to delight in poking fun at those who have now gone to the other extreme of allowing as much talk about God as one wishes as long as it is restricted to the realm of the mythological.

This point concerning James's philosophy of religion is well taken. James does not really discuss God at all, at least not in any Supernatural Theistic sense. As the subtitle to his *Varieties of Religious Experience* reads, it is a study in *human* nature, not divine nature. How effective can such an approach be when the whole issue is the reality of divine nature? The most such an approach can accomplish is not to explain God's existence and presence, but to explain them away. How then are we to continue using God as a sanction for civilized social behavior, and as a comfort to individuals in times of trouble?

Was James himself ever aware of the true meaning of his own position? It seems that he may have been. G. E. Myers, in his biography of William James, reports upon an incident in which A. O. Lovejoy pointed out to James that his whole approach to God was much too subjective to be taken seriously by the traditional believer. Myers notes that James "atypically" agreed with Lovejoy that his (James's) view was too subjective, but nevertheless he never revised it.[45]

Empiricists insist upon working with the facts of experience. James, for instance, defended a *radical empiricism* in which everything before the mind, including a "felt relationship," was on an equal footing, and in which something is real if it has real effects. This approach, though, has a major drawback.

If, for example, everyone in the bank thinks the bank robber has a gun in her pocket, what difference does it make in practice whether or not she really has a gun in her pocket? In those areas of action over which human beings have some willful control, what we *think* is the case is very important. The problem, though, is that we must *really* think it. As soon as any doubts creep in, the effectiveness of the whole system of beliefs comes apart. In other words, even in this area of human knowledge, in order to work it must be *objectively* true that the individuals involved in the interactions *really* believe, even if the beliefs are only subjective. But this is precisely what the pragmatic approach cannot provide.

This is especially true in matters of religion. James's approach to God and Kant's approach to God have an intimate connection with each other. For James, God is real because he produces real effects, at least in the context of interpersonal relationships. But it is quite easy to see that this is only one way of putting it. We could just as well say that the *idea* of God is real because it produces real effects, at least with respect to the person or persons possessing the idea of God. As soon as we see this, though, it becomes immediately obvious that there can be many different views of God, or that God could be only a creation of my own mind, and so on. I do not see how anyone claiming to be a *homo humanus* can be satisfied with this. Yet many today say they are.

In other words, even assuming that it is true to say that all sound philosophy is based upon experience, we still do not have an answer to the question: The experience of what? Of my own ideas? Of extramental things more or less as they really are in themselves? This is not an insignificant question. How the thinker answers it is the difference between an Epistemological Idealism and an Epistemological Realism. This is highly important to contemporary thought, especially if the thinker wants to put an emphasis upon sense experience in his or her empiricism. If matters of fact are paramount, what decides what the facts of the matter are: common sense, feelings, science? But then maybe this is not the way to go at all. Perhaps what we need is a purer form of Thinking and Being. Perhaps, after all, James was too hard on Hegel.

HEGEL AND KUENG:
PANTHEISM, THE POLITE
FORM OF ATHEISM

Sein ist die alleraermste Abstraktion. (Being is the poorest of all
abstractions.)

Georg Hegel
A Work on the Proofs of the Existence of God
"Amplification of the Ontological Proof"

The direct exposition [of the universal unity of everything] we find
in the Vedas, the fruit of the highest human knowledge and wisdom,
the kernel of which has at last reached us in the Upanishads as the
greatest gift of this century. . . . In India our religions will never
take root. The ancient wisdom of the human race will not be
displaced by what happened in Galilee. On the contrary, Indian
philosophy streams back into Europe, and will produce a
fundamental change in our knowledge and thought.

Arthur Schopenhauer
The World as Will and Idea (1844) Book IV, Second Aspect, 63

True to Descartes's Epistemological Idealism, both Kant and James
spun Being out of their own thoughts. As a result, they both ended up
identifying God with the self. But what if the self is itself only an
aspect of some much greater Self? In the manner of someone such as
A. N. Whitehead, for example, we could attempt to see God, the
earth, human beings, the farthest galaxies, flatworms, and so forth,
as all part and parcel of *one* reality. Perhaps from one point of view
God might be considered complete and perfect, while from another
perspective God is incomplete and imperfect.

It might even be possible to imagine a situation in which God is
an Absolute, something Perfect, but which nonetheless is constantly
evolving and developing. We might look upon the world as a passing
expression of the one and only God on his way to a complete self-
realization; forever becoming in order to become the Final For-Itself.
In such a world any statement which does not refer to the Whole

must necessarily be a partial and fragmentary truth, that is, an "abstraction" in the sense of something which, in the process of being stated positively, leaves out or abstracts from everything else. *Quoad nos* we must start with these abstractions because we ourselves are only partial realities, and only the abstractions are immediately present to us. Yet careful thinking may soon show us the one true reality, the one and only really real being, the one absolute ground and foundation for all change, development, differences, and abstractions. This can only be found in the Supreme Subject, the one organic, systematic, rational unity.

Thus we move from a theory of knowledge to a theory of reality, from epistemology to the philosophy of being. The world is transformed into objects of consciousness, but, unlike Descartes, for instance, for whom the world was still divided up into separately existing individual entities of a spiritual nature, the reality of the One can tolerate no such differences. All divisions must ultimately be absorbed into the single Ground of being, the only source for both self and non-self. All Idealisms begin with the idea and project it outward, but this does not automatically tell us about the nature of the active consciousness. Is it ultimately individuated, is it common to a certain subset of things in the world, is it common to the whole world or, more radically, is it God himself? If the last, is the Absolute as Ground of becoming the same as the Absolute as Completed Idea?

Kant left those who came after him with some serious problems. From Hegel's viewpoint the most serious was a deep-seated dichotomy between the scientific and the moral realms of experience. The world as studied in science is a strictly deterministic affair. There is no room for freedom or unexpected events, objectively speaking. On the other hand, the moral world demands freedom and a break in the iron-clad universality and necessity of the scientific laws of nature. This is also, in its own way, strictly deterministic and unyielding in its demands. In our moral life, according to Kant, there is a Categorical Imperative, that is, an absolutely necessary obligation placed upon the human subject, called Duty. Very often this Duty runs counter to what we want, as when we must restrain our sensual and egotistical desires in order to "please God" and preserve our civilized society. We must not steal, we must honor our contracts, we must have private and public censorship, and so forth. The obvious question is, How can these two spheres, the necessities of the starry heavens above and the moral law within, coexist in *one and the same* individual human being? Hegel's solution to this problem is to seek out a more fundamental unity underlying all apparent differences.

Coming to an understanding of Hegel is no easy task.[1] This is certainly the case as far as his view of God is concerned, especially since the place of God is so prominent in Hegel's philosophy. It might even be said that it is in fact his *whole* philosophy. In his Absolutism the whole of the world or reality is God in one way or another. This would also include the thinker who is thinking God. Indeed, it might be better to say that it is God who is thinking the thinker; or perhaps even better, it is God who is thinking himself through the thinker. As Hegel puts it, "Spirit is known as self-consciousness, and to this self-consciousness it is directly revealed, for it is this self-consciousness itself. The divine nature is the same as the human, and it is this unity which is intuitively apprehended (*angeschaut*)."[2]

The one central question that always arises with respect to Hegel's doctrine on God is exactly what sort of pantheism it is. Everyone is sure that Hegel was some sort of pantheist. This must be the case, if for no other reason than we can be sure that he was not a Supernatural Theist. Although he started off his intellectual life as a rather orthodox and traditional believer in the Judaeo-Christian tradition, he soon abandoned any serious and literal belief in the Perfect and Self-Subsisting God of the Scriptures.

As Hegel got older it became more and more clear to him that rational knowledge (science and/or philosophy) must hold the top position in any hierarchy of human learning. Religion, either in the form of popular religion or sacred theology, must have no more than a secondary place in the hierarchy of knowledge, even though religion could be regarded as superior to literature and the arts in the knowledge that it conveys to the human mind. For the better part of his academic life Hegel was well aware that this sort of thing could get him, as well as his students, into trouble with the civil authorities, to say nothing of the ecclesiastical authorities. According to the editors of Hegel's letters, even though Hegel saw little cognitive value in the term "atheist" (after all, everyone is a theist in one way or another), "Yet he realizes that his own philosophy, which elevates the standpoint of philosophy above that of religion, is exposed to the charge of 'atheism.'"[3]

To complicate matters, Hegel was always known as a Lutheran, and insisted upon referring to himself as a Lutheran. In a letter to the German theologian Friedrich Tholuck (1799–1877) of 3 July 1826 Hegel states that "I am a Lutheran, and through philosophy have been at once completely confirmed in Lutheranism."[4] As we know from the history of the last century, Sören Kierkegaard had a great deal to say on this subject, his main point being that if Hegel was a Lutheran, or religious at all in the Judaeo-Christian tradition as far as doctrine is concerned, then he (Kierkegaard) was the King of Denmark.[5]

Be this as it may, the more interesting point is the one of internal consistency with respect to Hegel's own thinking. If there was one thing that Luther hated with a passion it was speculative philosophy. He was absolutely opposed to any kind of "metaphysics," including natural theology. What he did support was a "back to the Bible" approach to life and salvation, the very sort of thing he claimed was lacking in medieval scholastic philosophy and theology.[6]

In sharp contrast, Hegel regarded speculative philosophy as the *only* kind of knowledge really worth having. In a letter to his friend Friedrich Niethammer (1766–1848) of 23 October 1812, on the subject of where, when, and how philosophy should be taught, Hegel makes it clear that the best and highest form of knowledge is speculative knowledge, that is, the knowledge of opposites that recognizes that all opposites are in truth really all one and the same reality. "Only this speculative stage is truly philosophical. It is naturally the most difficult; it is the truth."[7] In order to fully participate in the highest form of knowledge, one must pass beyond all forms of representationalism, whether of a pictorial, artistic, or religious nature. The nearer one gets to the purely conceptual level of pure reason, the closer one approaches true philosophy, "so much so that the content of the perfect religion is most speculative."[8]

In his early career, after rejecting the Bible and the church, Hegel embraced what the editors of his letters call a romantic form of Spinozistic pantheism. According to Clark Butler and Christiane Seiler, in his early university days, "Hegel, Hoelderlin, and Schelling all embraced a Romantic form of Spinozistic pantheism at Tuebingen."[9] One of the greatest influences on Hegel at this time was Johann Gottfried Herder (1744–1803) whose work on God was originally published in 1787. On this point, Butler and Seiler say that "Hegel's early development in the 1790s bore the imprint of Herder both in his rejection of pragmatic Enlightenment historiography in favor of empathetic understanding of past experience in its uniqueness, and in his espousal of a romanticized pantheism of the One and the All."[10]

His early attraction to Spinoza did not last, however. As he matured Hegel came to see Spinoza's doctrine of the One Substance as far too materialistic, much too static, cut off from the changing world, and anti-spiritual to suit the needs of a truly speculative system of knowledge which was totally pure in its conceptual approach to reality. Even though, according to Spinoza, *one* of God's infinite attributes was mind or consciousness, Hegel wanted a system in which reality was completely and totally akin to consciousness. To the extent, therefore, that Spinoza's doctrine was universally recognized as "pantheism," Hegel's doctrine was not a pantheism.

As pointed out by William Wallace, *The Encyclopaedia of the Philosophical Sciences in Outline* is the "only complete, matured, and authentic statement of Hegel's philosophical system."[11] Much of the Prefaces of the second and third editions is devoted to a defense of his system against criticisms by both secular philosophers and religious theologians. As Hegel became better known throughout Prussia, it became more and more obvious that his rational system of thought and the religious doctrines of the church and, indirectly, of the state, were at variance. Consequently he devoted more and more of his time and energies to defending himself against charges of heresy and disloyalty to the state.

To Hegel's own way of thinking, he was especially religious, and an especially good citizen. In later life he seems to have gone out of his way to defend the rights of the state and the monarchy relative to any subgroups or individuals within the state. The state, marching through the world on its way to self-completion and self-realization, was after all an even higher manifestation of the Idea or Divine Spirit than the individual. Although this aspect of his work is often played down today, it is no exaggeration to say that Hegel tended to deify the state. The state for Hegel is the Spirit on earth, the Divine Will, the free, rational, and thus ethical in its own right, expression of the Spirit as it consciously realizes itself in the world of human affairs.[12]

With respect to religion, Hegel regarded himself as supremely religious. His philosophy *is* his religion, and it is superior to the doctrines of any of the traditional religious churches. As Wallace states, "In ordinary moods of mind there is a long way from logic to religion. But almost every page of what Hegel has called Logic is witness to the belief in their ultimate identity."[13] To be truly religious is to be fully and rationally aware of the Divine Spirit. Hegel wants everyone to become fully aware of the *presence* of God. This can only occur in a complete and coherent system of the Absolute, Idea, or Concrete Universal.

The "concrete" for Hegel means a well-defined, circumscribed, clear and distinct concept. Hegel has no use for abstract thought or abstractions in general. The form of rationalism which deals only with abstractions in the sense of something fragmentary and incomplete, and hence empty and undetermined, is the enemy of all true philosophy for Hegel.

On the other hand, however, we cannot find true reality in sensations either. As expressed by Quentin Lauer, "Taking his cue from Plato rather than from Locke, he was convinced that reality was more concretely present (more real) in thought, in ideas, than in sensation."[14] Hegel makes this clear in his "Introduction" to his *Lectures on the History of Philosophy,* where he states that what is usually taken to be the concrete, namely, the sensible, is not; it is only the "so-called concrete."[15]

To the extent that religion makes the Supreme Being present to the consciousness of individual human beings, it is in fact contributing to the ultimate and final understanding of reality. "To this extent religions are the supreme work of reason."[16] Both philosophy and religion are directly related to the One and Only Reality, which is the Infinite Spirit or God. This Absolute Universality, or One and Only Absolute Concrete Infinite, is *best* known scientifically through philosophy. This is because the Spirit has for its primary task to know Itself.

It thereby becomes more and more free. "Freedom" for Hegel means that something is with itself; has a rational awareness of itself. Thus religion, to the extent it cooperates with and helps philosophy, is a source of human emancipation and freedom. The purpose of freedom "is to grasp the other in such a comprehensive way as to find itself in the other, to unite itself with itself in the other, there to possess and enjoy itself."[17]

Therefore religion and philosophy have a common content. They differ only in their form of understanding and expression. Later Hegelians, such as Hans Kueng, will be sure to agree with this. The philosopher must teach this important point to the theologians so that they may know their proper place. When this happens it will be seen that philosophy encompasses religion and provides it with the *system* it needs for its own perfection within a larger whole. "Thus, all that is required for philosophy is that the form of the concept be so far perfected as to be able to comprise the content of religion."[18] In this sense, then, and in a way very much like that of Spinoza, Hegel can be said to be very religious.

His critics, however, were not convinced. His efforts to deduce the main points of Judaeo-Christianity from his all-encompassing system seemed rather forced and peculiar, to say the least. His friend and confidant Johann Goethe (1749–1832) was certainly not convinced, and was troubled by Hegel's repeated attempts to Christianize the essentially pagan doctrine of pantheism, a doctrine in which Goethe himself believed.[19] Hegel's dream of uniting all of Christianity within his own supreme philosophy was certainly overly optimistic. In fact, at the time, Hegel was no more able to convince the vast majority of Lutheran ministers of his orthodoxy than Spinoza was able to convince the rabbis of his.

Hegel was not about to go down without a fight, however. In response to the charge of pantheism, which was later referred to in philosophical and theological literature as the polite form of atheism, Hegel insisted upon the ambiguity of the term and the way in which it could not be applied to his own doctrine once his own doctrine was properly understood. Butler and Seiler summarize Hegel's position for us very nicely in the following way. The theologian Tholuck had attacked Hegel, saying that he was much too rationalistic. Truth should be felt and taken in, not conceptualized. Hegel responded by pointing out the value of reason in theology. For the thinking human being, feeling is not enough. There must also be a speculative side to theology if the theologian expects to have any clear notion of what is being discussed. With respect to pantheism Butler and Seiler explain that

> The 1827 *Encyclopaedia* points out the ambiguity of the "pantheist" label which Tholuck attaches to philosophy: it may mean (*a*) that finite things as such are all divine, God being their aggregate, (*b*) that finite things are self-negated and annihilated within an undifferentiated divine substance beyond the worldly distinction of good and evil (acosmism, Brahmanism), or (*c*) that finite things are, though negated when viewed as absolute, preserved within God conceived as the self-differentiated infinite Spirit (Hegel's speculative philosophy of spirit).[20]

The last possibility is Hegel's own position, which, according to Hegel, is not really pantheism because it differs from *a* and *b*. In order to appreciate what Hegel is trying to say, we must explicate the various possibilities relative to one another. I think the situation can best be explained in the following way.

No Consciousness. The first possibility states that the world is composed of an innumerable host of individual finite beings which, when taken collectively, would constitute the whole of reality. Among these finite beings are human beings. But even though each human being possesses the power of consciousness and self-consciousness, no one human being can encompass the whole of reality. In effect, therefore, the whole of reality is characterized by a profound lack of consciousness of itself as a whole.

The extreme form of this position would be atomism, in which the whole of reality is composed of tiny, self-enclosed, completely unconscious particles of Greek being. Out of this world some human thinkers attempt to build up a doctrine of materialistic reductionism or physicalism based solely upon sensations. Such a world-view is pantheistic in the sense that *all* of the creative and directive powers of the universe must be attributed to this collection of finite beings, thereby taking over the traditional functions of a transcendent God.

Partial Consciousness. Baruch Spinoza viewed God as being in Itself wholly immutable, unchanging, and undifferentiated when viewed under the aspect of Its eternal mode of substantial reality. One of the infinite number of infinite attributes of the One Substance which is known to us is mind. However, it is doubtful if this could really play a large role in the eternal reality of the divine substance. In the world of human knowledge various things *appear* to us in various ways, one of which is mind, consciousness, and self-consciousness. The question is, What role can these finite appearances have in the one divine Substance?

Call It what you will — Nature, the One, God — It is beyond all such finite determinations. This is the acosmic aspect of Spinoza's doctrine. Relative to God the world is unreal and without development and novelty. In addition, God is static. God is being in the Greek sense of being the eternally stable, self-identical, unchanging, and existentially neutral one. If by the existence of things we mean that which is given to us in our day-to-day sensible experiences of the world, then God does not exist. But, and this is the important point with respect to Spinoza's approach to God, if we want to talk about the *reality* of God, we must transfer our attention from the sensible world to the world of ideas and concepts and thereby come to see that God *must* exist in the sense of being real. According to Spinoza, "as the potentiality of existence is a power, it follows that, in proportion as reality increases in the nature of a being, so also will it increase its strength for existence. Therefore a being absolutely infinite, such as God, has from himself an absolutely infinite power of existence, and hence he does absolutely exist."[21]

That is to say, God is certainly a reality or a being; in fact the one and only being in whom everything is eternally fixed and necessary. But then there is no real change or freedom in Spinoza's system, either for God or for the worldly manifestations of God. Our puny comings and goings, as well as those of all of material nature, are as nothing when compared to the timeless splendor of the divine.

Complete Consciousness. Hegel, though, sees himself as being quite different. God is not man or nature but completely and totally self-realizing spirit. God is not being in the Greek sense of the totally immutable. God is becoming. God is the eternally changing as he constantly strives to come to a complete self-knowledge of himself. God is reality, which is one dynamic whole of pure consciousness, freedom, and concreteness.

In a letter to a businessman, Edouard Duboc (1786–1829), Hegel attempts to explain his views in layman's terms. Hegel insists that his basic view is an *objective* approach to reality, not a purely subjective one. The Infinite Spirit is objectively real. It is not the result of our thinking; we are the result of its thinking. Hegel says to Duboc in his letter of 30 July 1822, "At this point I immediately take up what you point out in your letter, namely that I define the Idea as *becoming,* as the unity of being and nothing."[22]

All opposites, Hegel teaches, are only relative realities within the one Reality. Hegel wants to give a scientific, that is, a purely rational, account of what the really real is and how it operates. The Idea, which is constantly self-productive and self-developing, "is essentially concrete as a unity of the diverse, and the highest unity is that of the concept with its objectivity, just as truth, in relation to representations, is defined as their correspondence to objects."[23]

However, we must be careful here. Truth is not a mere correspondence between object and mind from the subjective viewpoint. Truth is objective; it stands for what something *ought* to be from the viewpoint of the really real. The idea *we* have *should* match the idea *God* has (or is). "The Idea in its highest sense, God, is thus alone truly true, is alone that in which the free concept no longer has any unresolved opposition to its objectivity. In other words, the concept is in no way entangled in the finite."[24]

God is the concept of all concepts, the coincidence of all contraries, and the summation of all realities. Remembering that "concrete" for Hegel means the conceptually all-inclusive, there can be only one concrete universal or infinite, namely, God, who is the Idea manifesting himself in various ways in his eternal quest for self-realization. Thus God shows up as material nature, human nature, the state, and so on, with human nature and human institutions being of special importance because it is via these that the Idea can come to a more perfect knowledge of itself and the history of its own development through time. In this sense Hegelianism is very much an anthropomorphism.

But how does this get Hegel off the hook with respect to this "twaddle about pantheism?"[25] It doesn't. Quite obviously Hegel is denying the existence of a transcendent God who freely created and sustains the completely unnecessary world of ordinary human experience. For Hegel the world *is* God, at least in the sense of being continuous with God. Talking about God as he might exist in some pure ideal state of complete self-possession is to talk about God as he in fact is not. The ideal, pure, self-conscious spirit has yet to be realized. God may be thought of by us, his agents, as being all there at once, but our very diversity is proof that God still has a long way to go before he is *all* there.

One recent attempt to defend Hegel against the charge of pantheism so backfires as to show just the opposite. In the interpretation of Hegel given by Lauer, the very logic of Hegel's reasoning forces him to identify God with the totality of reality. But how can anyone object to this? Lauer wonders. Imagine *not* doing so and see what happens. How can there be a reality which is not God?

If God created the world of nature and man in addition to himself, we would have a reality *in addition* to God, such that God plus the world would be a reality greater than God alone. How then could God be infinite? Would then not God be limited by the reality of the world? According to Lauer, being and God are the same thing, but operating in different ways, depending upon whether we are dealing with infinite or finite spirit. Divine spirit is creative; finite spirit recreative.[26]

In Hegel's system there can be no true free creation *ex nihilo*, only a necessary alienation or self-externalization of the For-Itself. The "created" universe is really only a continuation of God considered in himself. The infinite and the finite are continuous rather than identical. Although there may be a danger of identifying God and the world if we consider both in an abstract way, there cannot be any danger of this when we consider both in a concrete way. This is because mutual implications, which are necessarily dynamic or concrete, are best described as continuous rather than as identical. This must be the relationship between the finite and the infinite. Although there is only one reality, considered as infinite it is not the same as when considered as finite. Thus there is no need to take a supernatural approach to God.

In Lauer's view, the ability of human creatures to find God is maximized when they participate in the super-subjectivity of Infinite Spirit, that is, in God's power to bring all things back to himself in an immediate self-conscious and self-knowing way. For human beings it means letting God think through us rather than trying to maintain some sort of specious independence.[27]

It is easy enough to see how this sort of language can get all mixed up with orthodox Judaeo-Christian doctrine. Talk about union with God, about letting God work in us, about living in God, and so on, might possibly, as indeed it was with Hegel, be used in a non-Judaeo-Christian context as well as in a Supernatural Theistic context. This does not, however, alter the basic meanings of the two world-views, or bridge the irreconcilable gap which separates them from each other.

Lauer's question about the incompatibility of two or more realities (God and the world, God and creatures) is a variation on the basic problem of reconciling being and becoming. In modern times this objection goes back at least to the debate between Friedrich Jacobi (1743–1819) and Friedrich Schelling (1775–1854) at the beginning of the nineteenth century, and has been discussed in this century by A. O. Lovejoy in his *The Great Chain of Being* (1936). Siding with Schelling in his pantheistic claim that *one* reality is as much reality as the universe can take, Lovejoy claims that if there were already an infinitely perfect Supernatural God, and if he did create anything at all, the new combination of God plus the finite world must necessarily *reduce* the average amount of perfection in reality.

Given Hegel's pantheism, Lauer's question seems natural enough, but only on the assumption that the world and God are somehow homogeneous in a continuous way. In some other world-view, such as that of Saint Thomas Aquinas, there is no such homogeneity or continuity. In Aquinas's existential philosophy, for instance, God is Existence, while each creature, even though real, is only a *habens esse*. There is an absolute break between God and the world such that God could exist very well even if there were no world. If God does freely choose to create, it must be something discontinuous with himself since he is already perfect within himself. Thus the dilemma offered by Lauer and others is reversed, and becomes a matter of how, if God is already infinite perfection, anything he creates could possibly *not* be discontinuous with himself.[28]

An important question, though, still remains: Does Hegel, with all his emphasis upon rationalism, ever really prove the existence of God? In his *Lectures on the History of Philosophy,* when discussing Anselm's ontological argument, Hegel points out that Kant's criticism of the argument was completely justified. As Kant said, the mere concept of a hundred thalers in my mind in no way entails the actual existence of the money in my pocket.

But the reason Kant's criticism of Anselm is good is that Anselm made the initial mistake of separating thought and being. For Anselm there is first the naked intramental concept; next he tries to argue that such a thought really exists in the extramental world. This does not work. But what if the extramental world and the intramental world are really the same to begin with? What if the opposites of "the objective" and "the subjective" are really united in the one infinite being in the first place? Hegel replies to Kant: "To the proof which Kant criticises in a manner which it is the fashion to follow now-a-days, there is thus lacking only the perception of the unity of thought and of existence in the infinite; and this alone must form the commencement."[29]

Hegel's basic argument, if I may call it that, is that the reality of God is the condition against which all other conditions must be judged. God is the Ground of all being and understanding. As expressed by Lauer, Hegel is not arguing in exactly the same way as Anselm. "What Hegel is saying, rather, is that, because the *being* of the infinite is a necessary prerequisite for the very possibility of *thinking* the finite, the infinite really is — or else thinking is *not.*"[30]

In order for our thinking to be worthwhile it must be true. But no thought can be objectively true if it is simply and solely *my* thought alone. In order for thoughts to be true they must contact being or reality; they must identify "with the universality proper to the 'genus' to which they belong or to the 'purpose' to which they are ordered."[31] Consequently God must be real in order for any and all of our true thoughts to be real.

We must be careful here, as we were with Spinoza, not to confuse reality with existence, something those in the Judaeo-Christian tradition in theology, as well as anyone in a common-sense frame of mind, is inclined to do. *Existenz* for Hegel stands for the finite manifestations of the Infinite Spirit. This paper I am writing on exists. The pen I am writing with exists. My hand exists, and so forth. After moving to the mental level, we can still talk about existence in the sense that this or that particular idea or image or feeling or whatever, which I am having here and now, exists in me.

In this way, even my personal and private idea of God can be said to exist. The infinite, however, by its very definition as the objective summation of all conceptual contents, cannot be said to exist (be finite) even though it is certainly real, and even *more* real than the finite.

The best place to go for Hegel's attempted scientific (rational) proof for the existence of God is his *Logic* (or metaphysics, that is, God *per se* before "creation"), which makes up the first part of his *Encyclopaedia*. A truly rational approach must be *a priori*. We must go from the causes of things to the effects of those causes. This means that all philosophy, and hence all science and religion, must *start* with God. But how can this be if we supposedly do not yet know that God is real and must establish his reality by some reasoning process?

Hegel begins with the importance of thought. "Man — and that just because it is his nature to think — is the only being that possesses law, religion, and morality."[32] As soon as we think, though, we come to realize that thought and sensation are opposed to each other. As Parmenides and Plato saw so well, true knowledge (science) cannot be derived from the ever-shifting sands of sensation. But what is it to think something if not to be able to define it? A definition makes something more, not less, definite.

Hegel has no use for those who would reduce reality, and especially the highest reality, to some vague, undetermined, undifferentiated something or other. It is definition which gives us the quality of the thing. "Where there is no definite quality, knowledge is impossible. Mere light is mere darkness."[33] The only thing we can fruitfully keep from the metaphysical doctrine of abstractionism is the emphasis on the importance of thought. "Its good point was the perception that thought alone constitutes the essence of all that is."[34]

How, then, do we get to God? We reach God by taking into account the importance of negation. To be something definite entails not only a clear set of positive characteristics, but a whole set of negations telling us what a thing is not, that is, its distinctiveness. In this way, no matter where we start in the sensible world, we must negate the world of sensible experience as we complete our knowledge of reality. Imagine starting with our knowledge of a dog. In order to know a dog in a positive way we must know that it is a mammal, a vertebrate, and so on, until we have included all of its traits. The same holds for our knowledge of a banana, or anything else in the world.

On the negative side, we must realize that the essence of dogness includes non-dogness; bananaf ness, non-banananess, and so forth. When our clear and distinct understanding of *all* things is considered as a whole we will have arrived at the Concrete Infinite which includes in Itself both all positive and all negative determinations. God, therefore, is supremely Being, in the Greek sense of what is forever fixed and self-identical. But God is also supremely Non-being, in the sense of being the summation of all negations. Contradiction is thus at the very center and root of reality.

This is how Hegel accounts for becoming and development, so important in his world-view. He knows quite well from Parmenides that if God were only being (in the Greek sense) there could be no change at all. Thus Hegel feels rationally obligated to include non-being in the very definition of God. Briefly stated: No non-being, no change. Stated as a disjunctive argument we would have: Either there is non-being or there is no change. But there is change (there is not no change). Hence there is non-being.

If Hegel were an Aristotelian, he would have been able to explain change *within* being rather than having to insist upon the existence of that which is not. For Aristotle, the world is composed of separate beings, with change accounted for in terms of potency and act within each being. This prevented Aristotle from having to unify all beings in one and only one reality. In Aristotle's view, reality is made up of a long hierarchy of separate realities, from the lowest elements to the Prime Mover, who is the purest act (form) without any potential aspect. Even though ultimately an essentialist in his philosophy of being, that is, a philosophy of being in which "to be" means basically to be an essence, which applies especially to the *separated* (from matter) forms or essences (the gods) in the hierarchy of reality, each being is a separate thing for Aristotle.

For Hegel, however, this is not the case. As the mind moves from a particular experience of a particular thing, to its species, to its genus, and so on until everything is seen as united in the One, we get closer and closer to God. This is an inherent and unavoidable mode of behavior for human beings as thinkers. The result is that *to think at all* is to think God. Thinking and being are the same because essence and "to be" are the same thing for Hegel. God is necessarily there in human thinking because being (essence) is necessarily there in human thinking. As with Descartes, therefore, the existence (reality) of God is in a way innate and *a priori* within the human mind, and all because "Thought is thinghood, or thinghood is thought."[35] Put otherwise, the rational is the real, and the real is the rational. This is anthropocentrism plain and simple. As with Descartes, Kant, and James, it is Hegel's own mind that is creating God, not vice versa.

Can we say, then, that Hegel proves the existence and presence of God? Not exactly. He rather deduces the reality of a Great Spirit, which in itself is pure Idea or essence, from a certain characteristic of internal *human* thinking, namely, that it takes a *multitude* of concepts to know *one* thing in the extramental world. For example, a dime is a coin, which is money, which is a medium of exchange, and so on. This intellectual process, which is so natural to human beings, just as naturally leads to broader and broader categories, and finally to an ultimate genus, which encompasses all lesser classes.

Beginning with a *conceptual* analysis of what it means to be real, Hegel cannot comprehend how anyone could possibly not come to a *knowledge* of (not merely a belief in) God by simply thinking. To deny this would require the use of reason, the very thing which is being denied. Hence, finite consciousness necessarily entails Infinite Consciousness, and finite thought necessarily entails Infinite Thought.[36]

As with Aristotle's Prime Mover, this infinite thought is a self-thinking thought. Unlike Aristotle's First Cause, however, Hegel's Supreme Essence of Everything is not separated from the world of experience. It *is* the world of experience, or rather, the world of experience is a continuation and manifestation of Its own self-development. Call God what you will — Infinite Spirit, Nature, the Universe as a Whole, the One, the All, the For-Itself, the Absolute — one thing is certain and that is that God, who loves the world as he loves himself because the world is himself, is not separated from the world. The transcendent God of orthodox Judaeo-Christianity and Islam is regarded by Hegel as an empty and useless concept, a mere hollow abstraction when compared to the infinite richness of the Supreme Idea.

This must be the case since everything and anything which renders a being concrete, that is, which makes it conceptually clear and distinct, is, in fact, right here and now simultaneously present and all together in one unified whole. This can only be the case if the One is akin to consciousness, and is in fact Pure Consciousness or Self-Conscious and Self-Willing Mind (i.e., Spirit). A dime, a coin, money, and a medium of exchange are in fact *identical* with each other here and now. Even as we hold the dime in our hand it contains within itself *all* that it is and *all* that it is not, and all at the same time. Likewise for everything else in the whole universe. Therefore God, the synthesis of all concreteness, is real. In the end, Hegel is not so much interested in proving the truth of pantheism as he is in proving the truth of a certain kind of pantheism, the kind which guarantees to us a knowledge of God, that is, a knowledge of Reality.

This is Hegel's main message as found in his carefully written works destined for publication during his own lifetime. The same basic message, however, can also be found in his various lectures. For instance, Hegel's lectures on the philosophy of religion and the proofs for the existence of God neither add nor subtract anything substantial from his other works, especially his *Logic*. The main point of his philosophy of religion is that all religious *belief* is fulfilled and perfected in the *knowledge* of the real through philosophy. The main point of his lectures on the proofs for the existence of God is the inappropriateness of insisting upon the usual sort of syllogistic argumentation which goes from true and certain premises to an unavoidable conclusion.

In Hegel's system, the knowledge of the finite (the premises) must be negated in order to reach the infinite (the conclusion), something not allowed in formal abstract logical reasoning. Hegel is thus no friend of the logician. First he reasons his way into denying the principle of non-contradiction. Then he must also throw into doubt the value of all forms of basic syllogistic argumentation. And all so that he can successfully deconstruct the traditional theology of Supernatural Theism.

The only argument, in terms of its general approach, that is worth anything is the so-called ontological argument. Anselm was the first Christian to discover this approach. "It was then further developed by all the later philosophers, by Descartes, Leibnitz, and Wolff, yet always along with the other proofs, though it alone is the true one."[37] Hegel regarded himself as representing the final perfection of this approach.

Yet we can still inquire about just how useful this approach really is to an understanding of being and becoming. Hegel's basic problem is the same as that of Anselm and the others in the Idealistic camp: The dialectical hierarchy of classes, sets, and conceptual contents are fine as long as we remain within the mind. However, as soon as we come out of the mind and try to apply our categories to the concrete world as normally understood, we are bound to get wrecked on the rocks of real life. A purely rational science may be fine in the mind, but sooner or later it has to face the practical world. It may even be the case, as I think it is, that the intellectual process of conceptualization necessarily results in a synthesis of all ideas in one *summum genus,* which may also be the *summum bonum,* but this does not contact the realm of ordinary experience, regardless of how often Hegel insists that it must. In Hegel's case the conclusion (Universal Being, Infinite Spirit, God) is said to be immanent in the very beginning of the reasoning process, requiring only some attention and contemplation in order to bring it into full consciousness. This can only be achieved on the intellectual level.

The human mind, which is naturally inclined toward conceptual unification, and which attempts to explain effects in terms of causes which are as universal as possible (that is to say, the mind is naturally inclined toward science), must sooner or later push its thinking to the limit. This ideal limit, even though it may not provide us with a perfect knowledge of everything (at least not right away), is God. Thus, for instance, the scientist who discovers the cause of *all* cancers is universally regarded as superior to the one who finds the cause of only one particular kind of cancer. Likewise, the thinker who knows God is superior to one who has stopped short of this ultimate destination.

The difficulty with this approach, however, although very true in certain respects, is that it remains confined to the intramental sphere. The analogy with science fails precisely because the typical scientist begins, as well as ends, in the sensible existential world, while the philosopher of being who begins in the mind must also end in the mind. Rather than comparing this approach to all science, it might be better to compare it to a strictly abstract science such as mathematics. In a strictly formal setting the results are strictly formal as well, which means that contacting objective (extramental) reality requires one or more additional steps or stages. This puts us back where we started from, namely, in the world of ideas asking ourselves if God exists as anything more than the set of all sets.

In more recent years the dissident theologian Hans Kueng has made a concerted effort to rehabilitate Hegel as a Christian theologian. His long work *Does God Exist?* (1978) is, in effect, one long commentary on Hegel's *Phenomenology of Spirit*. God is defined as the Absolute, the One Reality, which includes within himself the whole universe and everything in it. There is a difference, though, between the two thinkers. Hegel must be updated and augmented by a much greater emphasis on biological evolution and the power of love in the world, and minus his dream of a complete knowledge of everything.

As far as Kueng is concerned, there is no going back before Hegel for our knowledge of God and his relationship to the world. All we can rationally do is to move forward from Hegel into the present and beyond, a beyond which will once and for all do away with the outdated Greek-Medieval world-view of the Catholic Church, replacing it with a demythologized, modernized, revitalized, thoroughly rationalized, Hegelian philosophy.

Kueng received his philosophical education early in the twentieth century when Thomism was interpreted largely through the mind and method of Désiré-Joseph Mercier. Unfortunately, Cardinal Mercier had made a great error, one which was passed on from teacher to student for many years. This error was to identify the purely philosophical parts of Aquinas's theology with the thought of Aristotle, somewhat modified in the light of Christian doctrine as filtered through Duns Scotus and Francis Suarez, so as, for instance, to be able to identify the Prime Mover with God and to defend the personal immortality of the soul and, ultimately, of the body as well. On this basis there seemed to be two Thomisms, one philosophical and the other theological. The former could be identified with the work of pure reason, that is, thinking as if revelation and Church tradition did not exist, but nevertheless reaching substantially the same conclusions about God, human nature, and morality, just the way that Descartes was to try doing later. The second Aquinas reasoned deductively from revelation and came out looking very much like St. Augustine.[38]

Based upon this commonly taught scheme of things, Kueng could compare Aquinas with Descartes in terms of a two-storied house. The first level is the purely philosophical one. On this level we find the preambles of faith, thought out and defended just as Aristotle would have done if he were to have examined the issues carefully in the light of reason. After this stage is completed, we would then be ready to move up to the next level, the theological level in which the various issues more closely connected with Scripture and revelation would be discussed. To get from the first to the second story, however, *requires* a rational ladder to cover the gap between the two. For this reason Kueng can put a hyphen between Aristotle and Aquinas, and also between Aquinas and Descartes. According to Kueng, "In this view, a Cartesian-Thomistic separation of the two cognitive powers (reason and faith) and the two spheres of knowledge (reason and revelation) cannot be defended in the light of either reason or faith: from the very outset, reason has to do with faith and faith also has to do with reason."[39] As it turns out at the end of his study, Kueng really has no use for supernatural faith at all. Such Thomistic faith can only be an obscure, completely unintelligible mystery.

Kueng wants nothing to do with such dualisms and divisions. What he wants is the absolute unity and truth of reality. This approach can best be found in Hegel, whose system for the unity of God and the world was basically correct, and who has accounted for such unity better than anyone before or after. With some modification, "we can recognize that Hegel is largely right when he both completes and surmounts the notion of the God of Greek metaphysics and — for genuinely Christian motives — tries to take seriously the unity of God and the world, God's coming to be and dialectic in God, as perhaps no other philosopher before or after him."[40]

In general, what Hegel is opposed to, for example, atheism, mechanism, the disintegration of organic wholes, anti-teleological explanations, and so on, Kueng is also opposed to. On the other hand, what Hegel is in favor of, so is Kueng. We must be especially devoted to God, states Kueng, and the reestablishment of the absolute need and value of the one, true God. Yet we must not advance an acosmic view of God, that is, one without reference to a becoming, changing, dynamic world. Spinoza, the prime example of pantheism, did that sort of thing, but not Hegel. We need a system in which God is *in* the world, transcendence is *in* immanence, and the hereafter is *in* the here and now. All such dichotomies must be overcome, just as we must eliminate other pre-Hegelian thought patterns, such as the oppositions between the natural and supernatural, nature and grace, reason and faith, theology and philosophy, in favor of one undivided reality.

After all, what is theology for Kueng? It is an extension of science and philosophy so as to include "questions of ultimate or primary interpretations, objectives, values, ideals, norms, decisions, attitudes."[41] Kueng would remove the Almighty, providential, miracle-working God of the old world-view and replace him with "the transcendent-immanent, all-embracing, all-permeating, most real reality in man and in the world" God of the post-modern, post-Hegelian world-view.[42]

Scripture is treated in the same way. Whatever parts of revelation fit in with Hegelian principles are retained, while those that do not are either completely eliminated or reinterpreted (deconstructed) to make them fit. So it is that monotheism is taken as the one central doctrine of the Christian religion (as well as of most other religions, for that matter). We must learn to concentrate on the totality, placing other issues in a relatively secondary position. This means, just as it did for Hegel, *not* concentrating on an *existential* interpretation of things, that is, on a view of things based primarily on sensual human experience. Recall that existence for Hegel stands for the finite manifestation of Infinite Spirit. If there is one passage in Scripture which can be quoted over and over again as a good indication of what revelation is really all about it is Deuteronomy 6:4: "Listen then, oh Israel, there is no Lord but the Lord our God." God is the one reality with no other realities beside him, no female consort, and no evil rival god or principle of action in the world.[43]

In contrast, many parts of Scripture must be eliminated because they do not fit into Hegel's *summa universalis,* the supreme *summa theologica* and true *philosophia perennis.* Most of the stories and images presented in the Bible cannot be taken as historical description. They are only myths, superstitions, old folks' tales, pious elaborations, and so forth. Their purpose is really only to indicate a spiritual truth behind the story. Thus all stories of miracles must be regarded, not as factual, but as rhetorical devices for the purpose of arousing our admiration for God. These lighthearted popular tales are really meant to show God's involvement in the world on a continuing basis.

So also for those parts of revelation which tell of the creation and end of the world, of a final judgment, of personal immortality with reward and punishment, and of divine providence in the sense of an existentially separate God directing the world order. None of these should be taken literally. For Kueng, for instance, believing in the creation of the world as a perfectly free act of God, out of nothing and beginning the process of time and becoming, is described as meaning that the world is a cosmos rather than a chaos. All of its parts have meaning and value, and that the universe, in its eternal duration, is ultimately explicable in terms of its primal ground.[44]

In a similar vein, the end of the world is not really the end of the world but only a way of talking about the relationship between the One Reality and its relative parts. Thus believing in God as the Finisher of the universe means that everything is in constant flux, never remaining the same from age to age. Even religious institutions, such as the Roman Catholic Church, are only temporary devices used by God to achieve his never-ending purposes.[45]

The traditional definition of God as a personal, separately existing supreme being must be replaced by the more modern notion of the One Reality. The best way to see the New God is as the Old God sublated (that is, affirmed, negated, and transcended) in the unity of the One Reality. Thus life after death cannot mean a personal immortality for each existential human being. Death and resurrection can only mean bursting out of the existential confines of space and time and going to "heaven," which means going *into* reality, not out of it. Sounding very much like Whitehead, Kueng describes Jesus as leading the way in this matter.

He can therefore rely with absolute confidence, explains Kueng, on going through the process of death and emerging on the other side as a renewed part of God. Like Jesus himself, Kueng will be "taken up" by God. Death is human; raising to new life is divine. We will all be accepted and saved by God, who is the "incomprehensible, comprehensive, last and first reality."[46]

Reading Kueng today, we can better understand why Kierkegaard was so upset by Hegel and, by extension, by the whole pantheistic process. The role of Christ is reduced to a minimum. In the one reality which is God, *all* other beings are of lesser importance. The Incarnation, for Kueng, is not the becoming man of the Second Person of the Trinity, first of all, because there is no Trinity. The Incarnation, which should be the central doctrine of Christianity, is explained away as a figurative means used by the Absolute to show his care for the world. Instead of concentrating on the one act of Christmas, we should look to Christ's life as a whole. There we see the true meaning of the Incarnation, which is only an emptying and abasement of God to show his love. It is foolish to think that God himself could be incarnated and made flesh. It would be like a whole organic being becoming one of its own cells. This would mean the whole becoming a part. That the Whole should want to show its care and love for the part, though, is acceptable to Kueng.[47]

Jesus, then, should not be regarded as God. Instead of this pious inclination toward deification, we should view Christ as the sublation of the finite in the infinite, best presented by his death and "resurrection." The special force of a specifically Christian religion is to be found in the sacrifice of Christ. Jesus is the real revelation of God in the world, whereby God encounters us in a unique and definitive fashion. In Jesus we see the face of God and live. It is the

Christ who leads the way for the rest of the human race. He shows us the continuing care of God for the world in a special way. By his life-long example we learn what it means to be truly finite yet also truly an aspect of the divine; how we can live and die and yet not die; how we can also do the will of the Father; how we can both be and not be God.

This leads Kueng to provide some reinterpretations of Scripture. What, for instance, is the proper name of God as found in Exodus 3:14? Contra Kueng, one of the main purposes of the Council of Nicea (325 A.D.) was to combat the influence of non-Platonism on Christian doctrine. In Platonism the highest reality is the One *Above* Being, an Absolute Unity without equal. Being is always second. The Nous (the Intelligible, the Word) is at most the First Emanation from the One. This is certainly an exalted status, a name above all names, far above anything else; nevertheless, it is still secondary. But this scheme of things cannot be compatible with Christianity. The God of Abraham, Isaac, and Jacob is Being, not Above Being. This would seem to be the message of God to Moses out of the burning bush (Exodus 3:14).

Kueng, however, takes the proper name of *I Am Who Am,* and squeezes it dry of all its existential content. The revelation becomes instead "I am present and I will be present forever." He offers this in opposition to the Thomistic *Ipsum Esse* of the old, outdated, pre-Hegelian theology. As Kueng repeats in various places, "being" can only mean Greek Being, that is, the immutable, static, and uninvolved. Kueng has no use for such a distant, non-present God. Now, even though it is true to say that taking Yahweh to mean "I am eternally present" does not *per se* entail Hegelian pantheism, it does, it seems to me, render the passage much more compatible with it.[48]

This interpretation is continued in his view of the relationship between Christ and the Father. The formula *homo-ousia* (one in being, of the same being) used in the Nicene Creed was *not* meant, claims Kueng, to say that the Son is equal to the Father, or to say that the Son is the same as God, but was really designed to avoid a renewed polytheism. Instead of strongly affirming the divinity of Christ, the intention of the Council Fathers was to *deny* Christ's divinity so as to avoid polytheism. This, he asserts, against all historical evidence, is the essential meaning of the "consub-stantiality" clause in the Creed. Its only meaning is that the Father is wholly present and active in Jesus, not that Jesus is God.[49]

One can easily see what could very well happen here as a result of Kueng's deconstruction of Jesus Christ. What need is there for Jesus to be God when we already have one, comprehensive, all-embracing reality; and when one is all we now need and will ever need? Jesus may be unique and unsurpassable, but the most we can claim for him relative to the One is to be God's advocate, deputy, representa-tive, and delegate, and who, by his death and return to God, shows us in a superlative way *how* God is present to us all. Only in this limited way, then, can we call Jesus Christ the Way, the Truth, and the Light.

Kueng is much more comfortable with the Council of Chalcedon (451 A.D.) which emphasized that Christ was fully human. Jesus was fully and truly a man, not merely something that looked human, or pretended to be human, or the like. This, after all, is what is really most significant to human beings. Talking about Christ as God cannot be of much interest to me unless I can see him as my brother in the flesh. It is the human Jesus, as opposed to the Greek "divine" Christ, who is of real and lasting significance to us.

But what about God then: Can we prove his existence and presence; can we prove the nature of God as the "being itself of all reality"?[50] Can we know about God as the "being itself in particular also of human life"?[51] Kueng's answer, in keeping with Hegel's, is that we really cannot prove God's nature and presence in the sense of traditional natural theology which saw reason alone as preparing the ground for faith and theology. Yet we can know with certainty about the presence of God by a sort of intuition concerning what is required in order to make sense out of anything at all.

Kueng, largely following Kant, gives four possible ways to prove God's existence: (1) The cosmological proof: Beginning with the fact of change, and armed with the principle of causality and the impossibility (supposedly) of an infinite regress, we arrive at a prime mover. (2) The teleological proof: From the orderliness, purpose-fulness, and lack of fulfillment we find in the finite, we proceed to a world-maker who is also the final goal of his product. (3) The ontological proof: From the innate idea of God which is perfect and necessary we deduce that it must really exist extramentally. (4) The moral proof: We must postulate God's existence in order to have morality and beatitude coincide; God is the necessary condition of the possibility of the highest good for human beings.[52]

Kueng rejects the first three out of hand as inconclusive. They are all based upon an old Greek and medieval world-view which can no longer be accepted. Even if we try working some minor variations within each proof, such as trying to see God as the first efficient cause rather than as a prime mover, we are left out in the cold. In addition, we are also left cold by the very nature of the proofs. They hold no personal appeal for us. We cannot feel the presence of God by means of what John Henry Newman called a smart syllogism. The only approach that might have some value today is the fourth one. Even here, though, it must be modified along Hegelian lines.

When approaching God in a rational way, we must avoid a certain set of extremes. We cannot proceed on the basis of traditional natural theology. This would give us a separate, non-present God. We cannot simply follow Kant's moral postulate. This is much too subjective. It would not give us the objective reality of God. Neither must we place our hope solely in the Bible and its testimony. This is much too dogmatic and rationally unfounded. The answer is to seek God in the very nature of reality itself; in the very conditions which are necessary to comprehend the world of our experience both intellectually and morally.

We proceed in two steps. First, we must see what the existence of God, as an hypothesis, without any claim to real being, would do for us. Next, we must decide how we are to move from the hypothetical to the real. *If* God exists, says Kueng, then we would have a lived-world in which things are grounded, supported, evolving, and without danger of falling into a void of meaninglessness and nothingness. It is a personal matter. There would be unity and identity in my life, truth and meaning in my actions, and goodness and value and hope in my present and future. All this can be the case for me *if* there is a primal source, meaning, value, and being which is objectively real.[53]

So now, what kind of life do we want? asks Kueng. The second step is to *choose*. As in the case of Pascal, for whom the existence of God was a scientifically neutral question, an "undecidable" in the language of modern mathematics, we cannot really prove his existence. But we can *risk* making a choice in favor of his existence, that is, if we want a meaningful life. So, like Pascal, and later Kierkegaard, we must "leap." It is a matter of faith and trust. Instead of a two-floor process, Kueng wants to combine reason and faith into a one-stage process. After the rational groundwork of experience is thought out, we can then, *within that same groundwork, decide* to believe in God. In one act we achieve *both* rationality *and* faith.

This is not a case, insists Kueng, of *creating* an object out of my own imagination. I am not *projecting* an illusion into the world. I am rather *receiving* something from outside. My free, unforced, decision to believe, which immediately grants me absolute certainty about God, as well as security, stability, value, and so on, for my life in all its aspects (scientist, artist, philosopher, religious), comes to me from reality itself. It is a gift of reality (God, the Absolute). My certainty about God "is not an object of immediate experience; he is not part of existing reality, he is not among the objects available to experience; no intuition or speculation, no direct experience or immediate perception, can provide a 'view' of him."[54] It is only "enigmatic reality itself" which can grant us this gift.

In his *Does God Exist?* Kueng never hesitates to pummel the Roman Catholic Church whenever he can. In this work he is especially critical of what he asserts to be the institutional Church's opposition to modern science and progress. This charge has been adequately answered many times in the past, but of more interest now is the way everyone is becoming more and more aware of the need for non-science agencies to supervise the work of the scientist, not *qua* scientist but *qua* the means and effects of science. Given our experiences since the middle of the century, it is not only legitimate but imperative that non-science agencies have an important say in what, where, when, and how science does things. It may be permissible to climb Mount Everest simply because "it's there," but this cannot apply to science. We cannot allow just any research to go on simply because it is possible, just any kind of experimentation to go on simply because we can, or just any sort of technology to be used simply because it is available, which all serious thinkers today realize. Kueng, though, does not seem to be aware.

Kueng is especially critical of the popes who have condemned *certain* aspects of some modern *interpretations* of science. Even though not opposed to science in principle, the Church is opposed to some philosophies, or even religions, of science. This could be the real foundation for Kueng's animosity. For instance, he is especially critical of Pope Pius XII's encyclical *Humani Generis*. In this encyclical Pope Pius XII does not in any way condemn Darwin's theory of evolution as a scientific theory. In fact, he urges continued thought and research on the topic. But he does condemn the doctrine of pantheistic evolutionism, of which Kueng himself seems to be a prime example. Could this be why Kueng is so intent upon stigmatizing *Humani Generis* as antediluvian?[55]

For Kueng the *only* metaphysics worth anything is one of becoming. He has no use for "being." He takes for granted that being must mean Greek Being. He attacks Aquinas for being too close to the Greek world picture to be modern. He sees Plato, with his "immutable, static order of things," as going hand-in-hand with traditional Christian theology.[56] As far as he is concerned, all of medieval scholasticism was based upon Greek metaphysics and was "essentially" connected with Greek physics and the ancient world-view.[57] As far as he is concerned, Greek metaphysics and Christian philosophy of being are the same thing.

Before Hegel, attempts to reconcile God and the world were static; afterward, a dynamic reconciliation is possible.[58] Now, in post-modern times, when discussing the existence and presence of God, it must be done "without Greek, medieval, or early-modern assumptions."[59] What he wants is an historical God. The old Father Figure, outside of time and change, is gone forever. He emphatically does not want a supra-historical God. "God is not static being itself," who sometimes miraculously intervenes in world history. Therefore a Greek-medieval-metaphysical notion of God cannot be allowed.[60]

When discussing Nietzsche's nihilism, which finally forced the modern world into an either-or situation concerning the meaningfulness of life, Kueng assumes that "being is being" and "being is not non-being" are the "two fundamental principles of the philosophy of being."[61] This conceptual approach to being is in keeping with Hegel.

But can we not know with certainty that these principles of identity and non-contradiction are true? Kueng says no; such an attitude is only the claim of the "naïve metaphysics of medieval scholasticism," the same attitude which insists that a purely philosophical natural theology is a necessary presupposition for faith.[62] The post-modern way, instead, is to recognize the central importance of subjectivity, and of its inescapable influence on our interpretation of reality.[63]

What is reality then? Everyone takes it for granted that the mere existence of things, their unquestionable facticity, is "simply given, a datum, a fact, an actuality, a true state of affairs: an unquestionable reality."[64] For Kueng, though, this is much too narrow a meaning. The purely factual, the bare reality, the actual, is not the really real. There must be something more, something more profound, underlying and encompassing the merely given. Reality for Kueng is not the factual, the actual, but "all strata, planes, dimensions of that which is."[65] Ultimately, there is only one reality, the all-encompassing being, the Infinite Spirit, God.

To the extent that Kueng is critical of the early twentieth-century version of Thomism, he is certainly justified. It was no service to the cause of a restoration of Christian philosophy in the schools to dissect the thought and works of Aquinas in order to segregate out those parts which were suitable to a scientific, rationalistic approach to the world, and then to claim that such segments were basically the same as taught by Aristotle. The creation of a Saint Aristotle was not what the Church needed. By the same token, though, it is no service to the cause of religious truth to attempt the creation of a Saint Hegel.

The overall effect of Kueng's approach is to collapse the second, supernatural story of the so-called Cartesian-Thomistic house into the first floor. He solves his architectural problem by deconstructing the upper level. In a completely rationalized system in which there is only one all-consuming God, there is no room for any essential separation of different things. Jesus is only a manifestation of the One Reality, while the Holy Spirit can only be the extension of Christ's influence in the world after he has died and has been reabsorbed into God.

We cannot even talk about the *existence* of God. Worldly, finite, partial, relative things, fragmentary parts, exist. God, though, is Real. The Absolute is the more divine God, the Being of beings, and, relative to any of its finite aspects, the Completely Other. We know that this *must* be the case because we have science, harmony, teleology, and, in general, intelligibility and value in our lived-world. In any event, there is no need for a second story in the Hegelian house. It is a case of Something or Nothing, All or None, on the level of human experience, and we must of course choose the positive. Thus reason and faith reside together quite well in the same living room because in the end they are the same.

Because he is not beginning on a natural level, and then later moving on to a supernatural level, Kueng claims that he is not doing natural theology. Nevertheless, from another perspective, his *whole* approach to the nature of God is nothing but natural theology. For him there is no existentially separate supreme being freely giving his people a supreme knowledge which must be accepted and believed as the ultimate truth. With Kueng it is just the other way around.

Not only that, his whole philosophical theology proceeds from the inside to the outside. I need God to maintain the connectedness and coherence of my thinking about the world and my valued place in the world. This integrity and coherence, though, cannot be purely subjective if the scheme is going to work. God must be an objective reality, so much so that I begin to think that it is not so much that I am thinking God as that God is thinking me. My thinking of God is a gift from God. Man, the goal and culmination of reality, is a gift of God to himself. At bottom, the philosophical theology of the One is still an Epistemological Idealism. This remains for Kueng the modern way, the way started by Descartes, institutionalized by Kant, and perfected by Hegel, Whitehead, and Kueng himself.

At one point, Kueng, repeating Karl Barth, wonders why Hegel did not become for Protestantism what Aquinas is (is supposed to be) for Catholic theology, to wit, the great synthesizer, the creator of a new paradigm against which all future thought would be judged and evaluated, the universal teacher, the *doctor communis*.[66] The answer is that from the viewpoint of orthodox monotheistic doctrine, Hegel was heterodox. Although he retained much of the language and wording of Scripture, as well as some of the traditional formulas of the Christian religion, he so emptied them of their original content that *only* the superficial wording remained. Whether it is called pantheism or panentheism, the fact remains that God is no longer the existentially separate supreme being who created a world which is existentially, actually, and completely not himself.

It is true that Kueng says that God is not man, just as Whitehead says that God is not the world. For Whitehead concrete reality consists entirely and completely of actual entities or occasions. God is also one of these actual entities. *No* actual entity is an enduring object in the sense of Greek Being, that is, forever substantial and self-identical. There is no unique seriality, no one and the same thing persisting through time. There is no *something* that becomes. The whole Aristotelian, common-sense, subject-predicate, substance-attribute way of looking at the world has to go. It is in fact a great evil in human thought, thinks Whitehead. The ultimate metaphysical truth is instead some sort of atomism. In such a world everything affects everything else in the universe. In the name of relativity physics, everything is implicated in everything else that exists. Each thing is all things.

But what does it mean to be? Each being for Whitehead is a bundle of relationships. Each one *is* its relations. But related to *what*? For Whitehead there are no essences; the *what* of each "thing" is nothing other than its set of relations. Does this mean that every time just one relation undergoes some alteration, the very nature of the entity also changes? Yes. Whitehead wants a *radical* desubstantialization of reality.

As Whitehead says in his *Process and Reality* (1929), "Actual entities perish, but do not change; they are what they are" (I: chap. 3, 2). Actual beings do not change and they do not move. Change for Whitehead is the continuing chain of differences between the perishing actual occasions in one event. An event is a series of closely related actual entities (II: chap. 2, 6). *To be* for a being is not *to be* but to be perpetually perishing in itself. Like time, in which the "now" never really is, these bundles of relations with "windows" always open to other bundles, never really are. As in relativity physics, in which all reality is seen through a rear-view mirror, the real things you see are no longer there. In effect, *every* change is a substantial change. Zillions and zillions of such transformations are taking place every moment. According to Whitehead (I: chap. 2, 4): "The ancient doctrine that 'no one crosses the same river twice' is extended. No thinker thinks twice; and, to put the matter more generally, no subject experiences twice. This is what Locke ought to have meant by his doctrine of time as a 'perpetual perishing.'"

Reality *is* process; being *is* becoming. This is so true that it cannot even be said that God is the ultimate ground of being. Rather, it is *Creativity,* that force or power which holds the whole universe in its grasp and perpetually moves it ahead into novelty. Yet how can such a world be understood? Pure becoming is totally unintelligible. Here is where God becomes indispensable. As a mathematician Whitehead knows that something is needed to provide stability. God is needed to provide the world with both Plato's Ideas (the eternal objects, God's "Primordial Nature"), so that actual entities can *be* something intelligible, and to act as a reservoir into which departed beings can flow, thus achieving "objective" immortality (God's "Consequent Nature").

By the ingress of these Concepts, presented by God and selected by the self-creating, newly developing beings, objective orderliness is achieved in the world. But not too much order. In this way the flux can be partially frozen, and we can *really* have something to understand. The eternal objects, however, are not actual *per se,* and we must be careful not to reify (make concrete) such abstractions. Consequently, although realizing that, in order to account for change, there must be something that does not change (the actual entities, the Ideas), the whole emphasis is on becoming.

Because of God's possession of the Ideas and of his never-ending absorption of dead beings, God is unique among actual entities. He alone is eternal. He is, nevertheless, still an integral part of the world. For an actual occasion to be what it is, both in its development and in its immortality, it must participate directly in God. The present entity is *constituted* of parts of God's Primordial Nature, while God's Consequent Nature is *constituted* of dead beings. Under such conditions it is impossible to think of God as transcending the world. At the same time, though, it is possible to say that God is not the world.

Kueng is aware of this; hence the desire to use some term other than pantheism to denote the situation. However, from the viewpoint of Supernatural Theism, the difference between pantheism and its attempted modification and compromise with orthodox monotheism is superficial. Even in panentheism God is still, in large part, the world.

If we add to this the incoherence of such a big man, bipolar, mind-body God, it must be unacceptable to both reason and the Church. Whitehead wishes to turn Spinoza upside down. Instead of actual things being inferior modes within the one substance, it is substance which is the illusion (II: chap. 2, 6). At another point Whitehead rejects as a basic fallacy the supposition of the independent existence of things in time and space (II: chap. 5, 3). In any case, though, he seems to be sure that God is a body, at least in part. Spinoza's One was supposed to contain both mind and extension (body) as infinite attributes. Whitehead's panentheism does something similar with respect to the unique being called God. We, that is, our zillions of ever-changing minute aspects, *are in* God now and *will be* God later. We are God's body, and it is precisely all the expired beings of the world that allow God to grow and develop. So in the end the extremes bend into a circle and meet. Whitehead's vibrating relations so blend together that they are hardly distinguishable from Spinoza's One.

From the religious viewpoint, even though God might be respected as some famous world leader, or as a Demiurge, such a God, who is himself subject to Creativity, would hardly be worthy of worship. Given Whitehead's doctrine on the self-creating power of each being (which is only "lured" by God in certain directions), each actual entity might as well worship itself. And since a human being is but a vast collection of such beings, which are choosing more or less the same eternal ideas, we might as well worship *them* (our own atoms) as our creators.

One must also ask how the ultimate inexplicable irrationality (Creativity) is to be viewed relative to the universe as a whole. It is not a being; but then neither is it nothing. It is certainly the Great Force. Is it the World Logos? The God above God? The World-Soul? Or perhaps Whitehead's *real* God?

Overall, in order to accommodate relativity physics, quantum mechanics, evolutionary doctrine, and also evil in the world, Whitehead must sacrifice the God of his fathers in favor of a new scientific God. Although certainly not just another actual entity, such a being is still nevertheless very much a creature, both of Creativity and of other (not so privileged) beings. Praying to such a God would be pointless because even if it were a coherent, unified, personal Being, which I do not think it can be, it would be powerless to help its brother and sister creatures.[67]

In the end we are left wondering whether we have paid too high a price for Hegel's unity. For instance, with respect to God's relationship to his creatures, for one thing to be present to another thing requires the existence of *two* things. Yet this is what we do not have in Hegel's case. I cannot be present to God, and God cannot be present to me, because I am God and God is me. The very condition for presence is removed in the case of the One Reality.

I still might be able to speak about presence, but only in a metaphorical way, as when I say I am present to myself when I think about myself. It is *as if* there were *two* things present to each other. Immanent activity, and the degree to which it is possessed, is a sign, not of being, but of superior being. This makes sense, but to what end? The ability I have to do this is very important in philosophical anthropology. My power of perfect reflection, whereby I am completely present to my own act of knowing, thus allowing me to judge the status (I know, I guess, I do not know) of the cognition, says something important about the superior spiritual nature of the human person. It does not, however, reveal to me the presence of God as a separate personal being with whom I, another separate personal being, can communicate. Yet this is a necessary condition for any literal meaning of the term "presence," or of the expression "to be present to."

Being present primarily and literally denotes one thing being near another; consciousness is not required. It is the opposite of *absentia,* not being near to each other. All cases of self-presence can only be understood in terms of this primary meaning, while all cases of self-presence in unconscious beings become so far removed from the primary meaning that it (self-presence) entirely loses its significance. In a psychosomatic context, insofar as anything is a natural substance, it has unity, which, in Aristotelian philosophy, is the result of its form and which in turn, in Thomistic philosophy, is due to its act of existing. In this sense, "self," "the thing itself," or "being present to itself" simply means unity or self-identity, a feature common to all beings of a substantial nature.

However, it does not mean that all beings are in fact, or can be, present to themselves. This conforms well to both common usage and philosophical terminology. Even in the case of mental entities, under active consideration by the mind here and now, we have to be careful about attributing to them self-presence in any literal sense. For instance, I can place together various ideas in a propositional form, say "Non-X is X," and say that the proposition is self-contradictory without meaning that the proposition is somehow present to itself. Yet even mental entities have a kind of being. In this case it would be better to say that the proposition is present to my mind, or better, to me. In this way I can treat it *as if* it were a separately existing thing, which in fact it really is not.

Thus, talking about being present to myself only makes sense in a derivative way (as if I were two things), while talking about a rock being present to itself is a most improper way of speaking. *A fortiori,* claiming that something (anything at all) *must* be present to itself *before* it can be present to another only makes sense as an indirect way of saying that it must possess an independent existence in order to be present to another independently existing being. In other words, contra the "subjective turn," presence and subjectivity are not primary; ideas or forms or essences are not the very substance of reality, but are themselves dependent upon substantial structures and their interrelationships.[68]

Consequently, Hegel's Absolutism is quite useless for the presence of God to me. The most that he can continue to affirm, assuming that God is the supremely immanent Idea, is that God is present to himself. To someone else, however, who continues to maintain the common-sense view that he is truly an independently real being, a view denigrated by Kueng, this is small comfort. Kueng is so enthralled with reconstructing Hegel that he manages to deconstruct the God of personal religion. Ironically, what he most wants is the last thing his philosophy will allow him to have. Not only that, both Hegel and Kueng have managed to deconstruct the human self. There really is no me. There is really only God. This non-being of the self is a common theme of modern Radical Hermeneutics and Deconstructionism, and fits in well with pantheism.

HEIDEGGER AND SARTRE: ESSENCE-PHOBIA, WITH A VENGEANCE

> Just as the assertion that everything is true means that nothing is true, so the assertion that everything is in motion means that there is no motion.
>
> S. Kierkegaard
> *Concluding Unscientific Postscript* (1941), 277

> *Schopenhauer's* question immediately comes to us in a terrifying way: *Has existence any meaning at all?* It will require a few centuries before this question can even be heard completely and in its full depth.
>
> F. W. Nietzsche
> *The Gay Science* V: 357

> I note this book [Derrida, *De la grammatologie*] for the importance of the subject, but the language [*langue*] which the author uses being often unintelligible to me, I do not feel myself authorized to relate its conclusions. . . . I had hoped to clarify them for myself by reading the study which M. Gerard Granel devoted to him, . . . but this study being written in the same language [*langue*] as the book, I found myself no further along. . . . One fears lest this linguistic [*langagière*] epidemic propagate itself. According to a review . . . "the masters of style, and also to a certain extent of philosophy," of this author "appear to be Heidegger and Hegel (in that order), which makes it difficult for the reader to follow him."
>
> E. Gilson
> *Linguistics and Philosophy* (1988), 194, note 8

In his 1971 essay on "Hegel and Heidegger," contained in his *Hegel's Dialectic* (1976), Hans-Georg Gadamer points out a fundamental difference between the two thinkers. Hegel was after a complete and absolute knowledge of the real, and the total attainment of a completely clear self-consciousness. Heidegger, however, saw this as impossible. The whole history of philosophy since the time of the ancient Greeks has been in the opposite direction. There has been an ever-increasing obliviousness to being. Heidegger thought that this forgetfulness of being had reached a climax in his own day, and that the time was then ripe for a radical reversal. Nietzsche's negating of being in favor of a complete becoming, even though modified and partially contradicted by his continued attraction for Greek stability as seen in his doctrine of the Eternal Return, marked the end of metaphysics. Around 1900 the heart of philosophy died, and with it the whole world of the past. Early in the twentieth century it was time to start anew.

Heidegger's intention was to go back to the beginning (parallel to the phenomenological "back to the things themselves") and recover what had been lost along the way. Even as positivism and nihilism were reaching their apex the light of the Pre-Socratic Greek thinkers was beginning to break through the darkness of modern thought. In this new light, according to Gadamer, Heidegger was going to give a new meaning to historical relativism. Unlike Hegel, who put the emphasis on the Great Spirit marching through time, progressing all the way as human self-consciousness became clearer and clearer in its realization of the Absolute, his latter-day countryman placed the emphasis upon the need to reverse the contemporary trend toward greater and greater self-determination and self-consciousness. We must allow being to speak through us; being must reveal and announce itself to us as it is; we must lay ourselves open to the being-there of being; we are the being-there of being (the *Dasein*).

The whole thrust and push of modern power and technology must be reversed. Our weakness and ignorance must be emphasized rather than our power and omniscience. We must return to the ancient fatalistic attitude of the pre-*logos* and the pre-*eidos,* to that frame of mind which existed before Plato invented the Idea and before Aristotle invented logic. It is not we who seize upon an intelligible reality; it is a mysterious and unintelligible I-know-not-what that seizes upon us, and it is our duty to allow the Force to flow through us unobstructed. Gadamer states that "it is a matter of what is allotted to man and by which he is so very much determined that all self-determination and self-consciousness remains subordinate" (109).

Heidegger does indeed endorse historical relativism, and an historical consciousness which binds intelligibility (or lack thereof) to the accumulated weight of language and history. In contrast to Hegel, though, there is no necessary progress in the world, and the universe does not revolve around human nature and human reason as it did in the post-Socratic period of Greek philosophy. What Heidegger was advocating, therefore, in Gadamer's view, is a dialectical reversal in which, as the forgetfulness of being increases, the expected "epiphany of being" also increases. The more rational and mechanical technology dominates the more the "eschatological expectation" of a profound turnabout also increases. Soon (the 1920s) the Primordial Force would reassert itself; soon All-Inclusive Being would overthrow Greek essences forever.

In this way Heidegger's hermeneutic (the revelation or showing forth of being as it is in itself) takes us back to the ever-flowing flux of the pre-rational Greeks, especially the world-view of Heraclitus, and even of the Sophists such as Gorgias and Callicles; to the metaphorical and the poetical; to the *Anwesen,* the coming into presence of that which is pure becoming. Those who go along with Heidegger must also go along with this basic insight into the ultimate meaning of reality. Among his disciples one finds Gadamer himself.

For Gadamer, *all* language is metaphorical, a crossing over from one mode of experience to another. The trouble is, we never do figure out what is literally true, what is *the* Truth according to which all local truths are measured and judged. His point is that, in principle, there never was, is not now, and never can be, any such thing as some objective truth. What temporary truths there are must be manufactured through convention and language. Everything is like something else, and it takes a great deal of creative footwork to get across (and around) the fact that the "something else" does not exist. In fact, there are not any *things* or *substances* at all.

And indeed this was the view of Heidegger himself. Allow me to present here a summary interpretation of Heidegger's world-view, especially as found in his early Marburg University lectures and in his *Sein und Zeit,* when as a young man he first experienced the exhilaration of discovering a new philosophical method with new results.

In Heidegger's world-view there is a real material world existing independently of anyone's private consciousness. Contra the whole Cartesian tradition, including Husserl, the existence of the material world is to be taken for granted; it is obviously there and its existence requires no proof. In agreement with many other Idealists, Heidegger rejects Ontological Idealism out of hand.

He does not, however, also in line with many other Idealists, reject Epistemological Idealism, that is, the process of deciding the *nature* of the objectively existing world by an analysis of ideas as found within the thinking of the knower. Generally speaking, Ontological Idealism is the only kind of Idealism known to post-Berkeley and non-Thomistic thinkers, the other kind being more or less taken for granted as the only proper way to proceed philosophically. When Heidegger attacks Idealism, it is the first sort that he is attacking.

When Kant, alerted by Hume, and after realizing that the best minds in Europe, after more than a hundred years of trying, had failed to restore reality, threw in the towel and surrendered any hope of doing so himself, Descartes's Epistemological Idealism was institutionalized. In the twentieth century Martin Heidegger sanctified it. It has now become a sacred cause for the post-moderns. For those secular-minded thinkers who have never been religious, post-modernism is the replacement for religion on the intellectual level, just as art substitutes for religion on the emotional level. For those religiously minded thinkers who still want to maintain some semblance of their past beliefs, post-modernism has become a new religion to replace the old. Let us examine this post-modern phenomenalism more closely.

As a Phenomenologist, Heidegger wanted to go to the *things themselves* as a way of reestablishing philosophy as a respectable and trustworthy branch of knowledge; in fact, as the one and only superior kind of knowledge. As it turned out, though, he did not really go back to the matters themselves as ordinary people would understand such matters, but rather to things *as presented to the conscious subject* themselves. *How* things are perceived is of primary importance. Likewise, he talked about talking about being *qua* being, but ended up talking about the *way* we should talk about being. In other words, he remained true to the Cartesian tradition of epistemology first and the philosophy of being second.

For Heidegger, Phenomenology means that we must take things as presented *a priori* in themselves. He claims that this is the *only* way to discover the truth (the identity of the intention with the intended) in an absolutely dependable way. This is something which cannot be done using the usual positivistic method of the physical and biological sciences, with science defined here by Heidegger as the interconnection of propositions about the unity of a particular domain of subject-matter (Marburg Lectures, Preliminary Part, II: 9, a-B).

It is difficult to talk about Heidegger's philosophy of science since he does not take the natural sciences as he finds them but rather as they should be according to his own broader interpretation of the world. Instead of a philosophy *of* science we have an interpretation of what science (supposedly) is really doing. In his phenomenology we do not perceive the entity in itself. What we perceive is the perception, that is, the thing as it shows itself in a concrete, here-and-now manner. Strictly speaking, the perceived as such *is* the thing according to the manner of its being-perceived. This is a roundabout way of saying that we do not know things first and foremost but only our ideas of things.

This then leaves Heidegger with a serious problem concerning truth, and the old medieval formula of *veritas est adequatio rei et intellectus*. It cannot mean the matching up of the mind with the thing as it really exists outside the mind, because, as it turns out, there are no things outside the mind. We certainly experience something. But apprehending the world is another matter. For Heidegger we can only live-in-the-truth, meaning that truth must somehow refer to something that is transpiring *within* the knowing subject. All knowledge, then, that is true and certain can refer only to what is internally coherent and expressed in various linguistic formulas designed to reflect these internal interrelationships. The *act* of knowledge is that aspect of our lived experience which has the character of an intentional (intramental) relation.

Science, therefore, cannot be the truth about the world. He deduces from his premises that it must be something else. Heidegger concludes that it is a form of discourse, which, like all discourse, can only be a human undertaking. And discourse, in its original Greek sense, means interpretation, letting something be exposed for what it is in itself. The outward manifestation is in the form of words, but the content is strictly functional. There is a practical dimension to the whole business. The *logos,* or inner meaning, is not simply a theoretical viewing of the many things in the world. Scientific knowledge is a way of getting around in the world, of getting things done, of rearranging things to suit our own human purposes. There is a methodology and discipline involved, a certain know-how which breaks down the division between the speculative and practical sciences.

In his *Sein und Zeit (Being and Time,* II: 4, 69-b) Heidegger makes it clear that the line between practice and theory must be largely erased. Scientific "objects" and categories are not so much discovered as constructed. Human beings must take an *attitude* toward the world. It is this "understanding" of being as manifested in nature that makes up the "themes" of science. Scientific activity is *thematizing* the world of lived experience. What used to be called scientific laws and formulas are translated by Heidegger into various themes constructed by humans for the purpose of "delimiting" the subject matter of the sciences. In this world there are really no bare facts. The whole of the world is constituted of the frames of reference created and maintained by the scientific investigation.

This is true even with respect to the main fortress of modern science, namely, mathematical physics. The universe as described by modern science, taking into account the methods of Newton and Einstein, is a mathematical projection in which something *a priori* is taken into account and disclosed to the student of nature. But where and how do we find that *a priori?* Is it Kant's set of categories? No, not if we understand by that that the categories must be the same everywhere and for everyone. However, regardless of the location of the *a priori* aspect of science (that aspect which gives us certainty, universality, and necessity), science is not an objective statement of the world's reality. It is as much the result of communication and discourse, which, through a process of self-reference, becomes binding upon us, as is anything else in which human beings engage.

Yet, he insists that his phenomenology is not a mere subjectivism, dealing with only mere appearances. He defends his view with the assertion that the idea of the thing clearly manifesting itself (*intentio*) *is* the thing itself (*intentum*). There is no real thing in itself standing behind the phenomenon; what the phenomenon gives us *is* the thing itself. Heidegger is not interested in mere descriptive psychology, in the meaning of life, or in the philosophical interpretation of some new scientific theory or other. In fact, he is not interested in any sort of hypothesizing or attempted explanations for things on some supposedly very profound level. What he wants is an absolute knowledge of "reality" which can stand completely on its own.

What this method nets Heidegger with respect to *being* is a realization that the being that raises the question of being in the first place must be the starting point for a true and certain understanding of being. We must proceed from the specific to the general. (In Aristotle and the Scholastics the understanding process is always from the general to the specific.) This questioning-being is a *Zu-sein*, an *Existenz*, a being here and now of a particular type (a *Dasein*), with the power to let itself reveal itself to itself if it works at it hard enough in a phenomenological way.

Practically repeating Hegel on the subject, for Heidegger there is no problem of knowledge in the sense of having to explain how something outside the mind can get inside, or vice versa. The particular-temporal-changing-questioning-being (*Dasein*) is already fully immersed in the general-temporal-changing-non-questioning world. To be a being questioning being is to be in the world. It knows the world from the inside out. Its consciousness is the world; what it knows from the inside is what is immediately present to its own consciousness. Any independently existing outside world, not given in consciousness, is, strictly speaking, incomprehensible. The fundamental phenomenological data of consciousness are a way of being in the being of the world, and no one can authoritatively say otherwise, claims Heidegger.

The world that *Dasein* knows is one unified world (universe, nature), the chief characteristic of which is its constant becoming (temporality). Phenomenology teaches us that the only being (truth, meaning) nature can have for us is that which we "see" in it. The only way to describe such a world in an analytic and reflective way is not in terms of fixed properties constantly present in the same way, but as process. Being is not a thing. To talk as if it were would be to talk physics rather than metaphysics. Thus someone such as Aquinas, who regarded God as *a* unitary being, or Hegel, who insisted upon one Concrete Universal or Absolute, or even Nietzsche, who taught the doctrine of the eternal recurrence of the same things over and over again, must be rejected.

Neither can there be any really ultimate and final separations and divisions within the world. All dichotomies and divisions, not only among different material things, but also among things such as object and subject, the world and the thinker, being and thought, and so on, must be rejected by the Heideggerian phenomenologist. Where such divisions seem to exist, such as in science, especially in the Cartesian-Newtonian tradition, as when the scientist speaks of separate things in separate spaces, of atoms, of objective knowledge, and so forth, it is only a matter of convenience. All such scientific objects, including space, and also time as some sort of evenly flowing objective thing, are only constructs created by the human knower for purposes of control and manipulation of his or her own environment.

Heidegger admits that his monism goes against the common sense of ordinary people. For the non-phenomenologist Aristotle's world-view is the common one. Ordinary people see the world as made up of separate substances possessing their own individual traits, properties, and accidental characteristics. These things are seen to interact with each other, thus bringing about the observed activities, changes, developments, and so on, in the world. They also form species of things which can be classified and studied scientifically in physics, biology, and so on. So, for example, we define a human being, for certain scientific purposes, as a rational animal. However, insists Heidegger, this is not the way nature really is.

In the totality of nature, thinks Heidegger, human nature holds a very special place. This is not because humans are somehow separate from, or spiritually superior to, the rest of nature. This is where people such as Augustine, Pascal, and Max Scheler went wrong, that is, in thinking that human nature is normally ordered to something out of this world (God). Instead, it is special because it is only in human nature that the true meaning of basic reality (being) can be revealed to itself.

The reason why there is something rather than nothing is not because without human awareness there would literally be nothing, or because the world was created by God, but because without human consciousness being would be unknown, undisclosed, undiscovered, unrevealed, and forever completely hidden in an unspeakable silence. The first law of being, the first rule of ethical authenticity, and the first obligation of *Dasein,* is to always remain open to the newest and more complete revelation of being in a pre-logical, intuitive, authentic way. Early on, then, Heidegger sets the stage for the superiority of the *avant-garde,* for modernity for the sake of modernity, for the current culture as an end in itself.

This talk about being open to "God" should not, however, be given a Supernatural Theistic interpretation. Heidegger's approach should rather be compared to that of Hegel or William James, thinkers who often used Christian-sounding terminology to say some very unchristian things, in a manner parallel to the way early Christian thinkers had to use the dominant language of Greek paganism to say some very unpagan things. For instance, in his *Sein und Zeit* (II: 2, 57) Heidegger treats the voice of conscience the same way that James treats the idea of God, namely, as something *apparently* coming from an external source. In reality, though, there is only *this* world, and our being is to be in *this* world. This is what the phenomenological method, which gives us a true reflection of reality (because what is true of the idea properly analyzed and attended to is true of reality), tells the post-modern philosopher.

Heidegger here is not referring to any one particular human being. He is thinking more in terms of the whole human species, of human nature in general. Human nature is *Dasein,* the locus of the revelation of being, the being of being-there, the coming to awareness of what would otherwise be forever hidden. It seems that there is a certain collectivistic tendency in Heidegger, which might help explain why he was attracted in the 1930s to Hitler's National Socialism.

Heidegger apparently does not see any conflict between being a strong supporter of a current culture, state, regime, and so on, even if the present power is a very anti-democratic, dictatorial one, and the general doctrine of historicism. All history is a vast museum and repository of past cultures, now dead and gone. Each one must be seen in the context of its own time and circumstances. What relevance could such modes of behavior have today? Some day the great German culture, language and all, will pass away, just like all the rest. However, *for the time being, it is the* modern way. Indeed, being open to the inner movement of Being could very well mean that one *must* go along with, and even be enthusiastic about, whatever is happening *now,* simply because it is happening now.

However, the meaning of being is not fully revealed to human beings as soon as they begin to employ the phenomenological method. Man is not the answer to the question of being, but the constant questioning of the mystery of being and the constant failure to receive a full answer. This may always be the case, in part at least, because becoming is in principle unintelligible. In order to try making it intelligible we must alter change to be non-change, we must freeze motion and duration as is done in mathematics and science, and in general we must destroy the very thing we are supposed to be revealing as it is in itself, which is the typical approach of modern science and technology. All bringing-to-a-standstill of nature is the work of a being who can never be non-historical.

This leads Heidegger to an understanding, if not of the whole world, then at least of the *human* condition. He regarded this as his most unique and original contribution to philosophy, and credited phenomenology with making it possible. The combination in human nature of the ability to come to some degree of self-consciousness concerning the true nature of being, and the realization of its ultimate precariousness, instability, ever-fluent character, uncontrollability, and scientific impenetrability, sets up in human nature in general (subconsciously in most people) a basic condition of deep tension, worry, anxiety, care, and concern (*Angst, Besorgnis, Sorge*). The very definition of man, which Heidegger claimed not to have arbitrarily invented but to have discovered from his analysis of the things (phenomena) themselves, is: that aspect of the world-process so structured as to be there (*Dasein*) in an anxious and worriful state. He thus explains the troubled human condition without any reference to God or Original Sin. Sartre will follow him on this point.

Another way of saying the same thing is to think in terms of death as the natural concomitant of life. Human nature is aware of death, exceedingly and excruciatingly so, and yet we try to hide this fact of experience from ourselves and from each other. Yet, given the ultimate nature of the world as becoming, without any ultimate and final being in the "traditional" sense of being finally fixed, eternal, self-identical, and constantly present in an unchanging way, each *Dasein* must be prepared to accept his or her own death as the ultimate affirmation of his or her own life. Realizing that we are racing toward death all our life, but that we are at the same time always holding it off (not committing suicide), and maintaining death as something always impending as long as possible, is the best way to handle this deep tension which can be neither eliminated nor relieved. Death is natural; and to let it pray upon your mind, instead of bravely facing it, is an inauthentic mode of human being.

In connection with death, Heidegger often speaks of "nothingness." The reader of Heidegger, though, must be careful here. By "nothing" he does not mean literally nothing or non-existence in some total and complete way. Instead, he uses the term in the same way the Pre-Socratics would talk about the amorphous state of the universe before it was formed into definite things and patterns. To be a nothing means only to be indeterminate. In fact, there never was a nothing, literally speaking. The world of nature is eternal and everlasting. There is no need for a God to create anything, as if there were a time when nothing of a phenomenal or sensual nature existed. As in so many other ways, the Pre-Socratics had the initial, and still correct, insight into things.

Finally, for Heidegger the best way to stabilize and pin down the meager understanding of reality that we have is to see being in terms of time. *Sein ist Dasein* in the sense that the recognition of the true nature of being can only take place in a certain subsection of

becoming, and even there with great difficulty (even today Heideggerian philosophy still has the aura of a mystery cult about it in some
quarters). Just as timelessness characterized the (false) metaphysics
of pre-phenomenological philosophy, so timefulness (temporality)
will now come to be seen as its proper and true modern replacement.

Time, like space, is not a thing. It is not something that *is*.
Rather, time is the very way in which *Dasein* comes to an
understanding of its very being. Becoming takes time. For *Dasein* to
be means for it to have been, and for it to move ahead of itself into the
future of what will be. For *Dasein* to be wholly and authentically it
must be aware of its past and be prepared to choose itself (to remain
in existence in a state of constant tension, a theme later picked up
and developed by Albert Camus and Jean-Paul Sartre) as it moves
ahead into an uncertain future.

Being is becoming, but to be "spread out" (temporalized) in terms
of before and after requires time, parallel to the way being spread out
in space requires three dimensions. Becoming is temporality, and
the disclosure of being takes place, at any given moment, in a certain
particular kind, and in a certain particular piece, of "spread out"
becoming, which is *Dasein,* a temporalized particularity (that is,
human nature).

In his 1925 summer session Marburg University lectures, which
formed the foundation for his *Sein und Zeit* (1927), Heidegger states
that he first came upon his basic insight into the importance of "care"
in 1918 while contemplating the ontological basis for St. Augustine's
philosophy of human nature. Sociologists of knowledge will be quick
to note that this was also the end of the horrors, previously unseen in
Europe, of World War I, which proved just how insecure human life
could be, especially in Germany. How could such evils exist if God
exists; but if God does not exist, how can human nature ever hope to
establish a rapport with being and replenish the reservoir of
philosophical knowledge? Heidegger finds his answer in the method
of Edmund Husserl and Max Scheler, a method which allows him to
carry on even when the Supernatural Theism of his teachers is
removed. At the very end of his 1925 lectures, published in English as
the *History of the Concept of Time: Prolegomena* (1985), Heidegger
summarizes his primordial insight for us:

> The time which we know everyday and which we take into
> account is, more accurately viewed, nothing but the Everyone
> to which Dasein in its everydayness has fallen. The being in
> being-with-one-another in the world, and that also means in
> discovering with one another the one world in which we are, is
> being in the Everyone and a particular kind of *temporality.*

The movements of nature which we define spatio-
temporally, these movements do not flow off "in time" as "in" a

channel. They are as such completely *time-free*. They are encountered "in" time only insofar as their being is discovered as pure nature. They are encountered "in" the time which we ourselves are.

According to Heidegger's basic *Anschauung* into reality, an orientation toward *being* which he never abandoned (later in life he denied that there ever was an "earlier" and a "later" Heidegger), we are all together in one world of change and becoming, a world which we ourselves to a large extent manufacture for ourselves. Thus we hammer out for ourselves society, ethics, time-keeping methods, language, space, scientific objects, things, substantial entities, and so forth. This would include the manufacture of the objects of religious worship as well as of anything else. For Heidegger, *homo faber* covers a great deal of ground indeed. In fact, in his totally anthropocentric view of things, without us there would be no organized world at all. Being is Duration-Temporality presence-ing itself in us.[1]

The emphasis on becoming and the lack of substantiality in the world is confirmed in later writings. By way of a few illustrations and examples, I will take a somewhat closer look at what he has to say about metaphysics and religion. Clearly, he was deeply concerned about the current state of metaphysics in the West, but at the same time he was not a follower of any of the great monotheistic religions of the world. Indeed, he did not even see how metaphysics and any actual religious doctrine involving a super-physical monotheism could ever be related to each other. As he makes clear near the beginning of his *An Introduction to Metaphysics,* metaphysics depends upon reason and religious doctrine depends entirely upon faith, and never the twain shall meet. There is no natural theology for Heidegger; but then there is also no unnatural theology in the sense of some definitive philosophical rejection of God, or the gods. On this point he sharply disagreed with Sartre. What he might mean by "God," though, is something else again.

For Heidegger, a Christian Philosophy is a contradiction in terms, but then so is an Atheistic Philosophy. Religion is an important part of human culture, something which cannot be eliminated, and the importance of which should not be played down. To this extent he is in full agreement with Hegel. However, it is also his view that no one religion can claim to be the true or right or best religion. Humans need their religions, but they also need to culturally invent their own religions. Different cultures in different times and places will have different needs and different religions. The job of the philosopher is not to attack these acts of faith, but, instead, to understand the very foundations of human nature that make religion possible in the first place. Thus, all religion is undermined, desubstantialized, and deconstructed.

For Heidegger, in the present age (the middle of the twentieth century) Nietzsche's dictum about the death of God has come true. But this does not mean that God is dead forever. Neither does it mean that the gods are gone forever. What it means is that we are now in a transitional period between one group of religions and other groups. Sooner or later the human race, either as a whole or in subsections, will hammer out new religions for itself, create new gods, and work out new forms of worship. Given the human condition, given our precarious position on the rim of the vast abyss of nothingness (indeterminateness), we must have our religions and our gods. The temporal world of pure becoming offers us no secure resting place, no forever fixed footing; it gives us only the opportunity for each new generation to make and remake its temporary shelters from the storms of our fleeting and passing lives.

Looked at objectively (philosophically) this state of affairs is sad. One sees a scene of human beings trying to do the impossible, desperately trying to achieve an absolute, to freeze time, to unite the fixity of Greek Being with the temporality of becoming. The sight is pitiful. These mice scurrying about, mostly unaware of their true condition, erecting an idol there, a monument here, some bulwark or other against change there, and so on, and all for nothing, for sooner than they think the great scythe of time will arrive to cut away all of their achievements, forcing them to start over again. To Heidegger, the place to search out the reason and meaning of this anxious state of affairs is in the house of metaphysics and in the way human language, if properly analyzed, expresses the most profound insights into the philosophy of being. In this way the house of language is the house of being.

Heidegger is noted for having emphasized the question, Why is there something rather than nothing? As interpreted by the well-known historian of philosophy Frederick Copleston, this should really be expressed as the question, Why are there many things rather than just One thing?[2] Put otherwise, it is not an existential question at all, but rather an essentialistic question about the relationship between unity and diversity in our experience of the world around us. This question brings us back to the Hegelian issue of the opposition between the intellect and the senses, the former always driving hard for unity while the latter is forever taking everything to pieces. In Hegel's case the One had to be a pure Mind Substance. But what is real for Heidegger?

When we look at what Heidegger has to say about metaphysicians previous to himself, we learn that he finds them all deficient. This is because they didn't know the difference between physics and metaphysics. Heidegger claims that "From the very first 'physics' has determined the essence and history of metaphysics. Even in the doctrines of being as pure act (Thomas Aquinas), as absolute concept (Hegel), as eternal recurrence of the identical will to power (Nietzsche), metaphysics has remained unalterably 'physics.'"[3]

What could Heidegger mean by such a statement when it seems so obvious that those mentioned were all interested in metaphysics, and maybe even in the philosophy of being, rather than physics? This is explained by Heidegger on the basis of their failure to pay sufficient attention to the "ontological difference," that is, the difference between Being in the singular and beings in the plural. Their fault was to begin and end in the world of individual things, of this plant and that man. Physics for Heidegger means the study of the being of a particular being (*ein Seiendes*). To be truly metaphysical the thinker must go beyond beings (*die Seienden*) to Being itself and the ground of beings. In the sense that for Aquinas, for instance, even God is *a* being, Aquinas does not fit Heidegger's notion of a true metaphysician. Such people have "forgotten" Being. According to a widely respected commentator on Heidegger:

> In other words, Being is reduced to a being. The confusion will mark the entire subsequent history of metaphysics. Token of the confusion will be the domination henceforth [Plato and after] of the conception of truth as conformity and a disregard of the original sense of truth as non-concealment. Since truth-as-non-concealment is what Heidegger understands by Being, it is easy to see in what sense he understands metaphysics as the perennial forgetfulness of Being.[4]

Instead of attempting to deal with things on an individual basis and, in many cases, such as Nietzsche, attempting to dominate and control them, the true metaphysician will aim for the intuitive and spontaneous non-concealment of Being; he will let Being be, and thereby gain an access to Being impossible to attain in any other way.[5]

And what is this truth of Being for Heidegger if not temporality? If we let Being be, we are, in effect, accepting the philosophical truth of Being as time, a truth which is revealed to the world by means of human consciousness. It may be that this truth is very unpleasant, disturbing, troubling, and so on, but it nevertheless must be accepted and will be accepted if we are brave and honest (authentic) enough to squarely face up to reality. In the end, regardless of how much we fight it, all attempts to suppress it, or circumvent it, or sweep it out of sight, will fail. In the past certain thinkers, even great thinkers, have tried to pin down Being, have tried to fix it and freeze it and cement it in place, but all to no avail. Often this impossible project has been aided and abetted by the world's great religions, especially the monotheistic ones.

It is certainly true that Heidegger was not a member, even secretly, of one of the great monotheistic world religions. If he were, it would seem, he should have been a Christian. Yet his denial of the central claims of Christianity was quite clear. Christianity, he thought, is a remythologizing of Plato's dichotomy between the Realm of Ideas (the eternally fixed) and the world below (appearances). In between there was a great gap. Heidegger states: "In that chasm Christianity settled down, at the same time reinterpreting the lower as the created and the higher as the creator. These refashioned weapons it turned against antiquity (as paganism) and so disfigured it. Nietzsche was right in saying that Christianity is Platonism for the people."[6]

Indeed, given his fundamental ontology of Being, Heidegger could not possibly have been a Christian. In all three of the world's great monotheistic religions God is a separate Supreme Being, in no way identified with the world. For Heidegger, though, Being is that out of which even human thought arises. Of even greater significance to his understanding of Being is the idea that it *is* human thought. We do not think Being. Being thinks us. Heidegger tells us with respect to the aim of his essay on *What Is Metaphysics?*: "Its sole thought is that thing which has dawned on Western thinking from the beginning as the one thing that has to be thought — Being. But Being is not a product of thinking. It is more likely that essential thinking is an occurrence of Being."[7] Thomas Langan translates the last two sentences as: "Being is not a product of thought; rather the opposite, essential thought is an event of Being."[8]

The same idea can be found in Heidegger's *An Introduction to Metaphysics.* Even though he certainly cannot agree with Parmenides's conclusion concerning the lack of change in the world, when discussing the meaning of the Parmenidean statement that "thinking and being are the same," Heidegger insists that its original meaning has been lost. Contrary to the usual interpretation, explains Heidegger, this expression should *not* be taken to mean that *only* what can be thought can be, and that what cannot be thought cannot be. The extension of this misinterpretation shows up later in Greek philosophy in the form of an unduly high status for logic and reasoning, as if logical reasoning *determines* what is or is not real. Heidegger finds this tendency throughout Western history, even including Hegel and Marx, and culminating in the especially obnoxious elevation of mathematical logic to such a high status in modern times. In fact, Being has no necessary internal logic, and addresses each age differently in an unpredictable way.[9]

For Heidegger the proper interpretation of Parmenides is that Being and its apprehension are *always* together, especially in human nature. Being is a great and mysterious reality, greater than the human mind. Where the truth of Being is allowed to present itself, apprehension occurs. "Apprehension is the receptive bringing-to-stand of the intrinsically permanent that manifests itself."[10] In human nature there is an event of Being called *noein,* knowledge, insight, intuition, and feeling. "Apprehension is not a function that man has as an attribute, but rather the other way around: apprehension is that happening that has man."[11] So, as with Hegel, a pure subjectivism is rejected by Heidegger. And what is this great permanence if not temporality? Thus is Parmenides turned upside-down and inside-out.

Everywhere we look in Heidegger we find the same central theme being played in different keys. Reality is both one and temporal, so that there is no place left for real substances (plural). For example, in his 1950 lecture "Das Ding," as translated by A. Hofstadter,[12] Heidegger explains how "thing" is to be taken as a verb.

In Greek, Latin, and Old German, that is, in its primitive, primeval meaning, thing *qua* thing does not mean a fixed object to be represented in the mind by a fixed concept. Nor does thing *qua* thing mean some object to be used by human beings for some utilitarian purpose. The original meaning of "thing" is that of a gathering and uniting together of people for social reasons, of a letting-be-here (*das Verweilen*) of Being in our experience. The notion of a thing as something *present* to us in a *stable* way is a secondary notion. By deconstructing *presence,* Heidegger means to steer us away from Aristotle and the Scholastics and *back* to the Pre-Socratics.

This social dimension, as we later find emphasized in Gadamer and Rorty, is all-important. *Res publica,* for example, did not mean the state, but a matter for public discussion, a common concern. Likewise for terms such as *Ding, causa, cosa,* and *chose.* Their basic meaning is that of doing, of handling matters and affairs, of dealing with the world, and so on. It is like handling a legal case in the courts. The *res* or *causa* refers to the contested case which must be worked out by the participants.

The notion of a thing as a stable enduring entity is all wrong according to Heidegger. It has come to us as a result of a basic misinterpretation of human experience carried out in Greek and medieval philosophy. Take the case of a water or wine jug, for instance. What is a thing *qua* thing and nearness *qua* nearness? In the case of a jug, its jugness does not reside in its material parts and shape but in its power to hold a liquid for us and to pour out that liquid for us. A jug is really a void, temporarily contained, so that it can work for us. In the jugness of the jug resides the coming together of many different aspects of the world, all combined in such a way as to bring us a gift of outpouring.

All reality, symbolized by Heidegger as the earth, sky, gods, and mortals, simultaneously comes together in the event of outpouring. Just as people might gather together to solve a common problem or deal with a common concern, so Being converges upon this one spot in time, curtailing nothingness (indeterminateness), circumscribing space through the medium of the artist, presenting us with an *ens,* an ontological reality, with a thing, with a something that is. In a parallel fashion, nearness is not a thing, but an act. Nearness removes farness. The near thing (for example, the jug) becomes present to us *in use.* Heidegger's affinity with pragmatism is obvious here.

Thus a thing is not an existentially separate substance. In the sense of substantial beings, *there are no things in the world.* Presence, and nearness, as the existence of substantial things in nature, is specious. A thing is really only a temporary gathering of the universal force and energy of Being. A thing is something which stays for a while. A thing is only a thing while it is "thinging," that is, only while it is the gathering together of earth, sky, divine, and mortal, in the vicinity of a human being open to Being, of a *Dasein.* Nearing is simply the presencing of nearness. Thinging is simply the presencing of thingness, that is, the concentration here and now of the universal forces of mysterious Being.

The world of things is a mirroring of the different aspects of the world, one in another. The world, which is just here, unexplainable in terms of something more intelligible (Being is the total All-in-All), is a mirror-play, an ever-ongoing set of events, circling round and round forever. Nearing is the nature of nearness. Thinging is the nearing (to us) of the world. In a flash of mirror-play the thing appears, temporarily freeing itself from the compliancy of the simple oneness of Reality. Heidegger's poetic, romantic, pantheistic monism seeps out from around every word he writes. At the very end of his lecture on "The Thing" he states:

> In accordance with this ring, thinging itself is unpretentious, and each present thing, modestly compliant, fits into its own being. Inconspicuously compliant is the thing: the jug and the bench, the footbridge and the plow. But tree and pond, too, brook and hill, are things, each in its own way. Things, each thinging from time to time in its own way, are heron and roe, deer, horse and bull. Things, each thinging and each staying in its own way, are mirror and clasp, book and picture, crown and cross. (p. 182)

All is flowing temporality. Ultimately unintelligible, the becoming which is Being must forever remain a mystery to us, and even to itself. Being is certainly not something personal with its own self-consciousness. Moreover, as with the Ultimate One and Unity of Plotinus, it is certainly at least doubtful that we can ascribe any characteristics to it at all. Also, as we have already seen with respect to Parmenides, Heidegger turns the great Greek father of metaphysics on his head. No longer is the Permanent the Real. But is it in any way personal? Can we ascribe to the One Reality intellect and will? Does Heidegger's inversion achieve personhood? Apparently not. It does, though, achieve the insubstantiality (deconstruction) of ordinary things.

Indeed, everything, in the plural, is deconstructed. I think I must agree with Frederick Copleston's interpretation of Heidegger mentioned earlier. Heidegger's main concern and constant preoccupation is with the problem of diversity within Unity. For Heidegger the Phenomenological Program of "getting back to the things themselves" really means getting back to *The* (whatever it may be) Itself. It seems that for Heidegger true Being can never be spoken of in the plural. It is always the *Singulare Tantum.*

In this inversion, although permanence no longer predominates, monism is still maintained. As Heidegger aged he became more clear about the basic nature of this one reality. This can be seen in his January 1962 lecture "Time and Being," delivered in the University of Freiburg in Breisgau. This lecture is important because it confirms and makes explicit what is implicitly contained in his *Being and Time,* in the works on metaphysics mentioned above, and in some of his other works, such as the *Letter on Humanism* (1947) and *Identity and Difference* (1957).

The main task of the lecture is to view both Being and time in terms of the more fundamental relationship of Appropriation (*Aneignung*). In effect Heidegger wishes to inaugurate the wholesale rejection of Greek Being. He wants to set up a revolutionary new world-view outside of, and separate from, the whole history of metaphysics, which is nothing more than the history of variations on Greek Being. This new philosophy is to be as far away from traditional metaphysics as possible, especially where traditional metaphysics turned into monotheistic theology.

Heidegger's whole aim is to explain the presence of reality without the God of the Bible or the Koran. He insists upon the psychological priority of presence. But what is present? Beings, in the plural. And what is it that is letting beings be present? Being itself, which is the same as presence *per se.* But Being is itself part of a broader scheme of understanding reality, not as a species within a genus, but as coextensive with a *process* of development.

For Heidegger there is change and destiny, but there is no divine providence, either in the traditional religious sense or in the Hegelian pantheistic sense of a Great Spirit and Infinite Idea necessarily progressing in a certain way. The broad process of change, which both withdraws from and comes toward us, which both conceals and reveals Being, which both shows us the presence (being) of things as a gift and which takes away this presence and, in general, which controls all aspects of the world, is called Appropriation by the "later" Heidegger.

Hegel's view of reality is rejected by Heidegger in part because it depends upon a conceptualizing of Being rather than upon an intuition, feeling, and direct experiencing of reality. Indeed, for Heidegger, as with Kierkegaard, there is an inverse relationship between the letting-be of Being (*aletheia*) and the conceptual knowledge of beings. The more you conceptualize the less you are, or at least the less you are in immediate contact with reality. So there is a sense in which Heidegger always was a mystic insofar as he saw an opposition between Being and thinking, at least in a certain sense of what it means to think.

Also, Hegel must be rejected because Being, like human nature, is finite rather than infinite. Both are bound by temporality, which is essentially finite, and which shows itself as finite in the finite process of Appropriation. Contra Hegel, Thinking is not Being, there is no Absolute, and hence the *question, problem,* and *mystery* of Being are recognized and preserved.

Neither does Heidegger want anything to do with the *poiesis*-God of the Jews, Christians, and Muslims. The old-fashioned idea of *presence* is parallel to the outmoded meaning of Being; namely, it is confused with the notion of production. Technological models have their place in the world of human society, but not in metaphysics. The creator-God who makes things, who is present to his creation via his productive power, must be replaced by the process of Appropriation, a process which expropriates rather than creates, which works with what is already there rather than one which makes things from nothing. There are no divine ideas to be *made* concrete.

Yes, but *what* is it that is appropriated and expropriated? What is appropriated by Appropriation? The answer, as found on page 42 of Joan Stambaugh's edition (1972) of Heidegger's lecture, is that "Appropriation appropriates, that is, brings into its own and retains in Appropriation: namely, the belonging together of Being and man. In this belonging together, what belongs together is no longer Being and man, but rather — as appropriated — mortals in the fourfold of world."

This quotation is from a summary of a series of six seminars concerned with explicating Heidegger's January 1962 lecture "Time and Being." They took place in Germany in September 1962 and were written by Alfred Guzzoni. This particular passage is especially interesting for bringing together the five key terms of Heidegger's view on the presence of Being, namely, Appropriation, Being, man, mortals (finitude), and the fourfold. The last refers to the trinity of true time (temporality), which is not the uni-dimensional succession of now instances, but which incorporates the past, present, and future into a whole, plus space, in which change in time takes place. Thus time-space (with shades of Einstein) forms a fourfold unity, with space rather than time as the fourth dimension. This emphasizes the point that time, not space, is primary.

What the explanation tells us is that the world is a finite process of change in time-space such that there are no things in the sense of absolute substances, either mental or physical. The traditional metaphysics of presence has been dismantled, deconstructed, desubstantialized. It is like being a guest at a celebration. There is no such *thing* as the celebration. The *presence* of the guests *is* the celebration. The guests *are* the celebration. Likewise for the whole of reality. Presence means the appropriation of the appropriating of that aspect of Being which is extended to man, approaches man, reaches to and recedes from man, in the abiding process of time-space. Being is temporality, but temporality always appears in a finite context, a context which must constantly be interpreted and reinterpreted by *Dasein* (man).

Guzzoni, at the beginning of the fourth seminar, says of Heidegger that his "usage of verbs is remarkable." This is indeed true, but not surprising. Throughout his writings and lectures, every time Heidegger approaches some fundamental area of the philosophy of being, or finds himself in a position where he can no longer put off giving a definition of some basic term, he attempts to turn nouns (substantives) into verbs. For instance, and perhaps most obviously, "man" as essential human nature disappears to be replaced by *Dasein,* the *process* of Being being there.

Where possible he eliminates nouns and pronouns altogether, or uses them only to later dissolve them away in a vat of verbs. Openness opens, appropriation appropriates, presence presences, and so on. We never do get an intelligible answer to the question, *What* is the *It* that gives Being, gives presence, gives temporality, gives the "and" between Being *and* time (the *neutrale tantum*), that sends, receives, withdraws, reaches out, withholds, conceals, unconceals, that provides the absence of presence, and so forth?

Dasein, which is the locus for the thought of Being, can only find itself by entering into the thinking of Appropriation, by awakening into It, by letting itself be expropriated by the process of Appropriation. Once this is achieved, we can see Being and time (that is, true time which is temporality), as well as human nature, as being encompassed within a possible Appropriation which has been actually appropriated.

Then humans belong to Appropriation rather than vice versa. Then and only then are we *with* Being, is our own being secured (as far as possible), and does one's own finitude really belong to one's self. The temporality of *Dasein* is then fully appreciated as a gift of something greater than one's self. At the end of the last (sixth) seminar (p. 54) we read: "For one can also speak about denial and withholding in Appropriation, since they have to do with the manner in which It gives time. The discussion of Appropriation is indeed the site of the farewell from Being and time, but Being and time remain, so to speak, as the gift of Appropriation."

From one viewpoint this can sound very religious, even traditionally religious. As humans we hold our finite existence as a gift from a mysterious God, and we come to a knowledge of this by releasing ourselves to the Power of God, a Force which appropriates what He himself has given, and as a result, we become more ourselves than we were before, and so forth. Similarly, because of his tendency to take "being" in its verb forms, and his emphasis upon the ultimate mystery of Being relative to human conceptualizations, it is also possible to confuse Heidegger with an existential Christian thinker such as Aquinas.

However, as soon as we realize that "God" is not God, but a World Process, that in fact there is no essence to man or anything else, we can see that Heidegger is as far removed from orthodox monotheistic theology as Heidegger claimed to be removed from Hegel. Like Jesus, Heidegger loved his paradoxes, but his were entirely secular. The *summum ens* as an existentially separate being is rejected by Heidegger. Beings (plural), and our awareness of Being, are not grounded in such *a* Being. The It that gives all is an action — and action actions.

We then also come to realize just how much Heidegger abused the term "presence." In religious matters he was absolutely opposed to the notion of a separately existing deity which somehow remains near to the creature. Yet the only reasonable way to talk about presence in any literal sense, as we have already seen with respect to Hegel and Kueng, is as the nearness to each other of at least two existentially different beings. Because I am not the chair and the chair is not me, the chair can be present to me when I am sitting on it, and I am present to the chair even though the chair is not aware of me. Where some degree of consciousness exists, say between a dog and its master, both can be consciously present to each other. On the human level of personal spiritual beings the intimacy can be much greater, and so on up the scale of being.

Heidegger's world-view, though, so lacking in substantial natures, cannot allow for such a thing, even in principle. Yet he continued to talk about presence, presences, and presencing. In the indissoluble unity of reality, of the wellspring and the stream that flows from it, terms such as awareness, secret giving (sending), withdrawing, approaching, nearness, concern about, caring for, and so on, lose their common-sense meaning. Although it is not necessary to separate Being and time (as thinkers such as Aquinas knew very well) after the fashion of Greek Being, it is nonetheless still necessary to have existentially separate beings (plural) if we are to make sense out of "presence."

So what is left of human nature in any substantial sense? What Heidegger does, in effect, is look around on all sides of human nature, examining how we do this or that, how we are related to this and that, how all of the scientific, artistic, religious, and so on, aspects of *our* world have a meaning and significance only in relationship to *our* needs and purposes, and so on. What, though, is left in the center of this great wheel of investigation and questioning? The answer can only be: Not very much. It would seem that there is an emptiness at the center; the hub of the wheel hides a nothingness, a vast amorphousness, of existence. The world is made up of events, but there are no substantial things in the world. There are events in time, but no substances (fixed beings).

What Heidegger has done, in effect, is to have deconstructed all of ordinary reality. It has not, however, been destroyed; it has been dissolved in the vat of time, and now flows out formed and reformed, cut and shaped, to fit the patterns of our historically conditioned times and needs. If it is true that there is no "later" Heidegger, this interpretation fits in well with the picture of a thinker who wanted, as he got older, to see more and more the full consequences of his original insight that Being *is* Time.

Sartre shared Heidegger's essence-phobia, except that he thought philosophy could at least disprove the existence of God. Even though self-consciousness comes from being, is born within being, and in a way depends upon being for its existence, as a hole in a donut depends upon the rest of the donut for its existence, it nevertheless derives its whole dignity and glory from the fact that it *opposes* being, and must fight against being every second in order to maintain its freedom of action. Sartre's whole anthropocentric, "humanistic" case for man and against God is based upon this division of the In-Itself (being) and the For-Itself, language gotten from Hegel via Heidegger.[13] The For-Itself, though, now refers exclusively to human nature.

Moreover, contact with the In-Itself, or being, is not a pleasant and wholesome condition to be in as far as the For-Itself, or human self-consciousness, is concerned. Relative to the For-Itself, it is in fact a terrible and oppressive condition to be in. Yet we live and have *our* being in the world. This love-hate relationship which Sartre has with the world exactly parallels the love-hate relationship which he has with Greek Being, that is, with the permanently fixed and self-identical.

In Sartre's case philosophy is relevant to natural theology in a negative way. Given his analysis of being, which, like Heidegger, takes us back into ancient Greek thought, Sartre cannot see any way to reconcile being and becoming, the absolute and time, reality and appearance, permanence and constant change, rootedness and alteration, security and novelty, conservatism and creativity, fixity and freedom, and so forth. What he does see is the great weight which being places upon our backs, how it holds us down and constrains us as we struggle to be free, to be ourselves in a world which everywhere seems to be warring against us. Again, going back to one's early days, to one's primordial insight into the human condition, can be as instructive in Sartre's case as it was in Heidegger's. To those not already familiar with Sartre, what he has to say about "being" can be shocking.

The tendency is to look upon nature as an evil, antagonistic force, an attitude reminiscent of the Platonists of ancient times, and the Manicheans of both ancient and medieval times. This tendency reached its culmination with Jean-Paul Sartre in the 1930s. He begins his early novel *La Nausée* (1938) slowly. Roquentin gradually comes to realize the precariousness and contingency of his existence, the filthiness of material bodies, and the isolated value of his own self-consciousness. As he later makes explicit in his *Being and Nothingness* (1943), one must learn to see human life in terms of a constant opposition between material nature, which he calls "being," and individualistic human self-consciousness, which he comes to talk about as "non-being."

At the beginning of *Nausea,* while sitting in a cafe, Roquentin begins to think that "The Nausea is not inside me. I feel it is *out there* in the wall, in the suspenders, everywhere around me. It makes itself one with the café; I am the one who is within it."[14] Later, material things are referred to as flabby masses. Still later, while having sexual relations with a local café owner, he imagines he is in a garden with hairy leaves, and ants, centipedes, and ringworm over everything. Horrible beasts walk and crawl over the ground. He also imagines a sign pointing to her sexual organs saying, "This park smells of vomit." As we proceed we learn that all flesh is dull, dirty, and disgusting.

About halfway through the novel Roquentin deliberately cuts his own hand. Right after this he goes out for a walk. His hand begins to hurt. He thinks to himself that "existence is an imperfection" (*"l'existence est une imperfection"*), and then, as his opening hand begins to hurt even more, he tells it to exist. "To expand; my cut hand hurts, exist, exist, exist." (*"S'épanouir; j'ai mal à la main coupée, existe, existe, existe."*)[15] By existing it will become like a material thing: inert, unfeeling, dull, dead, and removed from his consciousness.

A while later he decides that his only problem in life is that he exists. But this trouble is so vague and metaphysical that he is ashamed of it. Still later, while sitting in a park looking at the trees, he comes to the conclusion that existence is a deflection, a brute force working against his consciousness, an absurdity. The key to existence is the same key which unlocks the mystery of nausea, namely, the absurd nature of the world. The black, knotty, inert, nameless, cold tree root represents *all* of nature. The very multiplicity of existing things is a joke. One would be enough, and more than enough. "The abundance did not give the effect of generosity, just the opposite. It was dismal, ailing, embarrassed at itself."[16]

Even worse, the parts of the whole dismal mess do not even want to exist; they simply cannot help themselves. How foolish of Darwin and Nietzsche to talk about the struggle to survive and the will to life and power. The only reason all of nature did not die and go away a long time ago is because it is too weak to do so. "Every existing thing is born without reason, prolongs itself out of weakness and dies by chance."[17] Nature is not something good and wholesome; there is no reason to be proud of it. And neither is it good to be a part of nature.

By the end of the park scene, which is also nearing the end of the novel, Sartre's animosity reaches its height. The terms he uses to describe the world can leave no doubt concerning his opinion of nature. Existence is soft, sticky, soiling everything, and all thick like a jelly. It is an ignoble mess. It fills everything with its gelatinous slither. There are great depths upon depths of it. The naked world had revealed itself to Sartre as a great, gross, absurd being. Sartre has Roquentin say: "I shouted 'filth! what rotten filth!' and shook myself to get rid of this sticky filth, but it held fast and there was so much, tons and tons of existence, endless: I stifled at the depths of this immense weariness."[18]

And where does existence come from? Nowhere. The universe is eternal. Rotten, wasteful, and disgusting as it is, it remains a necessary being which cannot not exist.[19] Hence we cannot call upon God in a Supernatural Theistic sense to explain it. It is just there, and Sartre must have Roquentin make the best of it. And the only way to do that is to constantly wage war with it by means of the only weapon he has, namely, his own self-consciousness.

So it is that Sartre rejects being as bad. The material world is the same as being, which is equal to existence. This being-existence-nature is as necessary as it is repugnant. Even Sartre's own ideas in his own brain, insofar as they are something, are part of this filthy world of existence. It is a universe he is stuck with; he is thrown into it whether he likes it or not. And the only way he can handle it is to preserve the only thing he has which can be pitted against it; the only specifically human trait he possesses until he dies and becomes once and for all an inherent part of the inherently disgusting world, namely, his "non-being" or personal self-consciousness.

Even at the end of his life Sartre regarded *Nausea* as his best work. However, Sartre's foundational insight is presented in a much more formal way in his chief work *Being and Nothingness*. For Sartre existence precedes essence only in the sense that the human subject comes first, in an undetermined and open-to-all-possibilities way, possibilities which must, to a large extent, be determined by the subject himself or herself. Humans must then fill out their own nothingness so as to create themselves to be *what* they are by their own actions. This process must take place *within* the world of already given material being, but also in constant opposition to this world of fixed, dead, and antagonistic being. In such a world there is no essence, no *what* already given and fixed in advance, for the human subject. In fact, we cannot even talk about being as it might exist in itself unknown by human consciousness. It is *only* via the human subject that anything is apprehended and appreciated. And this subject *is* its actions.

As Sartre points out at the very beginning of his major work, the act is everything. Behind the act there is no being, no potency, no underlying habit, no dormant power waiting to be actualized. If there were, this would pull us back into the world of being, and thus our uniqueness would be suffocated and destroyed. By the same token, the appearance is everything. Appearance *is* reality, with nothing to support it. There are no substances in the world, no nature guiding things along fixed paths of predictable behavior. Sartre must, however, allow for time. Everything does not happen at once, and so we find that temporality, the predominance of process, is preeminent in all things. For Sartre, the potential is to the infinite as the actual is to the finite.

Appearances take time to manifest themselves and so their future manifestations are presently only potential. This future is infinite. Being and appearance are thus replaced with the infinite *in* the finite, which can be contrasted with Aristotle's view that the potential is *in* the actual. In Sartre's case, though, the significance is reversed. God, the Infinite Being of traditional theology, is unreal for Sartre, while the appearances of things, that is, the finite which must be successively manifested from moment to moment, is the *only* reality. Yet he still cannot escape the need for the potential, even if it is only in the temporal sequence of the phenomenal.

According to Sartre, if there were no distinction between appearance and reality, then there would be a problem involved in successfully maintaining a place for both the intramental and extramental worlds of existence, something which must be done in order to accommodate common linguistic usage and common-sense experience. But, if we identify appearance and reality in a spiritual soul, as was done by Descartes, Berkeley, and Kant, and as Husserl should have done if he had been consistent in the application of his own principles, then we would be forever stuck within our own minds. We would then be forced into Ontological Idealism as defined in post-Cartesian European philosophy, and as taught by Bishop Berkeley, namely, we would have to insist that *only* the intramental world is real, while the very existence of the extramental physical world would be called into question.

On the other hand, if there were only an extramental world of three-dimensional material things, and no inner world of consciousness at all acting on its own independently of the outside world of inert "being" (that is, being in the Greek sense of that which is forever fixed and immutable in itself), it would follow that there could be no freedom and no basis for any sort of true inner life for human beings. Such a consequence may be acceptable to the deterministic, scientific physicalists, but it cannot be taken seriously by Sartre or, for that matter, by anyone else who takes seriously ordinary human experience and the facts of human self-consciousness.

Sartre's solution to this dual problem is to sharply separate being-for-itself from being-in-itself. Being-in-itself is the deterministic, inert world of the scientists. Being-for-itself, though, cannot be being at all. It can only be something in opposition to being, namely, a relative non-being. The *only* contrary to being is non-being. Thus nothingness is at the very core and heart of human nature. It is what makes human nature to be human nature. It is what makes us unique and special in the world, the very center of all meaningful worldly activities. Our claim to goodness and dignity resides not in our being or existence but in our non-existence.

This same basic approach also extends to Sartre's views on God and creation. The material world must be eternal and uncreated for Sartre because he cannot understand how a creation *ex nihilo* could possibly result in a world separate from God. Anything God could possibly make would have to remain continuous with God. Anything thought by God could never get out of God's mind. What could a creator-God possibly give to his intentions? If a creature in itself is nothing, and must remain perpetually dependent upon God for its existence, then, thinks Sartre, its very existence must remain continuous with God's existence. Pantheism, therefore, is the necessary consequence. The influence of Hegel would seem to be especially strong here.

Moreover, even if, impossible though it be, a creature could "get out" of God, we would be no better off. Then we must embrace deism. This is the necessary alternative to pantheism, and the only form of Supernatural Theism that would make any sense to Sartre. Such a creature must break all ties with God and take on the traits of a completely independent thing. All trace of divine creation would have to be forever removed after the moment of creation. Thus, even if not in theory, we must all be atheists *in practice*. Sartre expects that this would be no comfort to the traditional believer.

At the end of his *Being and Nothingness* Sartre summarizes for us the metaphysical implications of the dichotomy between the In-Itself and the For-Itself. The distinctiveness of the For-Itself does not reside in a general sort of non-being or nothingness, but rather in a particular privation of being within a particularized temporal instance of material being. This "recoil" of non-being within being which we call human self-consciousness is the cause of all the upheaval and turmoil in the world. It is the *sine qua non* of the very being of the world; it is that whereby we can know the world, and know it as antagonistic to ourselves. Without it there would be no *significant* world at all. In this sense, self-consciousness is an absolute, but only relative to the *otherness* of being. "Thus the for-itself is an absolute *Unselbstaendig*, what we have called a non-substantial absolute. Its reality is purely *interrogative*."[20]

Sartre's debt to Heidegger here is quite clear. He is also indebted to Hegel. To understand the human condition requires *both* being *and* nothingess. These are not really two incommunicable parts. They are rather two factors making up one reality, one universe. Rather than being two heterogeneous realities, two separate genera, they constitute one integrated system in which each requires the other to be what it is. Even though they act *as if* they are two, in reality each without the other would be a mere abstraction. According to Sartre, the diversity of the structure of reality is "held within a unitary synthesis in such a way that each of them considered apart is only an abstraction."[21] This now sounds very much like Hegel.

Nevertheless, it is the For-Itself which constitutes the *significant* variable. The relationship of the two factors is not reciprocal. For Sartre, "the in-itself purely and simply is."[22] It is only the For-Itself which allows us any insight at all into the ontological foundations of the phenomenological appearances of things. To do this the For-Itself must be "what it is not and which is not what it is."[23] This is the best we can hope to do given our limited perspective on reality. It is not within our power to truly see things as a whole, to view the whole as if we stood outside of it and were viewing it as an objective observer. To do this we would have to be God.

But there is no God, and there can never be God. Here we see Sartre at odds with Hegel, to whom he otherwise owes so much. For Hegel, God does exist. He exists as the synthesis of Being and Non-Being, the combination of Something and Nothing. God is the one, unique Spirit, the Absolute, the Concrete Universal, the one and only For-Itself. But the very possibility of such a thing is denied by Sartre.

The For-Itself and the In-Itself, as they exist on the level of the finite and limited, can never coalesce into one thing regardless of how far down we penetrate into reality. At best, such a coalescence can only function as an imaginative ideal, something we might think about, but which can never actually be achieved. No doubt we can talk *as if* this were in fact the case, *as if* the *ens causa sui* were a real thing, but this is the best we can ever hope for. It will forever remain a futile and hopeless passion. Thus God, defined as the whole, as the One Supreme Being, *cannot* exist.

Nevertheless, human beings do exist, and they exist as at least a partial synthesis of being-in-itself and being-for-itself. Moreover, there are many of them. Hence the world of Sartre is full of little gods, each one pursuing his or her own purposes and creating his or her own universe, at least in theory. This also explains for Sartre the perpetual agony of human existence. "It is this perpetual failure [to be] which explains both the indissolubility of the in-itself and of the for-itself and at the same time their relative independence."[24] Just as on the macrocosmic level there can be no unity of the two into a common genus, so also on the microcosmic level of individual human existence. Such a failure to coalesce, despite the constant effort to do so, can be considered a certain sickness or disease within being. Like rats on a treadmill, we strive in vain to achieve an impossible destination.

Against this background we can understand why Sartre had to turn so outlandish on a topic such as presence. As long as we are dealing with material things, the ordinary meaning of "present to" will apply. Ordinarily things must possess independent existences before we can speak intelligently about one being present to another. The introduction of consciousness, however, serves to complicate matters. *Knowing* one thing to be present to another is a different kettle of fish from one thing of a material (being) nature being in the vicinity of another In-Itself. However many things may be present to each other in the world independent of the For-Itself, without at least one human mind to be *aware* of such presences, and thereby creating a new relationship of presence, the *whole* world of presencing would be meaningless.

But what about presence-to-self, something of special importance in a philosophy which wants to pit the individual consciousness of each separate human being against everything else in the universe? As Sartre explains in *Being and Nothingness,* Part II (Being for-itself), chapter 1 ("Immediate Structures of the For-Itself"), there are certain things he cannot allow. One is the existence of a spiritual soul capable of perfect reflection. Another is a pantheism in which "present to" becomes meaningless because ultimately there are no substantial divisions among things. Both Hegel and Heidegger, he feels, are too much into togetherness and solidarity. Still another is the possibility that the In-Itself might know and will, like the "thinking matter" of Locke and Voltaire. All these are rejected.

As a result, Sartre feels himself *forced* into an extraordinary account of presence-to-self, namely, that "nothingness," in the one unique case of human nature, must explain our power of self-consciousness. Because of a degeneration within being I can become an absolute event in the world. I am a perpetual alienation from my own being. To be me I must be what I am not. Within human-being there must be nothingness so I can be what I am. Since ordinary presence requires two things, Sartre must turn extraordinary and appeal to *nil* in order to account for the facts of experience.

Sartre's whole purpose in appealing to the *néant* is to get the human will out from underneath the great dead weight of unfree being. He takes great pains to convince us that the *nil* is a real cause. Imagination, perception, and intellection are all described in terms of their dependency upon nothingness. All specifically human acts are breaks with being. The For-Itself must be constantly nihilating its world; everywhere the In-Itself must be ruptured in order for a person to be a person. In practice this means a high regard for the pushing back of frontiers, for aggressiveness. We should not be surprised to learn that Sartre and people like Ernest Hemingway were friends.

Yet how can nothing explain anything, especially presence-to-self or to another? Ordinarily, things present to each other must be *qualified* realities with positive traits which can act upon one another. A "nothing" might mean simply an impossible being, such as a square circle. But this is not what Sartre means. He claims to be *forced* into asserting the reality of something unqualified, an absolute nothingness. Far from being impossible, "it" is supposed to explain being human in the most profound way. It seems that the absurd, *de trop* world, in order to be a significant something, must be explained by an equally absurd nothing.

In opposition to Sartre, though, we know that this cannot be. Even the "space" of science is not characterless. It is filled with forces, described in equations, shaped to matter, and so on. Even Aristotle's prime matter is not nothing. A totally unqualified, propertyless nothing cannot even be imagined, perceived, or thought. The best we can ever do is a relative negation or privation of something. On the *nil*-question, therefore, I think it is safe to give a negative decision on its rationality. Everything we know in any rational way tells us that "nothing" cannot account for anything. If one is *forced* into such a situation it does not mean that one is right about *nil*; it means that one's premises were wrong somewhere along the way. Neither common-sense nor foundational analysis is so tolerant as to allow the use of nothing to account for something. If Allan Bloom is correct in pronouncing the emperor of modern thought (Heidegger) intellectually naked, then I think the same must be said of Heidegger's erstwhile disciple Sartre.

As a consequence of this failure in the philosophy of being, Heidegger and Sartre are also ethically naked. Both thinkers produce an amorphous amoralism in terms of the concrete results of their doctrines. Heidegger's monism, and Sartre's last-ditch attempt to wring out of being some room for human freedom, both result in moral systems (or non-systems) which are capable of accommodating any sort of political and social policy. For Heidegger, we must go with what the cultural forces are saying to us *now*. For Sartre, who did not care for the restrictive nature of such a collectivism, hell is other people, and as he states in *Being and Nothingness* (III: 3, iii), "The essence of the relations between consciousnesses is not *Mitsein*; it is conflict." In neither case do we have any objective measure of right and wrong.[25]

Thus it stands with Sartre's desubstantializing of reality. In contrast to Heidegger, Sartre was more direct in his attack, but no less destructive in his doctrine. All this, according to foundational analysis, depends upon the acceptance of his initial premises. The deconstruction of Yahweh depends upon the previous construction of the non-reconcilable opposites of Being and Becoming, God and time, perfection and temporality. It may be that a different sort of "existentialism" would render such dichotomies inoperative. It may be that what is required is a return to the religious meaning of existentialism, one which goes back even beyond Kierkegaard and Pascal.

That "existentialism" did possess a religious meaning well before the advent of Sartre on the intellectual scene is clear from the writings of thinkers such as Gabriel Marcel. In the introduction to a collection of three of his essays, entitled *The Philosophy of Existentialism* (1956), Marcel claims that the main lines of French existentialism were set out in a 1925 essay of his entitled "Existence and Objectivity." At the time he had not yet read any of Kierkegaard, who was then almost unknown in France. This occurred, he reminds us, even before either Heidegger or Jaspers had published their main works. That its religious meaning was also known to the atheistic existentialists is clear from the writings of Sartre's contemporary, Albert Camus.

This can be seen, for example, in Camus's *Le Mythe de Sisyphe,* published in 1942. In this work Camus uses Kierkegaard as an example of the "sacrifice of the intellect" and the "almost intentional mutilation" of the mind and consciousness. Camus has no use whatsoever for Kierkegaard's "leap of faith" which was regarded as so necessary by Kierkegaard in order to overcome the failings of thought. Given the choice between a leap of faith in order to reach other persons and God, which would then make life meaningful, and the despair of having to live on in a meaningless world, maintaining and filling one's consciousness as best one can, the "absurd man" must choose the latter.

The world in which we live, claims Camus, is a muddled, unclear, unnerving, unsettling, precarious place which cannot be perfectly known and understood, even by science. Anyone who tries to overcome its meaninglessness by some leap of faith, whether in science, philosophy, or religion, is a basically dishonest person. And to be dishonest is to commit philosophical suicide; to die a death of self-consciousness; it is to kill the one thing which must be preserved above all else. And this is exactly what the "existentialists" do. "I am taking the liberty at this point of calling the existential attitude philosophical suicide," says Camus.[26]

Yet it is precisely this attitude which, Camus feels, must be invoked if we are to cross the line from naturalism to supernaturalism, from anthropocentrism to theocentrism. *Anyone* who claims, thinks Camus, that there is some world other than the one we live in, with our present senses and consciousness, such that if this world should perish the other one would continue to exist, is doing violence to his or her own consciousness. Camus is certainly not opposed to artistic imagination and creative fictionalizing. He did, after all, engage in such activity himself. What he cannot abide, however, is the assertion that these other worlds really and objectively exist. But this is exactly what Kierkegaard was saying, based upon his "leap."

Kierkegaard, as a religious thinker, had decided that philosophical rationalism and natural science had gotten *so* out of hand, especially as found in Hegel, that the only way to counteract them was to move to the opposite extreme. Objective scientific knowledge had to be pitted against subjective personal knowledge. He saw a fundamental dichotomy between knowing about love and being in love, or knowing about religion and being religious, for instance. As far as he could see, thinking and existence were absolutely opposed. The more you *think,* the less you *exist.*

Kierkegaard's "existentialism" was an intellectualized anti-rationalism in the name of religion. Its emphasis was on intuitive ethical-religious feelings of a personal nature. Consequently, to talk about such things in religion as proving the existence of God made absolutely no sense to him. Human beings exist, and a sure sign of this is their unavoidable involvement in time. God, though, is eternal, out of time, and, as such, *completely other* when compared with human existence. Because we exist in time we cannot be God, and because God is eternal he cannot exist with us in time. Nevertheless, he is sure that God is love and constantly cares for us as individuals. This assurance is derived from Scripture and the "leap."

This also holds for our interpersonal relationships while we live on earth. For Kierkegaard, the only being I can know in an immediate, personal way is myself. As much as he rejected Hegel, and Hegel's overly rationalistic ways which reduced Jesus Christ to a non-divine bit part in a philosophical play, Kierkegaard's own approach to the self sounds very Hegelian. Kierkegaard states: "Man is spirit. But what is spirit? Spirit is the self. But what is the self? The self is a relation which relates itself to its own self, . . . by relating itself to its own self and by willing to be itself the self is grounded transparently in the Power which posited it."[27]

Despair is the worst disease that can afflict the self. It would mean the worst sort of war, a civil war, in which the self was at war with itself. It is *the* sickness unto death. It is bad enough to have it suffer eternal death after death, but to have to begin the process while still alive is even worse. Kierkegaard's point is that despair is the result of being conscious of our lack of wholeness, integrity, and self-fulfillment. Hell is the state of being eternally separated from God, the only source of our self-completion and self-fulfillment. Hell is the personal conscious awareness that I (not somebody else) will *never* be whole, integral, and self-fulfilled. Hence despair is hell on earth. This is the condition of the *thinking* person who does not accept the personal existence and presence of God as a fact.[28]

In order to possess myself, therefore, I must possess God. Thinking, though, will not grant me such possession. Contra Descartes, I am not a thinking thing; if I think, I am not. For Kierkegaard, the only real thing I know subjectively is myself. Likewise for other subjects (persons). Each one is incommunicable. Everyone is radically alone. The only way to bridge the gap is through an individual leap of faith, wherein we do not reach the mere appearance of the other (the other as object, his or her body, words, documents left behind, and so forth), but the other as he or she is in himself or herself. Such a relationship is always immediate, present, individual, and personal. Likewise for our relationship to God. We must be like Abraham, who assented to God's will without knowing all the whys and wherefores. In a very Pelagian fashion we must hurl ourselves across the rational gap to God.

According to Kierkegaard, humans are always trying to do the impossible, namely, to synthesize eternity and time. If we could do it, we would achieve "being," but at the price of giving up our *human* existence. The very function of existence is to prevent this, that is, to exclude us from eternity. The only real *being* is God. Compared with human beings, therefore, God is *completely* other. Existence is what keeps us from being God. In contrast to human nature, God does not think, he wills; God does not exist, he is eternal.

Existence in humans is a constant failure to be real being, in the Greek sense of being, that is, the eternally immutable. This is a pathetic, comic, and miserable condition to be in. Hence our anguish, nausea, and absurdity. The doctrine of existence as the permanent rupture of being is the starting point of modern Atheistic Existentialism. This, however, was not Kierkegaard's intention. Nevertheless, his return to Greek Being (the divine, immutable, unchanging essence), which he placed in opposition to temporal existence, could easily lead in that direction. If we cannot have both essence (being) and existence (becoming in time), and if we want to remain in contact with human experience, we had better choose the latter and reject the former. It is either reason or religion.[29]

Sartre, in *L'Existentialisme est un humanisme,* states that "Dostoievsky once wrote 'If God did not exist, everything would be permitted'; and that, for existentialism, is the starting point."[30] This, though, is certainly an oversight on Sartre's part. The Death-of-God declaration cannot be the beginning of modern existentialism for the simple reason that it has obviously been around a long time before both Dostoyevski and Nietzsche. The real historical foundation for modern Atheistic Existentialism is the religious dilemma described by Kierkegaard in the first half of the nineteenth century, namely, the irreconcilable opposition he thought existed between the Absolute and time. Such a dichotomy, one which forces us to choose one side or the other as the significantly, meaningfully, and authentically real, would indeed rip apart the comfortable world of the petty bourgeois pseudo-intellectual, just as Sartre emphasized. The Death of God, as was done by Sartre himself in his *Being and Nothingness,* is then deduced from this starting point.

This is something Nietzsche himself knew very well. In his *Joyful Wisdom* (Book V, section 357) Nietzsche pinpoints the whole problem for us. Hegel, who taught that later kinds of things develop out of previously existing kinds, prepared the way for the last great scientific movement, namely, Darwin's evolutionism. At root the great modern problem is how to reconcile being and becoming, which also happens to be the great ancient problem as well. Unlike the Latins, says Nietzsche, the Germans are naturally evolutionists: "we hardly believe at all in the validity of the concept 'being.'"[31] By this he means immutable, self-identical Greek Being. With the passing of Being pessimism is sure to follow. Any "astronomer of the soul" worth his salt could have predicted to the day and hour the advent of Arthur Schopenhauer (1788–1860), the first true atheist. All of Europe, largely via the victory of scientific atheism, has contributed to the decay of the belief in the Christian God. This is now a universal European event in which all nations are to have their share of service and honor.

Ultimately, the Death of God is supposed to usher in a brave new world for all future generations. The door is now open for the advent of a true leader (the Superman) who will usher in an age of true progress. Because there is first the *Death of Being* there can be the Death of God, which in turn means the Death of Objective Morality. The twentieth century, as everyone now knows, has had enough of Supermen and their "progressive" ways; nevertheless the philosophical problem is still with us.

This great perennial problem is how to reconcile being-becoming, essence-existence, and so forth. In its later twentieth-century version, under the heading of Radical Hermeneutics and Deconstructionism, it becomes the fixed meaning vs. the changing interpretations, the content vs. the form, the truth vs. the symbol, sort of situation. If everything is a symbol, if everything is symbolic, then what is the symbol a symbol of? If the history of a thing is a part of the thing's essence (and maybe the whole of its essence), can the thing really have any essence at all? How can an ever-changing something-or-other have a fixed meaning? What is The Relative relative to?

Left in this form, the problem can only lead to the strangest modes of thought and expression, and very quickly to contradiction. We begin to hear that when X is present X is really absent, and vice versa. The blank is not blank, it is full, and vice versa. Science is really magic, and vice versa. The word is always a metaphor and what is "metaphor" but a word? There is no end to this sort of modern wordplay, and post-modern literature overflows with it.

God-talk must necessarily pass through the same grinder, and must come out as much minced as anything else. This is something which many modern atheistic existentialists share in common with many older theistic pantheists, namely, their inability to solve the being/becoming puzzle. Among the latter I would place thinkers such as Parmenides and Hegel. When speaking of Parmenides, for instance, Gilson points out that

> If we call *existence* the definite mode of being which belongs to the world of change such as it is given in sensible experience — and it should not be forgotten that we have no experience of any other type of reality — it then becomes obvious that there is a considerable difference between to be and to exist. That which exists [the world of the senses] is not, just as that which is [Being] does not exist. From the very beginning of the history of Western thought, it thus appears that, if being truly is, nothing should exist. In other words, there is nothing in being as such to account for the fact of existence. If there is such a thing as existence, either it has to be kept side by side with being, as something wholly unrelated to it — which is what Parmenides seems to have done — or else it will have already to pass for what modern existentialism says that it is: a "disease" of being.[32]

For Parmenides, Being (God, the Absolute) is, but does not exist.

When speaking in opposition to Hegel, Kierkegaard points out that

> Existence is always something particular, the abstract does not
> exist at all. . . . If thought could give reality in the sense of
> actuality [existence], and not merely validity in the sense of
> possibility, it would also have the power to take away existence,
> and so to take away from the existing individual the only
> reality to which he sustains a real relationship, namely, his
> own. . . . God does not think, he creates; God does not exist, He
> is eternal. Man thinks and exists, and existence separates
> thought and being, holding them apart from one another in
> succession. . . . Existence is not devoid of thought, but in
> existence thought is in a foreign medium.[33]

For Kierkegaard, simultaneously God is certainly real, is
certainly a particular being (that is, God exists), and is certainly
intimately present to those human beings who have faith. However,
he cannot *understand* how this can be the case. Hence the need for
his "leap of faith." We *believe* that God is completely other and yet also
close at hand. The Bible tells us so and *that* is what we must accept
as true even if our minds are not capable of grasping it.

Hegel, who insists that we must take Parmenides seriously as
the first philosopher of Pure Thought, cannot understand how
being and becoming can be compatible in one and the same world.
He is thereby forced into the very awkward position of having to
choose one over the other, the one being becoming.[34] That in turn
forces him into the ultimate irrationality of claiming to identify
Something and Nothing. Any modern who finds himself caught up
in Hegel's mind-set, such as Paul Tillich, Hans Kueng, John
Macquarrie, and even John Dewey must face the same insurmountable problems.

Kierkegaard wants nothing to do with Hegel's irrationalism and
pantheism, yet he is completely stymied by the philosophical problem
of reconciling the thinker and the religious believer. This then forces
Kierkegaard into the position of having to circumvent, and even
attack, reason in his deeply felt desire to preserve a place for religious
belief in human life.[35]

In modern times we find the same problem recurring. Heidegger
finds himself in the same situation when trying to speak of human-
being in relation to Being. In his 1949 introduction to his *What Is
Metaphysics?* (1929), Heidegger explains why his main work was
entitled *Being and Time* rather than "Existence and Time" or
"Consciousness and Time." The reason is that "existence" is too
restrictive a term. Existence is only a mode of Being. According to

Heidegger, *only* man exists. For Parmenides, anything that changes exists. For Kierkegaard, any particular thing exists. For Heidegger, however, the situation is much more restrictive. "Man alone exists. Rocks are, but they do not exist. Trees are, but they do not exist. Horses are, but they do not exist. Angels are, but they do not exist. God is, but he does not exist."[36] Man is the being that exists, but what of everything else? Being must somehow be, but the existence question is always subservient to the more fundamental issue of the concealed nature of Being, of that which is real, but which does not exist.

This shows us that we cannot take Heidegger at face value when he talks about God. Horses and God are all part and parcel of some more fundamental, but unintelligible, Great I-know-not-what. As with James, who uses the word "truth" but who does not mean it in any ordinary sense, as with Hegel, who uses the word "God" but who does not mean it in any traditional monotheistic sense, so with Heidegger who, for all his talk of "angels," "God," the "gods," the "divine," and so on, uses such terms simply to make a linguistic point. In his own mind their meanings have been so changed from their traditional monotheistic sense that only a follower of some monistic or pantheistic doctrine, such as Hinduism, would recognize what he is trying to say.

In addition the self is also deconstructed. The Hindu notion of *maya,* the illusion of the separate and independent existence of the individual human being, or anything else, comes to the fore once more. The manifold and variegated world of sense experience is only the superficial manifestation of something more profound (Brahman). Being, not beings, is the object of Heidegger's interest. All "things" are dissolved in this primeval force; all divisions, dichotomies, and oppositions are ultimately eliminated in the Singular Itself.

In other words, if God exists and if God is present to us, it can only be as a secondary and passing feature of Brahman. God, as a Supreme Being who cannot be identified with the world in any way, is only in the imagination, a symbol of something, a work of poetry, a metaphor. The harder we work at it, the more we realize we are running in circles. Even if we win some minor victories of understanding, we can never leave the social-linguistic game. It is like gambling in an ornate casino. Even if we win we can never leave the casino with our winnings; all we can do is to go on playing until we expire. It is an infinite process in which rocks, horses, gods, and people participate for a fleeting moment. In the end everything is a fiction, a fiction which we must joyfully accept as the ultimate wisdom — even while knowing it to be a fiction.

I would submit, however, that such a mental state is not even possible for the normal rational person. Self-consciously knowing that what we affirm as true, what we take as the foundation for our actions, what we claim as the justification for our decisions, and the like, is in fact false is not something which the normal person can live with. We can talk contradictions but we cannot really live them out. Nor is it necessary, I further submit, that the serious thinker be forced into such an outlandish position in the first place.

Why can we not have our religion and rationality, our eternity and temporality, and so on, simultaneously? What prevents us from being wholly integrated instead of being eternally torn asunder? Supermoderns such as Rorty look at the history of philosophy and despair. Others, such as Gilson, look at the history of philosophy and see that those who despair have missed the forest because of the trees. Realists contend that contained within the very history of its development can be found the reason philosophy might give such an impression to some. To the extent individual philosophers overlook, ignore, or deny the central importance of the philosophy of being, they are sure to fail in their efforts to comprehend reality in an integrated way. It is then an easy step to blame their failure on philosophy itself. In the later twentieth century Rorty is a perfect illustration of the syndrome Gilson was talking about early in the century.

Such a situation cannot last. The human person (as a whole), the true *homo humanus,* will not be satisfied with anything less than the full development of all of his or her capacities. To the extent one's deep-seated need for harmony and integration is not fulfilled and developed one is saddened and discontent; one suffers Kierkegaard's sickness unto death. This is true with respect to individuals, but it is also the foundation for all of our human social life. Thinkers such as Gadamer and Rorty, for instance, place a heavy emphasis upon the need for human community and solidarity. The human race belongs together, claims Gadamer, for better or for worse. It, and it alone, acting in unison, can hope to solve the problems of the world. God helps those who help themselves, and without God we have no choice but to help ourselves. In other words, the best Gadamer can offer us is a "for better or for worse" shotgun marriage.

Human or social solidarity seems to be the phrase *du jour.* What, though, is the foundation for such a claim? What is it that unifies the human race? How can we have a unified humanity when each human self is so deconstructed that it is not even there? Gadamer suggests that it is a doctrine carried over from the supposedly now defunct Judaeo-Christian tradition, but one important enough to be continued, simply because it is a necessity if the human race is to survive. If such an assertion does require a *fundamentum in re,* why not go back to the ancients, or to James, for some sort of World-Soul, One and Separate Intellect, or similar doctrine? In answer to the question, What is practice?, Gadamer states:

I would like to summarize: Practice is conducting oneself and acting in solidarity. Solidarity, however, is the decisive condition and basis of all social reason. There is a saying of Heraclitus, the "weeping" philosopher: The *logos* is common to all, but people behave as if each had a private reason. Does this have to remain this way?[37]

Contrary to Gadamer's pantheistic inclinations, the answer is yes. The alternative is to lose our individuality in the mass. Either that, or turn fanciful and eccentric in the fashion of Sartre and begin appealing to nothing to explain something. But what else can the Deconstructionist do? Having rejected the theocentric humanism of traditional monotheism, and having adopted the secular, anthropocentric humanism of Heidegger and Sartre, the typical post-modern is bound to make the best of an intellectually impossible situation.

Assuming that one fails to reconcile our dual human experiences of permanence and change, being and becoming, fixity (essence, science) and flux, and so forth, and then turns to an evolutionary pantheism, with or without Darwin's necessary progress, as a way of justifying the elimination of being in favor of becoming, one is bound to end up in a state of complete rational and moral confusion. The circle from an aimless pre-rationalized wandering about, to a rationalized account of becoming without being, and back to an aimless wandering about, adhered to via faith, in the form of pragmatism, is complete. This process parallels the geographical circle of moving from the Old World to the New World and then back again.

The post-rationalized situation, though, is different from the pre-rationalized situation, for *now* we *know* ourselves to be miserable, absurd, and in despair. And all because some philosophical runners, not just once but several times over the centuries, have not managed to make it over the first hurdle in the race to the goal of philosophical understanding.

THOMAS AQUINAS: SUPER-MODERNITY SUPERSEDED, "BEING" REMEMBERED

> Unde ipsum esse est actualitas omnium rerum, et etiam ipsarum
> formarum. (Hence existence is that which actuates all things, even
> their forms.)
>
> St. Thomas Aquinas
> *Summa Theologiae* I: 4, 1, ad 3

> Early in his *Summa* (q. 3, a. 4), Thomas establishes the funda-
> mental principle of his whole philosophy: only in God are essence
> (*quod est*) and existence (*esse*) identical; in creatures *esse* and *quod
> est* are really distinct, for creatures share, or participate, in the *esse*
> that is God. Upon this fundamental principle of his metaphysics
> Thomas constructs his theology of the One God, creation, and
> creatures.
>
> J. A. Weisheipl
> *Friar Thomas D'Aquino* (1974), 230

What has gone before does not contain anything absolutely new with
respect to the various thinkers discussed. What novelty there is
resides rather in the way certain aspects of their philosophies are
brought out and highlighted, in the way various factors within their
philosophies are juxtaposed and interrelated, and in the way the
thinkers are shown to be related to each other. Likewise for my
treatment of St. Thomas Aquinas. My intention here is to present a
highlighted version of just certain aspects of Aquinas's basic
philosophical vision, and to do it in a brief and concise manner.

In the preface to his *Being and Some Philosophers,* written at
mid-century, Gilson quotes at length a page from William James's
Some Problems of Philosophy (1911) in which James takes a moment
to define philosophy in the traditional way as the knowledge of things
in general by their ultimate causes as far as can be known by natural
reason. What happens next, though, from the viewpoint of an
existential philosophy of being, is not so good. James goes on to

interpret the definition to mean that one must develop a broad-minded attitude toward life and thought.

A philosophy is a world-view, a sweeping view of reality encompassing all aspects of one's life and environment. What this means, Gilson points out, is that philosophy is no longer a "wisdom" which comprehends some concrete ultimate thing or somebody, but is now only a general view of things which may or may not involve real beings. Instead of an ultimate real cause of things, we are left with an intramental attitude, disposition, and frame of mind. Realism has been squeezed out of philosophy, to be replaced with "broadness."

In Gilson's estimation this is a great loss. While the common-sense Realist can still be broad-minded, the Epistemological Idealist can no longer claim to *know* the real world. Although it is certainly true that all knowledge *qua* known resides in a personal subject, it should not be granted that the knowing subject determines all reality. From the intramental perspective it is possible for two or more philosophies to be equally sweeping yet mutually exclusive. But how then can they all be simultaneously true of reality in the ordinary meaning of the word "true"?

This highlights the need to seek out a *real* foundation for a theory of reality. A strictly personal truth will not do, even if every approach to truth is bound to be personal. There is no reason to suppose *a priori,* according to Gilson, that we cannot have both our personal view on the world and a true world-view simultaneously. To do it, though, means that we must be very careful about putting first things first.

> The only will that should be found at the origin of philosophy should be the will to know, and this is why nothing is more important for a philosopher than the choice he makes of his own philosophical principles. The principle of principles is that a philosopher should always put first in his mind what is actually first in reality.[1]

But what is first? Certainly *not* ideas. Only later do we come to reflect upon our own ideas of things. What is first are things or beings — something which possesses real extramental existence. In all of Thomistic philosophy there are only two principles: God and being. A principle is that from which something comes; it is the beginning, the origin, the source of whatever comes afterward. At the origin of everything that exists is God; and at the origin of our knowledge of anything is being. What we know first and foremost are not the *means* through which we know things (our ideas) but the things themselves, at least insofar as they are examples of something (essence) which is (existence). In fact we *never* know ideas directly; they are always the *means by which* we know the world.

This matter is not of belief or faith; it is a matter of knowledge. The *philosophical* knowledge we possess as ordinary human beings is not a matter of faith. And neither would be the moral system derived from it. It is rather something we do in fact see for ourselves. What is the difference between faith and the kind of knowledge I am talking about here? According to Bertrand Russell, for instance, faith is believing on the basis of nothing. He states:

> Christians hold that their faith does good, but other faiths do harm. At any rate, they hold this about the Communist faith. What I wish to maintain is that *all* faiths do harm. We may define "faith" as a firm belief in something for which there is no evidence. When there is evidence, no one speaks of "faith." We do not speak of faith that two and two are four or that the earth is round. We only speak of faith when we wish to substitute emotion for evidence.[2]

Saying something like this has a certain rhetorical effect, but just how accurate is it?

A better-balanced account can be found in St. Thomas Aquinas. Far from being based on nothing, faith must always have a firm foundation in the solid evidence of a trustworthy communicator of information. As even James realized, even in purely secular matters it is not possible to live without faith. As children growing up in a family, in working with others in society, in our law courts, in our study of history, and even as scientists who must trust the results obtained by other scientists, we cannot escape the need for trust and faith.

However, unlike seeing something directly for ourselves, faith must be based upon the word of another. Faith, for Aquinas, means the assent of the intellect to that which is believed. It is not an emotional response at all in its primary meaning, although, because of the psychosomatic character of human nature, it will ultimately involve the whole person. If we examine how the intellect operates in the process of assent, we find that it can assent directly to an object presented to it for consideration, as when we understand for ourselves that "Two and two are four" or that "John is mortal" because John is a man, and all men are mortal.

What, though, is the basis for assent when we either cannot or do not directly see something for ourselves? In such a case we must *choose* to assent based upon the word, testimony, evidence, and so on, presented to us by someone else, such as when a trustworthy traveler tells us about the existence of China, or when several independent witnesses tell us about some event which happened in the past.[3]

What is accepted on faith, however, need not always remain so. It is possible that something we now accept on faith will later become something which we see for ourselves. Even though I have never been to China, I have no doubt whatsoever about its existence on the basis of what I have heard from others. Some day, though, I might actually travel to China and witness for myself in a direct fashion the geography and people of that faraway land. In my present condition, though, I must continue to *believe* in China, not based upon nothing, but upon the accounts given to me in various ways by independent witnesses, with no reason to lie, and so on. "For whoever believes assents to someone's word."[4]

What does it mean to act on faith? Is it a sheer act of the will, founded on nothing? Is it an act of the will founded upon knowledge and supported by evidence? We have already seen in an earlier chapter how James, for instance, seems to treat it as a sheer act of the will. We also see in Sartre's *Being and Nothingness* and *Existentialism and Humanism,* for example, that the actor is expected to act without ulterior motives or excuses of any sort. He must never blame anyone or anything other than himself for his actions. By this Sartre does not mean merely that each normal human being is a responsible agent; even the religious thinkers he is attacking would agree with that. What he means is that we should not attempt to *justify* our actions by giving reasons for why we did or did not do such-and-such. The sheer fact that we *want* to do such-and-such should be a sufficient reason for us, according to Sartre.

With modification, this is still the situation we find among the post-moderns. Although there is a tendency among present-day post-modern thinkers to play down the hyper-individualistic side of anthropocentrism, since it can lead only to chaos in life, they nevertheless retain the collectivistic side of anthropocentrism. This is to say that both Hegel and Nietzsche, for example, despite their differences, were anthropocentric in their orientation. The same is true today with respect to thinkers such as Sartre and Rorty, or the Libertarians and Foucault, Derrida, and others directly inspired by Heidegger. The Individual Superman may be replaced by the Collective Superman, but human beings and only human beings continue to be the standard against which all right and wrong, true and false, are judged. The ancient Sophists, whether the more individualistic Protagoras or the more collectivistic and tribal Gorgias, are still the heroes of the day.

The situation with Aquinas is quite different. He too is firmly committed to human freedom, but it is a freedom operating within a natural world which is subject to fixed laws of operation. Wherever there is a nature there is a law. There is a great deal of determinism in the world, and if we are free it is not due to our complete exclusion from determinism, but to our ability for *self*-determination. In many ways we are not free to do whatever we want, either physically or psychologically. We are, for instance, fixed upon achieving our ultimate goal of happiness and self-fulfillment. There is also the necessary interplay of the intellect and the will. We are not, nor can we ever be, creatures of pure will. Although in our basic human nature we are fixed upon certain goals, for instance happiness, in our conscious lives we cannot want something we do not even know about.

In general the will follows the intellect. The operation of the will cannot be isolated from the intellect. There is a reciprocating relationship between these two powers. The will itself may be viewed in two ways: as a nature acting according to one predictable pattern, or as an agent allowing for variations in behavior. As a *nature* the will is no more free than sulfuric acid burning holes in your tablecloth, an acorn becoming an oak tree, or a cancer virus destroying the tissues of your small intestine. As a nature the will naturally and automatically inclines toward (loves) happiness and those goods which we intellectually judge will provide happiness. This means that there is no free will.

But what if there is nothing which the intellect *must* judge to be best here and now? The will need not necessarily desire things which do not clearly and obviously, as judged by the intellect, possess a necessary relationship to happiness. If there were such a known good (such as God) directly present to us, the judgment and consequent loving would be immediately predictable. However, God as our greatest good is not immediately and obviously present to us. Consequently, without some overpowering good attracting us, the will tends toward that finite good judged best here and now by the intellect. Now, since no finite good (for instance, a piece of pie as opposed to a piece of cake) necessarily determines the intellect, there is left open the possibility for the will to love one rather than the other. This means that there is free choice.

To know is to know something and to will is to will something. The intellect must specify the good. This, however, is insufficient to make the human agent act upon what is judged the "right" thing to do. It is the will which must determine the action actually to be done. Since no means to an end is absolutely necessary in the vast majority of our decision-making situations, the intellect cannot make a necessary judgment with respect to action. Another factor, the will, must come in to terminate deliberation and make the final choice. Since it is the will which terminates the reasoning, which decides the *last* choice, and the will is a power of the human agent, it is the person determining himself or herself. The result is freedom *within* necessity. You are determined by all sorts of forces as well as by your own nature. However, there is still the possibility for you to be *self-determined*.

Choice, then, is an act of the intellect *and* the will. It is not that there is a lack of motivation as if to be free means to act in a totally uncaused way. Quite contrary to the lack of a causal factor, there is a motivation, namely, the specific object of desire. When humans will, they always will something. Rather than being completely undetermined, in some cases we are undetermined by external forces. There is still determination, however, but it is a determination of one's self. We determine for ourselves how the means to an end (that is, the possible choices) are to be specified and at which point there will be a cutting off of deliberation. Therefore, human freedom is a *complex* act which cannot be explained by either a simple voluntarism or a simple intellectualism. All truly human decisions, both great and small, spring from the intellect and the will, knowledge and love, the head and the heart.[5]

These considerations, based upon real-life people and situations, are very important in understanding Aquinas's view of faith. Faith has a motive, and it does involve both the intellect and the will. This is true of both secular faith and religious faith. Faith, as is verified through everyday experience, is as much a secular necessity as it is a religious virtue. Faith, in its most fundamental meaning, does not mean belief based upon a total lack of evidence. It means belief based upon the word of another. *Whose* word determines whether it is anthropocentric or theocentric faith. And the reason for believing on the word of another is that the other person is judged to be worthy of our trust. Aquinas's approach to the definition of faith is therefore quite different from that commonly found today among those who take the "subjective turn." It is Realistic, based upon human nature as we actually find it to be.

We find that this is generally true of the whole approach of Aquinas to the world. He does not begin by arbitrarily defining things to suit himself, but rather begins with what is given and proceeds to build upon it. This "given" must be gotten from our fundamental experiences of the world in which we actually live. But what exactly is it that is given? What is most basic in our *Lebens-Welt* — our life situation as actually lived?

For Aquinas the ordinary human being comes before the scientific, philosophical, and theological human being. We know, feel, and think long before we ever start to act like a scientist, philosopher, or theologian. And later, when we do become active in one of these fields, the proper approach to take when analyzing reality is to keep first things first. This means that the philosophy of being must precede all other areas of philosophical inquiry. Thomists claim that this is in fact what happens, even though some groups of thinkers, such as the Stoics before Aquinas, and the post-moderns after him, make a habit of forgetting it. Especially since the time of Descartes, professional philosophers have been in the habit of trying to place logic, or the study of scientific methodology, or the study of human knowledge itself, first in the learning sequence. The result is always disastrous for the profession of philosophy, as we see in the post-moderns.

In the Thomistic arrangement of things, however, this should not be done. For example, the principle of non-contradiction is a secondary principle for Aquinas. The principle of non-contradiction states that something cannot both *be* and *not be* at the same time and under the same circumstances. Despite Hegel and the super-moderns, it is so fundamental to human thought that even to try denying it means having to use it. Yet, there is even something more fundamental in reality, the very foundation for the principle of non-contradiction itself, and that is *being*. The principle is basically about being, not about thoughts. The sheer fact that something should be, and be as a certain kind of thing, and exist in a certain way, is the rock-bottom foundation for all of human cognition and action. The principle of non-contradiction is founded upon being, not vice versa.

This approach, to be appreciated, should be seen in contrast to the approach of someone such as Russell. For example, with respect to the basic laws of logic, namely, the principles of identity, non-contradiction, and the excluded middle, he states that they are not the laws of *things* outside the mind but only linguistic devices within the mind. Outside the mind there are no real incompatibilities. The best we can do is to set up intramental linguistic conventions which allow us to talk about such really non-existent states of affairs. We see that intramentally you cannot both eat your cake and have it too, but (apparently) extramentally you can. This is exactly contrary to one's basic common sense. In the *real* world you cannot eat your cake and have it too, and it is this real world that is reflected in the logical world, not vice versa.[6]

The Thomistic claim is that this sort of thing is recognized by even the most uneducated human beings. There is a certain sort of complexity to reality which is known to all normal people. This complexity, inherent in both reality and in our knowledge of reality, may be called the distinction (of some sort) between essence and existence. This is the key to Thomistic *philosophy* that must always be kept in mind. In a Thomistic setting, ordinary human experience must be taken seriously by all concerned, especially by the philosophers and theologians who deal with the more ultimate reasons for things within our experience. And what could be more obvious than the fact that something exists? The problem is that maybe it is *too* obvious. Maybe we are too close to the side of the barn to see the barn. But then again, maybe, as we develop as *thinkers,* there is some other sort of peculiarity with existence which causes it to be pushed out of philosophy.

In fact, both of these problems are relevant to the situation we usually find in the philosophy of being. The tendency has always been to either overlook existence in our foundational analysis of reality because it is just there and should be taken for granted, or to dismiss it out of hand because it cannot be *thought,* that is, because it cannot be managed within the confines of a concept, a definition, a clear and distinct idea.

To develop this last point, in addition to our knowing *that* something is, another fundamental feature of our ordinary experience is our natural ability to know *what* something is. That is to say, our apprehension of some object, event, or state of affairs around us can be analyzed into at least *two* predominant parts. One is the apprehension of *what* the thing is, even if it is only as a "something." The other is an immediate judgment *that* the thing is. The first sort of knowledge is essentialistic; the second sort existentialistic. The first is of primary importance in science, mathematics, and logic; the second in philosophy. All of our knowledge, of any kind, even sense knowledge when incorporated into intellectual knowledge, which we as rational beings necessarily do, is by its nature *both* essentialistic *and* existentialistic knowledge. In this sense, *all* judgments, when first made about the world, are existential.

Furthermore, in contrast to essences, existence cannot be dealt with abstractly. There is no essence of existence. *What* a thing is always refers to the nature of *a* being; never to its existence. Yet existence is known, but it cannot be defined as we define a triangle as a plane closed three-sided figure or a human being as a rational animal. But how can we possibly claim to know something if we cannot say specifically *what* it is? A being is always an example of a particular *kind* of thing. But what *kind* of thing is existence?

This problem is sometimes taken as a reason for rejecting Aquinas's whole approach to being. In a nutshell, in the process of reasoning we must of course *think about* existence. As a result, we must conceptualize existence in the formal reasoning process. But, it is a fact that there can be no science of a subject without essences. If we are to understand the terms of the propositions used in the reasoning process, it is necessary to have an *idea* of existence; to *think* it as well as to grasp it via judgment. In this regard some comments by Joseph Owens are very much to the point.

Once again, the main problem seems to be with those who want to put logic and epistemology ahead of being. Owens readily admits that an existential proposition, like any other, may occur unasserted without any change of content. However, this is the case only when the thinker is carrying on like a logician, analyzing something which has *already* been conceptualized. It is possible to analyze the proposition "The weather is sunny" in front of a class taking place during a tropical hurricane, but no one *judges* that the day is sunny. The proper existential judgment is that the proposition in question exists in their minds as they analyze it. Likewise for "Dodos exist," and so on.

Owens also readily admits that unless conceptualized, existence cannot function as the subject of any discourse. "But how does the claim that existence is originally known through judgment entail the suicidal conclusion that existence is not conceptualizable?" Rather, it is the case that the actuality grasped via judgment is spontaneously conceptualized by the human knower as "existence." Aquinas is very clear about assigning the grasp of a thing's existence to a composing type of knowledge which goes beyond clear and distinct ideas. Owens states that: "In the texts the judgment grasps a composing actuality that is conditioned through and through by time, an actuality that is other than the timeless aspect of essence or nature represented through conceptualization."[7]

In any event, in our apprehension of the world around us we are as sure of the existence of things as we are of the fact that they have generic and specific natures. In fact, there is generally an inverse relationship between the certainty of our knowledge and its precision; that is, for example, you are more sure of the fact that you are alive and reading this here and now than you are of the exact number of words on the page or the specific nature of the kind of thing that is being discussed here.

It is for this reason that the old formula for the definition of knowledge, namely, the matching up of the thing and the intellect (*adequatio rei et intellectus*), must be very carefully interpreted if it is going to apply to Aquinas's theory of knowledge. It could be interpreted as meaning simply the matching up of a thought with itself, the correlation of one abstraction with another, for example, as with Descartes's equating of his idea of matter with three-dimensional extension or space. In this case, as with all Epistemological Idealisms, to talk about the *idea of something* and to talk about the *something,* would be a tautology. In a theory of reality in which the theory of knowledge comes first, the real is simply a projection of the rational, such that they *must* match up.

This is the root of Modern Philosophy (1600–1945) and something which the post-moderns have not yet managed to uproot. Descartes was the last of the decadent medieval scholastics and the first modern scholastic. Despite their difficulties with Descartes, later thinkers continued the "subjective turn." Locke and Hume, for instance, rejected innate ideas, claiming instead that the mind is like a blank tablet on which an impression is made. (For Hume, an idea is a faded impression.) This sounds like it should be very realistic, but it is not. The reason it is not is that, rather than knowing the thing which made the impression, according to such thinkers all we really know is the impression. It is not the thing we know but a *copy* or *representation* of the thing, like the mark left in wax by a ring.

This is in sharp contrast to Aquinas and common-sense realism, which maintains that there is in fact only *one* thing existing both extramentally and intramentally. To account for this state of affairs, though, it requires the real distinction between essence and existence, something we are not allowed to have according to the theory-driven views of the post-moderns. We are not even allowed to have essences, much less a real distinction between essence and existence.

In contrast, nonetheless, our experience tells us that conceptual knowledge *cannot* be a representation or copy of the thing known. For if this were the case there would be at least two things (the real thing and the concept) and hence there would arise an infinite regress as we desperately tried bridging one gap after another. The result would be no knowledge at all of anything, certainly not of anything outside of our own mind. Even though knowing them to be wrong, and knowing them to be the truly naïve ones in this particular matter, I can nevertheless sympathize with the post-mdoern thinkers. If I were in their shoes, I too would be forced into a position where it makes sense to reduce all human endeavor to play and parody.

But we do contact reality in our knowledge of the world. And we do this via judgment, the central act of human knowing. Only in judgment do we grasp existence. The verb, as Heidegger knew full well, is very important. What he did not understand is why this is the case. The verb is the only indispensable word in a sentence. We can see this by trying to construct one without a verb. This is because a sentence, in its most primary *human* meaning, is an expression of judgment, which is an expression of essence *and existence*. Merely joining together a series of "whats" (for example, "pink elephant") does not make a judgment. Neither does a logical copula, as in a definition, such as "A human being is a rational animal." Whereas logic always squeezes out existence, even when analyzing existential propositions, real-life judgments always say something about existence.

Because of this intimate connection with existence, the judgment is the proper home of truth and falsity. When we have judged properly concerning the existence (or non-existence) of something, then and only then can the thinker reflect upon that fact and say to himself or herself that the judgment is true. Thus truth and error, in their most fundamental meaning, reside *only* in the judgment, and not in an idea or some combination of ideas. Truth, fully understood, has a place only in the self-conscious mind which is in contact with the existential world. The reality, though, that is known by means of concepts and judgment, is not merely a creation of the mind.

In this sense, then, epistemology can never come first in our foundational analysis of our lived-world. Asking questions such as "What am I doing when I know something?", "What is doing that knowing?", and "What do I know when I know?" is an important philosophical undertaking, but it cannot be the primary consideration. The whole Epistemological Idealistic tradition from Descartes onward, including important twentieth-century religious thinkers such as Bernard Lonergan, maintains that it is primary. Common-sense experience, however, says otherwise.

Existentially speaking, *esse* is always first in cognition, and remains so even in self-knowledge. For an intellectual being, "to be" is to be a knower. Properly speaking, "thinking" is only knowing your own thoughts. "To know," however, is to think about an actually existing outside thing. All knowledge of the real is a vital interplay between two existences. This is immediate or natural realism, and what is meant by Aquinas's Realism. In the knowing process, to become another is also to be myself. This always takes place in a sensory empiricistic surrounding. In real life it always takes an existential act to answer another existential act. Specifically human relations, which always depend upon our specifically incarnated human powers of intellect *and* will, cannot avoid community if we are *to be* fully *what* we are.

Hence, for Thomas, humans are necessarily social beings. This does not mean, however, that we are somehow deprived of our own individuality. It means that there is much more to social relationships than merely biological or utilitarian considerations. Our very nature demands communication for fulfillment. This means that any philosophy, whether ancient sophistical or modern deconstructionist, which rules out in principle the very possibility for a real communication, a real meeting of the minds of different individuals who are truly unified selves, is in fact anti-humanistic, regardless of how much it might continue to talk about the *humaniora* or human solidarity.

The best beings to communicate with are God, angels, and humans. Normally, though, given the fact of Original Sin, we spend our time talking only to each other. Failing this, we try talking to our pet dog or the roses in the garden or to ourselves. However, since communication requires personal presence, talking to our pet dog or the flowers is not really satisfying to us. Even just talking to ourselves is not really satisfying for very long because, as we saw in an earlier chapter, we are not really two beings.

Also, our awareness of existence, the judgments we make affirming it, our comprehensions concerning what it is that exists, and our striving after what we judge to be good and what we consequently want to preserve in existence or bring into existence, are what make us personal beings on the level of empirical observation. The *explanation* of the fact is another matter. According to Aquinas, we do not know directly and immediately the nature of our own soul. It must be reasoned to on the basis of the facts of experience, especially of extramental events. In the reasoning process, though, we do not deny what is first and fundamental in all of our experience, namely, being (essence *and* existence), even in the experiences of our own ideas. Being is always first and remains present throughout the entire knowing process, even if it is just the process of knowing ourselves.

If what was said above is true, the question becomes: How are existential judgments possible? The answer is that in the real world there must be some sort of distinction between essence and existence that the human being is spontaneously capable of grasping. In other words, just as the realm of communication must exceed that of words, so the realm of the intelligible must exceed that of concepts. The reality described by words is always greater than its abstract definitions and characteristics. In the knowing process, abstractions (concepts) distinguish one thing from another. Judgments, however, unite and relate things existentially. Knowledge via concepts is essentialistic; that via judgments is existentialistic. In actual knowing situations the two always go together. Whereas mere naming need not be, all acts of judging, when first made, are existential.

But if there is some sort of distinction between the concept of the thing as it exists in the real world and the "to be" or "act of existing" of that same thing, what are our options when it comes to deciding exactly what sort of distinction is present and operative? To answer this question we must define "identity," "distinction," and the three types of distinction as they were understood by Aquinas.[8]

> *Identity*: Only one reality; a unity without duality or plurality.
> *Distinction*: Simply non-identical; there is some sort of multiplicity.
> *Logical, mental, rational, conceptual distinction*: A distinction made by the mind between at least two factors which are extramentally identical. Prior to thinking about it, there is only one thing; afterward, two or more distinct concepts refer to the *one* thing. For example, 60 minutes–1 hour; dime-coin-money.
> *Verbal distinction*: The use of different names for the same thing or for the same concept. If a distinction is between neither physical factors nor intentional factors, it is verbal. For example, Man-anthropos; you–your father's son or daughter.
> *Real distinction*: When two or more factors are extramentally non-identical.

A real distinction is not necessarily a separation. If the principles or factors upon which the distinction is based are not within the same being, we would have a separation. Sam and Sally are separate beings. All separations are real distinctions; *but only some real distinctions are separations.* Time and place, quality and quantity, height and weight, speed and direction, color and humanness, for instance, are really distinct without being separated in a real thing. Of much greater significance in philosophy are things like potency and act (matter and form) and essence and existence. The real distinction of essence and existence *means* that the essence of any extramental or intramental being is really other than the existence of that being as that being exists here and now.

We cannot arrive at the reality of the real distinction by comparing a real being (you, for example) with a fictitious being (Popeye, for example). You exist; Popeye does not. If it is to be established at all, it must be in a really existing thing, whether intramental or extramental. It is also more than the difference between a thing's definition and its instantiation. If there is a real distinction it must be *within* the instantiation of the thing. We can, however, get some notion of what a real distinction between essence and existence would be like by looking at the relationship between our comprehension of existence and logical-type distinctions.

Mentally, essence is always given priority over existence. This is the basis for Idealism, which begot pantheism, which begot intellectual fatigue and discouragement, which begot Deconstructionism. It then becomes very easy to try thinking of existence as something added to a somehow previously existing (in some very strange way) "possible." What does it mean to talk about a real possibility, or a remote possibility? It means that some essence is more or less close to being an actuality; a definition becomes progressively more instantiated.

But how can we talk about, or even think about, an essence without existence? The fact is we cannot. Even a concept is a being. It cannot be something upon which existence is conferred later. It must either exist now or be nothing at all. Rather than existence being added to an essence, it must be the other way around. Every essence is an aspect of a dynamic being. Possibles *qua* possibles have absolutely no existence at all. Every being is dynamic

We can, though, in many cases *logically* distinguish one thing from another. This is best shown by way of some examples. I know that iron is metal. Yet, I also know that I can *understand* metal without iron. Chemistry tells us that there are metals which are not iron. This makes them logically distinct, but not really distinct. In the real world every piece of iron *is* metal. Another example would be: All humans are animals. Here we use one concept for the subject and another for the predicate. But in reality every human being *is* an animal; every *real* human is a *real* animal. We can see from these examples what is meant by a logical distinction.

In general we can say that all differences between genera and species (for instance, metal-iron; animal-human), as well as all differences between genera and what accounts for the differences among species within the same genus (for example, human– *rational* animal), are only logical distinctions. If they were really distinct I would be able to say that iron *is not* metal, that humans *are not* animals, or that humans *are not* rational, and so forth.

In general with respect to essence and existence, Aquinas's main point is that existence must be prior to essence in all cases. We cannot even think of a being's essence outside of the mind except as something posterior to existence. Such a being must be an actuality, and must be viewed as such even mentally. Thus in *all* cases real being must precede logical being.

Let us see how this applies to something as basic as potency and act (matter and form). If there were no real distinction between potencies and actualities, any one thing would actually be everything it could possibly be here and now. You would be seated and standing, the water would be hot and cold to the same degree, at the same time, and under the same circumstances, and the like. In other words, there could be no change *within* being. To make sense of ordinary experience, potency and act (matter and form) must be more than logically distinct. Even though in *one* being, they are really distinct. This is something which Aristotle understood, and it marked a great advance over Plato.

The real distinction of potency and act divides every form of experienced being, whether intramental or extramental, substance or accident. Every genus, for example, is potential to its differences; the species come about via added forms or acts. For instance, this substance is generically metal and specifically iron. It is also at the base of all substantial changes. For example, this paper is actually paper but potentially ashes; this hydrogen and oxygen are actually hydrogen and oxygen, but potentially water. The list of examples could be extended indefinitely.

Within any one actually existing being we can also distinguish its *first act* (*what* it is) from its *second act* (its operations, its "actions"). All second acts presuppose first acts; all activity presupposes the existence of some definite sort of thing. Because my finger exists, I might be able to move it. When moving, the second and first acts exist simultaneously. A real unmoving finger is actually a finger, but potentially a moving finger. The first and second acts are really distinct. What this means is that no acting thing can be identified with its activities. A heart is *not* its beating. A human soul is *not* its thinking. Such a distinction is not a separation; the distinct elements exist in *one and the same* being.

Consider the situation if there were no real distinction between act and potency (form and matter). We would then be in the situation advocated by someone such as Sartre at the beginning of his *Being and Nothingness*. As we have already seen, for Sartre existence precedes essence only in the sense that the human subject comes first, in an undetermined and empty way, and then, via his or her "nothingness," makes himself or herself to be *what* he or she is. He or she *is* his or her actions.

The same sort of thing can be found tacitly stated in Kant. The philosopher Moses Mendelssohn (1729–1786), in his work *Phaedon* (1767), had defended the immortality of the soul on the speculative grounds that the soul is a simple substance and cannot in any way undergo a decomposition. Hence, once in existence, it must remain in existence forever (barring annihilation by God). Kant disagreed. Kant's rebuttal to this argument is, in effect, to deny a real distinction between the first and second acts of the soul. For Kant, in a very Cartesian fashion, the substance of the soul *is* its faculties, especially its consciousness. Even though without quantitative parts, its "intensive quantity" can gradually lose "parts" and thus fade away to nothingness. Consciousness comes in degrees, and we can imagine a gradual diminution of consciousness until nothing is left. Hence, even if not by decomposition, the powers of the soul can be lessened until it has been changed into nothing.[9]

If we were ever to accept such a situation, we would soon find ourselves face to face with insurmountable problems with respect to our personal self-identity. This problem existed long before Kant, Sartre, and the post-moderns and derived from the idea that we are merely a collection of loose parts. The body is a collection of little atoms; the mind is a collection of atomistic impressions and perceptions, as with David Hume, for instance. Especially with respect to the mind, how can someone be one thing, one and the same thing, for a long period of time if he or she is in fact only a subset of his or her actions? What could the person possibly be: a transitory series of chemical reactions, memories, rope-like pieces or strands of fiber which somehow hold together so as to provide a false and fake sort of unity for a while, or ... None of these, however, match up with the facts of experience.

Denying the real distinction between potency and act soon leads to the most unintelligible situations imaginable. If to be a human being means only to be a thinker, how could someone ever be a hearer, a runner, a lover, or anything else? A baseball pitcher would always have to be pitching. A computer would always have to be computing, and so on and so forth. But we know that these situations are contrary to fact.

It would also mean that any change from one activity to another must be a substantial change. For a living organism it would mean that every change in activity would be a death, to be reborn again as something else — over and over again, thousands and thousands of times a day. If a dog were equal to its seeing, it would have to die in order to be reborn immediately as a hearer, and so forth.

Also, as a development of what was just said above, if an agent were identical to its activity, there would be no potency to perform that activity at some other level. It would be forever stuck at whatever level of activity at which it was performing. For example, a thinker would never be able to learn anything new, and so on. There would be no degrees of consciousness or learning or anything else for one and the same being.

Let us look again at Descartes. When we talk about *what* something is, we are defining it. And once it is defined, we can expect the thing to remain what it is. If and when it does change into something else, we will also have to change its definition and start referring to it as something new and different. When hydrogen and oxygen get together under the right circumstances, for instance, they lose their identities as two separate substances and become something new, namely, water. We can still talk about water as hydrogen and oxygen, but only in terms of what it was, or what it may become in the future, not in terms of what it is now.

Another way of putting this is to say that whatever pertains to the essence of something is *always* with it. If something is defined as a thinking substance, it must always be thinking. Descartes identified his soul with a faculty; an action with a potency. Because he *started* his analysis with ideas, he was led to model extramental reality after his ideas. Now, all properly defined ideas are clear and distinct. But what happens if every mental distinction becomes an extramental separation? This means that every *real* thing is *essentially* individuated, that is, actually separated *in reality* from every other real thing. For Descartes, a real distinction is a real separation; he failed properly to distinguish the first and second acts of a being.

In order to avoid these impossible situations we must become more empirical. Just as existence must precede essence, so the philosophy of being must precede epistemology, phenomenological or otherwise. Failing to do this will lead to a confusion of distinction and separation, and the result of confusing distinction with separation is either an exaggerated realism or a nominalism. If *universality* is of the essence of a thing, it must exist extramentally as universal (hence Plato's Ideas). If *individuality* is of the essence of a thing, it must exist as an individual everywhere and anywhere, including within the mind (hence nominalism). In fact, both epistemologies begin within the mind, that is, with the way we approach things via ideas. However, regardless of which extreme we embrace, neither one matches up with experience which demands *both* universality (unity, science, commonality) *and* individuality (uniqueness, separatedness) *simultaneously* in the process of understanding our world as really lived.

The way to avoid these extremes is to be more empirical. We come to know what a thing is by observing what it does. In contrast, someone like Hume *was not* empirical; he *began* with the same identification of distinction and separation as did Descartes and *deduced* his conclusions. Not surprisingly, his results contradicted our ordinary common-sense experiences of practically everything. He ended up denying the reality of the self, the extramental reality of causality, the natural moral law, and so on. But to do so he had to begin by *not* observing the way things are.

For example, a bell is not a bell because we call it such, or because it rings. Rather, because it sometimes rings (in conjunction with other effects) we know it is a bell. An animal is not alive because it reproduces, but vice versa. Twins are not twins because they look alike, but vice versa. Does a weather vane change the wind's direction? Do the moving trees make the wind blow? The empirical realism of Aquinas tells us first to observe, and then offer some explanation for things which sticks to the facts of observation. This is being both empirical and rational.

And what does observation teach us? For one thing we learn that reality is not simple like a clear and distinct concept. It is complex; and any one real thing is complex. A real being is distinguishable (not necessarily separable) into various aspects and layers. And it may be that what is potential (material in the Aristotelian sense) on one level is actual (formal) on another level.

But exactly how is reality complex? How are the hierarchies that we see in nature, and the interacting substantial structures that we see around us, to be explained? To account for the facts of experience we must answer the question: What is it that everything has in common, but that no two things have in exactly the same way? This problem can be solved if we take "being" analogously. To say that being is analogous is to say that within each being there must be something which makes things *both* the same *and* different. If that something made things only the same, being would be univocal; that is, its meaning would be exactly the same every time it is applied, for example, when we say that Sam and Joe are *human beings*. If that something made things only different, being would be equivocal; that is, its meaning would be completely diverse every time it is applied, for instance, when we talk about the *bark* of a tree and the *bark* of a dog. As analogous, though, for example, when we refer to the *head* of a nail and the *head* of a man, being can account for unity *amid* diversity, change *within* being, and so on.

This can only be achieved by taking existence seriously. Each being has its own act of existing; *esse* is *diverse* in each being. Take, for example, the proportion 2/4 = 7/14. The numbers are not equal to each other, but the ratios are; 2 has no more in common with 7 than with 4 or 14. The parts of the ratio (a proportion among four elements) are not alike because they have the same components. If they did they would be univocal, as, for instance, animality and rationality in each human being. Humans are not *like* each other; insofar as each is a human, they are the *same*.

Analogously speaking, however, things are the same because they have the same relationship of component aspects. When being is understood in its proper and fullest sense, no two real things have numerically the same existence and essence. But the related components are the same. Saying that this angel is a being, this man is a being, this worm is a being, and so on, means, in general, that this individual's essence is to its *esse* as the other's is to its, and so forth. Having something in common does not mean that we are ultimately all one common being as in pantheism. Rather, in the hierarchy of beings, in which *all* beings are real, different things must contain *diverse* factors, but the *factors* (acts of existing) are not different; it is the beings which are different.[10]

Unless we are going to play arbitrary linguistic games, this linguistic usage makes perfect sense. Only things that differ can be alike. Obviously, *two* things must differ; just as two *things* must not differ. Difference presupposes composition. Difference means *both* diversity *and* sameness, just as does similarity. Saying that Toronto is *like* New York means that they have something in common. But it also means, as anyone can understand, that Toronto *is not* New York.

The division does not proceed to infinity. The explanation of how all beings can be real *and* of how there can be many unique individuals in the same species, can only be found within an existential philosophy of *being,* one in which diverse (not different) acts of existing are found in each being. The real distinction between essence and existence is the very heart of Aquinas's philosophy, the very foundation upon which rests the *explanatory* power of his form of faith seeking understanding.

By means of the real distinction, for example, Thomas can solve the ancient problem of universals in such a way that *all* the data of experience are preserved. This ancient philosophical problem asks, How can the same thing be predicated of many singulars in exactly the same literal way? John, Mary, Sam, and Sally, for instance, are all different, yet they are all *equally* human beings. How can this possibly be the case? What accounts for human solidarity? How can any *individual* thing be in a *species,* class, set, and so on?

Over the centuries various non-Thomistic thinkers have attempted to answer this question, but always in such a way as to deny at least part of the data. Some have said that *only* the class *name* is common, that in fact there are no real groups of things with something really in common outside of the name we apply to the individual members. There is, for instance, no such thing as *a* human species. There are only individual things which we arbitrarily cover with the same label for some private reason or other. This is nominalism.

Others have claimed that only the mental concept is really common to all the members of the set. Genera and species are only convenient mental constructions without any extramental counterparts in the natural world. This is conceptualism.[11]

Still others assert that the universal is indeed real, so much so that the individual becomes unreal. As far as this group is concerned the singular does not exist. The class is reified and is more real than the individual. This has traditionally been called exaggerated realism and can be found in Plato, Hegel, fascism (the State), and nazism (the *Volk,* the Race).

The Thomistic position is a fourth possibility, quite different from the others. According to Aquinas, there is a real distinction between the essence and existence of a thing, such that the same essence (nature, "what," definition) can exist in the human mind as a universal and outside the mind as a singular entity. The class has a real foundation in nature independent of the knower, which is reflected in the concept, and which is ultimately derived from its idea in God, while it is also objectively true that only the singular *exists* extramentally. The real world is populated with singulars, but they are nonetheless grouped into types of things which form a hierarchy in terms of their dignity and worth. In this hierarchy, it should be emphasized once again, *all* the beings are real.

With respect to human beings, one's uniqueness shows up in one's body, as we all know. My arm is my arm, not yours. My genes, warts, and so on, are mine, not yours, and so forth. Nonetheless, human individuality should not be confused with individuation. The only way to multiply an essence is via matter, thus making matter *a* principle of individuation within a species, considered essentially. However, the uniqueness of one's individuality, especially with respect to beings whose souls are subsisting entities, is ultimately derived from their private acts of existing, not their material component.

The chair I am sitting in is an individual thing in the sense of being separate from all other chairs. It has *its own* legs, seat, back, and so on. It is not, however, an individual in the sense that a human is. As an artifact it does not have *one* act of existing. And even if it were an organism, such as an individual dog, its act of existing would grant it only a dog nature rather than a human nature. Any "individuality" it might have would be greatly circumscribed by its essence, that is, its dog nature, which does not allow it to exceed certain limits.

With respect to human beings, however, the situation is quite different. For Aquinas, we have a spiritual dimension in addition to our material existence, a supernatural destiny in addition to our natural lives. Here also the real distinction between essence and existence serves Aquinas's religious purposes very well. Because of the uniqueness of each person, we are bound in charity to love each individual human being, not humanity in general. Charity begins with those actual, real people closest to us and works outward toward those individuals we meet as we go through life. On the other hand, because we are one with the rest of humanity through our essence, we can make sense of such things as the doctrines of Original Sin, respect for one's parents and children, and salvation history, in which the Son of Man can act on behalf of all humans, past, present, and future.[12]

Moreover, self-fulfillment means to be fully active according to the *kind* of being that the thing is. A thing *exists* in its fullest sense only when *acting* in its fullest sense. Fully "to be" is to fully do what a thing does when it is "what" it is. The second act must fulfill the first act in the highest and best way possible. The real world is not reductionistic, but hierarchical. There is a *scala naturae,* with each lower level acting as a foundation for a higher level. All real things are actual beings (that mineral, this plant, that animal, this woman — even each idea). But where does the hierarchy stop: humans, angels, God? For Aquinas the top of the scale is God.

This has important consequences for both individuals and society. There is no reason why either individuals *or* society should have an "identity crisis." Each person is unique with respect to having his or her own private act of existing. Each one is not unique with respect to the *kind* of essence he or she possesses. If each person did have his or her own essence, in the sense of a different kind of essence, there could not be *one* human race. This means that no one should be ashamed of having a feeling of solidarity with his or her fellow and sister human beings.

On the other hand, there is no need to think that you *must* be contrary simply to show the world and yourself that you are an individual. There is no need to feel guilty about "doing your own thing" so long as it does not violate the laws of God built into your nature. You are by natural right an individual with your own special talents and abilities. There is no need to ask anyone for permission to be yourself. This is not something you must fight against God to get; it is God who made you that way in the first place.

Returning now to our ability to make existential judgments, if we compare doing the philosophy of being with doing logic, the special role of existential judgments becomes even more apparent. The first trait of reality is to be. The *to be* as a copula in logic is well-chosen, not because logic decides what holds in the philosophy of being, but the other way around, because all judgments of predication (for instance, Sally is a human being, Sally is a mother, Sally is the president of GM) are meant to say *how* a thing actually *is.* In contrast to logically formulated propositions, though, existential judgments cannot be treated "formally" because they do not deal with forms (essences, concepts), but with existence. Logical propositions arise only when we start trying to relate something to the infinite ways of being. There are as many ways of expressing something logically as there are ways of existing.

An existential judgment, however, is always an either-or situation. In terms of actuality it is always a case of to be *or* not to be. Such judgments cannot be included in formal logic at all, yet they are understandable and meaningful to us. This is just another way of saying that we cannot get to the meaning of being via logic — intentional logic, mathematical logic, modal logic, or any other kind of logic. If we should try it in terms of intentional logic, as we saw in Hegel's case, we must end in pantheism. If we should try it in terms of symbolic, mathematical, mechanical logic, we arrive in a totally disconnected world of nothing but loose parts. The whole world is reduced to a digital system of merely juxtaposed on/off switches.[13]

In the former the individual disappears into the Absolute. In the latter the result is hyper-individualism, in which individual parts have no intrinsic commonality with anything else. The former produces an obnoxious collectivism in which the individual spirit is crused out; the latter produces social chaos in which one's privacy is the supreme value, so much so that interpersonal responsibility is crushed out, theoretically speaking at least. In either case, though, approaching being through concepts is bound to miss the true complexity and meaning of being in our *Lebens-Welt*. In this sense, at least, Aquinas can agree with Hegel and Heidegger about the danger of putting formal logic ahead of the philosophy of being, but without going to the extreme of attempting to eliminate the principle of non-contradiction.

According to Aquinas, we know from an analysis of ordinary experience that there is a real distinction between a thing's form (act) and matter (potency). In addition, we might strongly suspect, as an extrapolation from our analysis of matter and form, that there is also a real distinction between a thing's essence (which for Aquinas consists of both its matter and form) and its existence. If so, many serious philosophical problems could be solved, especially the problem of universals, thus avoiding the constant jumping back and forth between the extremes of exaggerated realism (only the universal is real) and nominalism (only the individual is real) with their concomitant political extremes of collectivism and licentious libertarianism, respectively.

As already pointed out, if there is a real distinction between essence and existence, there could be a nature (a "what," a definition) of something which could exist either extramentally or intramentally. As it exists outside the mind it would be an individual, and only an individual, thing. As it exists intentionally it would be an idea of that nature. Thus, "human being," for example, could be multiplied over many individuals, each one of whom would be truly and completely a human being, while at the same time we could have the idea of human nature in our intellects without any loss whatsoever to its extramental reality.

It would then be possible to make sense of ordinary language and thought. Extramentally, things could be *essentially* the *same* (Sam *is* a *human being*; Sally *is* a *human being*), which is a necessary condition for classification. The members of a species must have something *really* in *common*. A mere arbitrary name or label will not work. Simultaneously, however, each individual is *unique,* because each one possesses its own unique act of existing.

Such a view would have tremendously important consequences in all areas of life on earth, as well as for life after death. It would provide a basis for a political balance between collectivism and hyper-individualism. Both society and individuals would have *natural* rights, based upon the very structure of reality and the hierarchy of beings.

At the same time that each person claimed a special dignity for himself or herself, he or she would also have to acknowledge responsibility for other people, the common good of society, and the continued welfare of the natural goodness and beauty of the earth. Every day would be an Earth Day. Human beings, even though rulers of the earth, would not be the absolute rulers of all reality, but would be subject to the yet higher authority of God. Thus, there would arise the possibility for a truly universal morality with its ensuing promise of worldwide peace and harmony. In contrast to post-moderns such as Gadamer and Rorty, however, the possibility would be based upon something objectively true rather than upon mere wishful thinking and superstitions carried over from the past.

Moreover, although Aquinas, *qua* philosopher, approaches the world in such a way that not one of his conclusions is a deduction from any part of Scripture or Church teachings, there is, nevertheless, the possibility that reason and revelation can coincide on certain points. One example of this would be the question of the relation of God to the world, an issue of great importance to thinkers such as Kant, James, Hegel, Kueng, and many others. Is it really true that God and the world are so connected that one cannot avoid affecting the other and vice versa? Must this relationship be always and everywhere more or less symmetrical? And if it is not, how can this possibly be understood in our present post-modern world?

In Thomas's philosophy of being the relationship between God and the world is asymmetrical. God affects us; we do not affect God. God, for example, allows evil to exist because of the greater good derived from diversity, and because of human freedom, but evil acts do not change God. This is because the proper name for God is *to be*. God is *He Who Is*. God is not primarily the First Cause or the Author of Nature. To put this in another way, God would still be God even if he had never created the least little speck of sand. God defines himself to Moses in Exodus 3:14 not as a creator, not as infinite, not as spirit, and not as mind, but as Existence.

This passage from Scripture, and the way it fits in so well with ordinary human existence, goes a long way in showing the harmony of philosophy and Holy Writ. What does it mean "to be"? What is a being as experienced? Aquinas's answer to this most fundamental question in all of rational thought is that to be a created being means to be a *habens esse*. A created being is *that which has existence*. This is the basis for all human reasoning in all fields of theoretical and practical knowledge and action.

Consider, for instance, our understanding of something as basic as change and becoming. In ordinary usage "to change" means to become different from what something is now. What would a creationist philosophy of being make of this? According to Aquinas it must necessarily bring about some very radical changes in our most fundamental ways of viewing reality. For instance, "becoming" can no longer be viewed as synonymous with "change."

For the ancient Atomists all change was reduced to exchange, the exchange of position of the atoms (being) in space (non-being). For Aristotle this was only one type of accidental change. An accidental change is one which does not alter the essential nature of the thing. In Aristotle's philosophy of nature we also find, in addition to accidental-type changes, substantial changes, that is, changes in which the essential nature of something is altered. In all cases, though, "to change" means to become different, such that something is lost and something else shows up. For example, when hydrogen and oxygen become water (a substantial change) the hydrogen and oxygen, in terms of their sensible characteristics, disappear, to be replaced with water, something having entirely different properties. Also, when a Caucasian becomes suntanned (an accidental change) the white skin goes and the tanned skin appears in its place. Change here seems to exhaust the meaning of "become."

Not so for Aquinas, for whom even the very talk about change, as meaning to become different, would seem to call for a more profound understanding of the terms. Has the replacement notion of change really reached rock bottom? Can the inherent circularity of the definition of change (to become means to *become* different) be avoided? We can improve upon the situation, thinks Thomas, if we understand the usual meaning of change as being only a species of becoming. A more fundamental meaning for becoming might be "to come into being" either in some absolute sense or simply in some relative sense. A creation *ex nihilo* could then also be a becoming.

This could have important consequences, especially where the orthodox Catholic thinker must reconcile the immutable nature of God with the coming into human being of the Second Person of the Trinity. In a creationist philosophy of being it is not necessary to imagine that God must somehow be negated, alienated, or disappear, so that the Incarnation could take place. God "takes on" human nature in Mary's womb. Thus Jesus Christ, even though true God and true man, would continue to preserve the asymmetrical relationship between God and the world.

In such a philosophy of being (not a philosophy of existence in the more restricted sense of one that leaves out or plays down the role of essences, such as that of Kierkegaard or Sartre), even the immutable nature of God must be reinterpreted. God is indeed eternally unchanging, but not in the static and inert sense of Greek Being. There is instead in God, as expressed most perfectly in the Trinity, a becoming in the sense of a maximized dynamic and super-intensive activity which is so total and complete that it can in no way be augmented or made more perfect. In Aquinas's foundational analysis, which aims to balance science and spontaneity, rootedness and novelty, stability and creativity, and so forth, God's essence, which is to exist or *be*, marks the height of activity and life, not the nadir of stagnation.

Observe that common usage is not being denied here. It is instead being preserved, although within a more limited context. Just as divine grace, the undeserved help given by God to his intelligent creatures so that they might better attain eternal happiness, does not displace human nature, but instead presupposes it as a basis for development, so Thomistic "becoming" presupposes "change" as a basis for something more comprehensive. To use an analogy from contemporary science, we might say that common usage is to Thomistic philosophy as Newtonian physics is to Einsteinian physics. As currently understood, Einstein's relativity physics does not deny the basic principles and laws of Newtonian physics but rather preserves, justifies, and explains why Newtonian physics is so true and workable within its own proper, although more limited, context.

Other facets of human understanding are also well served by an approach to being that preserves both the fixed meaning and the many variations of the same thing. For example, Thomism is capable of avoiding both deism and pantheism. Yet God's presence to creatures is assured, not a partial or incomplete presence as in deism, but a complete and total presence. As we saw, pantheism does not allow for the presence of God at all. It deconstructs God in such a way that talking about God's presence to me as an individual consciousness no longer makes any sense. It is even doubtful if there can be a "me" in any self-identical sense, considering that God is supposed to be the *only* reality. As Miguel de Unamuno has described the situation:

> And if the belief in the immortality of the soul has been unable to find vindication in rational empiricism [e.g., Myers], neither is it satisfied with pantheism. To say that everything is God, and that when we die we return to God, or, more accurately, continue in Him, avails our longing nothing; for if this indeed be so, then we were in God before we were born, and if when we die we return to where we were before being born, then the human soul, the individual consciousness, is perishable. And since we know very well that God, the personal and conscious God of Christian monotheism, is simply the provider, and above all the guarantor, of our immortality, pantheism is said, and rightly said, to be merely atheism, disguised; and, in my opinion, undisguised.[14]

In contrast, for Aquinas, God as the creator and preserver of being is immediately with all things all the time. He is in all things by his essence, not because he is their essence, but because *his essence is existence*. As the cause of their very being (essence *and* existence) God is generally present to his creatures in the most immediate and intimate way possible. Because of his sustaining contact, all things, even the lowest, are subject to his omnipotence, all things are present *to him* and he is present *to them,* and he is in all things by his essence (existence) insofar as he is the cause of their very being.

God is not identified with any of his creatures, yet he remains in intimate contact with every one of them. Further, since God is not the one and only reality (pantheism), it is possible for God to be *meaningfully* present to his creatures. Beings can be meaningfully present to one another only if they are separately existing substantial entities. This is a necessary condition for presence; a condition which is fulfilled with respect to God and his creatures in Aquinas's foundational analysis. Thomas takes up this issue in his *Summa Theologiae,* Part I, question 8, "The Existence of God in Things." Of particular importance is article 3, "Whether God is Everywhere by Essence, Presence *(Praesentiam),* and Power?"

The presence of God must be defended against three main adversaries, namely, (1) those, such as the Manicheans, who say that God's influence extends only to spiritual (good) things in the world but not to material (bad) ones; (2) those, such as Moses Maimonides, who say that God is with all higher things, and maybe with the species, but not with inferior things, or at least not with the individual things in inferior species; (3) those, such as the Platonists, who say that God created only the higher beings in the universe, and these in turn created the lower levels of things. Thus God, like an aloof king, does not really have anything to do with the lower levels of things, including all those things on the earth.

In all of these cases Aquinas is dealing with various forms of deism. Pantheism is not seriously considered. In fact, in the first objection given in the article, the *rejection* of pantheism is used as an argument against God's presence. God is not in things essentially; he does not belong to the essence of anything. If he were in things essentially, they would be *one* with him, and hence pantheism. But this is not the situation. The basis for the objection seems to be that we have a choice between deism and pantheism with no possible intermediary position, and so, since pantheism is false, deism must be true.

The second objection is a continuation of the first. The objector says that to be present means not to be absent, hardly a very enlightening remark in and of itself. Yet, *if* God is in all things by his essence, then it must be said that he is present to all things. Hence, there would be no need to talk about God's presence. Again, pantheism is not taken as a serious possibility, but simply in terms of the description of God's relationship to the world, *if* pantheism were true then it would be superfluous to speak of God's presence. That is, if God *is* all things, he cannot meaningfully be present to all things.

The third objection moves on to the parallel between God's power and his knowledge and will. If God is in all things by the former, then he should also be there by the latter. But how can God be *in* something by his knowledge and will? God's knowing and willing are *in* God; they are not in his creatures. It follows then that he cannot be present by his power either.

The fourth objection states that, as we know from revelation and the teachings of the Church, God's divine grace can be added to the substantial structure of a human being. Therefore, should he not also be able to relate to human beings in an infinite number of other ways, depending upon the mode of divine perfection under consideration? In other words, is not limiting God's relationships to essence, presence, and power too restrictive?

Aquinas's response to the first three objections is based upon his foundational analysis of being. The real distinction of essence and existence in all beings except God means that there is *simultaneously* both an absolute difference between God and creatures and that there is an intimate presence of God to creatures at all times. Each creature, as an *esse habens,* is immediately and always dependent upon God in order to exist. God is perfect, and only God is perfect, yet each and every being is good and intimately related to God insofar as it exists. Even though God is *The* Being, and only God is Holy, God is not the one and only reality. *Every* creature is real, but not in exactly the same way as God is real or as any other creature is real. Being is that which is said of everything, but of no two things in the same way. Thus it is possible to compare God and creatures, as well as apples and oranges.

Can the ordinary person really understand such a thing? The answer is yes. We need have no fear of being yes-saying to Aquinas. For example, the ordinary word "early" can be used in many different ways in many different contexts. Yet there remains one basic meaning throughout all the different usages. "Early in the morning" does not mean the same as "early in the day," yet "early" is easily understood in both contexts. The basic meaning of "early" or "earlier" is that of being sooner than the other parts of, or events in, the series. We can thus set up a proportion among the various parts of the different series.

For example, six o'clock in the morning is to the morning as the morning is to the daylight hours of the whole day. Likewise for early in the year, early in the decade, early in the century, and so on. Also, let us not forget that the early bird gets the worm, and that early to bed and early to rise will make you healthy, wealthy, and wise.

We can see the same thing with respect to fractions. We are certain that 3/4, 5/9, 17/45, and so on, are fractions, but what, if anything, binds them all together? Maybe only the fact that they are fractions. But consider a subset of fractions such as 5/10, 25/50, 50/100, and so forth. Here they are all the same (0.5) while simultaneously being all different. This is something anyone can understand, and earlier rather than later at that.

As used in Aquinas's philosophy of being, this means that we can view the whole range of things in the world as equally real and yet as arranged in a hierarchy in which some things are truly superior to other things. All of reality is thus a long (we do not know how long) series of *analogous* relations which can be expressed in general terms as a series of proportions. So it is that the essence and existence of an angel is to that of a man as it is to that of a flatworm as it is to that of a rose, and the like.

Because of the real distinction of essence and existence in each thing, beings *must necessarily* be analogous to each other up and down the whole scale of reality. From this viewpoint, we can see that if being were univocal and God is being, then there could be only one reality (God, the World, pantheism). If being were equivocal there would then be no unity whatsoever to reality (no sets, species, classes). However, both extremes are contrary to human experience. What, then, is in conformity with human experience, remembering that the philosophy of being is the science of the ordinary?

The answer is the reality of all things in our world that we come to know originally via sensations, and of all things that are known as the contents of our own minds. The chair I am sitting on, even though an artifact, the person I am speaking to, who is an organic, natural substance, the idea in my mind, even though it may be of an extramentally non-existent thing, are all real beings. In each case there is a real distinction between essence and existence, with its own act of existing granting it a place in the real world of beings, either as a substance or as an accident of a substance.

Hence we see that there is no Thomistic "system," in the sense of an arrangement of unchangingly fixed parts with all the details spelled out in advance. It is rather a set of principles with various possible applications. God's essence is existence. A creature's being is to have existence, not to be existence. The real distinction of essence and existence means that in every creature its essence is really other than its existence even though there is no separation of the two. Our knowledge of existence does not come through clear and distinct ideas but via judgment. This means that, even though all knowledge is an immanent act of the knower, knowledge exceeds the limits of concepts.

As far as the answer to the fourth objection is concerned, Aquinas states that, theologically speaking divine grace is the *only* perfection, over and above the action of his continuing creativity, needed to make God known and loved by human persons. It is both necessary and sufficient to draw us to God. Except for the one special case of the Incarnation, in which there is a unique union of God and man, God's grace constitutes the normal and usual means whereby we may adhere to God in our personal spiritual lives. This special presence of God to a human being cannot, however, be obtained by philosophical knowledge, any more than mere intellectualism can cause a profound relationship to develop between the lover and the beloved. To have this special relationship requires God's grace, plus an active, sincere, and habitual response on the part of the human lover.[15]

Recently it has been argued that Thomas's account of the possibility of God's presence is faulty in certain ways. If God is present to all things by his essence (existence) and power, what are we to do with non-existent things such as empty space? God is supposed to be in all places because *being* is everywhere. "But if there are empty places, on this account, God does not exist in them. Surely an adequate treatment of omnipresence, however, should allow the possibility that God is present even in empty space; so this version of the doctrine is inadequate."[16]

Also, if God is present to everything by his power, and if his power is not directly and immediately exercised over everything, then God cannot be present to everything on that account. An analogy would be a king who operates via ministers so that the king is only indirectly present throughout his kingdom. "But just as a king is not really present as far as his power or rule extends, so the extent of God's power, if it is not direct control but rather some sort of potential power, does not seem to account for or to constitute his presence."[17]

Neither of these objections, however, is very telling. Taking them in order, first of all, there is no area of non-being in the universe. Everywhere in the world of nature, even in the farthest reaches of "space," something is happening. The very shape of space, in an unbounded but finite Einsteinian universe, is controlled by the matter it contains. Forces apply everywhere. At no point in space can we say that literally nothing is happening. But wherever there is something positive there also is God. Hence the objection fails.[18]

Also, with respect to the first problem, even if there were existing non-existing areas in the universe, this could not be used against God's creative power. A parallel situation would be the issue of whether or not God's power is limited by his inability to create a square circle, or to undo the past. The answer is no, because the object in question is a nothing, and the past no longer exists. God can do anything, not any no-thing. Consequently, the issue of what might or might not be present to a non-existent thing is meaningless.[19]

With respect to the second problem, it is a condition contrary to fact to say that God's power does not extend everywhere and to everything. Because of his existential relationship to his creatures his power extends directly and immediately to everything, whether necessary or contingent. The point is that his power *is not* like that of an earthly king. In the passage above from the *Prima Pars,* 8, 3, Aquinas is only speaking loosely about the different ways in which God's presence *might be* conceived from the viewpoint of several human analogies. These are (1) by indirect authority, (2) by inspecting something from a distance, and (3) by actually being in and with the present thing. It is only the last that is developed by Aquinas as his own position. The parallel with a king is not his own view.[20]

Overall, then, Thomism has succeeded in a philosophical way in establishing the presence of God to anything and everything real in an immediate and active fashion. On the basis of his philosophy of being, which not only sees the obvious but also understands its meaning, the shaky deconstructions of God's presence have been solidly reconstructed in an eminently rational way. And the beauty of it is that it has been done without in any way belittling the simple faith of the ordinary believer.

Neither is there any need for a two-tiered process of coming to a belief in the nearness of God only after a rational demonstration of the existence and nature of God. The only claim made by Thomism in this regard is that it is *possible* to know about the presence of God without divine revelation, not that it is necessary to do so in order to be a Christian. In actual practice, under ordinary circumstances, 99 percent of the faithful will not in fact ever actualize such a potential.

Nevertheless, this does not mean that such a possibility is not a permanent part of the human potential, a potential which *should* be activated when and where it can. After all, to see something directly for yourself *is* better than to believe it. Faith and hope are *means* to the end of knowing God (indeed, a way of knowing God even now), not ends in themselves. Faith *should* seek understanding, which is to say that the ideal situation is for every faithful Christian to be an orthodox theologian to the full extent of his or her ability. Even according to Scripture (1 Corinthians 13:1–13), it is not faith and hope which are meant to abide forever, but love.

Aquinas is thus able to do several things simultaneously. When God creates he creates beings, not either essences or naked existences separately. A being is both essence *and* existence in *one* thing. Therefore we can have the best of both worlds with respect to science and existentialism. In opposition to Greek Being, which is the basis for scientific and mathematical intelligibility, Aquinas's philosophy of being offers a dynamic view of reality which can incorporate into itself change and becoming even while preserving science and mathematics. As both Thomists and Deconstructionists know very well: No essences, no real science.

In opposition to modern "existentialism," often put forward as the basis for change, duration, becoming, temporality, and so on, Aquinas's philosophy of being offers the stability of essences even while preserving the primary importance of dynamic alteration and evolution. Certainly "historicism" and historical conditioning are a fact of life today, as they were at all times in the past, and will be in the future. However, they are not so central and important that they can usurp what can rightly belong only to essential natures. Thomism allows for both essence and historical development. No mean feat, but to do it requires the real distinction between potency and act, essence and existence, such that act is to potency as form is to matter as existence is to essence.

Another way of looking at this is in terms of what is and what is not "beyond nature." *Meta-physics* in Aristotle's world-system refers primarily to the beings which exist beyond the moon. Aristotle realizes that if such beings did not exist, metaphysics would not be First Philosophy. In that case physics would be First Philosophy. This is not the situation with Thomas.

Yes, but what about Kant? Did not Kant admit that "metaphysics" is in fact irrepressible, but nevertheless that it must remain empty and unproductive? This is because, according to Kant, who got his information from previous philosophers such as Christian Wolff (1679–1754), the philosophy of being deals exclusively with ideas and concepts. It has no contact with the sensible world of extramental existence. Its whole life is spent running round and round within the confines of one's own mind. If metaphysics, *by definition*, deals *only* with intramental ideas, how can the philosopher ever hope to contact reality? In such a case, any effort whatsoever to go from an idea to an extramental thing would be impossible. Thus, for instance, *all* philosophical approaches to God *must* be defective.

However, as we have seen, this need not be the case. The philosophy of being should begin in the world of the senses. Philosophers are ordinary people long before they are philosophers. Long before some of them talk themselves into an intellectual skepticism, usually by means of making certain unnecessary assumptions about the priority of ideas over the totality of human experience, including sense experience, they already possess the means for answering Kant. The whole history of philosophy seems at times to be the story of highly intelligent and well-meaning thinkers talking themselves out of ordinary experience and into some strange extraordinary scheme of things. This seems to be especially true in the philosophy of being, the most fundamental area of philosophy.

What does it mean to be real? Why is it necessary to think that to find reality the philosopher must go to the heavens? Why can he or she not begin right here in the world at hand? For Aristotle, metaphysics literally dealt with the extraordinary world of the unchanging heavens beyond the changing world of nature. For Wolff it dealt with the pure possibles of intramental thought, and Kant followed him in this. For Aquinas, however, philosophy proper does not begin in the stratosphere, but with the plumbing in the basement. Neither does it work solely with ideas. The real distinction of essence and existence applies from the ground up, and includes the realm of ideas. Kant was totally unaware of this.

True, there is something "beyond nature" for Aquinas, but it is not something separated from the changeable world. Every created being, regardless of whether it is near or far, here or there, is a "that which is," a *habens esse*. Insofar as it is a nature (essence) it is subject to scientific scrutiny. But insofar as it possesses its own act of existing, it is beyond the range of conceptual knowledge in its immediate apprehension even though it can be conceptualized later (thus losing its immediate existential character).

It is this *esse* which is beyond nature in the sense of being really distinct from the essence of the one being. It is not beyond nature in the sense of being literally out of this world (as with Aristotle). Thus science is *included within* the existential world, and even ideas, which exist *within* the existential world of human experience, require an act of existing to be real. Thus there is no need to assume an inherent incompatibility among the various branches of human learning such as science, philosophy, and theology. They can in fact be quite compatible and harmonious with each other in terms of their methodologies, and even in terms of their conclusions.

We have seen how being can be better understood by not taking existence for granted. Essences or natures are needed to found science, namely, necessary and universal knowledge explaining why things are the way they are, at least with respect to the physical world. Necessity and universality are required for predictability, and when a scientist can predict the future course of natural events we know that he is doing his work properly. This is the sort of thing for which Nobel Prizes are awarded, and for which professorships are awarded in the world's universities.

On the other hand, though, a purely scientific world can very easily become a very anti-humanistic world. A world in which determinism reigns supreme is a world without human free choice and without all the drama, joy, and tears which go with freedom. It is also a world in which essentialism so dominates all our thinking that humans cannot possess any individual independence at all. Everything can easily be identified with everything else until all of reality is swallowed up into one vast Absolutism. In this approach we solve the problem of classification by reifying abstractions, with devastating social and political consequences, as can be seen in twentieth-century fascism, nazism, and communism.

The reaction against this extreme is often another extremism, whether in the philosophical existentialism of Sartre or the economic hyper-individualism of someone such as Ayn Rand. The repugnance aroused by essentialism, collectivism, and the lack of human freedom becomes so pronounced that the *whole* scientific enterprise may be sacrificed in the name of humanism. Essence-phobia overpowers rational thought. *Too* much thinking may itself be regarded as undesirable; the more we think the less we *are*. Faith itself becomes segregated from the intellect; a deep opposition may develop between faith and reason, religion and science, and so on. Human life becomes a fragmented affair of internally warring factions, and where inner calm and tranquility is lacking, extra-mental conflict and physical violence are sure to follow.

But are these supposedly irreconcilable oppositions really necessary? The Thomistic answer is no. With the real distinction between essence and existence we can have *both* essence *and* existence related in such a way that the best of science and the best of personal worth, dignity, and integrity can be maintained simultaneously. Moreover, there is no need to choose either the natural world or the supernatural world, but not both, in our appreciation of reality, our own included. We can exist *and* God can exist *and* God can be present to us, without any insurmountable obstacles to overcome. Our individuality is in no way compromised by God's presence, just as God's providence and presence is in no way compromised by our own personal existence and freedom.

Insofar as God's presence is concerned, there is no one-sidedness about the Thomistic position. Contra Kueng's view of "classical" thought, philosophy is not a necessary first floor or stage on the way to faith and theology. If anything, it is the other way around. In any event, faith and reason can be two paths to the *same* destination. If the philosophy is an existential philosophy of being, it is possible to have both faith and reason within one integrated world-view. Having eliminated both the static, uncreative Greek idea of being and the duration-temporality-becoming idea of being as two mutually exclusive categories of interpretation, Aquinas has no need to choose one over the other. Instead, he can enjoy the benefits, both theoretical and practical, of change *within* being, disorder *within* order, freedom *within* determinism, contingency *within* providence, novelty *within* rootedness, diversity *within* hierarchy, immediacy *within* eternity, and human individuality *within* God's Presence.

Within an existential framework, one that also gives full credit to the role of essences, we can more clearly appreciate the interaction and *harmony* of science, philosophy, and theology. Even though distinct with respect to their own specific spheres of interest, their own special methods, and their own levels of analysis, they are not necessarily in contradictory opposition to each other. *One* human being can participate in all. As human beings we are immersed over our heads in nature while still possessing a non-mythical spiritual dimension. As human we sum up and integrate within ourselves the entire material universe of which we are an integral part, while simultaneously standing open to the uncovering and disclosure of an objective spiritual world, a world which is also very near to us — as close to us as our very own existence.

EPILOGUE: ON THE ETHICAL IMPORTANCE OF "AND"

> Instead, like a child begging for both, he must say that reality, or the sum of all things, consists of both the changeable and the unchangeable.
>
> Plato
> *The Sophist,* 249d

> Respondeo dicendum, quod persona significat id, quod est perfectissimum in tota natura, scilicet subsistens in rationali natura. (I answer that person signifies what is most perfect in the whole of nature, namely, a subsistent individual of a rational nature.)
>
> St. Thomas Aquinas
> *Summa Theologiae* I: 29, 3

What was said above has important theoretical and practical significance. On the speculative level it shows that post-modernism is resting on a very insecure foundation. As soon as one sees that being and becoming are not necessarily incompatible, the whole basis for post-modernism crumbles to dust. This can be seen when the contemporary thinker realizes that being need not mean Greek Being. There are other alternatives, one of which, that used by Aquinas in the thirteenth century, for example, can account very well for the harmony of change and permanence within the world as we actually experience it.

The implications of this for human solidarity are astonishing. If there is to be some sort of basic social and political inter-relationship, contractarianism, church membership, and so forth, among human beings, it must be based upon the fact of a common human nature shared by all humans alike. Aquinas is a very community-minded person; there is only *one* human race. In terms of our essence, I *am* you, regardless of sex, age, health, wealth, skin color, and so on. This is the *radical* foundation for social justice and harmony, more radical than any Hermeneutics, Deconstructionism, or Liberation Theology. The philosophical understanding of the religious dictate to love your neighbor as yourself is that, because there is only one and the same human nature in everyone, your neighbor *is* yourself. One could not ask for a stronger objective tie to bind us all together.[1]

Yet, in terms of my own act of existing, bestowed upon me by God in the act of creating me, and which binds me to God in a most direct and intimate fashion, I am me and not you. This is as legitimate and rational an explanation of my individuality as anything which can be offered by the phenomenology of the twentieth century or the pseudo-empiricism of Hume in the eighteenth century, and so forth.

As an individual human being I am both my own person and a member of society. I am both outer and inner-directed. My social nature does not contradict my own power of free choice. Contrary to Hobbes and Sartre, there is no opposition between authority and freedom. Some small reflection will show that *only* a *free* being can responsibly *obey* authority. It would make no sense for a traffic cop to stand on the seashore and order the waves not to roll in. It does make sense, though, assuming that the drivers possess the power of free choice, for a traffic cop to stand in an intersection of city streets and order some cars to go and others to stop.

A similar situation obtains in moral matters. Deconstructionists cannot get an ethics of liberation and toleration out of Heidegger's mysterious Being. Can we even speak of toleration under such circumstances? Very often people say "toleration" when what they really mean is "indifference." To be tolerant means to hold a very firm and strong position on some matter, but not to use physical force in order to make others hold the same view. A person without a firm commitment cannot be tolerant of others, only indifferent toward them. Toleration means *both* firm commitment *and* love of neighbor. Aquinas is tolerant *because of* his dogma.[2]

I think that one of the major criticisms of post-modernism, even assuming that we are taking it at its best, and that we are presenting it in its best light, is its failure to offer any objective justification for toleration as an attitude which all people must adopt. Richard J. Bernstein, for example, simply asserts that all people, and especially philosophers, should be tolerant of each other, regardless of how pretentious, obscure, woolly, and muddled the view of one may appear to another. Any response to intellectual differences must be peaceful. There must be a sincere desire to overcome one's biases, to avoid "tokenism," wherein one only pays lip service to the value inherent in the views of others while actually believing that there is really nothing to be learned from them. To be really tolerant, thinks Bernstein, we must adopt the "fallibilistic" position of pragmatism.[3]

One must really believe that no one is, or ever can be, really right in some fundamental way relative to others. *All* possible positions (except apparently the pragmatic one) are open to constant reevaluation, not merely with respect to their more or less superficial and secondary elements, but with respect to their most basic foundations. Why this would not apply to pragmatism, Radical Hermeneutics, and Deconstructionism is not explained. Neither are we told how to handle mutually exclusive views, positions which cannot be compromised without being destroyed, and the like.

True to the now-familiar pattern, Bernstein assumes the irreconcilable opposition of the absolute and the contingent and proceeds from there. According to Bernstein, pragmatism is more of an *ethos* than a philosophical position; it is a *moral* issue. Good people are tolerant; bad people are intolerant. To the good person there are no adversaries or opponents, only conversational partners with whom he or she can conduct a dialogue. Insofar as toleration is a positive thing, Aquinas can *wholeheartedly* agree. This is shown in his own works, in which he always attempts to put his "opponent's" views in the strongest terms possible, and in which he always takes as much truth from them as possible. He would, in addition, want to go even further and say that we should *love* our enemies.

Someone such as Plato proceeds in the same way. He even points out in the *Sophist* (246a–248a) that a certain group of "formidable" thinkers (the Atomists? the Sophists?) would have to have their *moral* character reformed before they could engage in a fruitful dialogue with himself. This is because they are much too slippery, always changing their premises and positions, always ready to go off on a tangent, never prepared to stick to the main point and issue at hand, and so forth. Plato, however, does not engage in such behavior.

In modern times, Allan Bloom, in his introduction to *The Closing of the American Mind,* points out that the hyper-modern mind-set makes a virtue out of relativism. Being an "absolutist" is comparable to being an anti-democratic dictator, or a believer in witches. Relativism, it is claimed, is a *moral* necessity in order to avoid wars, persecutions, slavery, xenophobia, racism, chauvinism, witch hunts, and other such evils. Bloom supports toleration in its positive aspect, but rejects the negative notion that it is wrong in principle to think that you are ever right, and that error has as much right to exist as truth.

In Heideggerian fashion, in the face of conflict, Bernstein says that we must "respond to others with responsiveness." But *why* we *should* be tolerant of others he does not say. He *implies* that it is to avoid the things mentioned above by Bloom. What he says explicitly is only that pluralism is a fact of life today (at least in some parts of the world). But, granted that this is in fact the *status quo,* why should we work to maintain it? Is this not much too conservative an attitude to be considered liberal? The defense of toleration turns out to be merely an assertion of what the post-moderns *want* to be the case, not what should be the case, or need be the case. If we examine the situation more carefully, we can see that persecution is not a necessary consequence of absolutism. Thus relativism in principle is not morally necessary. We can also see that "fallibilism" is not really toleration at all, but only indifferentism, especially on the level of foundational analysis.

But once we realize this we also realize that, whereas indifference would allow just anything to be, toleration cannot do so. Being tolerant does not mean giving up one's critical powers or allowing any actions whatsoever. In order to ensure a maximized degree of freedom in society we must necessarily put restrictions on some choices, such as the decision to kill others at will, to abuse or enslave others, to decide not to pay taxes, or not to help defend the nation during a just war, and so on. All of this, of course, as explained earlier, must be governed by an objective moral law and not simply by civil law. In order to maximize freedom for all, the actions of some must be restricted in accordance with objective measures that transcend all individual humans and all human societies.

This does not in any way violate our human freedom. Free choice, authority, and acting morally are all perfectly compatible within Aquinas's libertarianism. To act morally means to do *freely* what we *should* do. Only a free agent can freely conform to an objective standard of morality, that is, good defined in some *per se* way. Freedom does not mean simply doing whatever I feel like doing whenever I feel like doing it, regardless of how good it feels. In contrast to the hedonistic "If it *feels* good do it," the Thomistic approach is "If it *is* good do it."

This in no way impugns the authentic, genuine, honest nature of the mature, autonomous, rational agent. This can be made clear via a simple example. Imagine that you are at a track meet featuring a contest among several world-class highjumpers. Participating in the activities are the athletes, of course, but also the track officials and judges. We can presume that everyone is honest and sincere. Their intellectual integrity is beyond question. Nevertheless, there is also something else participating in the meet, namely, the cross-bar marking off the various heights to be jumped. Does this in any way lessen the honor of all concerned? Just the contrary. Instead of impeding their progress toward personal growth and self-fulfillment, the existence of the cross-bar is a necessary prerequisite for such development. Without it neither the athletes nor the judges would know how well anyone is doing.

Consequently we can lay to rest once and for all the very unrealistic notion that we are primarily self-assertive consciousnesses living in the midst of a mysterious, temporal Pure Becoming. Neither is it rational to maintain that our primary moral obligation is to preserve the state of amorphous moral ambiguity in our personal lives. Taking their cue from thinkers such as Heidegger and Sartre, modern-day Deconstructionists maintain the inherent relativity of all morals. But relative to what?

According to Sartre, for instance, human beings start out as nothing and must will themselves to be something. As we have already seen in an earlier chapter, it is me (my consciousness) against the world. Under the circumstances, all the naked ego can do is to invent for itself its own standards, which it can then hold up as something "objective," as something "over against itself" which it has an *obligation* to follow if it is to act "in good faith."

However, it does not require a great deal of reflection to realize that this standard of standardlessness is only a pseudo-standard at best. Nihilism is avoided, it is claimed, because there is a standard to follow. It turns out, however, that this standard is a purely subjective one. In a very Hegelian way it is doubly subjective, with the self returning to itself. Being sincere becomes the standard, and whether or not you are sincere is for *you* to say. The result is that an intramental idea is projected outwardly *as if* it were something objective. Seen in this light, the anti-Realism of the whole approach becomes quite obvious. In reality it is just a reassertion of the *de facto* situation as seen from within the subject.

When deciding what we sincerely want to do we must, of course, take into account what we *can* do. In his earlier days Sartre thought that this realm of free action was sky-high. This, at least, was the impression he gave in his *Being and Nothingness* of 1943. Later he insisted that the realm of what humans could do, and the limits within which humans could operate, were very much restricted by all kinds of conditions, especially economic ones. Nevertheless, Sartre never repudiated any of his earlier works; the same principle held good both early and late.

This explains both why he was rejected by the Marxists and yet remained a hero to Western "liberals." In the Western world it was like eating your cake and having it too. The hyper-individualists could say that we *do* have principles, that we *do* recognize the determining influences of material conditions and modes of production, but that we are still free to do whatever we want as individuals. Hence, while his lack of a collectivistic mentality made him unwelcome in the East at that time, his pseudo-standard of sincerity made him a truly post-modern man in the West. By rejecting all divine dictates, and keeping faith with subjectivism by being true only to yourself, because, as a unique and isolated individual there is no one else to whom you can be true, human nature would finally have been completely naturalized *à la* Nietzsche.

As we have seen, though, whether early or late, the principle is quite useless. If it is meant to preserve our dignity and honor as autonomous thinkers and actors, it is totally unnecessary. Far from denying it, acting *morally* according to an objective measure *presupposes* freedom.

If it is meant to be a deduction from the temporal flux of the world, that is, as a way of life necessarily implied by the Phenomenological-Atheistic Existentialistic "truth" about the way the world really is, and about the way we should let it be, then this too is totally unnecessary. Permanence and flux, being and consciousness, and so on, are not mutually exclusive. Likewise for liberty and authority, authority and personal morality, and so forth.

Sartre's *attitude* toward the world is typical of the hyper-moderns. One of Heidegger's chief desires was to overcome forever the old dichotomy between appearance and reality, semblance and essence, and the like. What has happened instead is just the opposite; everywhere today the dichotomy between appearance and reality abounds. In James, God only appears to be an existentially separate being; in reality God is only the self. Conscience appears to be working on the basis of objective measures; in reality it is only the self talking to itself. Science appears to be dealing with necessary physical connections in the real extramental world of nature, a world which appears to be made up of things with their own existential acts such that, if I should disappear, they would continue to exist as definite types of things, pursuing definite patterns of action, and so on. In reality it is only a case of individual and societal human projections that are really binding only in us and in the ways we choose to coherently interrelate our linguistic formulas with one another. Likewise in moral matters. What appear to be, at one time or another, the objectively true and eternally inspired norms of behavior are really only the results of a social consensus; they are only civil laws supported by the many and taken for granted as *our* way of doing things.

Every thinker has something worthwhile to say. All philosophies contain some portion of the truth. And any truth is of value. Thinkers such as Heidegger, Sartre, Gadamer, and Rorty are not exceptions to this rule. It is true that change and dynamic development are the order of the day, as it is true of all days. Temporality is of great importance, not primarily as the sort of time measured on a clock, but as the becoming of beings in the world. It is also true that existence is given to us, that the best understanding the human mind has of the existence of something is that it is *there* to be sensed and affirmed in judgments whose primary objects are worldly, material things. Nevertheless, there is an order to the importance of things and how they are known, and the thinker who gets that order more correctly stated must be regarded as the better thinker.

This would place Heidegger and his disciples below the level of Thomas, who at least took the "metaphysics of presence" seriously.[4]

Indeed, I am dubious about whether or not the post-moderns can take seriously anything of an objective nature, including their own doctrine. Under Deconstructionism, instead of all history being philosophy, as with Hegel, all philosophy is now a form of playful history, as with Derrida. The serious philosopher is no more; now all is play and parody. Unlike Plato's play of ideas in his Dialogues, and the Scholastic logic-play of the medieval university undergraduate Arts Faculty, both of which were constructive, truth-seeking instruments of learning, now we have the glorification of moral relativism, and play for the sake of play.

Others bypass Heidegger and turn back to the completely disintegrated atomistic world-view of Hume. The basic reason for this, though, is still their inability to understand how the absolute and the contingent, the intelligible and the sensible, and so on, can exist together simultaneously. To understand how this is possible one must be acquainted with the real distinction between essence and existence. A typical post-modern thinker, however, such as Mackie, trying to be true to both Nietzsche and Hume, shows no such acquaintanceship. When discussing Aquinas's "Five Ways," for instance, perhaps because he was misled by previous authors such as W. L. Craig and A. Kenny, he completely misses the existential nature of the core argument. Like Kant, he thinks that all rational arguments reduce to the ontological argument, which must fail. If he had been aware of Aquinas's existentialism, he at least might not have been troubled by problems such as, If God created the world, who created God?

Mackie's own position is that the universe is simply a collection of matter in motion (Epicurus) or energy and change (Einstein) which has existed forever and which will continue to exist forever, uncaused and completely rational and self-sufficient in itself. *It* is the one and only necessary being, in no need whatsoever of another one. This view is very common toady. It is, in effect, a form of pantheism. Even though broken up into countless atoms, the world *as a whole* possesses the divine attribute of eternal self-existence.

Because Mackie is absolutely certain of this, he can ask, Of what use would be a God arbitrarily introduced by definition as self-explanatory, and supposedly terminating the regress of explanatory principles?[5] Furthermore, what *kind* of a God is it who could create anything at all? Would not God be just another brute fact, in need of a creator himself rather than the source or cause of the brute fact of the world? God, as an unexplained given, as a postulate invented to explain something else but unexplained himself, should be an even greater embarrassment to the would-be theist than the unexplained universe which we can at least observe with our senses.[6]

Why continue looking for causes of the world, inquires Mackie, when anything postulated would be as unexplained as the world itself? Why not stop with the world itself and seek no further? Good questions, but Mackie it seems is not able to follow his own advice. Even for a disciple of Hume, the attraction of "metaphysics" and the lure of "ultimate questions" is too strong to resist. Mackie seems unable to resist becoming enmeshed in theological discussions, and even in biblical exegesis. We find evidence for this in the fact that, immediately after declaring the existence of God to be highly improbable, he moves into eight pages of discussion on why the Bible, *according to his interpretation,* cannot be used as a guide for morality.

Generally speaking, however, Mackie is on the right track. As all intelligent explanation requires, the explanation of something cannot be stated in the same terms as that which is to be explained. Saying, for instance, that something is red "just because," or because it is made up of little red parts, which in turn are composed of even smaller red parts, and so forth, will get us nowhere. Instead of just standing in awe of cloud formations, ocean tides, rusting iron, or whatever, the would-be scientist must offer some reason explaining *why* such events occur. Such explanations must be in conformity with all the available data and must represent nature as it really is.

As applied to the God Question this means that *if* the universe is not self-explanatory, then the explanation for its existence and traits *must be* different from the given universe which is to be explained. Rationally speaking, God cannot, especially as *He Who Is,* be a part of the world. *If* the explanation turns out to be just another "brute fact" as the world of nature is supposed to be, then it *cannot* be the explanation for the facts to be explained. Regardless of how far one must go in this process, sooner or later one must arrive at an explanation which is sufficiently different from the universe so as to act as a rational explanation. At that point it would be fruitless to keep repeating "just because," which is no explanation at all, or to insist that the cause is of exactly the same character as the effect, which is also a non-explanation. Yet this latter is exactly what Mackie does. Among rational people, this must be censured.

By merely postulating the whole universe as a self-sufficient, necessary being, Mackie is the one who is begging the question in favor of his own view, and engaging in his own form of the ontological argument. The approach of Aquinas, however, is quite different and much more in conformity with the canons of rational, scientific procedure. When carried on at the level of foundational analysis, the process of inquiry must examine the purported first principles of the very existence of things. Instead of examining the nature of Nature, however, Mackie takes it for granted that it exists in a completely materialistic fashion. In Mackie's "religion" the only God is Nature and the believer is strictly forbidden to have any other God; Mackie is very dogmatic in his rejection of idolatry.

In Aquinas's case, on the other hand, there is no need to give up scientific inquisitiveness because one believes in God's being and God's presence. The world remains *what* it is, to be investigated and analyzed. In principle the pursuit of knowledge can go on unhampered. In addition, though, we would also have a basis for moral behavior much more profound than the pragmatic and enlightened self-interest approach proposed by those who wish to deconstruct and desubstantialize both God and the human person.

Moreover, God's continuous presence, once fully recognized and appreciated, would provide human beings with the rational support needed to act morally in a scientific world. We would be our brother's keeper, as well as the world's keeper, and keepers of the peace. We could have our science and a clean environment and a peaceful, harmonious social life, and have it all simultaneously.

In the case of Aquinas we have someone who went beyond Hume long before Hume was born. Our whole knowing process is oriented toward the sensible world of material things. But how much can we know about God on the basis of such a starting point? We can know *that* God exists as *He Who Is* but not *what* God is in terms of a proper concept of God's essence. Sensible things, in whole or in part, says Thomas, are not equal to the total power of God. Hence, from God's effects, we cannot know God's whole essence or God's whole power. In this way Thomas anticipates, and agrees with, the case which Hume was to make centuries later, namely, that the God of the Bible cannot be proven from a scientific knowledge of the construction and operations of the physical universe.[7]

Our whole world, out to the farthest stars, cannot be regarded as exhausting God's power to create. This is not the best of all possible creations for Aquinas. To claim that it is would be to degrade, not elevate, God's infinite power. As the unique coincidence of essence and existence, the God of philosophy is far superior to the God of mere science (the Author of Nature). But even superior to that, especially in terms of our moral and psychological needs, is the God of revelation. They are, though, all one and the same Supreme Being. And what this Supreme Being has freely done is to create and conserve beings in being.

The whole post-modern movement is therefore based upon a totally unnecessary starting point. In modern times, the failure to reconcile being and becoming, essence and existence, fixed meaning and variation, and so on, in such a way as to preserve an honored place for both sides in philosophy, has usually led to pantheism, which in turn has produced nature worship, mystery cults, and the like, which in turn have produced a great deal of mental and moral confusion. The connection between the cause (pantheism) and the ultimate effect (utter confusion) is necessary, but the initial condition (pantheism) is not. The time has come to reevaluate the roots of post-modernism, hopefully before it is too late for human life on earth.

As Aquinas sees the situation, for example, only God can give what only God possesses, to wit, the very act of existing, which is the act of all acts, the perfection of all perfections. God creates beings. A created being is not just an essence; neither is it something without an essence. Each being is a *habens esse*. It is "being" which is first both in reality and in cognition. Moreover, the continuous action of God is required in order to maintain a being in existence. God is therefore with each thing always and everywhere, in its very substance as well as in every one of its operations. There is intimate contact, but not identity or continuity.[8]

Thus, by exposing its historical roots, Deconstructionism is deconstructed, and, if we follow Aquinas, it is done in a way which preserves our own selfhood, logic, science, freedom, good-naturedness, human solidarity, and God. In addition, in no way does this interpretation of being reduce the drama, challenge, and joy of human life. In place of the despair of Deconstructionism we would have both rationality and excitement in human life. Within the one human family there would be social and political stability, as well as ample opportunity for self-development and self-expression. Ethics would have a firm foundation in dynamic human nature.

The irony is that the post-moderns have brought their own deconstruction upon themselves. After all, there is a certain inconsistency and incoherence in their approach to what is really real. Nietzsche tells us that "The real philosophers of Greece are those before Socrates."[9] The only worthwhile thinker to come after Socrates was Pyrrho (365–275 B.C.), the extreme skeptic. Heidegger seems to agree. Yet how can it be that *all* philosophy after the Pre-Socratics is *all* downhill? Can we really believe that the height of human thought was, for instance, Anaximander's *apeiron* (indefinite, unlimited) or *aoriston ti* (indeterminate something), except perhaps to realize, as did the Sophists after Heraclitus and Parmenides, that morality is as equally undetermined?

In addition, how can someone be completely anthropocentric and still continue to talk as if human beings themselves are somehow only the passing product of some more fundamental Being? If the maxim *zu den Sachen selbst* (to the things themselves) does not apply to our own ideas, then what does it apply to? What is the really real? The Hindu Brahman mentioned earlier, Hegel's Absolute, Herbert Spencer's Great Unknown, Heidegger's Singular Itself, and so on? How can the *Dasein* be real if the One is real, but then how can the One be real without the *Dasein*? Deconstructionism sinks into the depression of deciding that everything is equally unreal, thus bringing some consistency into the picture. But at what cost?

The reason why Heidegger, following Hegel, is so difficult to follow is that he is trying to eat his cake and have it too. From one perspective, only the One is real; from another, only *Dasein* is real (exists). The human being is a product of Being, but Being is unknown without the human being. It is only because of *Dasein* that there is something rather than amorphous chaos (nothing). Being produces humans, but it is only humans who produce beings out of Becoming. Emanating from the I-know-not-what via an unknown process, *Dasein* returns the favor of existence, which it does not possess in its own right, by bestowing upon Becoming, unintelligible in itself, form and definition, something that Becoming does not possess in its own right. Incoherently, the one creates the other while the other creates the one, and all at the same time. Not surprisingly, ordinary logic and intelligibility must be ejected from the house of Being. In other words, there is no Being, no thing-in-itself, outside of human willing and cognition. The so-called later Heidegger is as anthropocentric as the early Heidegger.

Logical Positivism failed because it could not supply science with what it most needed, namely, a firm foundation for universality, necessity, and predictability in a truly objective manner. It thus had to be rejected by the very people (primarily those in the physical sciences) it was supposed to elevate above all others. This is deeply ironic, and points up the danger of attempting to take an extremist position, which means taking a very simplistic position, in the face of a complex world. The first victim of such a position is bound to be the position itself.

The devotees of Radical Hermeneutics and Deconstructionism are in a similar situation. *If* what they say about a universal historicism is true, then the Deconstructionist doctrine itself must be false. The first victim of a universal historicism is historicism. Likewise, the first victim of a universal relativism would be relativism; of a universal truthfulness, truth; of universal change, change, and so forth. Thinkers such as Plato, Aristotle, Aquinas, and Kierkegaard (all post-Socratics) knew this very well. Once we see where Deconstructionism is coming from, we see that it is the result of a completely unnecessary set of historical circumstances — an historical situation for which there was then, is now, and always will be a viable alternative quite capable of preserving the complexity of reality. The more eloquent the defense of Deconstructionism, the less convincing the argument. The more it struggles with language and logic, the more it sinks into the quicksand of its own historicism, and thereby self-destructs.

The best that a post-modern can do by way of a rebuttal to this state of affairs is to beg the question. Gadamer, for instance, in his *Truth and Method* (1989), when discussing Leo Strauss's critique of historicism in Supplement I, claims that Strauss has misunderstood the universal character of the hermeneutical approach. The statements that "All knowledge is historically conditioned" and that "This knowledge, namely, the immediately previous one, is true unconditionally," are not contradictory because they operate on different levels. It may be that some day the statement about all knowledge being historically conditioned will be regarded by social consensus as untrue. But even then *that* will itself be due to the influence of historical conditioning.

Even an unhistorical doctrine is historically conditioned. Why? Because *everything* is historically conditioned. This should be compared to the old claim of the Logical Positivists that if you cannot count it, it does not count. Only what is measurable is meaningful. Why? Because *everything* meaningful, in the way of synthetic statements, is measurable in some way, at least in principle. If the Logical Positivist extreme was not allowed to get away with this form of begging the question, I do not think the post-modern extreme should be allowed to get away with it either.

Moreover, even if one were to bend over backward in order to accommodate Gadamer's rebuttal he would still have missed the boat on this point. Regardless of the level on which one is working, there should be a complementarity among the different levels. A good explanation must always be in conformity with, not in contradiction to, the data to be explained. In direct opposition to this rational requirement, the post-modern program seems to be saying that this need not be the case. In any event, the post-moderns cannot be allowed to alter the rules of sound reasoning in order to accommodate a predetermined conclusion.

Given the truth of a universal proposition, such as "All human beings are liable to death," it can be immediately inferred that some human beings, say the ones living in Timbuktu, are indeed liable to death. This is very logical and reasonable, and, implicitly at least, is recognized by all normal people. We all know that if everyone in the room is wearing shoes, then it must be the case that some subsection of those in the room are wearing shoes, and so on. What is not reasonable and acceptable, however, is deliberately to invent the truth of a universal statement just so one can claim that its corresponding particular is true as well. Yet just this sort of reversal is typical of post-modern thinkers.

Failing to reconcile being and becoming, the post-modern emphasis is placed upon becoming as the only reality (a form of pantheism). In the area of cognitive theory this reinforces Descartes's Epistemological Idealism, and necessarily produces, as Hume saw, anthropocentrism. In morals it leads to cults and confusion. Ethics becomes as amorphous as the universe is supposed to be. One's morals reflect one's metaphysics. What we know decides in large part what we do.

The pervasive post-modern orthodoxy of the West, and to a larger and larger extent of the East as well, whether influenced by Western capitalism or Marxism, exhibits the same epistemological pattern of cognitive reversal. Descartes defined into existence a certain sort of material world which he wanted in order to suit his own purposes. Kant postulated the existence of a certain sort of God needed to complete his overall world-view. Hegel required non-being in order to account for change; *therefore* non-being existed.

Contrary to actual human social and economic experience (as economists, such as Friedrich Hayek, have shown quite well), Marx, now recognized by the Marxists themselves as being as much of a false prophet as Hitler and Mussolini, invented the proletariat class and the capitalist class so as to justify a war between two irreconcilable factions. This mirrored Hegel's contradiction at the heart of reality. James thought that society needed God in order to be civilized; therefore God is real. Heidegger achieved unity by imagining an all-encompassing, yet self-concealing, one great neuter *Ereignis* (event, happening). Gadamer, Rorty, and others reason in a similar way.

This, however, is certainly abnormal. It does have a place, I think, in fantasy art works, novels, and the like, but not in situations where human beings must act in the real world. A normal person, interested in fishing, let us say, would first make an effort to discover whether or not Big Lake really contains a large number of trout before fishing there and expecting to catch something. The post-modern, in contrast, reasons from theory to fact rather than vice versa. An example of such reasoning would be: I *want* to be successful on my fishing trip; therefore Big Lake is filled with trout eager to be caught by me.

It may be adventurous to go to Big Lake not knowing in advance whether or not it was well stocked with trout, but in such a situation one's judgment on the topic (i.e., one's existential act related to reality) would be suspended until one *discovered* the truth. To do otherwise would be to beg the question in favor of one's own theory. This may be an interesting diversion in fiction but is ruinous in real life, as the Communists, for instance, found out.

Nevertheless, this is what the post-moderns do. In his defense of post-modernism, Gadamer, for instance, presents us with a dilemma: Either something is historically conditioned or it is not. If it is historically conditioned, then it is historically conditioned. But, even if it appears not to be historically conditioned, it is still historically conditioned. Therefore, everything is historically conditioned.

Such a dilemma, though, can also be worked against Heidegger. On the basis of Heidegger's own phenomenological method one could argue: Either Heidegger is an Epistemological Idealist or he is an Epistemological Realist. If the former, then he is such. But, even if he thinks he is the latter, he is really still the former. Therefore, he is an Epistemological Idealist. This means that, for Heidegger, going back to the things themselves means going back no further than one's own ideas, wishes, and desires.

Although internally coherent, and although perhaps interesting as an intellectual game, no one could possibly *live* according to such a theory. The irony of it is that the *more* someone becomes aware of what post-modernism really means, the *less* someone can act on it. The more someone's consciousness is raised to an understanding of neo-pragmatism, the less pragmatic it becomes. Too much authenticity spoils the therapy. The more we are told about how opposed to a simple subjectivism the doctrine is, the less convincing the argument, as we realize just how much the meanings of ordinary words have been altered to fit a theory. If it is really the case that Being is a lie and an illusion, then the post-moderns cannot *be* any more than anything else.

Furthermore, this means that the post-modern program is doubly unnecessary. It is unnecessary from the standpoint of the foundational analysis of the meaning of being. It is also unnecessary from the viewpoint of the creative imagination and creative writing. Ironically, the more the post-modern thinker strains to be unique, the more pedestrian he or she becomes. It is still the case that truth is always stranger than fiction. The grandest fantasies of the greatest fantasy writers can never outstrip the wonders of nature. Drawing the dimensions of some fantastic landscape on some imaginary planet light-years away from us is certainly interesting. However, as intriguing, fascinating, and attractive as the results of an active imagination can be, they cannot compare to the wonders and mysteries of the real world. Without denying the truth of what we do know about the well-established laws of nature, as a reflection of God's essence, which is *to be,* the created world of real things contains more than we do now in fact imagine, and more than we are even capable of imagining.

A philosophically inclined person can get some hint of this from a consideration of the dual nature of human knowledge itself. With respect to knowledge, how much more exciting than reading a novel about dimensions of light-year proportions is it to contemplate the ordinary human experience of a thinking mind that has no dimensions at all. To know is to be united with the thing known. The potentially known object becomes actually present to the knower by specifying the being of the knower in a certain way. Thus knowledge is always an existential process in which one being interacts with another. There is always a relationship of at least two centers of activity. There must be a duality — the object is in the knower; the knower *and* the known are united. The manner of this unity is for the known to alter the non-essential existence of the knower, which can happen only because the knower exists, or is specified in the first place (primarily, essentially), as a being capable of knowing.

Such a union, which is more intimate than any imaginable physical contact, obviously cannot be a physical union. Nevertheless, as Sir Arthur Conan Doyle (Sherlock Holmes) is noted for having said, after eliminating the impossible, we must accept what is left even if it initially seems unlikely or improbable. If it is not possible to use the language of physical things to describe this union, then we need some other way of describing it. Let us call it, in traditional terminology, an *intentional* relationship. The thing as known possesses an intentional being (*esse intentionale*). Knowledge intends, tends to, or contains, other beings. In this way the knower becomes the thing known. As mentioned earlier, this uniting of the knower and the known, in philosophical language, is called Epistemological Realism. I personally become the other *as other*; i.e., not physically, for the other is not physically changed or destroyed as would happen, for instance, in the digestion of food

In this amazing process there is no physical change in the mind of the knower. If there were a physical change in the knower, *in the very act of intellectual knowledge itself,* we could never know anything. Imagine someone in thermodynamics actually becoming as hot as the sun while studying the sun. In fact, the scientist's knowledge of 1 million degrees of heat is no hotter than his or her knowledge of ten degrees of heat. Similarly, the idea of iron is no heavier than the idea of aluminum; justice can be the same for all regardless of how the word itself is spelled or pronounced, and so on. Although bodily changes certainly precede, accompany, and follow knowledge, knowledge *in itself* is not a physical change. We do not feel knowledge. We do not know water is hot because we feel it. This is because, as we can verify for ourselves through a reflection upon our own knowing, all such physical references are irrelevant to knowledge *qua* knowledge.

Conversely, if intellectual knowledge meant a physical change, then bending a tree branch should give the tree a knowledge of stress, tension, and strength-of-materials science. By the same token, a burning tree should really be knowledgeable about heat transfer. Even though physical changes may be a condition for knowledge, the knowledge itself is not something physical, something which somehow physically gets into the nervous system or brain. Claiming that it is something mechanical or physical does not conform to the data; it does not compute. The difference between knowing and not knowing is not merely physical. Hence, because they are simply physical instruments, cameras and computers really do not know, and can never, know anything at all.

Therefore, knowledge, considered as a fact of nature, is *immaterial* and *liberating*. A human being is essentially superior to machines (as well as to plants and animals) because we are *capable* of knowing scientifically, philosophically, and theologically, and, when *actually* knowing, we are exercising our nature to its fullest. Transcending the physical, even while being in the world, human beings can understand the universe in terms of *what* it contains and also in terms of *why* things are the way they are. Whereas subhumans possess only their own essences, knowers are capable of possessing all intelligible things other than themselves. This is the Realistic basis for all human culture, technology, science, philosophy, and theology.

As much as Heidegger and Gadamer insist upon the rejection of a mere subjectivism, they nonetheless remain in the subjective mode of thought. By begging the question with respect to the universality of historical conditioning, not only in regard to one's style of writing and localized social prejudices, but in regard to the *entire content* of one's science, philosophy, and theology, the post-moderns have in effect already prejudged the whole world in favor of the post-modern theory. Their sincerity and coherence notwithstanding, all this accomplishes is to forever trap them within their own minds. Their thoughts correspond only to their own thoughts; the world is a reflection of themselves in their own looking glasses and nothing more. God, the world, and everything are really only me, either alone or with others — that is, if there really is a me.

In contrast, for someone such as Aquinas, we can have both our selfhood and God at the same time. In morality, orthopraxis is greatly enhanced by orthodoxy. In no way does this rule out toleration and laughter in life. Justice is not opposed to charity among human beings any more than it is in God. There is no reason why we cannot have a hard-headed, tough-minded approach to logic, science, sin, and truth, on the one hand, and a soft-hearted approach to sinners and those in error, on the other hand. In real life it is not necessary to deny traditional theology in order to preserve our right to think for ourselves, as Heidegger implies in his Marburg Lectures (Preliminary Part, I: 4, e-a). And neither is it necessary to adopt the Neo-Paganistic, "the Earth is God's Body" sort of pantheism of someone such as Matthew Fox in order to justify a sincere concern for *our* natural environment.

In our real lived-world there *are* essences, moral absolutes, and *per se* goods. It *is* the case that Nature is an orderly array of natures; that there are real necessities in natural interactions. Appearance and reality, the phenomenal and the noumenal, and so forth, are not incongruent. The senses and the mind do in fact exist in one being. *How* this is possible is explained by the real distinction of essence and existence.

In the area of ethics, to deny the existence of fixed standards of moral action (practical knowledge) would be to act like the sailor who threw away his compass because the needle always pointed in the same direction. This can hardly be taken as making any sense in the real world of human experience. Every human being is a sailor who needs to know the location of the stars and the direction of the horizon if he or she is to act rationally. This means that it is absolutely necessary to have goals, and that these goals must be common to all human beings and all cultures throughout all history — basic goals founded upon the most basic aspects of human nature, that is, the basic principles of the natural moral law.

Gadamer, in the first Supplement to his new *Summa* of post-modern times (*Truth and Method*), insists that the hermeneutical turn is not merely another method on the philosophical scene. It is instead a description of the way things really are, whether or not anyone is aware of it. It is an exercise in consciousness-raising. And what we are raised to is the realization that everything is so historically conditioned by the peculiar set of circumstances of the time that there can be no privileged perspective from which to view the world. What he is revealing to us, in other words, is a new world-view, as complete and all-encompassing as anything previously known in the history of philosophical systems.

Nevertheless, Gadamer also insists in the Afterword to the same work that his new scheme of things is not a radical conservatism in human moral, social, and political life. Social mores *can* change. Such changes are brought about by an "emancipatory reflection" carried on within society and leading to the establishment of new goals and directions for society.

A social consciousness, a communal consensus, and a psychological reorientation can arise which break up the *status quo* and move society ahead in new and progressive ways. But surely this vague talk about progress can only be political-style rhetoric; it is not a philosophy of human morality. What Gadamer does not tell us, and cannot, by his own admission, tell us, is what these new horizons and north stars are going to be. Yet such information is exactly what a rational decision-making process needs. The efforts of later thinkers, such as Rorty, to add greater definition to the general scheme of things, as we have already seen, completely fails in this regard.

This state of affairs is to be expected. It fits the historic pattern stretching back into ancient times. No one maintaining an essentially anthropocentric doctrine, as we find, for instance, in Hegel, Marx, James, Whitehead, Heidegger, and Sartre, has been able to write a coherent work on personal ethical behavior. Even the ancient Stoics, for all their interest in ethics, could not overcome the amoral consequences of their pantheistic doctrine of the World-Soul. The best Stoicism could do was to urge its followers to write "ego" in huge letters across the sky, to be "bigger" than whatever happened to them, that is, to accept whatever happened and like it. In effect, it taught its disciples to actually do nothing. Post-modernism wants to regard the inherent moral ambiguity of pantheism as a great boon to human kind. In fact it is quite useless.

It is not even possible to rationally discuss progress without a fixed idea of what our ideal goal actually is. There must be some sort of ideal, *a priori*, "saving" knowledge if we are to measure our progress, either as individuals or as groups. There is only one way to stand upright in this matter, and an infinite number of ways to fall down. Without some fixed standard, such as the Word of God, an essential human nature which can support a natural moral law, or the like, we literally do not know where we are, what we are doing, or what we are talking about.

A similar situation holds for science. If we were to believe Heidegger when he asserts that science does not discover the truth about the way nature really is (speculative knowledge), but rather prescribes to nature its laws, we would be acting as if we were a school of fish living in an amorphous sea, inventing and projecting into the water the rules of hydrodynamics as we swim along. But this is as much opposed to well-established modern science as "emancipatory reflection" is to the demands of rational decision-making. Also in the Afterword to his *Truth and Method*, Gadamer insists that his aesthetic-hermeneutic and humanistic-historicism do not go against the objectivity of modern science.

It seems to me, however, that we have heard this sort of thing before. Was it not Bishop Berkeley who insisted that, even though there was in fact no material universe at all, science could go on as usual? Berkeley's Ontological Idealism left science exactly as it was; not one iota of Newton, or any other great scientist, need be altered. In more modern times, B. F. Skinner said the same sort of thing. Even though, in truth, there is no such thing as mind, we can still continue to use mental phraseology in ordinary language, and even in scientific papers, as long as we realize that reality is composed exclusively of material entities and their interactions. At least, unlike Rorty and Bernstein, neither Berkeley nor Skinner ever claimed to be pragmatists in any post-modern sense. After all, how pragmatic can a doctrine be when it makes no difference in practice?

It turns out that what Gadamer means by preserving the objectivity of science is the same thing that Heidegger meant by it, namely, that the objectivity of science *is not* being preserved. What is not, is; what is, is not. What is present is absent; what is absent is present. The interpretation is cancelled; the cancellation is interpreted. The greatest justice is the greatest injustice, and so on. What Gadamer wants to preserve is the *appearance* of objectivity. Science operates on one level, that of laboratory practice. That is what science is, says Gadamer, and it is wrong for the philosopher to tell science that it *ought* to be something else. All well and good. But what about *real* necessities in nature?

Here is where philosophy comes into the picture, howbeit on a different level. Knowing that the world is really only Becoming, and that there is no Being, we know that there cannot be, objectively speaking, any really universal and necessary laws operating in nature. Thus it is the task of philosophy to explain how science can thematize the experienced world through language, thus giving the finite human knower the *impression* of a scientific world which is really there independently of the human subject. But is this not too much like saying that, *for the time being,* there *never* will be new taxes?

When all is said and done, such views are certainly bizarre, to say the least. Nevertheless, the typical post-modern feels forced into such views. The alternative would be to admit that the world as known preexists, is pre-given, possesses a being unrelated to the human knower — something which is unthinkable in our post-modern age. The most telling pages in Gadamer's *Truth and Method* occur at the end of his work, in the chapter on language as the "horizon" (i.e., the ultimate foundation) of a hermeneutical ontology. In direct contrast to Aquinas's realism, which recognizes that the idea of something and the something are indeed one and the same thing (which is the *only* way to avoid Epistemological Idealism), Gadamer claims that only through the medium of language can human beings be related to the world. Finite, historical man meets the world in language.

In this way, claims Gadamer, the ancient philosophical problem and dialectical puzzle of the one and the many is finally resolved. Relegating to "medieval speculation" the notion of knowledge as a representation of a preexisting real order of things, Gadamer proposes instead to solve the problem on the basis of an internal capacity of human beings to use language to create the being of the world. Contrary to all common-sense realism, there are no things; there are only "things." The world is not "just there" waiting to be known; neither is language merely an arbitrary system of symbols useful for calculations, as in mathematics. Rather, language is the light which enlightens every man who comes into the world. It is the medium which explains why there is something rather than nothing. Being is wholly verbal in character.[10]

Such a view, though, is simply a continuation of Heidegger's final sanctification of Epistemological Idealism, which is believed by post-moderns, in the unexamined fashion of a basic tenet of a religious cult, to be a necessary consequence of the lack of Being in reality. A more true-to-life foundational analysis, however, shows us that this is in no way necessary theoretically speaking, and would certainly, if actually acted upon, be destructive of all human life and society practically speaking.

In his *Truth and Method* which, in effect, is a commentary on Heidegger's *Being and Time,* Gadamer makes it clear that there is no Being or substantial reality to be discovered by the investigator. He states that ". . . nor can one suitably describe what occurs here [in the process of interpretation] as the progressive knowledge of what exists, so that an infinite intellect would contain everything that could ever speak out of the whole tradition."[11] There are no real things to be discovered, only meanings to be invented. "The thing itself" that asserts its force and speaks through the poet, however, is really only the thinker himself or herself.

With respect to language, "To say what one means, on the other hand — to make oneself understood — means to hold what is said together with an infinity of what is not said in one unified meaning and to ensure that it is understood in this way."[12] This is plain Hegelianism. Sooner or later Something is Nothing, and everything becomes irrational at its very root.

The grain of truth in Gadamer's insight, from the existential perspective, is that because *esse,* which is the act of all acts and the perfection of all perfections, cannot be conceptualized as it is immediately grasped in judgment, there is no possible way to eliminate all mystery from beings, and especially spiritual beings. What we are in reality (essence *and* existence) must always exceed what can be *said* about us, and even what we can say about ourselves. It does not entail the ultimate irrationality of trying to reduce all being to becoming, with its ensuing confusion and unintelligible ambiguity in all areas of human life — from literature to morals, from liturgy to methodology, and from learning to motivation. This confusion will end only when everyone learns really to listen to what "being" is saying to us in the concrete.

Change *within* being and essence *within* being do not rule out the existence of human freedom, personal self-identity, and individual dignity. Being authentic, genuine, and true to yourself does not contradict being true to God, the Church, your husband or wife, your parents and children, or your promise to take out the garbage. The growth and flowering of a tree, for instance, is not the negation of the nature of the tree. A tiny acorn developing into a mighty oak tree is certainly a progression. Rather than being an alienation or a negation, however, it is the fulfillment and completion of what is primordial and ever-present in that being. In this way the conditioned must always exist *within* the unconditioned, and chaos *within* order and cosmos.[13]

So it is with all of reality. The individual members of the real world form a hierarchy in which no one substance is identified with any other one. In this complex, vertically integrated system different beings fulfill themselves in different ways. To the extent a being fulfills its nature it is content or, in the case of personal beings, happy. This is the very meaning of happiness and joy, namely, the by-product of fulfilling our own nature, of being more completely in an existential way what we already are in an essential way. Hence our rational nature provides an internal, objective standard against which we can judge progress and laws as good or bad.

Yet there is no disunity within the one being. Nor is there any opposition between the internal and the objective. Each being is existentially unique, even while belonging to a species; that is, each being is specified *in act* in a particular way; each being possesses an essence in an objective, extramental way. To understand how this is possible requires a knowledge of the real distinction of essence and existence, something well within our grasp to understand, as was shown above. However, for those who take for granted the truth of the roots of super-modernity there is no way they can ever hope to see and appreciate the far-ranging significance of the real distinction. For those who do see it, though, they also see that it does not belong only to Aquinas in an ancient age, but to everyone everywhere at all times. The foundational analysis of being belongs to all ages, and the meaning of *being*, although open to various interpretations, possesses at least one meaning which allows us to be both essentialistic *and* existentialistic at the same time.

To be *what* we are as human persons we must *act*, and the more we act in conformity with our nature the more we become what we are, and as a consequence, the closer we grow to God and to other human persons. We must *become* what we *are*. The fixed and the variable are not mutually exclusive; eternity and time, nature and *esse*, male and female, and so forth, are complementary.

The sacred, even while retaining its essential purity as the supernatural reality which it is in itself, is not mutually exclusive relative to the secular, either in theory or in practice. Taking existence seriously, in conjunction with essence, is the secret to both speculative and pragmatic success. God is not the world, and the world is not God. Yet God and the world, even though not identified with each other in any way, nor related as body and soul, are so intimate that God is closer to the individual human person than anything in the material world.

"It has arrived," announces Gilson, quoting the French poet J. N. A. Rimbaud; "What?" "Eternity." In light of the Thomistic foundational analysis, the contemporary thinker soon comes to realize that neo-modernity for the sake of neo-modernity, that "pop" culture and social consensus as the highest moral judge, supported by "The church of what's happening now," that the confusion of the style of writing and the peculiar prejudices of the writer with the eternal truth content the work may contain, and that the assumption that *all* truth is historically conditioned to the extreme point of always being only "truth," are doctrines which are themselves *always* passé. Where and when is eternity? It is *hic et nunc*.[14]

APPENDIX: A SUMMARY OF HUME'S DEDUCTION LEADING TO SKEPTICISM

MAIN REFERENCES: See Hume's *A Treatise of Human Nature,* Book I, Part III, sections V and XIV; Part IV, section V, as well as the "Appendix." See also his *An Inquiry Concerning Human Understanding,* Section 12, Part III.

According to A. J. Ayer, in his *The Central Questions of Philosophy* (N.Y.: Penguin, 1978), the world is composed of a long series of facts and events with no inherent relationship to each other. He tells us that "In nature one thing just happens after another. Cause and effect have their place only in our imaginative arrangements and extensions of these primary facts" (p. 183). If we take him at his word, this means, for instance, that, objectively speaking, lightning has nothing to do with forest fires nor sex with babies (which, theoretically speaking, should make forest rangers and teenagers very happy).

In addition, we are informed that there can be no such thing as an objective moral code of behavior. As a scientific determinist he must regard our feelings of personal freedom as misleading. Even though most people seem to regard their own moral standards as the best, and continue, even in our scientific age, to think themselves free, there is no foundation for such a view *in reality.* However the world may be ultimately pictured (atomistically or not), there is no room for freedom and moral evaluations in a physicalist universe of matter in motion, energy, and change. (See pp. 129–30, 226–27, 233–35.)

In his own way Ayer is an *avant-garde* Deconstructionist agnostic, holding a somewhat secret doctrine, about the way things really are. However, to the average human being Ayer's words are totally irrelevant. He has rendered himself meaningless as far as anything *human* is concerned. Even worse, insofar as he has ruled out any possible way of *evaluating* the facts of experience, which he regards, in their primary and fundamental mode of existence, as all disconnected and separated from each other, he has rendered him-self *sub-human*. It is part and parcel of human nature to make value judgments and to justify such judgments in some objective way.

In this regard a remark of Mark Van Doren is pertinent. He states, in reference to the ancient Atomist Lucretius, that the more eloquent the speaker the less convincing the argument.

> Beginning thus, he goes on with the excellent mind he has to prove that there is no mind — or rather, to explain mind as mechanics. The better the mind that does this, the falser the demonstration. For what Lucretius asks us to believe is no easier to believe than that the mind is a miracle. And it takes longer to say (*The Noble Voice* [N.Y.: Holt, 1947], p. 162).

Ayer, who takes his inspiration from Hume, sees Hume as being in the same situation, with the difference that Hume attempted to justify a more or less Judaeo-Christian moral code based upon sentiment, natural affection, and enlightened self-interest. Others, such as J. S. Mill, also attempted the same sort of thing. According to Ayer, Hume was fine as long as he remained in his study, abstractly thinking and writing about how impossible it was to draw any certain conclusions about anything based upon cause-effect reasoning. When he got up from his chair, however, and entered upon the concrete world of real-life existence, he may as well have never written anything concerning skepticism. Ayer says of Hume:

> He admitted that he was not able to adhere to this sceptical po-sition, outside his study. Like the rest of us, he allowed himself to be guided in the practical conduct of life by what he called his natural beliefs, but he did not claim that this was rational; indeed, even to speak of the beliefs on which he acted as natural beliefs, with the implication that they were shared by the generality of people over some period of time, was to make an inference which he could not rationally justify (p. 140).

As with so many other modern thinkers, a fundamental *ir*rationality is the best Hume can do.

As far as ordinary human life is concerned Hume is totally irrelevant. But how does he get himself into such a position? As a thinker Hume reaches his skeptical conclusions via a deductive process, not via some process of concrete experience and observation. He is, in fact, an Epistemological Idealist in the tradition of Descartes. As a result, we should not be surprised that he ends up being stuck only within his own mind after he deliberately starts out only within his own mind. Like Descartes, he is primarily interested in going from ideas to things rather than vice versa; he ends up going from ideas to ideas. This shows up very clearly in his use of the terms "distinct" and "distinction," terms which are of crucial importance when attempting to understand Humean "empiricism."

In 1644, under the title of *Renati Descartes Principia Philosophiae,* Descartes published the most complete exposition of his philosophy, which included a great deal of his (mostly wrong) science as well. In his preface to his *Principles of Philosophy* Descartes explains that this work should be regarded as the culmination of all his earlier works. It is divided into four parts, the first part, as we would expect, dealing with the principles of human knowledge. Only one point is of primary interest to me here, and that is what Descartes means by a "real distinction." In Part I, section 60, Descartes tells his readers that there are three kinds of distinctions: The "real," the "modal," and "of reason." As rendered into English by J. Veitch (*The Method, Meditations, and Philosophy of Descartes,* trans. J. Veitch, [Washington, D.C.: Dunne, 1901], p. 324) from the original Latin: "The real [distinction] properly subsists between two or more substances; and it is sufficient to assure us that two substances are really mutually distinct, if only we are able clearly and distinctly to conceive the one of them without the other." What does Descartes mean by a real distinction? He means a separation (what Aquinas would have called a *separatio*).

This way of defining a real distinction can be traced back to Giles of Rome, an immediate follower (and misinterpreter) of Thomas Aquinas. It is taken for granted by later "scholastics" as well, such as Francis Suarez (1548–1617), from whom much of Europe learned its philosophy in the early seventeenth century. (On this see Suarez's *On the Various Kinds of Distinctions* [*Disputationes Metaphysicae,* VII, II, 9–14] trans. C. Vollert, [Milwaukee: Marquette U. Press, 1947]; and his *On Formal and Universal Unity,* trans. J. F. Ross [Milwaukee: Marquette U. Press, 1964].)

This same approach is maintained throughout the whole modern Idealism tradition. Spinoza, for instance, when commenting on Descartes's *Principles of Philosophy,* reads him exactly in this way. Spinoza gives, under the heading of "Definitions," the following: "Two substances are said to be really distinguished when each one can exist without the other" (*Principles of Cartesian Philosophy,* trans. H. E. Wedeck, [N.Y.: Philosophical Library, 1961], p. 21).

It is no different with Hume. In the twelfth paragraph of the "Appendix" to his *A Treatise of Human Nature: Being An Attempt To Introduce The Experimental Method of Reasoning Into Moral Subjects,* Hume speaks in exactly the same terms:

Whatever is distinct is distinguishable, and whatever is distinguishable is separable by the thought or imagination. All perceptions are distinct. They are, therefore, distinguishable, and separable, and may be conceived as separately existant [sic], and may exist separately, without any contradiction or absurdity.

Earlier in the same work he had said basically the same thing, but in a longer form. At the end of the earlier statement he also brings in Descartes's definition of substance in order to declare that individually existing perceptions *are* substances. Perceptions, he states, "may exist separately, and have no need of anything else to support their existence. They are therefore substances, as far as this definition explains a substance" (Book I, Part IV, section V, "Of the Immateriality of the Soul").

This is confirmed in a general way in Book I of his *Treatise of Human Nature,* Part III, section V, "Of the Impressions of the Senses and Memory," where Hume states that, as far as the impressions which arise from the senses are concerned, "their ultimate cause is, in my opinion, perfectly inexplicable by human reason, and it will always be impossible to decide with certainty, whether they arise immediately from the object, or are produced by the creative power of the mind, or are derived from the Author of our being." The last possibility is meant to take into account the view of Bishop Berkeley who, on the basis of reductionistic materialism or physicalism, reasoned his way into the position that the existence of the entire extramental material world is an unnecessary hypothesis, even for science. All of our sense knowledge could just as well come *directly* from God.

Hume does not seem to think it is important to decide among the three alternatives. This is fine, provided one is in the Idealist philosophical tradition, for then we are primarily concerned with our own consciousness, and where our ideas come from can be regarded as relatively unimportant. Not so in a Realist tradition. For Hume to say that he is not sure about the existence of external objects as the source of his sense knowledge of those external objects, is for him to give away his hand as a follower of Descartes. The difference between being sure and not being sure is significant; it is the difference between Realism and Idealism.

What I have said of Hume is confirmed by Ayer's interpretation of the Scot. Logic, says Ayer in his *Central Questions,* does not apply directly to events in the real world. When we speak of logical relationships, we are really speaking only of the descriptions of the events as conveyed in propositional form. Reality is purely verbal. It is only our descriptions of the events as conveyed in propositional form. It is only our descriptions of the events which can be logically distinct relative to each other. But to be logically distinct means to be logically independent of each other. But what does that mean? Ayer says that he is not sure exactly what Hume meant by it, "but a reasonable definition would seem to be that two events are distinct if and only if they have no common part" (p. 140). In other words, projecting outwardly, to be distinct means to be physically separate.

Hume, who did not deny the existence of a material external world, was a very astute thinker, and a very stubborn person as well. Once he got on to something he was like a hound dog with a one-track nose. Hume knew exactly where the Cartesian trail would end up. To show clearly just how Hume's mind was working I will summarize his path in four arguments. Beginning in the same way as Descartes, Hume can demonstrate that all of the conclusions about God and the soul so highly prized by the Cartesians are rationally unfounded. All we really have to go on, concludes Hume, is a more or less extensive series of perceptions (or ideas, which for Hume are simply "faded" sense perceptions) associated together in a more or less orderly fashion based upon mere constant repetition. Hume, drawing upon the key figures of the Cartesian family (Descartes, Malebranche, Locke), proceeds:

> Whatever is clear and distinct (logically separated) intramentally is separated extramentally.
> All causes and effects are clear and distinct (logically separated) intramentally.
> Therefore, all causes and effects are separated extramentally.

This much was already taught by N. Malebranche, who went on to "see all things in God." The major premise is taken directly from Descartes. This, in fact, is the essence of his Epistemological Idealism, namely, whatever is thought in a certain way *is* the extramental thing itself.

But:

> No knowledge less evident to us than our knowledge of the world can give us a knowledge of causality.
> All knowledge of God is less evident to us than our knowledge of the world.
> Therefore, no knowledge of God can give us a knowledge of causality.

This he learned from Locke. There are no innate ideas, even of God. Thus there is no justification for some thinkers, such as Malebranche, appealing to God in order to explain the apparent interconnection of things and events in the world.

So *where* is causality to be found? Hume does not deny causality; he only relocates it. Assuming that all knowledge is an accumulation of sense perceptions:

All arrangements of perceptions are only within the mind.
All knowledge of causality is an arrangement of perceptions.
Therefore, all knowledge of causality is only within the mind.

All we can picture with our imagination is a series of before and after snapshots or still-frames (to use some anachronistic examples) which are always disconnected, yet juxtaposed, with respect to each other. We never can *picture* the causal connections.

How then are we supposed to know about "metaphysical" things such as teleology, God, and the soul, that is, things supposedly "beyond nature"?

Anything based upon the knowledge of causality is only within
the mind.
All reasoning about purpose in the world, God, and the soul, is
based upon the knowledge of causality.
Therefore, all reasoning about such things is only within the
mind.

So much then for all speculative knowledge about "higher things." We are back to the skepticism of M. Montaigne, but this time around *without* the support of faith.

This situation leaves Hume in a state of despair. All books not based upon the interrelationships of ideas (mathematics) and/or the associationships of sense perceptions are to be burned. Yet he is not happy. As he tells us in his *Treatise of Human Nature,* Book I, Part IV, section VII, "Conclusion":

> I am confounded with all these questions, and begin to fancy
> myself in the most deplorable condition imaginable, environed
> with the deepest darkness, and utterly deprived of the use of
> every member and faculty. . . . I dine, I play a game of
> backgammon, I converse, and am merry with my friends; and
> when, after three or four hours' amusement, I would return to
> these speculations, they appear so cold, and strained, and
> ridiculous, that I cannot find in my heart to enter into them
> any further.

Thus do we see in Hume's "empiricism" the necessary outcome of anthropocentrism. It is clear from the inner logic of Hume's position that it is not based upon any direct experience of the world on his part, but rather upon the thought of previous thinkers. He is, in effect, arguing from authority. Rather than being an independently minded "empiricist," he is in fact only one more part, although a very important part (because he shows what Cartesianism really leads to) of the Cartesian Epistemological Idealistic tradition.

Later, Hume begot Kant, who begot Hegel, and so forth. Kant realized that what Hume said would apply to the physical sciences as well as to religious matters. Anthropocentrism is as destructive of science as it is of religion. In his effort to save science he subdivided knowledge into several compartments, hermetically sealed relative to each other, which resulted in deep dichotomies within his view of reality. Hegel was the faced with the problem of overcoming these divisions and restoring unity to the world and human life. (Further to this see F. F. Centore, "Hume, Reid, and Skepticism," *Philosophical Studies* 28 (1981): 212–20.)

NOTES

CHAPTER 1

1. On the history of hermeneutics and the deconstructionist turn see H.-G. Gadamer, *Reason in the Age of Science,* trans. F. G. Lawrence, (Cambridge, Mass.: MIT Press, 1982); M. C. Taylor, *Deconstructing Theology* (N.Y.: Crossroad, 1982).

2. On the views of Gorgias see J. Owens, *A History of Ancient Western Philosophy* (N.Y.: Appleton-Century-Crofts, 1959), 160–64.

3. See Plato's *Meno,* 97e–98a.

4. On Protagoras see J. Owens, *Western Philosophy,* 157–60.

5. See J. Macquarrie, *In Search of Deity* (N.Y.: Crossroad, 1985), 233.

6. R. Rorty, *Philosophy and the Mirror of Nature* (N.J.: Princeton University Press, 1979), 170.

7. R. Rorty, *Consequences of Pragmatism* (Minneapolis: University of Minnesota Press, 1982), 165. This, however, does not rule out *per se* goods; in fact *it* is a good in itself, its own goal. "We are not conversing because we have a goal, but because Socratic conversation is an activity which is its *own* end" (172).

8. Ibid., 53

9. Ibid., 208.

10. Ibid., 229.

11. Taylor, *Deconstructing Theology,* 63, note 26. In his *Erring* (Chicago: University of Chicago Press, 1984), 76, Taylor states that "Christianity is a religion of the book, and the West is a book culture." This is very Protestant, but not very Catholic.

12. Taylor, *Deconstructing Theology,* 49. See also his *Erring,* cited above, 112–20.

13. Taylor, *Deconstructing Theology,* 102.

14. Ibid. According to Arthur Peacocke, among Protestants, pantheistic evolutionism, as it shows up in immanentism, pan-psychism, process philosophy, and process theology, is the dominant form of natural theology in America today. See "Biological Evolution and Christian Theology — Yesterday and Today," *Darwinism and Divinity,* ed. J. Durant (Oxford: Basil Blackwell, 1985), 113.

15. J. D. Caputo, *Radical Hermeneutics: Repetition, Deconstruction, and the Hermeneutic Project* (Bloomington: Indiana University Press, 1987), 280.

16. Ibid.

17. Ibid., 281.

18. See ibid., 288.

19. See ibid., 288–90.

20. Caputo does have one major criticism of Heidegger; namely, that he had no real sense of humor, especially with respect to someone like Kierkegaard. Heidegger was out to deconstruct traditional metaphysics; Kierkegaard wanted to demolish *all* metaphysics forever, but he let us know about it in an ironic way. This was Kierkegaard's great joke on Hegel, his loud last laugh on all "higher" learning. See also his "Presidential Address: Radical Hermeneutics and the Human Condition," *Proceedings of the A.C.P.A.,* 62 (1988): 2–14.

21. Cf. R. A. Knox, *University Sermons,* ed. P. Caraman (Montreal: Palm, 1963), 157: "Oh, to be sure, we all know good atheists. But we all have the feeling about them that they are, as it were, chewing the cud of that Christianity in which their ancestors believed; they are living up to a code which is in fact Christian, although they do not acknowledge it."

22. This, of course, can be reversed. For instance, Vaihinger, following Kant, states that if you *act* like a believer, then you *are* one regardless of what you may call yourself.

23. J. L. Mackie, *The Miracle of Theism* (N.Y.: Oxford University Press, 1982), 245. One of the people Mackie criticizes for insisting that God is needed to make even rationality itself rational is Hans Kueng. But he does not seem to be at all aware of the fact that Kueng is a pantheist, even though he does describe Kueng's God as being rather indeterminate, mysterious, incomprehensible, and complex. See 251, 262.

24. See ibid., 246.

25. On the existential meaning of *Yahweh* see G. Ricciotti, *The History of Israel,* 2d ed., Vol. I (Milwaukee: Bruce, 1958), 178. Cf. also E. Gilson, *The Spirit of Thomism* (N.Y.: Harper & Row, 1966), 120, note 18, where he makes reference to the Hebrew scholar E. Schild, who states that syntactically speaking the existential reading of the passage is the only correct one. See also F. F. Centore, "The 'Creative' Ethics of Nietzsche and Sartre," *Faith and Reason* 10 (1984): 222–41.

26. Mackie, *The Miracle of Theism,* 246.

27. Caputo, *Radical Hermeneutics,* 279.

28. On the ancient mystery cults see H. J. Rose, *Religion in Greece and Rome* (N.Y.: Harper, 1959); J. Ferguson, *The Religions of the Roman Empire* (Ithaca, N.Y.: Cornell University Press, 1970); W. Burkert, *Ancient Mystery Cults* (Cambridge, Mass.: Harvard University Press, 1987). See also M. Fox, *The Coming of the Cosmic Christ* (N.Y.: Harper & Row, 1988).

29. A. Bloom, *The Closing of the American Mind* (N.Y.: Simon and Schuster, 1987), 221.

30. Ibid., 222.

31. See ibid., 331.

32. Ibid., 154.

33. Ibid., 311. Bloom goes on, 311–12: "If I am right in believing that Heidegger's teachings are the most powerful intellectual force in our times, then the crisis of the German university, which everyone saw, is the crisis of the university everywhere." On page 208 Bloom states that Nietzsche, one of Heidegger's heroes, was the first philosopher to openly attack Socrates. The ideal human being for Bloom seems to be the ironic, lonely, isolated, misunderstood, unpopular man of reason; not the man of unreason, even though the Superman or poet may be just as much of an outsider. The university should be a haven for such people.

34. Rorty, *Consequences of Pragmatism,* 174.

35. To repeat, there is only one way to stand upright in this matter, which is to say that no other approach will work. For instance, A. MacIntyre's attempted

circumvention of relativism (perspectivism), in *Whose Justice? Which Rationality?* (Notre Dame, Ind.: University of Notre Dame Press, 1988), will not do. For one culture to offer something better to another culture according to *its own* standards in no way tells us that the standards of the one culture are better than those of the other culture. Despite the many historically conditioned aspects of life, to know that its own standards are better requires standards independent of *all* cultures. *If* someone denies the existence of such independent standards, then that thinker remains a post-modern regardless of how much he or she might wish for something else.

36. Ayer himself admits that "few of the principal theses of the Vienna Circle survive intact," that metaphysics is "no longer a term of opprobrium," and that the "pragmatic treatment of scientific theories is less in favour than scientific realism." *Philosophy in the Twentieth Century* (N.Y.: Random House, 1982), 140–41.

On the reintroduction of ancient and medieval ideas into modern science see W. Heisenberg, *Physics and Philosophy* (N.Y.: Harper, 1962), esp. 70 ff., 159 ff.; R. M. Augros and G. N. Stanciu, *The New Story of Science* (Lake Bluff, Ill.: Gateway, 1984); and R. M. Augros and G. N. Stanciu, *The New Biology* (Boston: New Science Library, 1988).

On the history of the Logical Positivism movement see F. C. Copleston, *Contemporary Philosophy* (London: Search Press, 1973); F. Waismann, *Wittgenstein and the Vienna Circle* (N.Y.: Barnes and Noble, 1979).

Even though twentieth-century philosophy generally is not, modern science is becoming more and more well disposed toward traditional philosophy. Einstein's finite but unbounded universe, the "Big Bang" theory of the origin of the universe, the current evidence that there are many aspects of light and energy more fundamental than the proton, pictures of matter taken with high-resolution scanning transmission electron microscopes (both showing that the atom can no longer be regarded as the ultimate level of material reality), important modifications in Darwin's special theory of evolution, and the present view of sexual reproduction as nature's way of "fooling" disease-causing organisms in the higher life forms (which seems to imply the contradictory notion that sexual reproduction came about both before and after natural selection) would be examples of how science has become more favorable toward traditional philosophy. Today it is scientifically possible to maintain that the world is not infinite, not eternal, and that Supernatural Theism is compatible with evolutionary theory. Perhaps of greatest significance is that we can now reject atomism in our philosophy of nature, thus leaving us free to frame a Unified Field Theory in terms of Aristotle's potency and act. Further to this see F. F. Centore, "Potency, Space, and Time: Three Modern Theories," *The New Scholasticism* 63 (1989): 435–62.

37. For Kant's view see his 1783 work *Prolegomena to Any Future Metaphysics,* trans. P. Carus and L. W. Beck, (Indianapolis: Bobbs-Merrill, 1950). In the tradition carried on by Kant, metaphysics deals with "mere concepts" and consists entirely of *a priori* concepts (8). Its knowledge cannot be empirical, and its principles can never derive from experience, whether internal or external (13). It deals with things that cannot be discovered or confirmed by any experience. These things are its essential goal (75). Its objects are only ideas in the mind (80). See also 87, 95, 110, 120.

38. Rorty, *Consequences,* 174–75.

39. Taylor, *Deconstructing Theology,* 81.

CHAPTER 2

1. Cf. H. Grenier, *Thomistic Philosophy,* vol. 3 (Charlottetown, Prince Edward Island: St. Dunstan's University Press, 1949), 83–84: "Actions by which a

thing tends to its natural end are naturally suited to it, i.e., are intrinsically good. . . . But man is naturally destined for God."

2. Cf. E. Gilson, *The Spirit of Mediaeval Philosophy*, trans. A. H. C. Downes (N.Y.: Scribner's, 1940).

3. See Plato's dialogue *Cratylus*; also Aristotle's *Metaphysics* IV: 5, 1010 a 10–16: Cratylus was someone who "thought one ought not to speak at all, but who simply pointed his finger and censured Heraclitus for saying that it is impossible to step twice into the same river — for he himself believed that one could not do this even once" (trans. R. Hope).

4. See Aristotle's *Metaphysics* IV: 5, 1010 a 22–25; XI: 6, 1063 a 22–29. See also F. F. Centore, "Atomism and Plato's *Theaetetus*," *The Philosophical Forum* 5 (1974): 475–85.

5. For a very contemporary discussion of the meaning of Epistemological Realism see M. J. Adler, *Ten Philosophical Mistakes* (N.Y.: Macmillan, 1987), Part I, 5–127.

6. Descartes's overall life-style, as well as the individual events in his life, point to his deeply felt religious outlook. For instance, when his illegitimate daughter died at a young age, he took it as a punishment for his sin; and at the end of his life, even though in a Protestant land, he insisted upon a Catholic funeral. Later his pupil, Queen Christina, converted to Catholicism (1654). On Descartes's life see J. R. Vrooman, *René Descartes: A Biography* (N.Y.: Putnam, 1970).

7. R. Descartes, *Discourse on Method and Other Writings*, trans. A. Wollaston, (Baltimore: Penguin Books, 1960), 127. This way of naming God is still with us today. Cf. R. Swinburne who, at the beginning of his *The Coherence of Theism* (N.Y.: Oxford University Press, 1977), defines God as an omnipresent perfect spirit, creator of the universe, and source of moral obligation.

8. Descartes, *Discourse*, 128.

9. Ibid., 133.

10. *Descartes: Philosophical Writings*, ed. and trans. E. Anscombe and P. T. Geach, (London: Nelson, 1966), 136–37.

11. Ibid., 143.

12. E. Gilson, *The Unity of Philosophical Experience* (N.Y.: Scribner's, 1947), 171.

13. John H. Hick, *Philosophy of Religion*, 3rd ed. (Englewood Cliffs, N.J.: Prentice-Hall, 1983), 120.

14. Ibid., 121.

15. If, *qua* human beings, the Chinese, for example, are as alert and intelligent as any Italian ever was, why did the Chinese not develop mathematics and physics as did the Europeans, and do it much sooner? On this see J. Needham, *Science in Traditional China* (Hong Kong: Chinese University Press, 1981); and Wen-yuan Qian, *The Great Inertia: Scientific Stagnation in Traditional China* (London: Croom Helm, 1985).

16. See Anselm, *Proslogium; Monologium; etc.*, trans. S. N. Deane (LaSalle, Ill.: Open Court, 1958). This is a basically decent translation. Another good translation would be M. J. Charlesworth, *St. Anselm's Proslogion* (N.Y.: Oxford University Press, 1965). Anselm's language is awkward even for medieval Latin. On some of the problems involved with translating Anselm properly, see G. Schufreider, "Reunderstanding Anselm's Argument," *The New Scholasticism* 57 (1983): 384–409.

Anselm is basically a Platonist in his thinking. The *really real* for Plato are only the Forms or Ideas. Above the Ideas is the One Above Being. As a Christian, though, there can be nothing above God (who is being, not non-being) for Anselm. This is not the case in the Platonic tradition. Cf. Plotinus, *The Enneads*, trans. S. MacKenna, (London: Faber, 1956), V, 5, 6: "The First must be without form, and, if without form, then it is no Being." "And this name, The One, contains really no more than the negation of plurality." V, 5, 13: "Thus we rob it of its very being as The Absolute Good if we ascribe anything to it, existence or intellect or goodness." Of course, like everyone else, Plotinus cannot speak of, or even think, nothingness in any direct way. Like it or not, when discussing the One Above Being he must clothe it with positive attributes, even though, logically speaking, it cannot have any.

17. I. Kant, *Critique of Pure Reason,* trans. J. M. D. Meiklejohn (N.Y.: Wiley, 1900), 359. The translation by N. K. Smith is basically the same: *Critique of Pure Reason,* trans. N. K. Smith (N.Y.: St. Martin's Press, 1965), 531 (A642, B670).

18. I. Kant, *Critique of Practical Reason,* trans. L. W. Beck, (Indianapolis: Bobbs-Merrill, 1956), Introduction, xix.

19. Kant, *Practical Reason,* 129. Cf. Kant's *Critique of Judgment,* 87–88.

20. Kant, *Practical Reason,* 129.

21. See ibid., 130–36.

22. H. Vaihinger, *The Philosophy of As If,* 2d ed., trans. C. K. Ogden (London: Routledge and Kegan Paul, 1935), 311.

23. Ibid., 312.

24. Ibid., 307. The phrases are: "You act with rectitude, therefore you believe," and "I think, therefore I am."

25. See ibid., 313–18.

26. See Voltaire, *Philosophical Letters,* trans. E. Dilworth (Indianapolis: Bobbs-Merrill, 1961), "On the Pensées of M. Pascal," 123–24.

27. W. James, *Essays in Pragmatism,* ed. A. Castell (N.Y.: Hafner, 1948), 147. This passage is from *Pragmatism* (1907), Lecture II.

28. Ibid., 99. This passage is from *The Will to Believe* (1896) VI.

29. Ibid., 166 (*Pragmatism* VI).

30. Ibid., 171 (*Pragmatism* VI). Cf. 149: "The new contents [facts] themselves are not true, they simply *come* and *are*" (*Pragmatism* II).

31. Ibid., 91 (*The Will to Believe* II).

32. The language of the gambling table may not have been congenial to Harvard, Yale, and Brown students in 1896, but apparently the language of the New York Stock Exchange was. James forgets that a large part of Pascal's audience was composed of pseudo-sophisticates who spent many hours gambling. In his own way, James does the same sort of thing. His works are filled with terms such as credit, commerce, bank notes, cash value, pay off, working values, cash basis, prosperity, profit, and success, language suitable to the upsurge in capitalism at the time.

33. James, *Essays in Pragmatism,* 22 (*The Sentiment of Rationality,* 1880).

34. Ibid., 25 (*The Sentiment of Rationality,* 1880).

35. Ibid., 108 (*The Will to Believe* X, note 1).

36. See W. James, *The Varieties of Religious Experience: A Study in Human Nature* (N.Y.: Collier-Macmillan, 1961), 393–94.

37. Ibid., 396. James does not make reference to Freud here, but to Frederic W. H. Myers (1843–1901), noted for his work in spiritualism and psychical research.

38. Ibid., 396–97.

39. Ibid., 399.

40. Ibid.

41. Ibid., 400

42. Ibid., 407.

43. E. Gilson, *Reason and Revelation in the Middle Ages* (N.Y.: Scribner's, 1938), 96–97.

44. A. J. Ayer, *The Central Questions of Philosophy* (N.Y.: Penguin, 1978), 234–35. Cf. Ayer's *Ludwig Wittgenstein* (N.Y.: Penguin, 1986), 92: "I am not myself a religious believer but if I were I doubt if I should be content to be told that I

was playing a game in accordance with a canonical set of rules. Rather, I should wish for some assurance that my beliefs were true."

45. See G. E. Myers, *William James: His Life and Thought* (New Haven, Conn.: Yale University Press, 1986), 604, note 16.

CHAPTER 3

1. Some modern thinkers, such as Sigmund Freud in his *New Introductory Lectures on Psychoanalysis,* claim to find Hegel completely unintelligible. For examples of the sort of thing he may have had in mind, cf. *Hegel's Philosophy of Nature (Encyclopaedia,* Part II), trans. A. V. Miller (London: Oxford University Press, 1970):

> Fire is the existent being-for-self, negativity as such: only not the negativity of an other but the negation of the negative which results in universality and exact likeness. The first universality (air) is a dead affirmation; the veritable affirmation is fire. In fire, that which is not is posited as being, and vice versa; fire is accordingly active (*rege*) Time (110).
>
> *Zusatz.* Water is the Element of selfless opposition; it is a passive being-for-another, while fire is an active being-for-another (111).
>
> It is here [in the reactions of acids, alkalis, and water to form salts] especially that formation (*Gestaltung*) and crystallization have their seat. The process, in general, is this: one neutrality is sublated, but another one is brought forth in its place. The neutrality is therefore here engaged in conflict with itself; for the neutrality which is product is mediated by the negation of neutrality. We have, therefore, particular neutralities of acids and bases in mutual conflict (262).

Further to this see B. Blanshard, *On Philosophical Style* (Manchester, England: Manchester University Press, 1954).

2. G. Hegel, *The Phenomenology of Mind,* trans. J. B. Baillie, 2d ed. (London: Allen and Unwin, 1964), 759–60.

3. *Hegel: The Letters,* ed. and trans. C. Butler and C. Seiler (Bloomington: Indiana University Press, 1984), 465.

4. Ibid., 520.

5. For a comprehensive view of Kierkegaard's position see his *Concluding Unscientific Postscript,* trans. D. F. Swenson and W. Lowrie (Princeton, N.J.: Princeton University Press, 1941).

6. On Martin Luther see B. Lohse, *Martin Luther: Eine Einfuehrung in sein Leben und sein Werk* (Munich: Beck, 1981).

7. *Hegel Letters,* 282.

8. Ibid. It is possible that Hegel's emphasis upon his Lutheranism and lack of atheism was politically motivated. Just as likely, however, he really believed that his supreme philosophical wisdom could encompass, save, and absorb the best of any and all religious traditions and doctrines.

9. *Hegel Letters,* 51.

10. Ibid., 85, note.

11. W. Wallace, "Bibliographical Notice on the Three Editions and Three Prefaces of the Encyclopaedia," in *Hegel's Logic,* trans. W. Wallace, 3rd ed. (New York: Oxford University Press, 1975), xxxi.

12. For Hegel's political philosophy see *Hegel's Philosophy of Right,* trans. T. M. Knox (N.Y.: Oxford University Press, 1967), especially the Supplement or Additions, sections 258, 270, 281, 324–39; pp. 279, 283–85, 289, 295–97. See also sections 270 and 360 in the main work, pp. 164–74, 222–23. On the relationship between Hegel and twentieth-century European politics see L. Azar, *Twentieth Century In Crisis: Foundations of Totalitarianism* (Dubuque, Iowa.: Kendall/Hunt, 1990).

13. Wallace, *Hegel's Logic,* xlii.

14. Q. Lauer, *Hegel's Idea of Philosophy, with a New Translation of Hegel's Introduction to His Lectures on the History of Philosophy* (Bronx, N.Y.: Fordham University Press, 1971), 2.

15. Ibid., 73.

16. Ibid., 106.

17. Ibid., 107.

18. Ibid., 115.

19. On Hegel and Goethe see *Hegel Letters,* 681 ff.

20. Ibid., 517–18.

21. B. Spinoza, *Philosophy of Benedict de Spinoza,* trans. R. H. M. Elwes (N.Y.: Tudor, n.d.), 47: *Ethics* I: Prop. XI, "Note."

22. *Hegel Letters,* 492.

23. Ibid., 493.

24. Ibid.

25. Letter from Hegel to Georg Gabler (1786–1853) of 4 March 1828.

26. See Q. Lauer, *Hegel's Concept of God* (Albany: State University of New York Press, 1982), 281.

27. Lauer, *Hegel's Concept,* 264–65.

28. For more on this topic see F. F. Centore, "Lovejoy and Aquinas on God's 'Need' to Create," *Angelicum* 59 (1982): 23–36.

29. G. Hegel, *Lectures on the History of Philosophy,* trans. E. S. Haldane and F. H. Simson, as contained in the Introduction to the Deane edition of Anselm's *Proslogium,* xx.

30. Lauer, *Hegel's Concept,* 228.

31. Ibid., 99.

32. *Hegel's Logic,* 5 (*Logic* I: 2).

33. Ibid., 58 (*Logic* III: 36).

34. Ibid., 59 (*Logic* III: 36).

35. G. Hegel, *The Phenomenology of Mind,* 594.

In his 1943 essay on Hegel's idea of experience, contained in his *Holzwege* (1950), Heidegger is critical of Hegel's approach to reality, which wants to actively penetrate into being rather than simply allowing being (truth) to reveal itself. This means that, in order to be present, being (ultimately God) must be represented in some rational way. Not only does this confuse theology with ontology, claims Heidegger, but it also serves to complicate ontology because its end result is only a long series of concepts, all reflecting back upon each other. Phenomenology then becomes identified with logic, with the result that truth becomes conceptual certitude and *reason (ideas) become the very substance of all reality.* Cf. W. J. Richardson, *Heidegger,* 2d ed. (The Hague: Nijhoff, 1967), 359:

> All this is crystallized in the key-word of all post-Cartesian philosophy: Awareness, sc. Being-aware (*Bewusst-sein*); for Being (*-sein*) means "to be" in the manner of a "knowing" (*Bewusst-*), sc. of a *cogitatio,* of a pro-posing (re) present-ation.

36. See *Logic* VII: 88.

37. G. Hegel, *Lectures on the Philosophy of Religion, Together with a Work on the Proofs of the Existence of God,* trans. E. B. Speirs and J. B. Sanderson, 3 vols. (Atlantic Highlands, N.J.: Humanities, 1974), 3: 361.

38. See, for instance, Mercier's *A Manual of Modern Scholastic Philosophy,* trans. T. L. and S. A. Parker, 2 vols., 8th ed. (London: Kegan Paul, Trench, and Trubner, 1921–1922):

> We might go further and say that the substance or substantial being we abstract from the world of sensible nature forms the object of *all* metaphysics both special and general (I: 418).

> In other words, as apart from its existence, a thing may be called *real being, essence, quiddity*; whereas, in as far as it is an existing thing, it is called *existential, actual* being (I: 421).

> Metaphysics has nothing to do with the *verb* "to be" [here he means the copula] nor with *notional being [entia rationis vel entia secundae intentionis]*, which it leaves to be treated of in grammar and logic; it deals solely with *real* being (I: 442).

> He [Aquinas] enlarged the scope of the Peripatetic tradition and developed its teachings in the direction of a very pronounced individualism. In fine, he succeeded in welding [together] the main tenets of Aristotelianism and the most important doctrines given to us by St. Augustine (II: 405; the section on the history of philosophy was written by M. deWulf.).

> *Real* distinction is that which exists between different objects independently of our knowledge, either because they exist separately or because they are the physical parts of a whole (II: 511; the Glossary was written by G. Simons).

For a discussion of John Duns Scotus, O.F.M. (1266–1308) and Francis Suarez, S.J. (1548–1617), from whom much of Mercier's metaphysics was derived, see E. Gilson, *Being and Some Philosophers,* 2d ed. (Toronto: Pontifical Institute of Mediaeval Studies, 1952), chapter 3.

The main points of difference between the original Aquinas and the later "manual" tradition are (a) that Scotus, Suarez, and Mercier completely misunderstood Aquinas on "being" (for Thomas there is only *one* kind of real being and that is actual, existential being; "possibles" do not have any kind of real, independent existence at all); and (b) that a real distinction is not necessarily a separation.

39. H. Kueng, *Does God Exist?,* trans. E. Quinn (Garden City, N.Y.: Doubleday, 1980), 63.

40. Ibid., 183.

41. Ibid., 333 (italics removed).

42. Ibid., (italics removed).

43. See ibid., 332, 494, 617.

44. See ibid., 641–42.

45. See ibid., 659. God the Creator and God the Finisher should be compared to Whitehead's Primordial and Consequent natures of God. However, while Whitehead's God is less than perfect, lacking complete power and knowledge, Kueng wants the Absolute to also be "always the selfsame" and "eternally perfect" (188). This, I think, is the main reason why Hegel rather than Whitehead heads his list of thinkers, although he does claim that "Whitehead thinks of God wholly in Hegelian terms" (179).

46. Ibid., 679.

47. In this context we should not be surprised to find that Kueng gives the Virgin Mary no status whatsoever. On the possibility of an incarnation without pantheism, the orthodox theologian R. Garrigou-Lagrange, *The One God,* trans. B. Rose (St. Louis: Herder, 1946), explains:

> Even if God were to unite Himself hypostatically to all created natures, this would not result in pantheism, for there could not be a fusion of the assumed natures with the divine nature. We know from revelation that God is hypostatically united only with Christ's humanity, and if He were united with the humanity of other human beings, these would be impeccable as Christ is, which is manifestly not so (199).

48. See Kueng, *Does God Exist?,* 621. E. Gilson, quoting the Hebrew scholar E. Schild, states that the existential interpretation of the text is the only natural and syntactically correct one. See Gilson, *The Spirit of Thomism,* (N.Y.: Harper & Row, 1966), 120.

49. See Kueng, *Does God Exist?,* 687.

50. Ibid., 566 (italics removed).

51. Ibid., 568 (italics removed).

52. See ibid., 531.

53. See ibid., 566–68.

54. Ibid., 575.

55. See ibid., 519–20.

56. See ibid., 36.

57. See ibid., 117.

58. See ibid., 178.

59. Ibid., 181.

60. See ibid., 187 (italics removed).

61. Ibid., 417.

62. See ibid., 418.

63. In orthodox monotheism, in the beginning there was intelligibility, rationality, and harmony. Kueng keeps neglecting the fact that for Hegel in the beginning there was unintelligibility, irrationality, and disharmony. Hegel's whole system is built upon the assertion that Something is the same as Nothing, which cannot even be thought, much less accepted as reasonable. At the very root of Hegel's (and Marx's) metaphysics is contradiction.

For an attempted defense of Hegel on this point see B. Croce, *What Is Living and What Is Dead in the Philosophy of Hegel,* trans. D. Ainslie, 3rd ed. [1912] (Lanham, Md.: University Press of America, 1985), 24–32. Croce claims that when we think about them rightly and truly, "being" and "nothing" are not identical but in conflict with each other. This conflict is "becoming." Outside of becoming, being and nothing are mere abstractions and unreal shadows. In other words, becoming is the *only* Reality. If someone should think Hegel mad for destroying barren and formal logic, he or she would be on the right track, because everything does dissolve into everything else and in this sense Reality itself is mad. Neither is the denial of the principle of non-contradiction irrational. What Hegel did was to transform it from its erroneous condition in ordinary thinking into its true meaning. Ordinary people see the world as subdivided into many separate things, while true philosophy knows everything to be One. "That fallacious use exists, because we are unwilling to recognize that opposition or contradiction is not a defect . . . but that it is indeed the true being of things. All things are contradictory in themselves, and thought must think this contradiction." In other words, the *true* principle of identity (the positive form of the principle of non-contradiction) is the *thinking* of the *unity* of contradictories, especially on the most basic level of Something and Nothing.

The objection against Hegel is that contradictories cannot be thought. We cannot think of nothing *per se*. For instance, a square-circle is literally a non-entity, a non-being, and hence unthinkable. It seems obvious that in his defense of Hegel, Croce is begging the question; but why should this trouble someone who has transcended normal logic? Perhaps today we are in a better position to pass judgment on the issue than was Croce. History in the twentieth century, in the form of Fascism, Nazism, and Communism, has shown us what actually happens in real life when devoted disciples of Hegel's anthropocentrism put Hegel's "madness" into practice. Under the circumstances, it is incredible that a post-modern should demand that someone else, the Pope for instance, "get modern" and adopt a process philosophy and theology world-view.

Kierkegaard makes much more sense when he says of Hegel:

> The dialectic of the beginning must be made clear. This, its almost amusing character, that the beginning is, and again is not, just because it is the beginning — this true dialectical remark has long enough served as a sort of game played in good Hegelian society.

S. Kierkegaard, *Concluding Unscientific Postscript,* trans. D. F. Swenson and W. Lowrie (Princeton, N.J.: Princeton University Press, 1941), 101.

64. Kueng, *Does God Exist?,* 419.

65. Ibid.

66. See ibid., 152.

67. See A. N. Whitehead's *Religion in the Making* (N.Y.: Macmillan, 1926), II: 3; IV: 4–5. See also L. Azar, *"Esse* in the Philosophy of Whitehead," *The New Scholasticism* 37 (1963): 462–71; "Whitehead: Challenging a Challenge," *The Thomist* 30 (1966): 80–87. In the first article, Azar states: "For Whitehead, then, God is not, strictly speaking, a creator. As the first instance of creativity, He does not exist *before* creation; He rather exists *with* it" (469). See in addition F. F. Centore, "Whitehead's Conception of God," *Philosophical Studies* 19 (1970): 149–71, for an analysis of the incoherence of his process notion of God.

68. Also, if presence-to-self *(Bei-sich-sein)* is a necessary sign of any real being, as seems to be the case, for instance, with Karl Rahner (being is being-present-to-self, being is subjectivity), who wanted to combine Epistemological Idealism with Thomism, then it follows that unconscious things are unreal. The only way around this problem is to either adopt a panpsychism (everything is conscious however dimly) or to change presence-to-self to self-identity, which could then apply to individual rocks, trees, and so on. The latter way, though, is really only a metaphor which equivocates on the term "self." See B. Hurd, "Being is Being-Present-To-Self: Rahner's Key to Aquinas's Metaphysics," *The Thomist* 52 (1988): 63–78, for an attempt to view universal self-presence as a proper analogy.

CHAPTER 4

1. In 1962 Heidegger himself stated that there was no inversion, conversion, or reversal in his position between his earlier and later writings. If anything, his thought developed so as to grow closer to his original insight, and he wished that the "boden- und endlosen Geredes" concerning the so-called later Heidegger would stop. See W. J. Richardson, *Heidegger,* 2d ed. (The Hague: Nijhoff, 1967), Preface, xvi–xviii.

2. See F. Copleston, *Religion and the One: Philosophies East and West* (N.Y.: Crossroad, 1982), 165–66.

3. M. Heidegger, *An Introduction to Metaphysics,* trans. R. Manheim, (Garden City, N.Y.: Doubleday, 1961), 14 (hereinafter *Introduction*); cf. also 118. Originally a series of 1935 lectures, this work was somewhat redone and published in 1953. The lines quoted are in square brackets, indicating that they are later (after 1935) additions.

4. Richardson, *Heidegger,* 17; cf. also 18–19. Langan puts it this way: "Failure to see that Being is not a thing (whether *Idea, energeia,* or God) nor the totality of things, but that *Sein* and *Seiende* are radically different even though one cannot be without the other, is disastrous, both for the tradition as a whole, and for the existence of the individual *Dasein*." E. Gilson, T. Langan, and A. A. Maurer, *Recent Philosophy* (N.Y.: Random House, 1966), 147.

5. See Richardson, *Heidegger,* 20.

6. Heidegger, *Introduction,* 90; cf. also 107. Cf. also the 1949 Introduction ("The Way Back Into The Ground Of Metaphysics") to Heidegger's 1929 lecture *What Is Metaphysics?* contained in *Existentialism from Dostoevsky to Sartre,* ed. W. Kaufmann (N.Y.: Meridian Books, 1975), 276: Heidegger asks, When will Christianity realize that *for it* philosophy can only be foolishness, and should therefore be abandoned?

Does this mean that he is really a clandestine Christian, perhaps of the pre-Scholastic kind? I do not think so. What he is really saying is that religion should not try to supersede philosophy by pretending to give ultimate and final answers. *Any* religion is only a passing mode within Being, and should not try to be more than it is, namely, a temporary expression of the changing times. Further to this see C. H. Malik, "A Christian Reflection on Martin Heidegger," *The Thomist* 41 (1977): 1–61.

7. From Heidegger's 1943 *Postscript to What Is Metaphysics?* contained in *Existence and Being,* ed. W. Brock (Chicago: Gateway, 1949), 355–35.

8. E. Gilson et al., *Recent Philosophy,* 152. The same outlook can be found among the non-reductionistic materialists. For example, John Dewey talks about the way Nature owns thoughts and ideas. Rather than saying "*I* am thinking a stone," it would be much more accurate to say that "a stone is being thought by nature here and now in this human locus." See his *Experience and Nature,* 2d ed. (N.Y.: Dover reprint, 1929), 69, 232–34. On non-reductionistic materialism see F. F. Centore, *Persons* (Westport, Conn.: Greenwood, 1979).

9. See Heidegger, *Introduction,* 115–16. Cf. also Richardson, *Heidegger,* 383–86.

10. Heidegger, *Introduction,* 117.

11. Ibid., 119. Rudolf Allers points out that "being" for Heidegger is never an "object" since an object for Heidegger, true to his Epistemological Idealism, is only what is present to the conscious subject. But if there is one thing being is not, it is a clear and distinct idea. Even more fundamental than this, though, is Heidegger's conviction that being must be an univocal term; whatever it is, it is the same everywhere and always. See R. Allers, "Heidegger on the Principle of Sufficient Reason," *Philosophy and Phenomenological Research* 20 (1959–1960): 365–73.

Also, it might be asked, was Heidegger as much impressed by Emerson as was Nietzsche? Did Heidegger ever read Emerson's 1844 essay "Nominalist and Realist"? According to this ex-Unitarian American Hegelian:

> It is the secret of the world that all things subsist, and do not die,
> but only retire a little from sight, and afterwards return again.
> Whatever does not concern us, is concealed from us. As soon
> as a person is no longer related to our present well-being, he is

concealed, or *dies*, as we say. Really, all things and persons are related to us, but according to our nature, they act on us not at once, but in succession, and we are made aware of their presence one at a time. All persons, all things which we have known, are here present, and many more than we see; the world is full. As the ancient [Parmenides] said, the world is a *plenum* or solid; and if we saw all things that really surround us, we should be imprisoned and unable to move.

R. W. Emerson, *Essays: First and Second Series* (N.Y.: Allison, 1895), 238.

12. M. Heidegger, "Das Ding," trans. A. Hofstadter, in *Poetry, Language, Thought* (N.Y.: Harper & Row, 1975), 165–82.

13. For a more comprehensive treatment of Sartre, both early and late, see F. C. Copleston, *Contemporary Philosophy* (London: Search Press, 1973); T. R. Flynn, *Sartre and Marxist Existentialism* (Chicago: University of Chicago Press, 1984); F. Jeanson, *Sartre and the Problem of Morality*, trans. R. V. Stone (Bloomington: Indiana University Press, 1980); T. M. King, *Sartre and the Sacred* (Chicago: University of Chicago Press, 1974).

14. J.-P. Sartre, *Nausea*, trans. L. Alexander (N.Y.: New Directions, 1964), 19–20.

15. Ibid., 101. Cf. Sartre, *La Nausée* (Paris: Librairie Gallimard, 1938), 145.

16. Sartre, *Nausea*, 133.

17. Ibid.

18. Ibid., 134.

19. See ibid.

20. J.-P. Sartre, *Being and Nothingness*, trans. H. E. Barnes (N.Y.: Washington Square Press, 1966), 757.

21. Ibid., 761.

22. Ibid., 763.

23. Ibid., 755.

24. Ibid., 762.

25. See J.-P. Sartre, *Existentialism and Humanism*, trans. P. Mairet (London: Methuen, 1982), 37–38. Sartre recounts how a young man came to him during the war asking for advice on how he should behave *vis-à-vis* the Germans. Sartre's reply was that he should make up his own mind. Sartre himself was working for the Resistance and so obviously was not neutral on the subject. However, let us not miss the subtle message written between the lines. Sartre's advice could have been looked upon with favor by the Germans; after all, the young man could have decided, *in all sincerity and good faith*, to become a Collaborator. On a more fundamental level, it might be mentioned, the position of having no position is itself a position. Further to this see F. F. Centore, "The 'Creative' Ethics of Nietzsche and Sartre," *Faith and Reason* 10 (1984): 222–41.

26. A. Camus, *The Myth of Sisyphus and Other Essays*, trans. J. O'Brien (N.Y.: Vantage, 1955), 31.

27. S. Kierkegaard, *The Sickness Unto Death* I: 1, A, in *Fear and Trembling and The Sickness Unto Death*, trans. W. Lowrie (Princeton, N.J.: Princeton University Press, 1941), 146–47.

28. I think Camus understood Kierkegaard very well. Cf. Lord Byron's 1816 poem *The Prisoner of Chillon* XIV:

At last men came to set me free;
   I asked not why, and recked not where;
It was at length the same to me,

Fettered or fetterless to be,
    I learned to love despair.

29. These themes are best developed in Kierkegaard's *Concluding Unscientific Postscript,* trans. D. F. Swenson and W. Lowrie (Princeton, N.J.: Princeton University Press, 1941). The religious person should be *proud* of being unscientific, thinks the Dane.

From Kierkegaard's perspective, Hegel is worse than a heretic insofar as his rationalism is concerned. He was not merely heterodox on some point or other; he wanted to completely usurp Christianity. The Dane writes in his diary on Friday, 14 April 1854:

> But now the only Christianity we have is a falsity — and here is the greatest danger. So there is no philosophy so harmful to Christianity as the Hegelian. For earlier philosophies were honest enough to let Christianity be what it is — but Hegel had both the stupidity and the effrontery to solve the problem of speculation and Christianity by altering Christianity — and then everything was splendid.

S. Kierkegaard, *The Last Years: Journals 1853–1855,* ed. and trans. R. G. Smith (N.Y.: Harper & Row, 1965), 30.

See also N. Thulstrup, *Kierkegaard's Relation to Hegel* (Princeton, N.J.: Princeton University Press, 1980).

30. Sartre, *Existentialism and Humanism,* 33.

31. *The Joyful Wisdom* is also known as *The Joyous Science* or *The Gay Science,* the last after an Italian subtitle given to the work by Nietzsche himself. See *The Gay Science,* trans. W. Kaufmann (N.Y.: Random House, 1974), 304–10.

With respect to Nietzsche's (usually overlooked) views on the absolute need, given our present state of evolutionary development, for fictions (such as substance, soul, God, freedom) in order to sustain human life, see H. Vaihinger, *The Philosophy of As If,* trans. C. K. Ogden, 2d ed. (London: Routledge and Kegan Paul, 1935), 341–62.

32. E. Gilson, *Being and Some Philosophers,* 2d ed. (Toronto: Pontifical Institute of Mediaeval Studies, 1952), 9–10.

33. S. Kierkegaard, *Concluding Unscientific Postscript,* 294–96.

34. See Hegel, *Logic,* trans. W. Wallace, 3rd ed. (N.Y.: Oxford University Press, 1975), chapter 7; sections 86–88.

35. See Kierkegaard, *Concluding Unscientific Postscript,* 101.

36. M. Heidegger, "The Way Back Into The Ground Of Metaphysics," *Existentialism from Dostoevsky to Sartre,* 272. Cf. also Heidegger's 1969 reemphasis on what he had already said in his 1927 *Being and Time*: "Higher than actuality stands *possibility*" (241). Put otherwise, existence is only a mode of Reality. As with Parmenides and Hegel, the possible (the abstract) is as real, if not more real, than the actual (the concrete). Contrast this with Kierkegaard and Aquinas, for whom the abstract *is not real at all.*

37. H.-G. Gadamer, *Reason in the Age of Science,* trans. F. G. Lawrence (Cambridge, Mass.: MIT Press, 1982), 87.

CHAPTER 5

1. E. Gilson, *Being and Some Philosophers,* 2d ed. (Toronto: Pontifical Institute of Mediaeval Studies, 1952), ix. A consequence of *beginning* with existential-empirical reality is that one may *end* with it. Among the ancients, for

instance, Aristotle's metaphysics is about the gods, real beings, not about abstract principles, however "broad."

2. As quoted in *B. Russell's Best,* ed. R. E. Egner (N.Y.: Mentor, 1958), 30.

3. See Thomas Aquinas, *Summa Theologiae* II-II: 1, 4. Cf. also II-II: 2, 1.

4. *Summa* II-II: 11, 1.

5. On Aquinas's doctrine concerning free will and free choice see *Summa* I: 82–83; I-II: 8–10. See also C. W. Grindel, ed., *Concept of Freedom* (Chicago: Regnery, 1955). See especially Grindel's "Freedom of Autonomy" (57–73) wherein he takes into account the greater emphasis put upon the will as an efficient cause by Aquinas in his *Quaestiones Disputatae de Malo,* written and/or revised after the 1270 Paris condemnation of thirteen Averroistic propositions, some of which (nos. 3 and 9) denied freedom in human beings.

6. See B. Russell, *My Philosophical Development* (London: Allen and Unwin, 1959), chapter IX, "The External World," 102: "But there are other matters [since 1913] on which my views have undergone important changes. I no longer think that the laws of logic are laws of things; on the contrary, I now regard them as purely linguistic."

A similar move can be seen in twentieth-century Marxism. When some Russian logicians wanted to reestablish the teaching of formal logic in the 1950s, they carefully worded the principle of non-contradiction so as to have it apply only intramentally. They thought it should be acceptable as a law of thought even if not as a law of being. Recall that the denial of the principle of non-contradiction was a basic dogma of Marxist-Leninism. Its three basic laws were the transformation of quantity into quality, the unity and struggle of opposites, and the negation of the negation. See G. A. Wetter, *Dialectical Materialism,* trans. P. Heath (N.Y.: Praeger, 1958), 531–34.

The same can be found in many modern textbooks in philosophy. See, for instance, R. C. Solomon, *The Big Questions,* 2d ed. (N.Y.: Harcourt Brace Jovanovich, 1986), 282: "*contradiction:* two statements, both of which cannot be true; neither can they both be false." The implication here is that the principle of non-contradiction operates only on the linguistic ("statements") level.

7. J. Owens, "The Causal Proposition Revisited," *The Modern Schoolman* 44 (1967), 150, note 12. See also the Appendix to E. Gilson's *Being and Some Philosophers,* 216–32. The Aquinan texts in question are discussed in Owens's article "Diversity and Community of Being in St. Thomas Aquinas," *Mediaeval Studies* 22 (1960): 285–97.

8. On the types of distinctions in Aquinas see J. Owens, *An Elementary Christian Metaphysics* (Milwaukee: Bruce, 1963), chapter 7; and his *Aquinas on Being and Thing* (Niagara Falls, N.Y.: Niagara University Press, 1981). See also Mary T. Clark, ed., *An Aquinas Reader* (Garden City, N.Y.: Doubleday, 1972), 39–112.

9. See Kant's *Critique of Pure Reason,* trans. J. M. D. Meiklejohn (N.Y.: Willey, 1900), 221–27. Cf. also the translation by N. K. Smith (N.Y.: St. Martin's Press, 1965), 372–80 (B414–B426). On 373 we read: "For consciousness itself has always a degree, which always allows a diminution, and the same must also hold of the faculty of being conscious of the self, and likewise of all the other faculties."

10. On analogy and its history in Aquinas see J. Owens, *An Elementary Christian Metaphysics,* 86–92. See also D. B. Burrell, *Knowing the Unknown God* (Notre-Dame, Ind.: University of Notre Dame Press, 1986).

11. Following Darwin, this approach is widely accepted today in biology. Cf. Harvard's S. J. Gould:

> A classification is not an observation; only the discredited
> inductivist model of science would ever lead us to believe that it

might be. *A classification is a human decision, constrained by a bevy of facts, about how best to order nature.*

Book review of *Numerical Taxonomy* in *Science* 183 (22 February 1974): 740.

12. Aquinas's solution to the problem of classification is found in chapter 3 of his early (1255) work *On Being and Essence.* On the principle of individuation see Gilson's Gifford Lectures, *The Spirit of Mediaeval Philosophy,* trans. A. H. C. Downes (N.Y.: Scribner's, 1940), 464–66, notes 5, 6, 7.

For a mathematical logic treatment of the problem of species, see I. M. Bochenski, "The Problem of Universals," in L. R. Ward, ed., *The Problem of Universals* (Notre Dame, Ind.: University of Notre Dame Press, 1956), 35–54. At the very end of the article the author states, "It is not implied that there is no correct solution of the fundamental aspects of the PU; on the contrary, the author thinks that such [a] solution has been found many centuries ago [by Aquinas]."

13. On the history of mathematical logic see I. M. Bochenski, *A History of Formal Logic,* trans. I. Thomas (Notre Dame, Ind.: University of Notre Dame Press, 1961); W. and M. Kneale, *The Development of Logic* (N.Y.: Oxford University Press, 1962).

In mechanical logic there can be no group concepts in any immaterial sense. All classes are extrinsic and external; they are *only* collections of individuals. In intentional logic, "men" in the statement "All men are mortal" stands for a nature. Not so in mathematical logic. But in intentional logic, at least, there is no "problem of induction." If you have the nature of one thing correctly stated, you have the nature of *all* such things correctly stated. To the extent science cannot be reduced to mathematics, intentional logic is more scientific than mathematical logic. But *qua* logic (any logic) extramental existence remains irrelevant. Whether T or F, "All dinosaurs are reptiles" is a perfectly good statement for logical analysis even though there are now in fact no dinosaurs.

14. M. de Unamuno, *The Tragic Sense of Life* [1921], trans. J. E. C. Flitch (N.Y.: Dover, 1954), 88–89.

For a summary of Aquinas's argument for the existence of God, following the "Toronto School" interpretation, especially J. Owens, which results in a Being who is both non-deistic and non-pantheistic, see F. F. Centore, "Logic, Aquinas, and *Utrum Deus Sit,*" *Angelicum* 63 (1986): 213–26.

15. Further to this see R. Garrigou-Lagrange, *The One God,* trans. B. Rose (St. Louis, Herder, 1946), 265. He also observes that we must not confuse God's "immensity" with his omnipresence, that is, God's "aptitude to exist in all things" with his "actual existence in them" (267). This point is well taken. It is precisely God's existentially perfect nature which allows for the *possibility* of his perfect presence, even if he had never created the least little grain of sand.

By the same token, once God's proper name (*He Who Is*) is known we also know implicitly many other things about God, things, such as his providence, omnipotence, and sole right to be worshipped, which the pagan philosophers could not fully know or appreciate. See Aquinas's *Summa* II-II: 1, 8, the second objection and its answer. This would apply to God's presence as well.

16. E. Wierenga, "Anselm on Omnipresence," *The New Scholasticism* 62 (1988): 40.

17. Ibid., 41.

18. Further to this see F. F. Centore, "Aquinas on Inner Space," *Canadian Journal of Philosophy* 4 (1974): 351–63.

19. On this see Aquinas's *Summa* I: 25, 3, "Whether God is Omnipotent."

20. Wierenga prefers to emphasize God's knowledge of everything, including our most intimate and secret thoughts, as a basis for God's presence. This would be recognized by Aquinas as well. The advantage of Thomas over Wierenga,

however, is that Thomas avoids the danger of deism, whereas Wierenga does not. In various forms of deism it is possible for God to know what is happening, and even to punish wrongdoers on the basis of such knowledge, but to still be providentially remote from the world, as, for example, in Voltaire.

On deism in general and Voltaire in particular see Rosemary Z. Lauer, *The Mind of Voltaire* (Westminster, Md.: Newman Press, 1961). Concerning deism in general, she states:

> *Deism*, however, is a term broad enough and varied enough in its meanings to cover a number of quite divergent intellectual enterprises. There are, nonetheless, certain minimal conditions required that the term may be applied justly to anyone's religious or philosophical thinking: the author must eschew Christian revelation or regard it as only a reformulation of a natural religion known through reason alone; he must offer arguments proving, from observation of the world of nature, that God exists; he must show by reason that God rules the world of nature by eternal, immutable laws; and, finally, he must explain how practicable rules of morality can be deduced from knowledge of nature and man's place in nature (vii).

Concerning divine retribution, see the third stanza of Voltaire's poem "Épitre CIV: A L'Auteur du Livre des Trois Imposteurs" (1769), which can be found in volume 10 of *Oeuvres Complètes de Voltaire*, ed. L. Moland (Paris: Garnier, 1877), 403. This need for God, sounding very much like the second Psalm, was no *boutade* or *plaisanterie* on Voltaire's part, but the expression of a basic requirement for social justice.

> If heaven, stripped of its solemn vocation,
> Could ever cease to show forth its function,
> If God did not exist, it would be necessary to invent him.
> Let the sage announce him, let kings fear him.
> Kings, if you oppress me, if your Excellencies disdain
> The tears of the innocent which you cause to flow,
> My avenger is in heaven: Learn to tremble.
> At least such is the fruit of a useful dogma.
>   (trans. J. Finn)

EPILOGUE

1. Further to this see Aquinas's *On the Perfection of the Religious Life*, chapters 13 and 14, contained in *An Aquinas Reader*, ed. Mary T. Clark (Garden City, N.Y.: Doubleday, 1972), 279–89.

This in turn opens the door to a natural law ethics founded upon a stable human nature. Without such a nature humans are left with nothing but a naked will; it is my consciousness against the world and everything in it, including other people. Happiness then becomes a ratio of what I want to what I get (H = G/W). See, for example, R. J. Hollingdale's commentary on Nietzsche's *Beyond Good and Evil*, trans. R. J. Hollingdale (N.Y.: Penguin, 1973), 216:

> If one understands correctly what is meant by the word "happiness" (and especially if one distinguishes it from "pleasure"), it is a tautology to say: all men desire happiness.

"Happiness" is the state of possessing what one desires: pain can constitute happiness if pain is what one desires.

To be happy I must then either lower the denominator (Stoicism, Buddhism, even Epicureanism) or increase the numerator. But the latter path has no common nature to guide it and thus, theoretically at least, chaos should reign.

The fact that chaos does not reign points to the fact that we *do* have a stable nature with fixed *needs,* rather than simply wants, which must be satisfied. Regardless of what deconstructionists may say, this is the only reason some thinkers can even begin to imagine that enlightened self-interest, utilitarianism, contractarianism, and other forms of non-natural law ethics, might work at all. Power is getting what I want. Happiness is getting what I need. Holiness is getting the two together.

2. Although it must occur within an atheistic, tragic context, it might be noted in passing that this sort of thing can also occur within a religious context. Some people appeal to their religious feelings, to their private consciences, or to their personal "love," as a means for justifying their actions. Such feelings, however, cannot be used to confirm the fact that God is on their side, even though it does appear to be a convenient and honest way of circumventing the authority of a denominational church. Nonetheless, experience shows that a conscience without an objective measuring rod to guide it, or a vague and amorphous feeling of "love," can very easily and honestly lead to the most harmful forms of immorality, and usually does. Further to this see R. A. Knox, *Enthusiasm* (N.Y.: Oxford University Press, 1961).

3. See R. J. Bernstein, "Pragmatism, Pluralism and the Healing of Wounds," *Proceedings and Addresses of the American Philosophical Association* 63 (November 1989): 5–18.

4. Cf. G. Marcel, *The Philosophy of Existentialism,* trans. M. Harari (N.Y.: Citadel, 1964), 83–84: "[Modern] Existentialism (I have surely not abused this word) has developed historically as a reaction against the Hegelian system; yet it is now seen to emerge — like the tunnels on the St. Gothard railway — considerably *below* the level from which it had started."

5. See J. L. Mackie, *The Miracle of Theism* (N.Y.: Oxford University Press, 1982), 92, 250.

6. See ibid., 252–53.

7. See Aquinas, *Summa Theologiae* I: 12, 12.

8. As already pointed out in the previous chapter, on the presence of God to creatures see the *Summa* I: 8, 3; see also I: 43, 3. The term "contact" (*attingit*) used by Aquinas in this place need not imply a physical meeting of three-dimensional parts. It can also mean: To be in communication with, to be similar to, to belong to, to be related to, to be concerned with. Minds can contact each other intellectually, and so on. It is even permissible these days to use it as a verb: "For more information contact your local Christian philosopher."

9. F. W. Nietzsche, *The Will To Power,* trans. W. Kaufmann and R. J. Hollingdale (N.Y.: Vintage, 1968), 240, section 437.

10. See H.-G. Gadamer, *Truth and Method* (N.Y.: Crossroad, 1989), 457–58. Earlier in the twentieth century, some British and American philosophers, notably G. E. Moore and A. O. Lovejoy, did attempt a renewed realism, but with disappointing results. In their reaction, on the one hand, against Hegelian abstractionism and, on the other hand, against the ever-growing scientific reductionism of the time, some thinkers desired a return to a philosophical position which honored both body and mind. However, they returned no further than post-Cartesian philosophy and, as a result, found themselves facing the same insurmountable problems that Descartes's more immediate disciples were unable

to solve. By and large, they wanted to be non-reductionistic physicalists, but their *a priori* commitment to a universal materialism made it impossible for them to do justice to the abundant evidence supporting the existence of at least an immaterial mind. Their empiricism was nowhere as empirical as they said. Later, Sartre would run to the opposite extreme, asserting that the distinctively human consciousness was founded upon a nothingness. Attempting to maintain such a position, though, was to jump from the frying pan into the fire, since such a view is both empirically and logically impossible. Further to this see E. Gilson et al., *Recent Philosophy* (N.Y.: Random House, 1966), chapters 20, 25.

  11. Gadamer, *Truth and Method,* 461.

  12. Ibid., 469.

  13. One of the best works on this as applied to religion, even though old (1845), is J. H. Newman's *An Essay on the Development of Christian Doctrine* (Garden City, N.Y.: Doubleday, 1960).

  14. See E. Gilson, *Being and Some Philosophers,* 167. In closing, I wish to emphasize the point that there is no substitute for a really existing, extramental foundation for faith, hope, and charity. If indeed some form of naturalistic theism has replaced supernatural theism in our post-modern times, then there are certain inevitable consequences which can be neither denied nor ignored. It seems to me that most post-moderns have yet to face up to this fact of real life. As Plato realized long ago, lying to others is bad enough, but lying to ourselves is even worse. Cf. C. P. Snow, *The Two Cultures: And a Second Look* (New York: Cambridge University Press, 1964), 84: "One can teach a myth: but when the myth is seen as fact, and when the fact is disproved, the myth becomes a lie. No one can teach a lie."

BIBLIOGRAPHY

Abraham, W. J. *An Introduction to the Philosophy of Religion.* Englewood Cliffs, N.J.: Prentice-Hall, 1985.

Adams, R. M. *Nil.* N.Y.: Oxford University Press, 1966.

Adler, M. J. *The Idea of Freedom.* 2 vols. Garden City, N.Y.: Doubleday, 1958–1961.

_____. *Ten Philosophical Mistakes.* N.Y.: Macmillan, 1987.

Allers, R. "Heidegger on the Principle of Sufficient Reason." *Philosophy and Phenomenological Research* 20 (1959–1960): 365–73.

_____. *The Philosophical Works of Rudolf Allers: A Selection.* Ed. J. A. Mann. Washington, D.C.: Georgetown University Press, 1965.

Anderson, R. F. *Hume's First Principles.* Lincoln: University of Nebraska Press, 1966.

Anselm. *Proslogium; Monologium; an Appendix in Behalf of the Fool by Gaunilon; and Cur Deus Homo.* Trans. S. N. Deane. LaSalle, Ill.: Open Court, 1958.

Aquinas, T. *Summa Theologica; Summa Contra Gentiles.* 6 vols. Rome: Forzanii, 1894.

_____. *Opera Omnia.* 25 vols. N.Y.: Musurgia, 1948–1950.

_____. *De Ente et Essentia.* 3rd ed. Rome: Marietti, 1948.

_____. *On Being and Essence.* Trans. A. Maurer. Toronto: Pontifical Institute of Mediaeval Studies, 1949.

_____. *Aristotle: On Interpretation: Commentary by St. Thomas and Cajetan.* Trans. J. T. Oesterle. Milwaukee: Marquette University Press, 1962.

_____. *An Aquinas Reader.* Ed. M. T. Clark. Garden City, N.Y.: Doubleday, 1972.

Arendt, H. *Eichmann in Jerusalem.* N.Y.: Penguin, 1977.

Aristotle. *The Basic Works of Aristotle.* Ed. R. McKeon. N.Y.: Random House, 1941.

_____. *Metaphysics.* Trans. R. Hope. Ann Arbor: University of Michigan Press, 1960.

_____. *The Complete Works of Aristotle.* 2 vols. Ed. J. Barnes. Princeton, N.J.: Princeton University Press, 1984.

Augros, R. M., and Stanciu, G. N. *The New Story of Science.* Lake Bluff, Ill.: Gateway, 1984.

_____. *The New Biology.* Boston: New Science Library, 1988.

Augustine, A. *Basic Writings of Saint Augustine.* 2 vols. Ed. W. J. Oates. N.Y.: Random House, 1948.
Ayer, A. J. *Language, Truth and Logic.* 2d ed. N.Y.: Dover, n.d.
____. *The Central Questions of Philosophy.* N.Y.: Penguin, 1978.
____. *Philosophy in the Twentieth Century.* N.Y.: Random House, 1982.
____. *Ludwig Wittgenstein.* N.Y.: Penguin, 1986.
Azar, L. *"Esse* in the Philosophy of Whitehead." *The New Scholasticism* 37 (1963): 462–71.
____. "Whitehead: Challenging a Challenge." *The Thomist* 30 (1966): 80–87.
____. *Philosophy and Ideology: An Adventure.* 2d ed. Dubuque, Iowa: Kendall/Hunt, 1983.
____. *Man: Computer, Ape, or Angel?* Hanover, Mass.: Christopher, 1988.
____. *Twentieth Century in Crisis: Foundations of Totalitarianism.* Dubuque, Iowa: Kendall/Hunt, 1990.
____. *Evolution and the Humanities: Friends or Foes?* Forthcoming.
Bacon, F. *The New Organon and Related Writings.* Ed. F. H. Anderson. N.Y.: Liberal Arts, 1960.
Balthasar, H. U. von. *The Office of Peter and the Structure of the Church.* Trans. A. Emery. San Francisco: Ignatius Press, 1986.
Barrett, W. *Irrational Man.* N.Y.: Doubleday, 1990.
Barthes, R. *A Barthes Reader.* Ed. S. Sontag. N.Y.: Hill and Wang, 1982.
Bergmann, G. *The Metaphysics of Logical Positivism.* N.Y.: Longmans Green, 1954.
Bergson, H. *Creative Evolution.* Trans. A. Mitchell. N.Y.: Modern Library, 1944.
____. *The Two Sources of Morality and Religion.* Trans. R. A. Audra, et al. Garden City, N.Y.: Doubleday, 1954.
Berkeley, G. *The Principles of Knowledge: Three Dialogues Between Hylas and Philonous.* N.Y.: Meridian, 1963.
Bernstein, H., et al. "Genetic Damage, Mutation, and the Evolution of Sex." *Science* 229 (20 September 1985): 1277–81.
Bernstein, R. J. "Pragmatism, Pluralism and the Healing of Wounds." *Proceedings and Addresses of the American Philosophical Association* (University of Delaware, Newark) 63 (1989): 5–18.
Bildstein, W. J. *Radical Response.* Hicksville, N.Y.: Exposition Press, 1974.
Blanshard, B. *On Philosophical Style.* Manchester, England: Manchester University Press, 1954.
Bloom, A. *The Closing of the American Mind.* N.Y.: Simon and Schuster, 1987.
____. *Giants and Dwarfs: Essays 1960–1990.* N.Y.: Simon and Schuster, 1990.
Bochenski, I. M. *A History of Formal Logic.* Trans. I. Thomas. Notre Dame, Ind.: University of Notre Dame Press, 1961.
____. *Contemporary European Philosophy.* Trans. D. Nicholl and K. Aschenbrenner. Berkeley: University of California Press, 1964.
____. *The Logic of Religion.* N.Y.: New York University Press, 1965.
Boethius, A. M. S. "Liber de Persona et Duabus Naturis." *Patrologiae Latinae.* Vol. 64. Ed. J.-P. Migne. Paris: 1860.
____. *The Consolation of Philosophy.* Trans. R. Green. Indianapolis: Bobbs-Merrill, 1962.
Bonjour, L. *The Structure of Empirical Knowledge.* Cambridge, Mass.: Harvard University Press, 1987.
Bork, R. H. *The Tempting of America.* N.Y.: Free Press, 1989.
Bourke, V. J. *Aquinas' Search for Wisdom.* Milwaukee: Bruce, 1965.
Bowler, P. J. *Evolution: The History of an Idea.* Berkeley: University of California Press, 1984.

Boyd, G. W. *On Stress, Disease, and Evolution.* Hobart: University of Tasmania Press, 1989.

Bricke, J. *Hume's Philosophy of Mind.* Princeton, N.J.: Princeton University Press, 1980.

Brock, W., ed. *Existence and Being.* Chicago: Gateway, 1949.

Brougham, H. *Dissertations on Subjects of Science Connected with Natural Theology.* London: Knight, 1839.

Burkert, W. *Ancient Mystery Cults.* Cambridge, Mass.: Harvard University Press, 1987.

Burrell, D. B. *Knowing the Unknowable God.* Notre Dame, Ind.: University of Notre Dame Press, 1986.

Callahan, J. P. *Four Views of Time in Ancient Philosophy.* N.Y.: Greenwood, 1968.

Campbell, G. "Sartre's Absolute Freedom." *Laval Theologique et Philosophique* 33 (1977): 61–91.

Campbell, J., and Moyers, B. *The Power of Myth.* Garden City, N.Y.: Doubleday, 1988.

Camus, A. *The Myth of Sisyphus and Other Essays.* Trans. J. O'Brien. N.Y.: Vintage, 1955.

_____. *The Rebel.* Trans. A. Bower. N.Y.: Vintage, 1956.

Caputo, J. D. *Heidegger and Aquinas.* Bronx, N.Y.: Fordham University Press, 1982.

_____. *Radical Hermeneutics: Repetition, Deconstruction, and the Hermeneutic Project.* Bloomington: Indiana University Press, 1987.

Carr, D. *Time, Narrative, and History.* Bloomington: Indiana University Press, 1986.

Centore, F. F. "Hospers' Understanding of Necessary Being." *The New Scholasticism* 43 (1969): 449–53.

_____. *Robert Hooke's Contributions to Mechanics: A Study in Seventeenth Century Natural Philosophy.* The Hague: M. Nijhoff, 1970.

_____. "Whitehead's Conception of God." *Philosophical Studies* 19 (1970): 149–71.

_____. "Mechanism, Teleology, and Seventeenth Century English Science." *International Philosophical Quarterly* 12 (1972): 553–71.

_____. "The Philosophy of Heliocentrism in Pre-Newtonian English Science." *Organon* 10 (1974): 75–85.

_____. "Aquinas On Inner Space." *Canadian Journal of Philosophy* 4 (1974): 351–63.

_____. *Persons: A Comparative Account of the Six Possible Theories.* Westport, Conn.: Greenwood, 1979.

_____. "Camus, Pascal, and the Absurd." *The New Scholasticism* 54 (1980): 46–59.

_____. "Hume, Reid, and Skepticism." *Philosophical Studies* 28 (1981): 212–20.

_____. "Lovejoy and Aquinas on God's 'Need' to Create." *Angelicum* 59 (1982): 23–36.

_____. "Is Darwin Dead?" *The Thomist* 47 (1983): 550–71.

_____. "The 'Creative' Ethics of Nietzsche and Sartre." *Faith and Reason* 10 (1984): 222–41.

_____. "Logic, Aquinas, and *Utrum Deus Sit.*" *Angelicum* 63 (1986): 213–26.

_____. "Potency, Space, and Time: Three Modern Theories." *The New Scholasticism* 63 (1989): 435–62.

_____. "Thomism and the Female Body as Seen in the *Summa Theologiae.*" *Angelicum* 67 (1990): 37–56.

_____. "A Note on W. J. Hill's 'The Doctrine of God After Vatican II'." *The Thomist* 54 (1990): 531–40.

____. "On Talking Positive But Being Negative." *Faith and Reason.* Forthcoming.

Charlesworth, M. J. *Saint Anselm's Proslogion.* N.Y.: Oxford University Press, 1965.

Chesterton, G. K. *What's Wrong with the World.* 2d ed. London: Cassell, 1910.

____. *Saint Thomas Aquinas.* Garden City, N.Y.: Doubleday, 1956.

Clarke, D. M. *Descartes' Philosophy of Science.* University Park: Pennsylvania State University Press, 1982.

Cohen, H. *Reason and Hope.* Ed. and trans. E. Jospe. N.Y.: Viking, 1973.

Collingwood, R. G. *The Idea of Nature.* Oxford: Oxford University Press, 1945.

Collins, J. D. *The Existentialists: A Critical Study.* Chicago: Gateway, 1952.

____. *God in Modern Philosophy.* Chicago.: Regnery, 1959.

____. *Crossroads in Philosophy.* Chicago: Regnery, 1962.

____. *The Emergence of Religion.* New Haven, Conn.: Yale University Press, 1967.

____. *The Mind of Kierkegaard.* Princeton, N.J.: Princeton University Press, 1983.

Comte, A. *Auguste Comte and Positivism: The Essential Writings.* Ed. G. Lenzer. N.Y.: Harper & Row, 1975.

Confucius. *The Sayings of Confucius.* Trans. J. R. Ware. N.Y.: Mentor, 1955.

Copleston, F. C. *Contemporary Philosophy.* London: Search Press, 1973.

____. *Religion and the One: Philosophies East and West.* N.Y.: Crossroad, 1982.

Crewe, A. V. "High-Resolution Scanning Transmission Electron Microscopy." *Science* 221 (22 July 1983): 325–30.

Croce, B. *What Is Living and What Is Dead in the Philosophy of Hegel.* Trans. D. Ainslie. 3rd ed. [1912]. Lanham, Md.: University Press of America, 1985.

Cuellar, O. "Animal Parthenogenesis." *Science* 197 (26 August 1977): 837–43.

Cushing, J. T., and McMullin, E., eds. *Philosophical Consequences of Quantum Theory,* Notre Dame, Ind.: University of Notre Dame Press, 1989.

Dahlstrom, D. O., ed. *Hermeneutics and the Tradition.* Proceedings of the American Catholic Philosophical Association, Washington, D.C. 62 (1988).

Darwin, C. *The Origin of Species; The Descent of Man and Selection in Relation to Sex.* N.Y.: Modern Library, n.d.

____. *Charles Darwin: His Life Told in an Autobiographical Chapter and in a Selected Series of His Published Letters.* Ed. F. Darwin. N.Y.: Appleton, 1892.

____. *The Life and Letters of Charles Darwin, Including an Autobiographical Chapter.* 2 vols. Ed. F. Darwin. N.Y.: Appleton, 1898.

____. *More Letters of Charles Darwin.* 2 vols. Ed. F. Darwin and A. C. Seward. N.Y.: Appleton, 1903.

____. *Charles Darwin's Diary of the Voyage of H.M.S. Beagle.* Ed. N. Barlow. London: Cambridge University Press, 1933.

____. *The Autobiography of Charles Darwin, 1809–1882.* Ed. N. Barlow. N.Y.: Harcourt Brace, 1958.

____. *The Origin of Species (A Variorum Text).* Ed. M. Peckham. Philadelphia: University of Pennsylvania Press, 1959.

____. *The Correspondence of Charles Darwin: 1837–1843.* Vol. 2. Ed. F. Burkhart and S. Smith. N.Y.: Cambridge University Press, 1986.

____. *Charles Darwin's Notebooks, 1836–1844.* Ed. P. H. Barrett et al. Ithaca, N.Y.: Cornell University Press, 1987.

Dawson, C. *Religion and Culture.* N.Y.: AMS Press, 1948.

____. *Progress and Religion.* Westport, Conn.: Greenwood, 1970.

DeMarco, D. *In My Mother's Womb.* Manassas, Va.: Trinity Communications, 1987.

_____. *The Incarnation in a Divided World*. Front Royal, Va.: Christendom College Press, 1988.

Derrida, J. *Of Grammatology*. Trans. G. C. Spivak. Baltimore: Johns Hopkins University Press, 1976.

_____. *Spurs*. Trans. B. Harlow. Chicago: University of Chicago Press, 1979.

_____. *Positions*. Trans. A. Bass. Chicago: University of Chicago Press, 1981.

_____. *Margins of Philosophy*. Trans. A. Bass. Chicago: University of Chicago Press, 1982.

_____. *The Post Card: From Socrates to Freud and Beyond*. Trans. A. Bass. Chicago: University of Chicago Press, 1987.

_____. *Of Spirit: Heidegger and the Question*. Trans. G. Bennington and R. Bowlby. Chicago: University of Chicago Press, 1989.

Descartes, R. *The Method, Meditations and Philosophy of Descartes*. Trans. J. Veitch. Washington, D.C.: Dunne, 1901.

_____. *Discourse on Method and Other Writings*. Trans. A. Wollaston. Baltimore: Penguin, 1960.

_____. *Descartes: Philosophical Writings*. Ed. and trans. E. Anscombe and P. T. Geach. London: Nelson, 1966.

Dewey, J. *Reconstruction in Philosophy*. Boston: Beacon, 1957.

_____. *Experience and Nature*. 2d ed. N.Y.: Dover, 1958.

Dickson, D. "Was Galileo Saved by Plea Bargain?" *Science* 233 (8 August 1986): 612–13.

Diderot, D. *The Encyclopedia: Selections*. Ed. and trans. S. J. Gendzier. N.Y.: Harper & Row, 1967.

Dougherty, J. P., ed. *The Good Life and Its Pursuit*. N.Y.: Paragon House, 1984.

Dupree, A. H. *Asa Gray*. Baltimore: Johns Hopkins University Press, 1988.

Durant, J., ed. *Darwinism and Divinity*. Oxford: Basil Blackwell, 1985.

Eckhard, C. D. "A Commonsensical Protest Against Deconstruction, Or, How The Real World At Last Became A Fable." *Thought* 60 (1985): 310–21.

Einstein, A. *Ideas and Opinions*. Trans. S. Bargmann. N.Y.: Crown, 1954.

_____. *Relativity*. 15th ed. Trans. R. W. Lawson. N.Y.: Crown, 1961.

Eiseley, L. *Darwin and the Mysterious Mr. X*. N.Y.: Dutton, 1979.

Eldredge, N. *Time Frames*. N.Y.: Simon and Schuster, 1985.

Eliade, M. *The Sacred and the Profane: The Nature of Religion*. Trans. W. R. Trask. N.Y.: Harper & Row, 1961.

_____. *History of Religious Ideas*. 3 vols. Chicago: University of Chicago Press, 1979–1985.

_____. *The Myth of the Eternal Return*. Trans. W. R. Trask. Princeton, N.J.: Princeton University Press, 1985.

Eliade, M., ed. *The Encyclopedia of Religion*. 16 vols. N.Y.: Macmillan, 1985.

Eliade, M., and Tracy, D., eds. *What Is Religion?* N.Y.: Seabury, 1980.

Emerson, R. W. *Essays: First and Second Series*. N.Y.: Allison, 1895.

Engels, F. *The Part Played by Labour in the Transition from Ape to Man*. Peking: Foreign Language Press, 1975.

Fackenheim, E. L. *God's Presence in History*. N.Y.: New York University Press, 1970.

_____. *To Mend the World: Foundations of Future Jewish Thought*. N.Y.: Schocken, 1982.

Falck, C. *Myth, Truth and Literature*. N.Y.: Cambridge University Press, 1989.

Farias, V. *Heidegger and Nazism*. Philadelphia: Temple University Press, 1989.

Ferguson, J. *The Religions of the Roman Empire*. Ithaca, N.Y.: Cornell University Press, 1970.

Ferry, L., and Renaut, A. *French Philosophy of the Sixties: An Essay on Anti-Humanism*. Amherst: University of Massachusetts Press, 1989.

Festugière, A. M. J. *Epicurus and His Gods*. Trans. C. W. Chilton. Oxford: Blackwell, 1955.

Feuerbach, L. *The Essence of Christianity*. Trans. G. Eliot. N.Y.: Harper, 1957.

_____. *Thoughts on Death and Immortality*. Trans. J. A. Massey. Berkeley: University of California Press, 1980.

Feynman, R. P. *QED: The Strange Theory of Light and Matter*. Princeton, N.J.: Princeton University Press, 1985.

Finocchiaro, M. A., ed. *The Galileo Affair: A Documentary History*. Berkeley: University of California Press, 1989.

Fishkin, J. S. *Beyond Subjective Morality*. New Haven, Conn.: Yale University Press, 1984.

Flannery, A. P., ed. *Vatican Council II: The Concillar and Post Concillar Documents*. 2 vols. Northport, N.Y.: Costello, 1984.

Fletcher, J. *Situation Ethics*. Philadelphia: Westminster, 1966.

Flew, A. *God and Philosophy*. London: Hutchinson, 1966.

Flynn, T. R. *Sartre and Marxist Existentialism*. Chicago: University of Chicago Press, 1984.

Fogel, S. *The Postmodern University*. Toronto: ECW Press, 1988.

_____. Review of A. Bloom, *The Closing of the American Mind* in *Rubicon* 10 (1988): 375–77.

Fogothey, A. *Right and Reason*. 5th ed. St. Louis: Mosby, 1972.

Ford, L. S. *The Emergence of Whitehead's Metaphysics*. Albany: State University of New York Press, 1984.

Fothergill, P. G. *Historical Aspects of Organic Evolution*. London: Hollis and Carter, 1952.

Foucault, M. *Michel Foucault: Politics, Philosophy, Culture*. Ed. L. D. Kritzman. N.Y.: Routledge Chapman and Hall, 1988.

Fox, M. *The Coming of the Cosmic Christ*. N.Y.: Harper & Row, 1988.

Freud, S. *Totem and Taboo*. Trans. A. A. Brill. N.Y.: Vintage, 1946.

_____. *A General Introduction to Psychoanalysis*. Trans. J. Riviere. N.Y.: Washington Square Press, 1952.

_____. *Civilization and Its Discontents*. Trans. J. Strachey. N.Y.: Norton, 1961.

_____. *New Introductory Lectures on Psychoanalysis*. Trans. J. Strachey. N.Y.: Norton, 1965.

_____. *Moses and Monotheism*. Trans. K. Jones. N.Y.: Vintage, 1967.

Gadamer, H.-G. *Hegel's Dialectic*. Trans. P. C. Smith. New Haven, Conn.: Yale University Press, 1976.

_____. *Philosophical Hermeneutics*. Ed. D. E. Linge. Berkeley: University of California Press, 1976.

_____. *Reason in the Age of Science*. Trans. F. G. Lawrence. Cambridge, Mass.: MIT Press, 1982.

_____. *The Idea of the Good in Platonic-Aristotelian Philosophy*. Trans. P. C. Smith. New Haven, Conn.: Yale University Press, 1986.

_____. *Truth and Method*. 2d ed., rev. Trans. J. Weinsheimer and D. G. Marshall. N.Y.: Crossroad, 1989.

Gard, R. A., ed. *Buddhism*. N.Y.: Washington Square Press, 1963.

Garrigou-Lagrange, R. *The One God*. Trans. B. Rose. St. Louis: Herder, 1946.

Gasman, D. *The Scientific Origins of National Socialism*. N.Y.: Elsevier, 1971.

Gauthier, D. *Morals By Agreement*. N.Y.: Oxford University Press, 1987.

Geach, P. *Providence and Evil*. N.Y.: Cambridge University Press, 1977.

Gelinas, J.-P. *Summary of the Revival of Thomism under Leo XIII*. Washington, D.C.: Catholic University of America Press, 1959.

Gilson, E. *Reason and Revelation in the Middle Ages*. N.Y.: Scribner's, 1938.

____. *The Spirit of Mediaeval Philosophy.* Trans. A. H. C. Downes. N.Y.: Scribner's, 1940.

____. *God and Philosophy.* New Haven, Conn.: Yale University Press, 1941.

____. *The Unity of Philosophical Experience.* N.Y.: Scribner's, 1947.

____. *Being and Some Philosophers.* 2d ed. Toronto: Pontifical Institute of Mediaeval Studies, 1952.

Gilson, E., ed. *The Church Speaks to the Modern World: The Social Teachings of Leo XIII.* Garden City, N.Y.: Doubleday, 1954.

____. *History of Christian Philosophy in the Middle Ages.* N.Y.: Random House, 1955.

____. *A Gilson Reader.* Ed. A. C. Pegis. Garden City, N.Y.: Doubleday, 1957.

____. *The Philosopher and Theology.* Trans. C. Gilson. N.Y.: Random House, 1962.

____. *The Spirit of Thomism.* N.Y.: Harper & Row, 1966.

____. *From Aristotle to Darwin and Back Again.* Trans. J. Lyon. Notre Dame, Ind.: University of Notre Dame Press, 1984.

____. *Linguistics and Philosophy.* Trans. J. Lyon. Notre Dame, Ind.: University of Notre Dame Press, 1988.

Gilson, E., Langan, T., and Maurer, A. A. *Recent Philosophy.* N.Y.: Random House, 1966.

Girodat, C. R. "The Thomistic Theory of Personal Growth and Development." *Angelicum* 58 (1981): 137–50.

Gleick, J. *Chaos.* N.Y.: Penguin, 1987.

Golovchenko, J. A. "The Tunneling Microscope: A New Look at the Atomic World." *Science* 232 (4 April 1986): 48–53.

Gottlieb, A. "Heidegger for Fun and Profit." *The New York Times,* Sec. 7, Book Reviews, 7 January 1990, 21–23.

Gould, S. J. Review of P. Sneath and R. Sokal, *Numerical Taxonomy* (1973) in *Science* 183 (22 February 1974): 739–40.

Gray, A. *Natural Science and Religion.* N.Y.: Scribner's, 1891.

____. *Darwiniana.* Ed. A. H. Dupree. Cambridge, Mass.: Harvard University Press, 1963.

Greene, W. C. *Moira: Fate, Good, and Evil in Greek Thought.* N.Y.: Harper & Row, 1963.

Greenwood, D. J. *The Taming of Evolution.* Ithaca, N.Y.: Cornell University Press, 1984.

Greisch, J. *Heidegger et la Question de Dieu.* Paris: Grasset, 1980.

Grenier, H. *Thomistic Philosophy.* Vol. 3: *Moral Philosophy.* Trans. J. P. E. O'Hanley. Charlottetown, Prince Edward Island: St. Dunstan's University Press, 1949.

Griffin, D. R. *God and Religion in the Postmodern World.* Albany: State University of New York Press, 1989.

Grindel, C. W., ed. *Concept of Freedom.* Chicago: Regnery, 1955.

____. *God, Man, and Philosophy.* N.Y.: St. John's University Press, 1971.

Gruber, H. E., and Barrett, P. H. *Darwin on Man.* N.Y.: Dutton, 1974.

Haller, J. S. *Outcasts From Evolution.* Urbana: University of Illinois Press, 1971.

Hansma, P. K., et al. "Scanning Tunneling Microscopy and Atomic Force Microscopy: Application to Biology and Technology." *Science* 242 (14 October 1988): 209–16.

Hansot, E. *Perfection and Progress: Two Modes of Utopian Thought.* Cambridge, Mass.: MIT Press, 1982.

Harre, R. *The Philosophies of Science.* 2d ed. N.Y.: Oxford University Press, 1985.

Hartshorne, C. E. *Anselm's Discovery.* LaSalle, Ill.: Open Court, 1965.

____. *Aquinas to Whitehead: Seven Centuries of Metaphysics of Religion.* Milwaukee: Marquette University Press, 1976.

Hawking, S. W. *A Brief History of Time.* N.Y.: Bantam, 1988.

Haworth, L. *Autonomy.* New Haven, Conn.: Yale University Press, 1986.

Hayek, F. A. *The Road to Serfdom.* Chicago: University of Chicago Press, 1944.

____. *The Constitution of Liberty.* Chicago: University of Chicago Press, 1960.

____. *New Studies in Philosophy, Politics, Economics and the History of Ideas.* Chicago: University of Chicago Press, 1978.

Healey, R. *The Philosophy of Quantum Mechanics.* N.Y.: Cambridge University Press, 1989.

Hegel, G. F. W. *The Phenomenology of Mind.* Trans. J. B. Baillie. 2d ed. London: Allen and Unwin, 1964.

____. *Hegel's Philosophy of Right.* Trans. T. M. Knox. N.Y.: Oxford University Press, 1967.

____. *Hegel's Philosophy of Nature.* Trans. A. V. Miller. London: Oxford University Press, 1970.

____. *Werke.* 20 vols. Frankfurt am Main: Suhrkamp, 1969–1979.

____. *Hegel's Lectures on the History of Philosophy.* Trans. E. S. Haldane and F. H. Simson. 3 vols. Atlantic Highlands, N.J.: Humanities, 1974.

____. *Lectures on the Philosophy of Religion, Together with a Work on the Proofs of the Existence of God.* Trans. E. B. Speirs and J. B. Sanderson. 3 vols. Atlantic Highlands, N.J.: Humanities, 1974.

____. *Hegel's Logic.* Trans. W. Wallace. 3rd ed. N.Y.: Oxford University Press, 1975.

____. *Hegel: The Letters.* Ed. and trans. C. Butler and C. Seiler. Bloomington: Indiana University Press, 1984.

Heidegger, M. *Holzwege.* Frankfurt am Main: Klostermann, 1950.

____. *What Is Philosophy?* Trans. W. Kluback and J. T. Wilde. N.Y.: Twayne, 1958.

____. *The Question of Being (Concerning the Line).* Trans. W. Kluback and J. T. Wilde. N.Y.: Twayne, 1958.

____. *An Introduction to Metaphysics.* Trans. R. Manheim. Garden City, N.Y.: Doubleday, 1961.

____. *Being and Time.* Trans. J. Macquarrie and E. Robinson. N.Y.: Harper, 1962.

____. *What is a Thing?* Trans. W. B. Barton and V. Deutsch. Chicago: Regnery. 1967.

____. *Identity and Difference.* Trans. J. Stambaugh. N.Y.: Harper & Row, 1969.

____. *On the Way to Language.* Trans. P. Hertz. N.Y.: Harper & Row, 1971.

____. *On Time and Being.* Trans. J. Stambaugh. N.Y.: Harper & Row, 1972.

____. *What Is Called Thinking?* Trans. J. G. Gray and F. D. Wieck. N.Y.: Harper & Row, 1972.

____. *Poetry, Language, Thought.* Trans. A. Hofstadter. N.Y.: Harper & Row, 1975.

____. *Basic Writings.* Ed. D. F. Krell. N.Y.: Harper & Row, 1977.

____. *History of the Concept of Time: Prolegomena.* Trans. T. Kisiel. Bloomington: Indiana University Press, 1985.

____. *Hegel's Concept of Experience.* N.Y.: Harper & Row, 1989.

Heisenberg, W. *Physics and Philosophy.* N.Y.: Harper, 1962.

Hick, J. H., ed. *Faith and the Philosophers.* N.Y.: St. Martin's, 1964.

____. *Faith and Knowledge.* London: Collins-William, 1974.

____. *Philosophy of Religion.* 3rd ed. Englewood Cliffs, N.J.: Prentice-Hall, 1983.

____. *Problems of Religious Pluralism.* N.Y.: St. Martin's, 1985.

_____. *An Interpretation of Religion: Human Responses to the Transcendent.* New Haven, Conn.: Yale University Press, 1989.

Hill, W. J. "The Doctrine of God after Vatican II." *The Thomist* 51 (1987): 395–418.

Himmelfarb, G. *The New History and the Old: Critical Essays and Reappraisals.* Cambridge, Mass.: Harvard University Press, 1987.

Hobbes, T. *Leviathan.* Ed. F. B. Randall. N.Y.: Washington Square Press, 1964.

Hollander, P. *The Many Faces of Socialism.* New Brunswick, N.J.: Transaction Books, 1983.

Holton, G. J. *Introduction to the Concepts and Theories in Physical Science.* 2d ed. Ed. S. G. Brush. Princeton, N.J.: Princeton University Press, 1985.

The Holy Bible. Trans. R. A. Knox. London: Burns and Oates, 1960.

Hook, S. Review of A. Bloom, *The Closing of the American Mind* in *The American Scholar* 58 (1989): 123–35.

Houlgate, S. *Hegel, Nietzsche and the Criticism of Metaphysics.* N.Y.: Cambridge University Press, 1986.

Hull, D. L. *Science as a Process.* Chicago: University of Chicago Press, 1988.

_____. *The Metaphysics of Evolution.* Albany: State University of New York Press, 1989.

Hume, D. *An Enquiry Concerning the Principles of Morals.* LaSalle, Ill.: Open Court, 1938.

_____. *Dialogues Concerning Natural Religion.* Ed. N. K. Smith. Indianapolis: Bobbs-Merrill, 1947.

_____. *A Treatise of Human Nature.* Garden City, N.Y.: Doubleday, 1961.

_____. *On Human Nature and the Understanding.* Ed. A. Flew. N.Y.: Collier, 1962.

_____. *The Natural History of Religion.* Ed. H. E. Root. Stanford, Cal.: Stanford University Press, 1975.

Huntley, W. B. "David Hume and Charles Darwin." *Journal of the History of Ideas* 33 (1972): 457–70.

Hurd, B. "Being Is Being-Present-To-Self: Rahner's Key to Aquinas's Metaphysics." *The Thomist* 52 (1988): 63–78.

Husserl, E. *Cartesian Meditations.* Trans. D. Cairns. The Hague: M. Nijhoff, 1960.

_____. *Ideas.* Trans. W. R. B. Gibson. N.Y.: Collier, 1962.

_____. *Phenomenology and the Crisis of Philosophy.* Trans. Q. Lauer. N.Y.: Harper & Row, 1965.

Huxley, T. H. *Collected Works.* 10 vols. N.Y.: Appleton, 1895.

_____. *The Life and Letters of T. H. Huxley.* 2 vols. Ed. L. Huxley. N.Y.: Appleton, 1900.

James, W. *Essays in Pragmatism.* Ed. A. Castell. N.Y.: Hafner, 1948.

_____. *The Will to Believe, etc.; Human Immortality.* N.Y.: Dover, 1956.

_____. *Psychology: The Briefer Course.* Ed. G. W. Allport. N.Y.: Harper & Row, 1961.

_____. *The Varieties of Religious Experience: A Study in Human Nature.* N.Y.: Collier-Macmillan, 1961.

_____. *Some Problems of Philosophy.* Westport, Conn.: Greenwood, 1968.

_____. *Essays in Pragmatism.* N.Y.: Free Press, 1974.

_____. *Essays in Radical Empiricism.* Cambridge, Mass.: Harvard University Press, 1976.

_____. *A Pluralistic Universe.* Cambridge, Mass.: Harvard University Press, 1977.

_____. *Pragmatism and the Meaning of Truth.* Cambridge, Mass.: Harvard University Press, 1978.

Jeanson, F. *Sartre and the Problem of Morality*. Trans. R. V. Stone. Bloomington: Indiana University Press, 1980.

Jones, E. E. "Interpreting Interpersonal Behavior: The Effects of Expectancies." *Science* 234 (3 October 1986): 41–46.

Jones, G. *Social Darwinism and English Thought*. Atlantic Highlands, N.J.: Humanities, 1980.

Josephson, E., and Josephson, M., eds. *Man Alone: Alienation in Modern Society*. N.Y.: Dell, 1962.

Jung, C. G. *Modern Man in Search of a Soul*. N.Y.: Harcourt, Brace and World, 1933.

Kaku, M. *Beyond Einstein*. N.Y.: Bantam, 1987.

Kant, I. *Critique of Pure Reason*. Trans. J. M. D. Meiklejohn. N.Y.: Willey, 1900.

____. *Kants Opus Posthumum*. Ed. E. Adickes. Berlin: Reuther and Reichard, 1920.

____. *The Philosophy of Kant: Moral and Political Writings*. Ed. C. J. Friedrich. N.Y.: Modern Library, 1949.

____. *Prolegomena to Any Future Metaphysics*. Trans. P. Carus and L. W. Beck. Indianapolis: Bobbs-Merrill, 1950.

____. *Critique of Judgment*. Trans. J. C. Meredith. London: Oxford University Press, 1952.

____. *Critique of Practical Reason*. Trans. L. W. Beck. Indianapolis: Bobbs-Merrill, 1956.

____. *Perpetual Peace*. Trans. L. W. Beck. Indianapolis: Bobbs-Merrill, 1957.

____. *Foundations of the Metaphysics of Morals; What Is Enlightenment?* Trans. L. W. Beck. Indianapolis: Bobbs-Merrill, 1959.

____. *Religion Within the Limits of Reason Alone*. Trans. T. M. Greene and H. H. Hudson. N.Y.: Harper, 1960.

____. *Groundwork of the Metaphysics of Morals*. Trans. H. J. Paton. N.Y.: Harper, 1964.

____. *Critique of Pure Reason*. Trans. N. K. Smith. N.Y.: St. Martin's, 1965.

Kater, M. H. *Doctors Under Hitler*. Chapel Hill: University of North Carolina Press, 1990.

Kaufmann, W., ed. *Existentialism from Dostoevsky to Sartre*. N.Y.: Meridian, 1975.

Kearney, R. *The Wake of Imagination: Ideas of Creativity in Western Culture*. London: Hutchinson, 1987.

Kenny, A. *Wittgenstein*. London: Allen Lane, The Penguin Press, 1973.

____. *Faith and Reason*. N.Y.: Columbia University Press, 1983.

Kierkegaard, S. *Fear and Trembling; Sickness Unto Death*. Trans. W. Lowrie. Princeton, N.J.: Princeton University Press, 1941.

____. *Concluding Unscientific Postscript*. Trans. D. F. Swenson and W. Lowrie. Princeton, N.J.: Princeton University Press, 1941.

____. *The Last Years: Journals 1853–1855*. Ed. and trans. R. G. Smith. N.Y.: Harper & Row, 1965.

____. *A Kierkegaard Anthology*. Ed. R. Bretall. Princeton, N.J.: Princeton University Press, 1973.

____. *Parables of Kierkegaard*. Ed. T. C. Oden. Princeton, N.J.: Princeton University Press, 1989.

King, T. M. *Sartre and the Sacred*. Chicago: University of Chicago Press, 1974.

Knasas, J. F. X. "Transcendental Thomism and the Thomistic Texts." *The Thomist* 54 (1990): 81–95.

Kneale, W., and Kneale, M. *The Development of Logic*. N.Y.: Oxford University Press, 1962.

Knox, R. A. *The Epistles and Gospels for Sundays and Holidays.* London: Burns Oates Washbourne, 1947.
____. *Essays in Satire.* London: Sheed and Ward, 1955.
____. *The Belief of Catholics.* New ed. Garden City, N.Y.: Doubleday, 1958.
____. *Enthusiasm.* N.Y.: Oxford University Press, 1961.
____. *University Sermons.* Ed. P. Caraman. Montreal: Palm Publishers, 1963.
Kobler, J. F. *Vatican II and Phenomenology.* The Hague: M. Nijhoff, 1985.
Koch, G. A. *Republican Religion: The American Revolution and the Cult of Reason.* N.Y.: Holt, 1933.
Kockelmans, J. J. *Heidegger on Art and Art Works.* The Hague: M. Nijhoff, 1985.
____. *On the Truth of Being: Reflections on Heidegger's Later Philosophy.* Bloomington: Indiana University Press, 1985.
Kolenda, K. *Rorty's Humanistic Pragmatism.* Tampa: University of South Florida Press, 1990.
Kovacs, G. "Philosophy and Faith in Heidegger." *Proceedings of the American Catholic Philosophical Association* 54 (1980): 135–43.
Kueng, H. *Freud and the Problem of God.* Trans. E. Quinn. New Haven, Conn.: Yale University Press, 1980.
____. *Does God Exist?* Trans. E. Quinn. Garden City, N.Y.: Doubleday, 1980.
____. *Theology for the Third Millenium.* Trans. P. Heinegg. N.Y.: Anchor, 1990.
Kuhn, T. S. *The Structure of Scientific Revolutions.* 2d ed. Chicago: University of Chicago Press, 1970.
Kuklick, B. *Churchmen and Philosophers: From Edwards to Dewey.* New Haven, Conn.: Yale University Press, 1985.
Lambert, L. A. *Tactics of Infidels.* Buffalo, N.Y.: Peter Paul, 1887.
____. (Simon Fitz Simons). *A Refutation of Agnosticism: A Tract for the Times.* Printed privately, 1889.
Langan, T. *The Meaning of Heidegger.* Westport, Conn.: Greenwood, 1983.
____. *Self-Discovery.* San Francisco: Golden Phoenix Press, 1985.
Lao Tzu. *Tao Te Ching.* Trans. D. C. Lau. Baltimore: Penguin, 1963.
Lauer, Q. *Hegel's Idea of Philosophy.* Bronx, N.Y.: Fordham University Press, 1971.
____. *The Triumph of Subjectivity.* 2d ed. Bronx, N.Y.: Fordham University Press, 1978.
____. *Hegel's Concept of God.* Albany: State University of New York Press, 1982.
Lauer, R. Z. *The Mind of Voltaire.* Westminster, Md.: Newman, 1961.
Leibniz, G. W. *Monadology and Other Philosophical Essays.* Trans. P. and A. M. Schrecker. Indianapolis: Bobbs-Merrill, 1965.
Leland, J. *A View of the Principal Deistical Writers that Have Appeared in the Last and Present Century.* 2 vols., 4th ed. London: Dodsley and Longman, 1764.
LeMahieu, D. L. *The Mind of William Paley.* Lincoln: University of Nebraska Press, 1976.
Levin, D. M. *The Opening Vision: Nihilism and the Postmodern Situation.* N.Y.: Routledge, 1988.
Lewin, R. "A Heresy in Evolutionary Biology." *Science* 241 (16 September 1988): 1431.
Lewis, C. S. *The Four Loves.* Glasgow: Collins, 1977.
____. *Mere Christianity.* N.Y.: Macmillan, 1986.
Lifton, R. J. *The Nazi Doctors.* N.Y.: Basic Books, 1988.
Livingstone, D. *Darwin's Forgotten Defenders.* Grand Rapids, Mich.: Eerdmans, 1987.
Llewelyn, J. *Beyond Metaphysics? The Hermeneutic Circle in Contemporary Philosophy.* London: Macmillan, 1985.

Locke, J. *Treatise of Civil Government; Letter Concerning Toleration*. Ed. C. L. Sherman. N.Y.: Appleton-Century, 1937.

____. *An Essay Concerning Human Understanding*. 2 vols. Ed. J. W. Yolton. N.Y.: Dutton, 1961.

Loewenberg, B. J., ed. *Darwin, Wallace and the Theory of Natural Selection*. Cambridge, Mass.: Arlington, 1959.

Lohse, B. *Martin Luther: Eine Einfuehrung in sein Leben und sein Werk*. Munich: Beck, 1981.

Lonergan, B. *Insight*. San Francisco: Harper & Row, 1977.

____. *Understanding and Being*. Ed. F. E. Crowe and R. M. Doran. Toronto: University of Toronto Press, 1989.

Longino, H. E. *Science as Social Knowledge*. Princeton, N.J.: Princeton University Press, 1990.

"[*Los Angeles Times*] Study Notes Media Bias In Abortion Coverage," *The Catholic Register* (Toronto), 28 July 1990, 17.

Lovejoy, A. O. *The Great Chain of Being*. N.Y.: Harper, 1960.

Lowrance, W. W. *Modern Science and Human Values*. N.Y.: Oxford University Press, 1985.

Lucas, G. R. *The Rehabilitation of Whitehead*. Albany: State University of New York Press, 1989.

Lucretius. *De Rerum Natura*. Trans. W. H. D. Rouse. 3rd ed. Cambridge, Mass.: Harvard University Press, 1959.

Macdonald, S. "The *Esse/Essentia* Argument in Aquinas's *De Ente et Essentia*." *Journal of the History of Philosophy* 22 (1984): 157–72.

MacIntyre, A. *Whose Justice? Which Rationality?* Notre Dame, Ind.: University of Notre Dame Press, 1988.

Mackie, J. L. *The Miracle of Theism: Arguments For and Against the Existence of God*. N.Y.: Oxford University Press, 1982.

Macquarrie, J. *Existentialism*. N.Y.: Penguin, 1973.

____. *Twentieth Century Religious Thought*. N.Y.: Scribner's, 1981.

____. *In Search of Deity*. N.Y.: Crossroad, 1985.

Mahon, J. "Consciousness and the Marxist Tradition." *Philosophical Studies* 27 (1980): 143–58.

Maimonides, M. *The Guide for the Perplexed*. Trans. M. Friedlaender. 2d ed. N.Y.: Dover, 1956.

Malik, C. H. "A Christian Reflection on Martin Heidegger." *The Thomist* 41 (1977): 1–61.

Marcel, G. *The Philosophy of Existentialism*. Trans. M. Harari. N.Y.: Citadel, 1964.

Maritain, J. *Existence and the Existent*. Trans. L. Galantiere and G. B. Phelan. N.Y.: Pantheon, 1948.

____. *Bergsonian Philosophy and Thomism*. Trans. M. L. and J. G. Andison. N.Y.: Philosophical Library, 1955.

____. *An Essay on Christian Philosophy*. Trans. E. H. Flannery. N.Y.: Philosophical Library, 1955.

____. *St. Thomas Aquinas*. Trans. J. W. Evans and P. O'Reilly. N.Y.: Meridian, 1958.

____. *The Degrees of Knowledge*. Trans. G. B Phelan. N.Y.: Scribner's, 1959.

____. *God and the Permission of Evil*. Trans. J. W. Evans. Milwaukee: Bruce, 1966.

Maritain, J., and Cocteau, J. *Art and Faith*. Trans. J. Coleman. N.Y.: Philosophical Library, 1948.

Marshall, E. "A Controversy on Samoa Comes of Age." *Science* 219 (4 March 1983): 1042–45.

Marx, K. *Capital.* Ed. F. Engels. Trans. S. Moore and E. Aveling. N.Y.: International Publishers, 1947.

Marx, K., and Engels, F. *Marx and Engels: Basic Writings on Politics and Philosophy.* Ed. L. S. Feuer. Garden City, N.Y.: Doubleday, 1959.

Mascall, E. L. *He Who Is.* London: Longmans Green, 1943.

____. *Existence and Analogy.* London: Longmans Green, 1949.

____. *Christian Theology and Natural Science.* London: Longmans Green, 1957.

____. *The Secularization of Christianity.* N.Y.: Holt, Rinehart, and Winston, 1966.

Maslow, A. H. *The Farther Reaches of Human Nature.* N.Y.: Viking, 1971.

Masson, J. *The Assault on Truth: Freud's Suppression of the Seduction Theory.* N.Y.: Penguin, 1985.

Maurer, A. A. *St. Thomas and Historicity.* Milwaukee: Marquette University Press, 1979.

May, R. *The Art of Counseling.* N.Y.: Gardner Press, 1989.

May, W. E. *Moral Absolutes.* Milwaukee: Marquette University Press, 1989.

Maydole, R. "A Modal Model for Proving the Existence of God." *American Philosophical Quarterly* 17 (1980): 135–42.

Mayo, T. F. *Epicurus in England: 1650–1725.* Dallas: Southwest Press, 1934.

McCosh, J. *The Religious Aspect of Evolution.* N.Y.: Scribner's, 1890.

McMullin, E., ed. *The Concept of Matter in Modern Philosophy.* Notre Dame, Inc.: University of Notre Dame Press, 1978.

____. *Evolution and Creation.* Notre Dame, Ind.: University of Notre Dame Press, 1986.

Medved, M. "Why Hollywood Hates Religion." *Reader's Digest* 137 (August 1990): 139–43.

Megill, A. *Prophets of Extremity: Nietzsche, Heidegger, Foucault, Derrida.* Berkeley: University of California Press, 1985.

Meissner, W. W. *Psychoanalysis and Religion.* New Haven, Conn.: Yale University Press, 1984.

Menninger, K. *Whatever Became of Sin?* N.Y.: Hawthorn, 1973.

Mercier, D. *A Manual of Modern Scholastic Philosophy.* Trans. T. L. and S. A. Parker. 8th ed. 2 vols. London: Kegan Paul, Trench, and Trubner, 1921–1922.

Messenger, E. C. *Evolution and Theology.* London: Burns Oates Washbourne, 1931.

Michelfelder, D. P., and Palmer, R. E., eds. *Dialogue and Deconstruction: The Gadamer-Derrida Encounter.* Albany: State University of New York Press, 1989.

Midgley, M. *Evolution as a Religion.* London: Methuen, 1985.

Mill, J. S. *The Positive Philosophy of Auguste Comte.* Boston: Spencer, 1866.

____. *Three Essays on Religion.* N.Y.: Holt, 1874.

____. *J. S. Mill's Philosophy of Scientific Method.* Ed. E. Nagel. N.Y.: Hafner, 1950.

____. *Nature and Utility of Religion.* Ed. G. Nakhnikian. Indianapolis: Bobbs-Merrill, 1958.

____. *The Essential Works of J. S. Mill.* Ed. M. Lerner. N.Y.: Bantam, 1961.

Milton, J. *Complete Poetry and Selected Prose.* N.Y.: Random House, n.d.

Molnar, P. D. "Is God Essentially Different From His Creatures? Rahner's Explanation From Revelation." *The Thomist* 51 (1987): 575–631.

Moore, J. R., ed. *History, Humanity and Evolution.* N.Y.: Cambridge University Press, 1990.

Morewedge, P., ed. *Philosophies of Existence: Ancient and Medieval.* Bronx, N.Y.: Fordham University Press, 1982.

Morris, R. *Time's Arrow: Scientific Attitudes Toward Time.* N.Y.: Simon and Schuster, 1985.

Morris, T. V. *The Logic of God Incarnate.* Ithaca, N.Y.: Cornell University Press, 1986.

_____. *Anselmian Explorations.* Notre Dame, Ind.: University of Notre Dame Press, 1987.

Mueller-Hill, B. *Murderous Science: Elimination by Scientific Selection of Jews, Gypsies, and Others.* Trans. G. R. Fraser. N.Y.: Oxford University Press, 1988.

Murdoch, D. *Niels Bohr's Philosophy of Physics.* N.Y.: Cambridge University Press, 1987.

Murdoch, I. *Sartre: Romantic Rationalist.* New Haven, Conn.: Yale University Press, 1960.

Myers, G. E. *William James: His Life and Thought.* New Haven, Conn.: Yale University Press, 1986.

Narveson, J. *The Libertarian Idea.* Philadelphia: Temple University Press, 1988.

Needham, J. *Science in Traditional China.* Hong Kong: Chinese University Press, 1981.

Newman, J. H. *Selections.* Ed. L. E. Gates. N.Y.: Holt, 1895.

_____. *An Essay on the Development of Christian Doctrine.* Garden City, N.Y.: Doubleday, 1960.

_____. *The Argument from Conscience to the Existence of God According to J. H. Newman.* Ed. A. J. Boekraad and H. Tristram. Louvain, Belgium: Nauwelaerts, 1961.

_____. *Newman Against the Liberals.* Ed. M. Davies. Devon, England: Augustine Publishing Co., 1978.

_____. *An Essay in Aid of a Grammar of Assent.* Ed. I. T. Ker. N.Y.: Oxford University Press, 1985.

Nietzsche, F. W. *Jenseits von Gut und Boese.* Leipzig: Naumann, 1886.

_____. *The Complete Works of Friedrich Nietzsche.* 18 vols. Ed. O. Levy. London: Foulis, 1910–1913.

_____. *Thus Spoke Zarathustra.* Trans. R. J. Hollingdale. Baltimore: Penguin, 1966.

_____. *The Portable Nietzsche.* Ed. W. Kaufmann. Baltimore: Penguin, 1968.

_____. *The Will to Power.* Trans. W. Kaufmann and R. J. Hollingdale. N.Y.: Vintage, 1968.

_____. *Beyond Good and Evil.* Trans. R. J. Hollingdale. N.Y.: Penguin, 1973.

_____. *The Gay Science.* Trans. W. Kaufmann. N.Y.: Random House, 1974.

Nijenhuis, J. "To Be or To Exist: That is the Question." *The Thomist* 50 (1986): 353–94.

Nisbet, R. *History of the Idea of Progress.* N.Y.: Basic Books, 1979.

Norris, C. *The Deconstructive Turn.* N.Y.: Methuen, 1983.

_____. *Derrida.* Cambridge, Mass.: Harvard University Press, 1988.

_____. *Deconstruction and the Interests of Theory.* Norman: University of Oklahoma Press, 1989.

Oates, W. J., ed. *The Stoic and Epicurean Philosophers.* N.Y.: Modern Library, 1940.

Ockham, W. *Philosophical Writings: A Selection.* Trans. P. Boehner. Indianapolis: Bobbs-Merrill, 1964.

O'Connor, B. "Overcoming the Heideggerian Critique of Metaphysical *Ousia.*" *Proceedings of the American Catholic Philosophical Association* 61 (1987): 151–63.

Oesterle, J. A. Review of W. and M. Kneale, *The Development of Logic* (1962) in *The New Scholasticism* 37 (1963): 373–76.

Oesterreicher, J. M. *Walls Are Crumbling.* N.Y.: Devin-Adair, 1952.

Ogden, U. *Antidote to Deism. The Deist Unmasked; or, An Ample Refutation of All the Objections of Thomas Paine against the Christian Religion.* Newark, N.J.: Woods, 1795.

Orange, D. M. *Peirce's Conception of God: A Developmental Study.* Lubbock: Texas Tech University Press, 1984.

Ormiston, G. L. and Schrift, A. D., eds. *The Hermeneutic Tradition.* Albany: State University of New York Press, 1990.

Orwell, G. *Nineteen Eighty Four.* N.Y.: New American Library, 1983.

____. *Animal Farm.* London: Secker and Warburg, 1987.

Ospovat, D. *The Development of Darwin's Theory.* N.Y.: Cambridge University Press, 1981.

Owens, J. *A History of Ancient Western Philosophy.* N.Y.: Appleton-Century-Crofts, 1959.

____. "Diversity and Community of Being in St. Thomas Aquinas." *Mediaeval Studies* 22 (1960): 285–97.

____. *An Elementary Christian Metaphysics.* Milwaukee: Bruce, 1963.

____. "The *Analytics* and the Thomistic Metaphysical Procedure." *Mediaeval Studies* 26 (1964): 83–108.

____. "The Causal Proposition Revisited." *The Modern Schoolman* 44 (1966–1967): 143–51.

____. *St. Thomas Aquinas on the Existence of God: Collected Papers of Joseph Owens.* Ed. J. R. Catan. Albany: State University of New York Press, 1980.

____. *Aquinas on Being and Thing.* Niagara Falls, N.Y.: Niagara University Press, 1981.

____. Review of A. Kenny, *Aquinas* (1980) in *Dialogue* 23 (1984): 352–53.

____. *Human Destiny.* Washington, D.C.: Catholic University of America Press, 1985.

Paley, W. *The Works of William Paley.* 5 vols. Ed. D. S. Wayland. London: Cowie, 1837.

____. *Natural Theology.* Hallowell, England: Goodale, 1819.

Parel, A., ed. *Calgary Aquinas Studies.* Toronto: Pontifical Institute of Mediaeval Studies, 1974.

Parkes, G., ed. *Heidegger and Asian Thought.* Honolulu: University of Hawaii Press, 1987.

Pascal, B. *Pensées and Provincial Letters.* Trans. W. F. Trotter. N.Y.: Modern Library, 1941.

Patt, W. "Aquinas's Real Distinction and Some Interpretations." *The New Scholasticism* 62 (1988): 1–29.

Pegis, A. C., ed. *The Wisdom of Catholicism.* N.Y.: Random House, 1949.

Péguy, C. *Basic Verities.* Trans. A. and J. Green. N.Y.: Pantheon, 1943.

Penelhum, T. *God and Skepticism.* Hingham, Mass.: Kluwer Academic, 1983.

Perotti, J. L. *Heidegger on the Divine.* Athens: Ohio University Press, 1974.

Phelan, G. B. *Saint Thomas and Analogy.* Milwaukee: Marquette University Press, 1948.

Piel, G. "Natural Philosophy in the Constitution." *Science* 233 (5 September 1986): 1056–60.

Pius XII. *Humani Generis.* N.Y.: Paulist Press, 1950.

Plantinga, A. *God and Other Minds.* Ithaca, N.Y.: Cornell University Press, 1967.

____. *God, Freedom, and Evil.* Grand Rapids, Mich.: Eerdmans, 1978.

____. *The Nature of Necessity.* N.Y.: Oxford University Press, 1979.

____. *Does God Have a Nature?* Milwaukee: Marquette University Press, 1980.

Plato. *The Collected Dialogues of Plato.* Ed. E. Hamilton and H. Cairns. N.Y.: Pantheon, 1963.

Plotinus. *The Enneads*. Trans. S. MacKenna. London: Faber, 1956.
Pois, R. A. Review of R. Proctor, *Racial Hygiene* (1988) in *Science* 242 (4 November 1988): 785–87.
Polybius. *The Histories of Polybius*. Trans. E. S. Shuckburgh. 2 vols. Bloomington: Indiana University Press, 1962.
Pool, R. "Chaos Theory: How Big An Advance?" *Science* 245 (7 July 1989): 26–28.
Popper, K. R. *Conjectures and Refutations*. 2d ed. London: Routledge and Kegan Paul, 1965.
____. *Realism and the Aim of Science*. Totowa, N.J.: Rowman and Littlefield, 1983.
____. *The Poverty of Historicism*. N.Y.: Routledge Chapman and Hall, 1988.
Poster, M. *Sartre's Marxism*. N.Y.: Cambridge University Press, 1982.
Powers, J. *Philosophy and the New Physics*. London: Methuen, 1982.
Preus, J. S. *Explaining Religion*. New Haven, Conn.: Yale University Press, 1987.
Prichard, H. A. *Knowledge and Perception*. N.Y.: Oxford University Press, 1970.
Proctor, R. *Racial Hygiene*. Cambridge, Mass.: Harvard University Press, 1988.
Qian, Wen-yuan. *The Great Inertia: Scientific Stagnation in Traditional China*. London: Croom Helm, 1985.
Quine, W. V. O. *Word and Object*. Cambridge, Mass.: MIT Press, 1960.
____. *Ontological Relativity and Other Essays*. N.Y.: Columbia University Press, 1969.
____. *From a Logical Point of View*. 2d rev. ed. Cambridge Mass.: Harvard University Press, 1980.
____. *Quiddities: An Intermittently Philosophical Dictionary*. Cambridge, Mass.: Harvard University Press, 1987.
____. *Pursuit of Truth*. Cambridge, Mass.: Harvard University Press, 1990.
Reichmann, J. B. "Language and the Interpretation of Being in Gadamer and Aquinas." *Proceedings of the American Catholic Philosophical Association* 62 (1988): 225–34.
Renou, L. *Hinduism* N.Y.: Washington Square Press, 1963.
Rescher, N. *Pascal's Wager*. Notre Dame, Ind.: University of Notre Dame Press, 1985.
Ricciotti, G. *The Life of Christ*. Trans. A. I. Zizzamia. Milwaukee: Bruce, 1947.
____. *The History of Israel*. Trans. C. D. Penta and R. T. A. Murphy. 2d ed. 2 vols. Milwaukee: Bruce, 1958.
____. *The Age of Martyrs*. Trans. A. Bull. Milwaukee: Bruce, 1959.
____. *Julian the Apostate*. Trans. M. J. Costelloe. Milwaukee: Bruce, 1960.
Richards, R. J. *Darwin and the Emergence of Evolutionary Theories of Mind and Behavior*. Chicago: University of Chicago Press, 1988.
Richardson, R. A. "Biogeography and the Genesis of Darwin's Ideas on Transmutation." *Journal of the History of Biology* 14 (1981): 1–41.
Richardson. W. J. *Heidegger*. 2d ed. The Hague: M. Nijhoff, 1967.
____. "Pyschoanalysis and the God-Question." *Thought* 61 (1986): 68–83.
Ricoeur, P. *Time and Narrative*. Trans. K. McLaughlin and D. Pellauer. Chicago: University of Chicago Press, 1984.
Ridley, M. *The Problems of Evolution*. N.Y.: Oxford University Press, 1985.
Robinson, A. L. "Atomic Physics Tests Lorentz Invariance." *Science* 229 (23 August 1985): 745–47.
Rohrlich, F. *From Paradox to Reality: Our New Concepts of the Physical World*. N.Y.: Cambridge University Press, 1987.
Rorty, R. *Philosophy and the Mirror of Nature*. Princeton, N.J.: Princeton University Press, 1979.

____. *Consequences of Pragmatism.* Minneapolis: University of Minnesota Press, 1982.
____. *Contingency, Irony, and Solidarity.* N.Y.: Cambridge University Press, 1989.
Rose, H. J. *Religion in Greece and Rome.* N.Y.: Harper, 1959.
Roszak, T. *The Cult of Information.* N.Y.: Random House, 1986.
Roth, R. J. "Hume's Theory of Human Nature and Community." *The New Scholasticism* 57 (1983): 331–51.
Rothschild, R. C. *The Emerging Religion of Science.* Westport, Conn.: Praeger, 1989.
Rousseau, J.-J. *The Social Contract.* Trans. W. Kendall. Chicago: Regnery, 1954.
____. *Religious Writings of Rousseau.* Ed. R. Grimsley. London: Claredon, 1970.
____. *Emile: or, On Education.* Trans. A. Bloom. N.Y.: Basic Books, 1979.
Russell, B. *Mysticism and Logic.* Garden City, N.Y.: Doubleday, n.d.
____. *The Scientific Outlook.* London: Allen and Unwin, 1931.
____. *Bertrand Russell's Best.* Ed. R. E. Egner. N.Y.: Mentor, 1958.
____. *My Philosophical Development.* London: Allen and Unwin, 1959.
____. *Religion and Science.* N.Y.: Oxford University Press, 1961.
Ryle, G. *The Concept of Mind.* London: Hutchinson, 1949.
Sartre, J.-P. *La Nausée.* Paris: Gallimard, 1938.
____. *Existentialism and Human Emotions.* N.Y.: Philosophical Library, 1957.
____. *No Exit and Three Other Plays.* N.Y.: Vintage, 1960.
____. *Critique de la Raison Dialectique.* 2 vols. Paris: Gallimard, 1960.
____. *Les Mouches.* N.Y.: Harper & Row, 1963.
____. *Nausea.* Trans. L. Alexander. N.Y.: New Directions, 1964.
____. *Being and Nothingness.* Trans. H. E. Barnes. N.Y.: Washington Square Press, 1966.
____. *L'Existentialisme est un humanisme.* Paris: Nagel, 1966.
____. *Search for a Method.* Trans. H. E. Barnes. N.Y.: Random House, 1968.
____. *The Transcendence of the Ego: An Existential Theory of Consciousness.* Trans. F. Williams and R. Kirkpatrick. N.Y.: Octagon, 1972.
____. *Sartre: Between Existentialism and Marxism.* Trans. J. Mathews. N.Y.: Pantheon, 1974.
____. *Existentialism and Humanism.* Trans. P. Mairet. London: Methuen, 1982.
Schiller, F. C. S. *Plato or Protagoras?* Oxford: Blackwell, 1908.
____. *Logic for Use: An Introduction to the Voluntarist Theory of Knowledge.* N.Y.: Harcourt Brace, 1930.
Schmidt, W. *The Origin and Growth of Religion.* Trans. H. J. Rose. 2d ed. N.Y.: Dial, 1935.
____. *Primitive Revelation.* Trans. J. J. Baierl. St. Louis: Herder, 1939.
____. *The Religion of Earliest Man.* London: Catholic Truth Society, 1952.
Schopenhauer, A. *The Philosophy of Schopenhauer.* Ed. I. Edman. N.Y.: Modern Library, 1928.
____. *The Essence of Religion.* Albuquerque, N.M.: American Classical College Press, 1985.
Schufreider, G. "Reunderstanding Anselm's Argument." *The New Scholasticism* 57 (1983): 384–409.
Shapiro, G., ed. *Postmodernism.* Albany: State University of New York Press, 1989.
Shea, W. M. *The Naturalists and the Supernatural: Studies in American Philosophy of Religion.* Macon, Ga.: Mercer University Press, 1984.
Sheehan, T., ed. *Heidegger: The Man and the Thinker.* Chicago: Precedent, 1981.

Shook, L. K. *Etienne Gilson*. Toronto: Pontifical Institute of Mediaeval Studies, 1984.

Shurkin, J. *Engines of the Mind: A History of the Computer*. N.Y.: Norton, 1984.

Sia, S. *God in Process Thought*. The Hague: M. Nijhoff, 1985.

Skinner, B. F. *Beyond Freedom and Dignity*. N.Y.: Knopf, 1971.

____. *About Behaviorism*. N.Y.: Random House, 1976.

____. "Selection by Consequences." *Science* 213 (31 July 1981): 501–4.

Smith, A. *The Theory of Moral Sentiments*. Ed. D. D. Raphael and A. L. Macfie. N.Y.: Oxford University Press, 1976.

Smith, J. E. *Purpose and Thought: The Meaning of Pragmatism*. New Haven, Conn.: Yale University Press, 1978.

Smith, J. H. *The Death of Classical Paganism*. N.Y.: Scribner's, 1976.

Smith, V. E. *The Elements of Logic*. Milwaukee: Bruce, 1957.

____. *Science and Philosophy*. Milwaukee: Bruce, 1965.

Smith, V. E., ed. *The Logic of Science*. N.Y.: St. John's University Press, 1963.

____. *Philosophical Problems in Biology*. N.Y.: St. John's University Press, 1966.

Snow, C. P. *The Two Cultures: And a Second Look*. N.Y.: Cambridge University Press, 1964.

Solomon, R. C. *The Big Questions*. 2d ed. N.Y.: Harcourt Brace Jovanovich, 1986.

Spencer, H. *Illustrations of Universal Progress: A Series of Discussions*. N.Y.: Appleton, 1889.

____. *The Inadequacy of Natural Selection*. N.Y.: Appleton, 1897.

____. *First Principles*. 5th ed. N.Y.: Burt, n.d.

Spinoza, B. *Philosophy of Benedict de Spinoza*. Trans. R. H. M. Elwes. N.Y.: Tudor, n.d.

____. *The Principles of Cartesian Philosophy*. Trans. H. E. Wedeck. N.Y.: Philosophical Library, 1961.

Sprigge, T. L. S. *Theories of Existence*. London: Penguin, 1984.

Staub, E. *The Roots of Evil*. N.Y.: Cambridge University Press, 1989.

Steiner, G. *Real Presences*. Chicago: University of Chicago Press, 1989.

Stern, K. *The Third Revolution: A Study of Psychiatry and Religion*. Garden City, N.Y.: Doubleday, 1961.

Stewart, I. *Does God Play Dice?* N.Y.: Basil Blackwell, 1989.

Stewart, W. K. "My Sister and I: The Disputed Nietzsche." *Thought* 61 (1986): 321–35.

Strauss, L. *The Political Philosophy of Hobbes*. London: Oxford University Press, 1936.

____. *Natural Rights and History*. Chicago: University of Chicago Press, 1965.

____. *Spinoza's Critique of Religion*. Trans. E. M. Sinclair. N.Y.: Schocken, 1982.

____. *Persecution and the Art of Writing*. Chicago: University of Chicago Press, 1988.

____. *The Rebirth of Classical Political Rationalism*. Chicago: University of Chicago Press, 1989.

Strawson, P. F. *Skepticism and Naturalism: Some Varieties*. N.Y.: Columbia University Press, 1985.

Suarez, F. *On the Various Kinds of Distinctions*. Trans. C. Vollert. Milwaukee: Marquette University Press, 1947.

____. *On Formal and Universal Unity*. Trans. J. F. Ross. Milwaukee: Marquette University Press, 1964.

Sussman, H. *The Hegelian Aftermath: Readings in Hegel, Kierkegaard, Freud, Proust, and James*. Baltimore: Johns Hopkins University Press, 1982.

Swinburne, R. *The Coherence of Theism*. N.Y.: Oxford University Press, 1977.

____. *The Existence of God*. N.Y.: Oxford University Press, 1979.

____. *Faith and Reason.* N.Y.: Oxford University Press, 1981.
Tawney, R. H. *Religion and the Rise of Capitalism.* London: Murray, 1928.
Taylor, M. C. *Deconstructing Theology.* N.Y.: Crossroad, 1982.
____. *Erring.* Chicago: University of Chicago Press, 1984.
____. *Deconstruction in Context.* Chicago: University of Chicago Press, 1986.
Teilhard de Chardin, P. *The Phenomenon of Man.* N.Y.: Harper & Row, 1961.
Teixidor, J. *The Pagan God: Popular Religion in the Greco-Roman Near East.* Princeton, N.J.: Princeton University Press, 1977.
Thornton, E. M. *The Freudian Fallacy.* Garden City, N.Y.: Doubleday, 1984.
Thulstrup, N. *Kierkegaard's Relation to Hegel.* Princeton, N.J.: Princeton University Press, 1980.
Tillich, P. *The Courage To Be.* New Haven, Conn.: Yale University Press, 1952.
____. *Theology of Culture.* N.Y.: Oxford University Press, 1964.
____. *What is Religion?* Ed. J. L. Adams. N.Y.: Harper & Row, 1969.
Toulmin, S. *The Return to Cosmology: Postmodern Science and the Theology of Nature.* Berkeley: University of California Press, 1982.
Turner, D. *Commitment to Care.* Old Greenwich, Conn.: Devin-Adair, 1978.
Turner, J. *Reckoning with the Beast: Animals, Pain, and Humanity in the Victorian Mind.* Baltimore: Johns Hopkins University Press, 1980.
Unamuno, M. de. *The Tragic Sense of Life.* Trans. J. E. C. Flitch. N.Y.: Dover, 1954.
Urban, P. L., and D. Walton, eds. *The Power of God.* N.Y.: Oxford University Press, 1978.
Vaihinger, H. *The Philosophy of As If.* Trans. C. K. Ogden. 2d ed. London: Routledge and Kegan Paul, 1935.
Van Der Leeuw, G. *Religion in Essence and Manifestation.* Trans. J. E. Turner. Princeton, N.J.: Princeton University Press, 1986.
Van Doren, M. *The Noble Voice.* N.Y.: Holt, 1947.
Vattimo, G. *The End of Modernity: Nihilism and Hermeneutics in Postmodern Culture.* Trans. J. R. Snyder. Baltimore: Johns Hopkins University Press, 1988.
Veatch, H. B. *Two Logics.* Evanston, Ill.: Northwestern University Press, 1969.
____. *Human Rights: Fact or Fancy?* Baton Rouge: Louisiana State University Press, 1986.
Vickers, B., ed. *Occult and Scientific Mentalities in the Renaissance.* N.Y.: Cambridge University Press, 1984.
Viney, D. W. *Charles Hartshorne and the Existence of God.* Albany: State University of New York Press, 1984.
Vitz, P. S. *Psychology as Religion: The Cult of Self-Worship.* Grand Rapids, Mich.: Eerdmans, 1977.
____. Letter on secular humanism in the schools to the editor of *Science* 235 (27 February 1987): 955.
Voltaire, F. M. A. *Oeuvres Complètes de Voltaire.* 52 vols. Ed. L. Moland. Paris: Garnier, 1877–1885.
____. *Lettres Choisies de Voltaire.* Ed. R. Naves. Paris: Garnier, 1955.
____. *Philosophical Letters.* Trans. E. Dilworth. Indianapolis: Bobbs-Merrill, 1961.
____. *Philosophical Dictionary.* Trans. P. Gay. 2 vols. N.Y.: Basic Books, 1962.
Vos, A. *Aquinas, Calvin, and Contemporary Protestant Thought.* Washington, D.C.: Christian University Press, 1985.
Vrooman, J. R. *René Descartes: A Biography.* N.Y.: Putnam, 1970.
Waismann, F. *Wittgenstein and the Vienna Circle.* N.Y.: Barnes and Noble, 1979.

Walsh. J. J. *The Popes and Science.* Bronx, N.Y.: Fordham University Press, 1908.

Ward, L. R., ed. *The Problem of Universals.* Notre Dame, Ind.: University of Notre Dame Press, 1956.

Weindling, P. *Health, Race and German Politics Between National Unification and Nazism.* N.Y.: Cambridge University Press, 1989.

Weinsheimer, J. C. *Gadamer's Hermeneutics.* New Haven, Conn.: Yale University Press, 1985.

Weisheipl, J. A. *Friar Thomas D'Aquino: His Life, Thought, and Work.* Garden City, N.Y.: Doubleday, 1974.

____. *Nature and Motion in the Middle Ages.* Ed. W. E. Carroll. Washington, D.C.: Catholic University of America Press, 1985.

Weiss, S. F. *Race Hygiene and National Efficiency.* Berkeley: University of California Press, 1988.

Wernham, J. C. S. *James's Will-To-Believe Doctrine: A Heretical View.* Montreal: McGill-Queen's University Press, 1987.

Wetter, G. A. *Dialectical Materialism.* Trans. P. Heath. N.Y.: Praeger, 1958.

Wheat, L. F. *Paul Tillich's Dialectical Materialism: Unmasking the God Above God.* Baltimore: Johns Hopkins University Press, 1970.

Whewell, W. *Indications of the Creator.* 2d ed. Philadelphia: Carey and Hart, 1845.

____. *History of the Inductive Sciences, from the Earliest to the Present Time.* 2 vols. 3rd ed. N.Y.: Appleton, 1859.

Whitehead, A. N. *Religion in the Making.* N.Y.: Macmillan, 1926.

____. *The Function of Reason.* Boston: Beacon, 1958.

____. *Process and Reality.* N.Y.: Harper, 1960.

____. *Science in the Modern World.* N.Y.: Mentor, 1964.

Wickham, H. *The Unrealists.* N.Y.: Dial, 1930.

Wierenga, E. "Anselm on Omnipresence." *The New Scholasticism* 62 (1988): 30–41.

Wilhelmsen, F. D. *Christianity and Political Philosophy.* Athens: University of Georgia Press, 1978.

Wippel, J. F. *Metaphysical Themes in Thomas Aquinas.* Washington, D.C.: Catholic University of America Press, 1984.

Wippel, J. F., ed. *Studies in Medieval Philosophy.* Washington, D.C.: Catholic University of America Press, 1987.

Wittgenstein, L. *On Certainty.* N.Y.: Harper & Row, 1972.

____. *Wittgenstein: Conversations, 1949–1951.* Ed. J. L. Craft and R. E. Hustwit. Indianapolis: Hackett, 1986.

Wolfson, H. A. *The Philosophy of Spinoza.* Cambridge, Mass.: Harvard University Press, 1983.

Wood, A. W., ed. *Self and Nature in Kant's Philosophy.* Ithaca, N.Y.: Cornell University Press, 1984.

Wright, J. P. *The Sceptical Realism of David Hume.* Minneapolis: University of Minnesota Press, 1983.

____. "Ignorance and Evidence in Hume Scholarship." *Dialogue* 26 (1987): 731–33.

Wyschogrod, E. *Spirit in Ashes: Hegel, Heidegger, and Man-Made Mass Death.* New Haven, Conn.: Yale University Press, 1985.

Yates, F. A. *Giordano Bruno and the Hermetic Tradition.* London: Routledge and Kegan Paul, 1964.

Yolton, J. W. *Thinking Matter.* Minneapolis: University of Minnesota Press, 1983.

Young, R. M. *Darwin's Metaphor: Nature's Place in Victorian Culture.* N.Y.: Cambridge University Press, 1985.

Zaehner, R. C., ed. *Hindu Scriptures*. London: Dent, 1968.

____. *Hinduism*. London: Oxford University Press, 1970.

Zimmerman, M. E. "On Vallicella's Critique of Heidegger." *International Philosophical Quarterly* 30 (1990): 75–100.

____. *Heidegger's Confrontation with Modernity*. Bloomington: Indiana University Press, 1990.

INDEX

Abortion, 6–9, 61
Absolute, the, 90, 105, 193; as ground of becoming, 106
Absolutism, 204
Affirming the consequent, fallacy of, 64
Agnosticism, modern, 24
Alienation, 162
Analogous usage, 99
Animal Farm (Orwell), 19
Anselm, Saint, 76, 115
Anthropocentrism, 32–33; collectivistic side of, 176; essence of, 6; and ethical behavior, 223; Hegelian, 117; and legal positivism, 9; Sartre's, 155; theocentrism and, 33
Antichrist (Nietzsche), 25–27, 31
Appearance and reality, 158–59
Apprehension, 149
Appropriation, 151–54
Aristophanes, 11
Aristotle, 14, 73, 117, 121; Prime Mover of, 118
Atheism and pantheism, 105–33
Atheist: first true, 166; naïveté of, 52, 93
Atheistic Existentialism, 3; starting point of, 166
Atheistic policy, reversal of, 61–62
Atomists, 195
Augustine, Saint, 57
Authority, freedom and, 19–20, 208, 210
Avant-garde, 141
Ayer, A. J., 102–3, 229–30

Barth, Karl, 129
Beck, Lewis White, 85
Becoming, 5, 21; the Absolute as ground

of, 106; change and, 195; one world of, 22; and time, 144; as unity of being and nothing, 112
Being, 21, 27, 127; convergence of, 150; God as creator and preserver of, 197; love-hate relationship with, 90; question of, 67–68; rejection of, 157; return to, 28; and thought, 148, 152; as truth-as-non-concealment, 147; weight of, 156
Being and Nothingness (Sartre), 158, 161, 211
Being and Some Philosophers (Gilson), 173–74
Being and Time (Heidegger), 1, 168, 255. See also *Sein und Zeit*
Berkeley, George, 85, 224
Bernstein, Richard J., 208–9
Beyond Good and Evil (Nietzsche), 21, 60
The Birds (Aristophanes), 11
Birth control, 7–8, 61
Bloom, Allan, 6, 19, 26, 43–47, 209
Bohr, Niels, 22
Brahman, 111, 169, 216
Butler, Clark, 108, 110–11

Camus, Albert, 39, 163–64
Capitalism, myth of, 9–10
Caputo, John D., 38–39, 42
Categorical Moral Imperative, 29, 106
The Central Questions of Philosophy (Ayer), 229
Cervantes, Miguel de, 11
Chalcedon, Council of, 125

Dewey, John, 90 [handwritten annotation]

Change, 195
Chesterton, G. K., xii
City of God (Augustine), 57
Civil law, 48
Cleese, John, 13
The Closing of the American Mind
    (Bloom), 19, 26, 43, 209
Cognitive reversal, 219
Comedy, contemporary, 9–13
Common standards, 57
Concluding Unscientific Postscript
    (Kierkegaard), 135
Conformity, 91–92
Conscience, 55; voice of, 142
Consciousness: complete, 112–13; in
    degrees, 187; lack of, 111; partial,
    111–12
Consequences of Pragmatism (Rorty),
    35–36, 71
Contingency, Irony, and Solidarity
    (Rorty), 51
Contractarianism, 59
Conversation, 35
Copleston, Frederick, 146
Cosmological argument, 84
Craig, W. L., 213
Cratylus, 73
Creativity, 131
Critique of Pure Reason (Kant), 83–85
Cults, 42–43

Darwin, Charles, 7–8, 76; on morality,
    55–56
Dasein, 140, 217; first obligation of, 141;
    and the human condition, 142–43
Death as affirmation, 143
Deconstructing Theology (Taylor), 37
Deconstruction, 2, 47; of
    deconstructionism, 216; dogmatism
    of, 18–19; of Jesus Christ, 124; in
    literary circles, 24; of ordinary
    reality, 155; of presence, 149; of
    scripture, 122–24; of the self, 22;
    universal nature of, 23
Democratic personality, 6
Derrida, Jacques, 21, 32
Descartes, René, 72–83, 188, 231–32
Descent of Man (Darwin), 7–8, 55
Despair, 165
Determinism: freedom and, 176–77,
    204; rejection of, 3–4
Deus absconditus, 38
The Development of Darwin's Theory
    (Ospovat), 56

Dialectical theism, 33
Dialogues Concerning Natural
    Religion (Hume), 40
Dionysian Mystery Cults, 43
Distinction, 184–86
Divine grace, 196
Does God Exist? (Kueng), 120, 126
Don Quixote (Cervantes), 11
Dostoyevski, Fyodor, 166
Doyle, Arthur Conan, 221
Dualism, 21
Duboc, Edouard, 112

Einstein, Albert, 22, 196, 213
"Emancipatory reflection," 233
The Encyclopaedia of the Philosophical
    Sciences in Outline (Wallace), 108
Epicurus, 55, 213
Epistemological Idealism, 73–74, 101,
    220, 225; institutionalization of, 137;
    as a holy cause, 138, 225
Essays in Satire (Knox), 12
Essences, phobia for, 73
Evil: existence of, 194–95; meaning of,
    47–49; nature as, 156
Evolutionary theory, 100; pantheistic,
    127
Existence: filthy world of, 157; thinking
    and, 164, 180
Existentialism, religious meaning of,
    163
Existentialism is a Humanism
    (Sartre), 60, 166
Existential judgment, 193

Faith: action and, 97, 176; Aquinas's
    view of, 178; definition of, 95–96;
    knowledge and, 175; leap of, 96, 163–
    65; reasoned, 85; in the scientific
    method, 102; as secular
    phenomenon, 94–95; understanding
    and, 202, 205
Fallibilism, 208–10
Financial matters, 13–16
Fourfold unity, 153
Fox, Matthew, 43, 222
Free choice, 40, 177, 210
Freedom: authority and, 19–20, 208, 210;
    as complex act, 178; determinism
    and, 176–77, 204; religion and,
    110
Free love, 8
Free will, 86
Freud, Sigmund, xii

Friar Thomas D'Aquino (Weisheipl), 173

Funny walks, 12

Gadamer, H.-G., 33, 135–37, 170–71, 217–18, 223–26; vs. existentialism, 226

The Gay Science (Nietzsche), 1, 135

Gilson, E., 81, 102, 135, 167, 173–74, 227

God: ability to find, 114; as the Absolute, 105–6; attempts to prove the existence of, 83–85, 118–19, 125; Consequent Nature of, 130–31; as creator and preserver of being, 197; deconstruction of, 83, 89, 109; Descartes's idea of, 77–83; essence of, 200; eternality of, 165; existence of, 40, 86, 126; as Higher Self, 98–99; negation and, 116–17; of the post-modern world-view, 122; practical belief in, 88; presence of, 197–201, 215; Primordial Nature of, 131; proper name of, 124, 195, 214; reality of, 112, 115, 128; of revelation, 215; Sartre's rejection of, 160–61; as separate personal being, 132; as Supreme Moralist, 87; thinking about, 76, 107; the Trinity and, 196; the unconscious and, 98; the world as, 113

God-Is-Dead doctrine, 5, 36, 47, 146, 166

Goethe, Johann, 110

Good and evil, objective measure of, 49

Gorgias, 23

Gray, Asa, 76

The Great Chain of Being (Lovejoy), 114

Gulliver's Travels (Swift), 11

Guzzoni, Alfred, 152–53

Hayek, Friedrich, 219

Hegel, George, 32–33, 105–29, 132, 135, 168

Heidegger, Martin, 1, 22, 25, 43, 135–55, 168–69, 217, 222; on Christianity, 148; earlier and later, 145; fourfold unity of, 153; Nazism and, 46–47, 142; phenomenology of, 138

Hell on earth, 165

Hemingway, Ernest, 162

Heraclitus, 27, 137, 171

Herder, Johan Gottfried, 108

Herd mentality, 36

Hick, John, 81

Hinduism, 169

Historical relativism, 136, 219

History of the Concept of Time: Prolegomena (Heidegger), 144–45

Hitler, Adolf, 43, 48

Hobbes, Thomas, 59, 79–80

Holmes, Sherlock, 221

Human condition, 142–43

Humani Generis (Pius XII), 127

Human nature, 75–76, 208; divine grace and, 196; nothingness and, 159, 162; social, 183

Hume, David, 32, 40, 54–57, 189, 230, 232–35

Huxley, Thomas Henry, 102

Ideals, need for, 59

Identity, 184, 192

Immortality, in Kueng, 123

Incarnation, the, 123

Indifferentism, 208, 210

In Search of Deity (Macquarrie), 33

Intellect and will, 177

Intellectual knowledge, 221

Internal Revenue Service, 16–17

Interpretation as game, 24

Intolerance, 7

An Introduction to Metaphysics (Heidegger), 145, 148

Jacobi, Friedrich, 114

James, William, 9, 33, 41, 68, 89–104, 142, 173–74

Jesus, 25, 33, 123, 196; deconstruction of, 124; as fully human, 125

Kant, Immanuel, 29–30, 67, 83–88, 115, 187, 202–3; categorical imperative of, 29, 106

Kenny, A., 213

Kierkegaard, Sören, 107, 135, 163–69, 196

Knowledge: Aquinas's theory of, 181; dual nature of, 220–21; the fact of, 73; faith and, 175; liberating, 221–22

Knox, Ronald, 12

Kueng, Hans, 25, 41, 42, 120–33

Langan, Thomas, 148

Lauer, Quentin, 109, 113–15

Law, 48–49; of nature, 66

Leap of faith, 96, 163–65

Lectures on the History of Philosophy (Hegel), 109, 115

Legal positivism, 9

Liberal democracy and consensus, 6

Linguistics and Philosophy (Gilson), 135
Literary circles, deconstructionism in, 24
Locke, John, 80
Logic, 116; religion and, 109; judgments and, 192–93
Logical Positivism, 3, 217; rise and fall of, 63; temporary detour of, 67
Love, 25
Lovejoy, A. O., 103, 114
Luther, Martin, 107–8

Mackie, J. L., 25, 40–42, 213–14
Macquarrie, John, 33
Malebranche, N., 233
Mao Tse-tung, 52
Marcel, Gabriel, 163
Maritain, Jacques, xiii
Marx, Karl, 219; reinterpretation of, 44
Mathematical logic, 148
Mathematical physics, 139
Maya, 169
Meditations (Descartes), 75–79, 82
Mendelssohn, Moses, 187
Mercier, Désiré-Joseph, 120
Metaphysics, 52, 67, 214
Mill, J. S., 52, 230
Mind, existence of, 75–76
The Miracle of Theism (Mackie), 40
Modernity, 21
Money and prayer, 15–16
Monotheism, 99
"Moral holiday," 33
Morality: coincidence of happiness with, 86–87; consistency and, 62; science and, 106; truly universal, 194
Moral relativism, 5–7, 211; glorification of, 213
Les Mouches (Sartre), 60
Mussolini, Benito, 219
Myers, G. E., 103
Myers, Frederick W. H., 197
Mystery cults, 42–43
Le Mythe de Sisyphe (Camus), 163

Nabokov, Vladimir, 54
Nature, 271; beyond, 203; as evil force, 156–57; immersion in, 205; will as a, 177; wonders of, 220
La Nausée (Sartre), 156
Nazism, 46, 142
Negation, 116–17

New Age, 3, 43
Newman, John Henry, 71, 125
Newton, Isaac, 21, 84, 196, 224
Nicene Creed, 124
Niethammer, Friedrich, 108
Nietzsche, Friedrich Wilhelm, 1, 3–4, 21, 27–32, 135, 166; eternal return doctrine of, 136; nihilism of, 36; phobia of, 25; on slave mentality, 41–42; as subversive figure, 39; on suicide, 68; Superman of (*see* Superman)
Nihilism, 5, 36
Nominalism, 190; Descartes's, 188; Rorty's, 53
Norris, John, 80
Nothingness, 143, 159, 162

Objectivity, 2
Obligations, 86
Opus Posthumum (Kant), 88
Original Sin, 38, 183
Orwell, George (Eric Blair), 19, 54
Orwell's Reversal, 61
Ospovat, D., 56
Owens, Joseph, 180–81

Panentheism, 131
Pantheism, 33, 43, 105–33, 167, 169, 196–97
Paradigm shift, 20
Parmenides, 148–49, 167–68
Pascal, Blaise, 71, 92–93, 95–96
Pensées (Pascal), 71
Phaedon (Mendelssohn), 187
Phenomenology, Heidegger's, 138
Phenomenology of Spirit (Hegel), 120
Philosophy and the Mirror of Nature (Rorty), 34
The Philosophy of Existentialism (Marcel), 163
Phobia: for essences, 73; of Nietzsche, 25
Pius XII, 127
Plato, 18, 32, 73, 207, 209
Play, 213
Plotinus, 157
Pollution, 9
Polytheism, 99
Post-modernism, 2; and comedy, 13; and finance, 13–16; libertarian branch of, 17; major false assumption of, 26–27; moral imperative of, 7–8, 18; prevalence of, 9; reevaluation of, 215–16; as

replacement for religion, 138; root
of, 20; ultimate foundation for, 5
Potency and act, 186–89, 193
Pragmatism, 30, 35–36; context for, 100;
doctrine of, 89–91
Prayer and money, 15–16
Presence, 149, 154, 161
Pre-social existence, mythical, 59
Principles, 174
Principles of Morals (Hume), 57
Principles of Philosophy (Descartes),
231
The Principles of Psychology (James),
99
Process and Reality (Whitehead), 130
Progress, 223–24
Protagoras, 32
Pseudo-Christianity, 154
Psychology: The Briefer Course
(James), 99
Pyrrho, 216

Quine, W. V. O., 35

Radical empiricism, 103
Radical Hermeneutics (Caputo), 43
Rand, Ayn, 204
Reality: appearance and, 158–59;
complexity of, 189; first in, 174; as
process, 130; as series of proportions,
199; unity and truth of, 121, 128
Reasoned faith, 85
Religion, 28; freedom and, 110; logic
and, 109; need for, 146; as protest
against suffering, 38; secondary
place for, 107; as social
phenomenon, 96–97
Revelation, reason and, 194
Rhetoric (Aristotle), 14
Rights, obligation and, 86
Rimbaud, J. N. A., 227
Rorty, Richard, 34–37, 47, 51–56, 68–69,
71, 219
Russell, Bertrand, 96, 175, 179

Salvation, 97
Sartre, J.-P., 1, 4, 39, 60, 155–63, 166, 176,
196, 211–12; anthropocentrism of,
155; intellectual and ethical
nakedness of, 163
Satire, 11–12
Schelling, Friedrich, 114
Schopenhauer, Arthur, 105, 166
Science, 30; the Church and, 127;

inclination toward, 119; moral
realms and, 106; the reasonable
and, 85; reliability of, 63–66, 224;
thematizing and, 139
Scientific method, 102
Scripture, reinterpretation of, 122–24
Secular faith, 94–95, 102
Segregation, 57–58
Seiler, Christiane, 108, 110–11
Sein und Zeit (Heidegger), 137, 139, 142,
144
Selections (Newman), 71
Self: deconstruction of, 22; Higher, 98–
99; nonexistence of, 28
Self-consciousness, 160
Self-fulfillment, 192
Sellars, Wilfrid, 35
Simonides, 14
Sin, 28
Skinner, B. F., 224
Slapstick comedy, 12
Socialism, myth of, 9–10
Society, 26
Socrates, 46, 216
Some Problems of Philosophy (James),
173
Sophist (Plato), 207, 209
Soul, 86; existence of, 74–75;
immortality of, 187, 197; peace of, 99;
World, 99–100
Sour grapes syndrome, 68
Speculative knowledge, 30, 107–8
Spencer, Herbert, 216
Spinoza, Baruch, 33, 108, 111–12
Spurs (Derrida), 21
Stalin, Joseph (Iosif Vissarionovich
Dzhugashvili), 19
Stambaugh, Joan, 152
State, deification of, 109
State religion, 17
Stevens, Wallace, 69
Stillingfleet, Edward, 80–81
Stoicism, 223
Strauss, Leo, xi, 217
Suffering, protest against, 38
Suicide, 68
Summa Theologiae (Aquinas), 173, 197,
207
Superman, 8; collective, 176; as leader,
166–67; nihilism and, 36; role of, 26
Supreme Moralist, 87
Sweden, 61
Swift, Jonathan, 11
Swinburne, Richard, 40

Taxes, 14–17
Taylor, Mark C., 37, 69
Television, 11–12
Temporality, which is man, 144
Terrorism, 51, 53
Theaetetus (Plato), 73
Theatre of the Absurd, 13
Theism, as-if, 71–104
Theocentrism, 33
"The Thing" (Heidegger), 149–50
Tholuck, Friedrich, 107
Thomas Aquinas, Saint, 1, 114, 120–21,
    173, 175–207, 213, 215; realism of,
    183; view of faith, 178
Thomism, 120–21, 128; class in, 191;
    key to, 179; the presence of God and,
    197–201; principles of, 174, 200
Tillich, Paul, 37
Time, 144
"Time and Being" (Heidegger), 151–52
Toleration, 36, 208–9
Treatise of Human Nature (Hume), 56,
    232
The Trinity, 196
Truman, Harry S, 19
Truth, 182; the factual and, 92; fiction
    and, 31, 220; instrumentalist view
    of, 91; redefinition of, 89–90; search
    for, 66–67; as self-consciousness,
    101; simple, 100; temporary, 137;
    unity and, 121
Truth and Method (Gadamer), 33, 217,
    223–26
Twilight of the Idols (Nietzsche), 27, 30

Unamuno, M. de, 197
The Unconscious, 97–98
Underachievement, 10
Universalized ethnocentrism, 52
Universals, problem of, 188, 190–92
University, politicization of, 45–47

Vaihinger, Hans, 87–88
Values, 35
Van Doren, Mark, 230
Varieties of Religious Experience
    (James), 97, 99
The Verb, 182

Wager Argument, 92–93
Wallace, William, 108
Weisheipl, J. A., 173
What is Metaphysics? (Heidegger), 148,
    168
Whitehead, A. N., 105, 129–32, 223
Wider Self, 98
Will: deficiencies of the intellect and,
    96; following intellect, 177
The Will to Believe (James), 92–93,
    101
Wolff, Christian, 202
*A Work on the Proofs of the Existence of
    God* (Hegel), 105
The World as Will and Idea
    (Schopenhauer), 105
World-Soul, 99–100, 223

Zu den Sachen selbst, 216

ABOUT THE AUTHOR

F. F. CENTORE is Professor of Philosophy and Chairman of the Department at St. Jerome's College in the University of Waterloo, Canada. He is the author of *Persons: A Comparative Account of the Six Possible Theories* (Greenwood Press, 1979), *Robert Hooke's Contributions to Mechanics,* and has co-authored *Philosophy Today.* His numerous articles have appeared in *Angelicum, International Philosophical Quarterly,* and *The Thomist,* among other scholarly journals.

A MYTHIC TALE: In 1864, while on a secret mission to Europe to raise money for the war, a fifty-five-year-old Abraham Lincoln asked a twenty-year-old Friedrich Wilhelm Nietzsche: If I should decide to call the tail of a cow a leg, how many legs will the cow have? The deeply thinking Nietzsche answered sharply and confidently: Why, five legs, of course. To which Lincoln retorted in good humor: Nonsense, my intense young man! It would still have only four legs; merely calling a cow's tail a leg doesn't make it one — not really. After thinking about this for twenty-five years, and not being able to find a convincing rebuttal, Nietzsche went insane.